What They Said® In 1995

The Yearbook Of World Opinion

Compiled and Edited by
ALAN F. PATER
and
JASON R. PATER

MONITOR BOOK COMPANY

TWENTY-SEVENTH ANNUAL EDITION

Printed in the United States of America

Library of Congress catalogue card number: 74-111080

ISBN number: 0-917734-28-9

WHAT THEY SAID is published annually by Monitor Book Company, Palm Springs, California 92263. The title, "WHAT THEY SAID," is a trademark owned exclusively by Monitor Book Company and has been duly registered with the United States Patent Office. Any unauthorized use is prohibited.

To

The Newsmakers of the World . . .

May they never be at a loss for words

Table of Contents

PART THREE: GENERAL

Preface to the First Edition (1969)

Words can be powerful or subtle, humorous or maddening. They can be vigorous or feeble, lucid or obscure, inspiring or despairing, wise or foolish, hopeful or pessimistic . . . they can be fearful or confident, timid or articulate, persuasive or perverse, honest or deceitful. As tools at a speaker's command, words can be used to reason, argue, discuss, cajole, plead, debate, declaim, threaten, infuriate, or appease; they can harangue, flourish, recite, preach, discourse, stab to the quick, or gently sermonize.

When casually spoken by a stage or film star, words can go beyond the press-agentry and make-up facade and reveal the inner man or woman. When purposefully uttered in the considered phrasing of a head of state, words can determine the destiny of millions of people, resolve peace or war, or chart the course of a nation on whose direction the fate of the entire world may depend.

Until now, the *copia verborum* of well-known and renowned public figures—the doctors and diplomats, the governors and generals, the potentates and presidents, the entertainers and educators, the bishops and baseball players, the jurists and journalists, the authors and attorneys, the congressmen and chairmen-of-the-board—whether enunciated in speeches, lectures, interviews, radio and television addresses, news conferences, forums, symposiums, town meetings, committee hearings, random remarks to the press, or delivered on the floors of the United States Senate and House of Representatives or in the parliaments and palaces of the world—have been dutifully reported in the media, then filed away and, for the most part, forgotten.

The editors of *WHAT THEY SAID* believe that consigning such a wealth of thoughts, ideas, doctrines, opinions and philosophies to interment in the morgues and archives of the Fourth Estate is lamentable and unnecessary. Yet the media, in all their forms, are constantly engulfing us in a profusion of endless and increasingly voluminous news reports. One is easily disposed to disregard or forget the stimulating discussion of critical issues embodied in so many of the utterances of those who make the news and, in their respective fields, shape the events throughout the world. The conclusion is therefore a natural and compelling one: the educator, the public official, the business executive, the statesman, the philosopher—everyone who has a stake in the complex, often confusing trends of our times—should have material of this kind readily available.

These, then, are the circumstances under which *WHAT THEY SAID* was conceived. It is the culmination of a year of listening to the people in the public eye; a year of scrutinizing, monitoring, reviewing, judging, deciding—a year during which the editors resurrected from almost certain oblivion those quintessential elements of the year's *spoken* opinion which, in their judgment, demanded preservation in book form.

WHAT THEY SAID is a pioneer in its field. Its *raison d'etre* is the firm conviction that presenting, each year, the highlights of vital and interesting views from the lips of prominent people on virtually every aspect of contemporary civilization fulfills the need to give the *spoken* word the permanence and lasting value of the *written* word. For, if it is true that a picture is worth 10,000 words, it is equally true that a verbal conclusion, an apt quote or a candid comment by a person of fame or influence can have more significance and can provide more understanding than an entire page of summary in a standard work of reference.

The editors of *WHAT THEY SAID* did not, however, design their book for researchers and scholars alone. One of the failings of the conventional reference work is that it is blandly written and referred to primarily for facts and figures, lacking inherent "interest value." *WHAT THEY SAID*, on the other hand, was planned for sheer enjoyment and pleasure, for searching glimpses into the lives and thoughts of the world's celebrities, as well as for serious study, intellectual reflection and the philosophical contemplation of our multifaceted life and mores. Furthermore, those pressed for time, yet anxious to know what the newsmakers have been saying, will welcome the short excerpts which will make for quick, intermittent reading—and rereading. And, of course, the topical classifications, the speakers' index, the subject index, the place and date information—documented and authenticated and easily located—will supply a rich fund of hitherto not readily obtainable reference and statistical material.

Finally, the reader will find that the editors have eschewed trite comments and cliches, tedious and boring. The selected quotations, each standing on its own, are pertinent, significant, stimulating—above all, relevant to today's world, expressed in the speakers' own words. And they will, the editors feel, be even more relevant tomorrow. They will be re-examined and reflected upon in the future by men and women eager to learn from the past. The prophecies, the promises, the "golden dreams," the boastings and rantings, the bluster, the bravado, the pleadings and representations of those whose voices echo in these pages (and in those to come) should provide a rare and unique history lesson. The positions held by these luminaries, in their respective callings, are such that what they say today may profoundly affect the future as well as the present, and so will be of lasting importance and meaning.

ALAN F. PATER
JASON R. PATER

Beverly Hills, California

Editorial Treatment

ORGANIZATION OF MATERIAL

Special attention has been given to the arrangement of the book–from the major divisions down to the individual categories and speakers–the objective being a logical progression of related material, as follows:

(A) The categories are arranged alphabetically within each of three major sections:

Part one:	"National Affairs"
Part two:	"International"
Part three:	"General"

In this manner, the reader can quickly locate quotations pertaining to particular fields of interest (see also *Indexing*). It should be noted that some quotations contain a number of thoughts or ideas–sometimes on different subjects– while some are vague as to exact subject matter and thus do not fit clearly into a specific topic classification. In such cases, the judgment of the Editors has determined the most appropriate category.

(B) Within each category the speakers are in alphabetical order by surname, following alphabetization practices used in the speaker's country of origin.

(C) Where there are two or more quotations by one speaker within the same category, they appear chronologically by date spoken or date of source.

SPEAKER IDENTIFICATION

(A) The occupation, profession, rank, position or title of the speaker is given as it was *at the time the statement was made* (except when the speaker's relevant identification is in the past, in which case he is shown as "former"). Thus, due to possible changes in status during the year, a speaker may be shown with different identifications in various parts of the book, or even within the same category.

(B) In the case of a speaker who holds more than one position simultaneously, the judgment of the Editors has determined the most appropriate identification to use with a specific quotation.

(C) The nationality of a speaker is given when it will help in identifying the speaker or when it is relevant to the quotation.

THE QUOTATIONS

The quoted material selected for inclusion in this book is shown as it appeared in the source, except as follows:

(A) *Ellipses* have been inserted wherever the Editors have deleted extraneous words or overly long passages within the quoted material used. In no way has the meaning or intention of the quotations been altered. *Ellipses* are also used where they appeared in the source.

(B) *Punctuation and spelling* have been altered by the Editors where they were obviously incorrect in the source, or to make the quotations more intelligible, or to conform to the general style used throughout this book. Again, meaning and intention of the quotations have not been changed.

(C) *Brackets* ([]) indicate material inserted by the Editors or by the source to either correct obvious errors or to explain or clarify what the speaker is saying. In some instances, bracketed material may replace quoted material for sake of clarity.

(D) *Italics* either appeared in the original source or were added by the Editors where emphasis is clearly desirable.

Except for the above instances, the quoted material used has been printed verbatim, as reported by the source (even if the speaker made factual errors or was awkward in his choice of words).

Special care has been exercised to make certain that each quotation stands on its own and is not taken "out of context." The Editors, however, cannot be responsible for errors made by the original source, i.e., incorrect reporting, mis-quotations, or errors in interpretation.

DOCUMENTATION AND SOURCES

Documentation (circumstance, place, date) of each quotation is provided as fully as could be obtained, and the sources are furnished for all quotations. In some instances, no documentation details were available; in those cases, only the source is given. Following are the sequence and style used for this information:

Circumstance of quotation, place, date/Name of source, date:section (if applicable), page number.

Example: *Before the Senate, Washington, Dec.4/The Washington Post, 12-5:(A)13.*

The above example indicates that the quotation was delivered before the Senate in Washington on December 4. It was taken for *WHAT THEY SAID* from *The Washington Post,* issue of December 5, section A, page 13. (When a newspaper publishes more than one edition on the same date, it should be noted that page numbers may vary from edition to edition.)

(A) When the source is a television or radio broadcast, the name of the network or local station is indicated, along with the date of the broadcast (obviously, page and section information does not apply).

(B) An asterisk (*) before the (/) in the documentation indicates that the quoted material was written rather than spoken. Although the basic policy of *WHAT THEY SAID* is to use only *spoken* statements, there are occasions when written statements are considered by the Editors to be important enough to be included. These occasions are rare and usually involve Presidential messages and statements released to the press and other such documents attributed to persons in high government office.

INDEXING

(A) The *Index to Speakers* is keyed to the page number. (For alphabetization practices, see *Organization of Material*, paragraph B.)

(B) The *Index to Subjects* is keyed to both the page number and the quotation number on the page (thus, 210:3 indicates quotation number 3 on page 210); the quotation number appears at the right corner of each quotation.

(C) To locate quotations on a particular subject, regardless of the speaker, turn to the appropriate category (see *Table of Contents*) or use the detailed *Index to Subjects.*

(D) To locate all quotations by a particular speaker, regardless of subject, use the *Index to Speakers.*

(E) To locate quotations by a particular speaker on a particular subject, turn to the appropriate category and then to that person's quotations within the category.

(F) The reader will find that the basic categorization format of *WHAT THEY SAID* is itself a useful index, inasmuch as related quotations are grouped together by their respective categories. All aspects of journalism, for example, are relevant to each other; thus, the section *Journalism* embraces all phases of the news media. Similarly, quotations pertaining to the U. S. President, Congress, etc., are in the section *Government.*

MISCELLANEOUS

(A) Except where otherwise indicated or obviously to the contrary, all universities, organizations and business firms mentioned in this book are in the United States; similarly, references made to "national," "Federal," "this country," "the nation" etc., refer to the United States.

(B) In most cases, organizations whose names end with "of the United States" are Federal government agencies.

SELECTION OF CATEGORIES

The selected categories reflect, in the Editors' opinion, the most widely discussed public-interest subjects, those which readily fall into the over-all sphere of "current events." They represent topics continuously covered by the mass media because of their inherent importance to the changing world scene. Most of the categories are permanent; they appear in each annual edition of *WHAT THEY SAID*. However, because of the transient character of some subjects, there may be categories which appear one year and may not be repeated the next.

SELECTION OF SPEAKERS

The following persons are always considered eligible for inclusion in *WHAT THEY SAID*: top-level officials of all branches of national, state and local governments (both U.S. and foreign), including all United States Senators and Representatives; top-echelon military officers; college and university presidents, chancellors and professors; chairmen and presidents of major corporations; heads of national public-oriented organizations and associations; national and internationally known diplomats; recognized celebrities from the entertainment and literary spheres and the arts generally; sports figures of national stature; commentators on the world scene who are recognized as such and who command the attention of the mass media.

The determination of what and who are "major" and "recognized" must, necessarily, be made by the Editors of *WHAT THEY SAID* based on objective personal judgment.

Also, some persons, while not generally recognized as prominent or newsworthy, may have nevertheless attracted an unusual amount of attention in connection with an important issue or event. These people, too, are considered for inclusion, depending upon the specific circumstance.

SELECTION OF QUOTATIONS

The quotations selected for inclusion in *WHAT THEY SAID* obviously represent a decided minority of the seemingly endless volume of quoted material appearing in the media each year. The process of selecting is scrupulously objective insofar as the partisan views of the Editors are concerned (see *About Fairness,* below). However, it is clear that the Editors must decide which quotations *per se* are suitable for inclusion, and in doing so look for comments that are aptly stated, offer insight into the subject being discussed, or into the speaker, and provide—for today as well as for future reference— a thought which readers will find useful for understanding the issues and the personalities that make up a year on this planet.

ABOUT FAIRNESS

The Editors of *WHAT THEY SAID* understand the necessity of being impartial when compiling a book of this kind. As a result, there has been no bias in the selection of the quotations, the choice of speakers or the manner of editing. Relevance of the statements and the status of the speakers are the exclusive criteria for inclusion, without any regard whatsoever to the personal beliefs and views of the Editors. Furthermore, every effort has been made to include a multiplicity of opinions and ideas from a wide cross-section of speakers on each topic. Nevertheless, should there appear to be, on some controversial issues, a majority of material favoring one point of view over another, it is simply the result of there having been more of those views expressed during the year, reported by the media and objectively considered suitable by the Editors of *WHAT THEY SAID* (see *Selection of Quotations*, above). Also, since persons in politics and government account for a large percentage of the speakers in *WHAT THEY SAID*, there may exist a heavier weight of opinion favoring the philosophy of those in office at the time, whether in the United States Congress, the Administration, or in foreign capitals. This is natural and to be expected and should not be construed as a reflection of agreement or disagreement with that philosophy on the part of the Editors of *WHAT THEY SAID*.

Abbreviations

The following are abbreviations used by the speakers in this volume. Rather than defining them each time they appear in the quotations, this list will facilitate reading and avoid unnecessary repetition.

ABA:	American Bar Association
ABM:	anti-ballistic missile
ACLU:	American Civil Liberties Union
AIDS:	acquired immune deficiency syndrome
AIM:	American Indian Movement
ANC:	African National Congress
ATF:	Bureau of Alcohol, Tobacco and Firearms
AT&T:	American Telephone & Telegraph Company
BBC:	British Broadcasting Corporation
CBO:	Congressional Budget Office
CBS:	Columbia Broadcasting System (CBS, Inc.)
CCC:	Civilian Conservation Corps
CD:	compact disc
CEO:	chief executive officer
CIA:	Central Intelligence Agency
C.I.S.:	Commonwealth of Independent States
CNN:	Cable News Network
CUNY:	City University of New York
DLC:	Democratic Leadership council
EPA:	Environmental Protection Agency
FAA:	Federal Aviation Administration
FBI:	Federal Bureau of Investigation
FCC:	Federal Communications Commission
FDA:	Food and Drug Administration
F.D.R.:	Franklin Delano Roosevelt
GOP:	Grand Old Party (Republican Party)
HHS:	Department of Health and Human Services

HIV:	human immunodeficiency virus (AIDS virus)
HMO:	health maintenance organization
HUD:	Department of Housing and Urban Development
IPO:	initial public (stock) offering
I.Q.:	intelligence quotient
IRS:	Internal Revenue Service
LP:	long-playing (phonograph record)
MBA:	Master of Business Administration
MIA:	missing in action
MPAA:	Motion Picture Association of America
NAACP:	National Association for the Advancement of Colored People
NAFTA:	North American Free Trade Agreement
NASA:	National Aeronautics and Space Administration
NATO:	North Atlantic Treaty Organization or National Association of Theater Owners
NBC:	National Broadcasting Company
NEA:	National Endowment for the Arts
NFL:	National Football League
NPT:	(nuclear) Non-Proliferation Treaty
NRA:	National Rifle Association
OECD:	Organization for Economic Cooperation and Development
PAC:	political action committee
PBS:	Public Broadcasting Service
PC:	personal computer
PLO:	Palestine Liberation Organization
POW:	prisoner of war
PRI:	Institutional Revolutionary Party (Mexico)
REA:	Rural Electrification Administration
SAARC:	South Asian Association for Regional Cooperation
SEC:	Securities and Exchange Commission
TV:	television
UN:	United Nations
UNPROFOR:	United Nations Protection Force

U.S.:	United States
U.S.A.:	United States of America
USIA:	United States Information Agency
V-E:	victory in Europe (World War II)
WTO:	World Trade Organization

Party affiliation of United States Senators, Representatives, Governors and state legislators:

D: Democrat

I: Independent

R: Republican

The Quote of the Year

I don't think anybody who carries a rifle carries the future. Because I don't believe that you can really change the world by killing and shooting. You have to change it by creating and competing. And the people who don't understand this will disappear, not by the kinds of enemies we have seen in the past, but by the judgement of history.

—SHIMON PERES
Foreign Minister of Israel;
In an interview, July.

PART ONE

National Affairs

The State of the Union Address

Delivered by Bill Clinton, President of the United States, at the Capitol, Washington, D.C., January 24, 1995.

Mr. President, Mr. Speaker, members of the 104th Congress, my fellow Americans, again we are here in the sanctuary of democracy. And once again, our democracy has spoken.

So let me begin by congratulating all of you here in the 104th Congress, and congratulating you, Mr. Speaker.

If we agree on nothing else tonight, we must agree that the American people certainly voted for change in 1992 and in 1994.

And as I look out at you, I know how some of you must have felt in 1992.

I must say that in both years we didn't hear America singing, we heard America shouting. And now all of us, Republicans and Democrats alike, must say: We hear you. We will work together to earn the jobs you have given us. For we are the keepers of the sacred trust and we must be faithful to it in this new and very demanding era.

Preserving the American Idea

Over 200 years ago, our founders changed the entire course of human history by joining together to create a new country based on a single, powerful idea. We hold these truths to be self-evident, that all men are created equal, endowed by their creator with certain inalienable rights. Among these are life, liberty and the pursuit of happiness.

It has fallen to every generation since then to preserve that idea—the American idea—and to deepen and expand its meaning in new and different times. To Lincoln and to his Congress, to preserve the Union and to end slavery. To Theodore Roosevelt and Woodrow Wilson, to restrain the abuses and excesses of the Industrial Revolution and to assert our leadership in the world. To Franklin Roosevelt, to fight the failure and pain of the Great Depression and to win our country's great struggle against fascism.

And to all our Presidents since, to fight the cold war. Especially, I recall two who struggled to fight that cold war in partnership with Congresses where the majority was of a different party. To Harry Truman, who summoned us to unparalleled prosperity at home and who built the architecture of the cold war. And to Ronald Reagan, whom we wish well tonight, and who exhorted us to carry on until the twilight struggle against Communism was won.

In another time of change and challenge, I had the honor to be the first President to be elected in the post-cold-war era, an era marked by the global economy, the information revolution, unparalleled change in opportunity and in security for the American people.

Goals and Accomplishments

I came to this hallowed chamber two years ago on a mission: To restore the American dream for all our people and to make sure that we move into the 21st century, still the strongest force for freedom and democracy in the entire world.

I was determined then to tackle the tough problems too long ignored. In this effort I am frank to say that I have made my mistakes. And I have learned again the importance of humility in all human endeavor.

But I am also proud to say tonight that our country is stronger than it was two years ago.

Record numbers, record numbers of Americans are succeeding in the new global economy. We are at peace, and we are a force for peace and freedom throughout the world. We have almost six million new jobs since I became President, and we have the lowest combined rate of unemployment and inflation in 25 years.

Our businesses are more productive and here we have worked to bring the deficit down, to expand trade, to put more police on our streets, to give our citizens more of the tools they need to get an education and to rebuild their own communities. But the rising tide is not lifting all the boats.

While our nation is enjoying peace and prosperity, too many of our people are still working harder and harder for less and less. While our businesses are restructuring and growing more productive and competitive, too many of our people still can't be sure of having a job next year or even next month. And far more than our material riches are threatened, things far more precious to us: our children, our families, our values.

Our civil life is suffering in America today. Citizens are working together less and shouting at each other more. The common bonds of community which have been the great strength of our country from its very beginning are badly frayed.

What are we to do about it?

Government's Role

More than 60 years ago, at the dawn of another new era, President Roosevelt told our nation new conditions impose new requirements on Government and those who conduct Government. And from that simple proposition he shaped the New Deal, which helped to restore our nation to prosperity and defined the relationship between our people and their Government for half a century.

That approach worked in its time but today we face a very different time and very different conditions. We are moving from an industrial age built on gears and sweat to an information age demanding skills and learning and flexibility.

Our Government, once a champion of national purpose, is now seen by many as simply a captive of narrow interests putting more burdens on our citizens rather than equipping them to get ahead. The values that used to hold us all together seem to be coming apart.

So tonight we must forge a new social compact to meet the challenges of this time. As we enter a new era, we need a new set of understandings not just with Government but, even more important, with one another as Americans.

The "New Covenant"

That's what I want to talk with you about tonight. I call it the New Covenant but it's grounded in a very, very old idea that all Americans have not just a right but a solemn responsibility to rise as far as their God-given talents and determination can take them. And to give something back to their communities and their country in return.

Opportunity and responsibility—they go hand in hand; we can't have one without the other, and our national community can't hold together without both.

Our New Covenant is a new set of understandings for how we can equip our people to meet the challenges of the new economy, how we can change the way our Government works to fit a different time and, above all, how we can repair the damaged bonds in our society and come together behind our common purpose. We must have dramatic change in our economy, our Government and ourselves.

My fellow Americans, without regard to party, let us rise to the occasion. Let us put aside partisanship and pettiness and pride. As we embark on this course, let us put our country first, remembering that regardless of party label we are all Americans. And let the final test of everything we do be a simple one: Is it good for the American people?

Let me begin by saying that we cannot ask Americans to be better citizens if we are not better servants. You made a good start by passing that law which applies to Congress all the laws you put on the private sector—and I was proud to sign it yesterday.

Lobbyists

But we have a lot more to do before people really trust the way things work around here. Three times as many lobbyists are in the streets and corridors of Washington as were here 20 years ago. The American people look at their capital and they see a city where the well-connected and the well-protected can work the system, but the interests of ordinary citizens are often left out.

As the new Congress opened its doors, lobbyists were still doing business as usual—the gifts, the trips—all the things that people are concerned about haven't stopped.

Twice this month you missed opportunities to stop these practices. I know there were other considerations in those votes, but I want to use something that I've heard my Republican friends say from time to time: There doesn't have to be a law for everything.

So tonight I ask you to just stop taking the lobbyists' perks, just stop.

We don't have to wait for legislation to pass to send a strong signal to the American people that things are really changing. But I also hope you will send me the strongest possible lobby reform bill, and I'll sign that, too. We should require lobbyists to tell the people for whom they work what they're spending, what they want. We should also curb the role of big money in elections by capping the cost of campaigns and limiting the influence of PAC's.

Political Reform

And as I have said for three years, we should work to open the air waves so that they can be an instrument of democracy, not a weapon of destruction, by giving free TV time to candidates for public office.

When the last Congress killed political reform last year, it was reported in the press that the lobbyists actually stood in the halls of this sacred building and cheered. This year, let's give the folks at home something to cheer about.

More important, I think we all agree that we have to change the way the Government works. Let's make it smaller, less costly and smarter. Leaner, not meaner.

I just told the Speaker the equal time doctrine's alive and well.

New Approach to Governing

The New Covenant approach to governing is as different from the old bureaucratic way as the computer is from the manual typewriter. The old way of governing around here protected organized interests; we should look out for the interests of ordinary people. The old way divided us by interests, constituency or class; the New Covenant way should unite us behind a common vision of what's best for our country.

The old way dispensed services through large, top-down, inflexible bureaucracies. The New Covenant way should shift these resources and decision making from bureaucrats to citizens, injecting choice and competition and individual responsibility into national policy.

The old way of governing around here actually seemed to reward failure. The New Covenant way should have built-in incentives to reward success.

The old way was centralized here in Washington. The New Covenant way must take hold in the communities all across America, and we should help them to do that.

Our job here is to expand opportunity, not bureaucracy, to empower people to make the most of their own lives and to enhance our security here at home and abroad.

We must not ask Government to do what we should do for ourselves. We should rely on Government as a partner to help us to do more for ourselves and for each other.

I hope very much that as we debate these specific and exciting matters, we can go beyond the sterile discussion between the illusion that there is somehow a program for every problem, on the one hand, and the other illusion that the Government is the source of every problem that we have.

Our job is to get rid of yesterday's Government so that our own people can meet today's and tomorrow's needs.

And we ought to do it together.

Cutting Government

You know, for years before I became President, I heard others say they would cut Government and how bad it was. But not much happened.

We actually did it. We cut over a quarter of a trillion dollars in spending, more than 300 domestic programs, more than 100,000 positions from the Federal bureaucracy in the last two years alone.

Based on decisions already made, we will have cut a total of more than a quarter of a million positions from the Federal Government, making it the smallest it has been since John Kennedy was President, by the time I come here again next year.

Under the leadership of Vice President Gore, our initiatives have already saved taxpayers $63 billion. The age of the $500 hammer and the ashtray you can break on David Letterman is gone. Deadwood programs like mohair subsidies are gone. We've streamlined the Agriculture Department by reducing it by more than 1,200 offices. We've slashed the small-business loan form from an inch thick to a single page. We've thrown away the Government's 10,000-page personnel manual.

Government Is Working Better

And the Government is working better in important ways. FEMA, the Federal Emergency Management Agency, has gone from being a disaster to helping people in disaster.

You can ask the farmers in the Middle West who fought the flood there or the people in California who've dealt with floods and earthquakes and fires and they'll tell you that.

Government workers, working hand-in-hand with private business, rebuilt Southern California's fractured freeways in record time and under budget.

And because the Federal Government moved fast, all but one of the 5,600 schools damaged in the earthquake are back in business.

Now, there are a lot of other things that I could talk about. I want to just mention one because it'll be discussed here in the next few weeks.

University administrators all over the country have told me that they are saving weeks and weeks of bureaucratic time now because of our direct college loan program, which makes college loans cheaper and more affordable with better repayment terms for students, costs the Government less and cuts out paperwork and bureaucracy for the Government and for the universities.

We shouldn't cap that program, we should give every college in America the opportunity to be a part of it.

Previous Government programs gather dust; the reinventing Government report is getting results. And we're not through—there's going to be a second round of reinventing Government.

We propose to cut $130 billion in spending by shrinking departments, extending our freeze on domestic spending, cutting 60 public housing programs down to 3, getting rid of over a hundred programs we do not need, like the Interstate Commerce Commission and the Helium Reserve Program.

And we're working on getting rid of unnecessary regulations and making them more sensible. The programs and regulations that have outlived their usefulness should go. We have to cut yesterday's Government to help solve tomorrow's problems.

Federal/Local Aspect

And we need to get Government closer to the people it's meant to serve. We need to help move programs down to the point where states and communities and private citizens in the private sector can do a better job. If they can do it, we ought to let them do it. We should get out of the way and let them do what they can do better.

Taking power away from Federal bureaucracies and giving it back to communities and individuals is something everyone should be able to be for. It's time for Congress to stop passing onto the states the cost of decisions we make here in Washington.

I know there are still serious differences over the details of the unfunded mandates legislation but I want to work with you to make sure we pass a reasonable bill which will protect the national interest and give justified relief where we need to give it.

Unnecessary Spending

For years, Congress concealed in the

budget scores of pet spending projects. Last year was no different. There was a million dollars to study stress in plants and $12 million for a tick removal program that didn't work. It's hard to remove ticks; those of us who've had them know.

But I'll tell you something, if you'll give me the line-item veto, I'll remove some of that unnecessary spending.

But, I think we should all remember, and almost all of us would agree, that Government still has important responsibilities.

Our young people—we should think of this when we cut—our young people hold our future in their hands. We still owe a debt to our veterans. And our senior citizens have made us what we are.

Now, my budget cuts a lot. But it protects education, veterans, Social Security and Medicare, and I hope you will do the same thing. You should, and I hope you will.

And when we give more flexibility to the states, let us remember that there are certain fundamental national needs that should be addressed in every state, north and south, east and west.

Immunization against childhood disease, school lunches in all our schools, Head Start, medical care and nutrition for pregnant women and infants—all these things are in the national interest.

Regulatory Reform

I applaud your desire to get rid of costly and unnecessary regulations, but when we deregulate let's remember what national action in the national interest has given us: safer food for our families, safer toys for our children, safer nursing homes for our parents, safer cars and highways and safer workplaces, cleaner air and cleaner water. Do we need common sense and fairness in our regulations? You bet we do. But we can have common sense and still provide for safe drinking water. We can have fairness and still clean up toxic dumps and we ought to do it.

The Budget and the Deficit

Should we cut the deficit more? Well, of course we should. Of course we should. But we can bring it down in a way that still protects our economic recovery and does not unduly punish people who should not be punished, but instead should be helped.

I know many of you in this chamber support the balanced-budget amendment. I certainly want to balance the budget. Our Administration has done more to bring the budget down and to save money than any in a very, very long time.

If you believe passing this amendment is the right thing to do, then you have to be straight with the American people. They have a right to know what you're going to cut, what taxes you're going to raise, how it's going to affect them.

And we should be doing things in the open around here. For example, everybody ought to know if this proposal is going to endanger Social Security. I would oppose that, and I think most Americans would.

The Welfare System

Nothing is done more to undermine our sense of common responsibility than our failed welfare system. This is one of the problems we have to face here in Washington in our New Covenant. It rewards welfare over work, it undermines family values, it lets millions of parents get away without paying their child support, it keeps a minority—but a significant minority—of the people on welfare trapped on it for a very long time.

I worked on this problem for a long time—nearly 15 years now. As a Governor, I had the honor of working with the Reagan Administration to write the last welfare reform bill back in 1988.

In the last two years we made a good start in continuing the work of welfare reform. Our Administration gave two dozen states the right to slash through Federal rules and regulations to reform their own welfare systems and to try to promote work and responsibility over welfare and dependency.

Last year, I introduced the most sweeping welfare reform plan ever presented by an Administration. We have to make welfare what it was meant to be—a second chance, not a way of life.

We have to help those on welfare move to work as quickly as possible, to provide child care and teach them skills, if that's what they need, for up to two years. But after that, there ought to be a simple, hard rule. Anyone who can work must go to work.

If a parent isn't paying child support, they should be forced to pay.

We should suspend driver's licenses, track them across state lines, make them work off what they owe. That is what we should do. Governments do not raise children, people do. And the parents must take responsibility for the children they bring into this world.

I want to work with you, with all of you, to pass welfare reform. But our goal must be to liberate people and lift them from dependence to independence, from welfare to work, from mere childbearing to responsible parenting. Our goal should not be to punish them because they happen to be poor.

We should—we should require work and mutual responsibility. But we shouldn't cut people off just because they're poor, they're young or even because they're unmarried. We should promote responsibility by requiring young mothers to live at home with their parents or in other supervised settings, by requiring them to finish school. But we shouldn't put them and their children out on the street.

And I know all the arguments pro and con and I have read and thought about this for a long time: I still don't think we can, in good conscience, punish poor children for the mistakes of their parents.

My fellow Americans, every single survey shows that all the American people care about this, without regard to party or race or region. So let this be the year we end welfare as we know it.

But also let this be the year that we are all able to stop using this issue to divide America.

No one is more eager to end welfare.

I may be the only President who's actually had the opportunity to sit in the welfare office, who's actually spent hours and hours talking to people on welfare, and I am telling you the people who are trapped on it know it doesn't work. They also want to get off.

So we can promote, together, education and work and good parenting. I have no problem with punishing bad behavior or the refusal to be a worker or a student or a responsible parent. I just don't want to punish poverty and past mistakes. All of us have made our mistakes and none of us can change our yesterdays, but every one of us can change our tomorrows.

And America's best example of that may be Lynn Woolsey, who worked her way off welfare to become a Congresswoman from the state of California.

Crime

I know the members of this Congress are concerned about crime, as are all the citizens of our country. But I remind you that last year we passed a very tough crime bill—longer sentences, three strikes and you're out, almost 60 new capital punishment offenses, more prisons, more prevention, 100,000 more police—and we paid for it all by reducing the size of the Federal bureaucracy and giving the money back to local communities to lower the crime rate.

There may be other things we can do to be tougher on crime, to be smarter with crime, to help to lower that rate first.

Well, if there are, let's talk about them and let's do them. But let's not go back on the things that we did last year that we know work—that we know work because the local law-enforcement officers tell us that we did the right thing. Because local community leaders, who've worked for years and years to lower the crime rate, tell us that they work.

Let's look at the experience of our cities and our rural areas where the crime rate has gone down and ask the people who did it how they did it and if what we did last year supports the decline in the crime rate, and I am convinced that it does, let us not go back on it, let's stick with it, implement it—we've got four more hard years of work to do to do that.

Gun Control

I don't want to destroy the good atmosphere in the room or in the country tonight, but I have to mention one issue that divided this body greatly last year. The last Congress also passed the Brady bill and in the crime bill the ban on 19 assault weapons.

I don't think it's a secret to anybody in this room that several members of the last Congress who voted for that aren't here tonight because they voted for it. And I know, therefore, that some of you that are here because they voted for it are under enormous pressure to repeal it. I just have to tell you how I feel about it.

The members who voted for that bill and I would never do anything to infringe on the right to keep and bear arms to hunt and to engage in other appropriate sporting activities. I've done it since I was a boy, and I'm going to keep right on doing it until I can't do it anymore.

But a lot of people laid down their seats in Congress so that police officers and kids wouldn't have to lay down their lives under a hail of assault-weapon attacks, and I will not let that be repealed. I will not let it be repealed.

I'd like to talk about a couple of other issues we have to deal with. I want us to cut more spending, but I hope we won't cut Government programs that help to prepare us for the new economy, promote responsibility and are organized from the grass roots up, not by Federal bureaucracy.

Americorps

The very best example of this is the National Service Corps—Americorps. It passed with strong bipartisan support and now there are 20,000 Americans—more than ever served in one year in the Peace Corps—working all over this country, helping person to person in local grass-roots volunteer groups, solving problems and in the process earning some money for their education.

This is citizenship at its best. It's good for the Americorps members, but it's good for the rest of us, too. It's the essence of the New Covenant and we shouldn't stop it.

Illegal Aliens

All Americans, not only in the states most heavily affected, but in every place in this country are rightly disturbed by the large numbers of illegal aliens entering our country.

The jobs they hold might otherwise be held by citizens or legal immigrants. The public services they use impose burdens on our taxpayers. That's why our Administration has moved aggressively to secure our borders more, by hiring a record number of new border guards, by deporting twice as many criminal aliens as ever before, by cracking down on illegal hiring, by barring welfare benefits to illegal aliens.

In the budget I will present to you, we will try to do more to speed the deportation of illegal aliens who are arrested for crimes, to better identify illegal aliens in the workplace as recommended by the commission headed by former Congresswoman Barbara Jordan.

We are a nation of immigrants, but we are also a nation of laws. It is wrong and ultimately self-defeating for a nation of immigrants to permit the kind of abuse of our immigration laws we have seen in recent years, and we must do more to stop it.

The Economy

The most important job of our Government in this new era is to empower the American people to succeed in the global economy. America has always been a land of opportunity, a land where, if you work hard, you can get ahead. We've become a great middle-class country; middle-class values sustain us. We must expand that middle class and shrink the underclass even as we do everything we can to support the millions of Americans who are already successful in the new economy.

America is once again the world's strongest economic power: almost six million new jobs in the last two years, exports booming, inflation down, high-wage jobs are coming back. A record number of American entrepreneurs are living the American dream.

If we want it to stay that way, those who work and lift our nation must have more of its benefits.

Today, too many of those people are being left out. They're working harder for less. They have less security, less income, less certainty that they can even afford a vacation, much less college for their kids or retirement for themselves.

We cannot let this continue. If we don't act, our economy will probably keep doing what it's been doing since about 1978, when the income growth began to go to those at the very top of our economic scale. And the people in the vast middle got very little growth and people who worked like crazy but were on the bottom then, fell even further and further behind in the years afterward, no matter how hard they worked.

We've got to have a Government that can be a real partner in making this new economy work for all of our people, a Government that helps each and every one of us to get an education and to have the opportunity to renew our skills.

That's why we worked so hard to increase educational opportunities in the last two years from Head Start to public schools to apprenticeships for young people who don't go to college, to making college loans more available and more affordable.

That's the first thing we have to do: We've got to do something to empower people to improve their skills.

Taxes

Second thing we ought to do is to help people raise their incomes immediately by lowering their taxes.

We took the first step in 1993 with a working family tax cut for 15 million families with incomes under $27,000, a tax cut that this year will average about $1,000 a family.

And we also gave tax reductions to most small and new businesses. Before we could do more than that, we first had to bring down the deficit we inherited and we had to get economic growth up. Now we've done both, and now we can cut taxes in a more comprehensive way.

But tax cuts should reinforce and promote our first obligation: to empower our citizens through education and training to make the most of their own lives. The spotlight should shine on those who make the right choices for themselves, their families and their communities.

Middle Class Bill of Rights

I have proposed a middle-class bill of rights, which should properly be called the bill of rights and responsibilities, because its provisions only benefit those who are working to educate and raise their children and to educate themselves. It will, therefore, give needed tax relief and raise incomes, in both the short run and the long run, in a way that benefits all of us.

There are four provisions:

First, a tax deduction for all education and training after high school. If you think about it, we permit businesses to deduct their investment, we permit individuals to deduct interest on their home mortgages, but today an education is even more important to the economic wellbeing of our whole country than even those things are. We should do everything we can to encourage it, and I hope you will support it.

Second, we ought to cut taxes $500 for families with children under 13.

Third, we ought to foster more savings and personal responsibility by permitting people to establish an individual retirement account and withdraw from it tax free for the cost of education, health care, first-time home buying or the care of a parent.

And fourth, we should pass a G.I. bill for America's workers. We propose to collapse nearly 70 Federal programs and not give the money to the states but give the money directly to the American people, offer vouchers to them so that they—if they're laid off or if they're working for a very low wage—can get a voucher worth $2,600 a year for up to two years to go to their local community colleges or wherever else they want to get the skills they need to improve their lives. Let's empower people in this way. Move it from the Government directly to the workers of America.

Now, any one of us can call for a tax cut, but I won't accept one that explodes the deficit or puts our recovery at risk. We ought to pay for our tax cuts fully and honestly. Just two years ago it was an open question whether we would find the strength to cut the deficit.

Thanks to the courage of the people who were here then, many of whom didn't return, we did cut the deficit. We began to do what others said would not be done: We cut the deficit by over $600 billion, about $10,000 for every family in this country. It's coming down three years in a row for the first time since Mr. Truman was President and I don't think anybody in America wants us to let it explode again.

In the budget I will send you, the middle-class bill of rights is fully paid for by budget cuts in bureaucracy, cuts in programs, cuts in special interest subsidies. And the spending cuts will more than double the tax cuts. My budget pays for the middle-class bill of rights without any cuts in Medicare, and I will oppose any attempts to pay for tax cuts with Medicare cuts. That's not the right thing to do.

I know that a lot of you have your own ideas about tax relief. And some of them I find quite interesting. I really want to work with all of you.

My tests for our proposals will be: Will it create jobs and raise incomes? Will it strengthen our families and support our children? Is it paid for? Will it build the middle class and shrink the underclass?

If it does, I'll support it. But if it doesn't, I won't.

The Minimum Wage

The goal of building the middle class and shrinking the underclass is also why I believe that you should raise the minimum wage.

It rewards work—two and a half million Americans, often women with children, are working out there today for four-and-a-quarter an hour. In terms of real buying power, by next year that minimum wage will be at a 40-year low. That's not my idea of how the new economy ought to work.

Now I studied the arguments and the evidence for and against a minimum-wage increase. I believe the weight of the evidence is that a modest increase does not cost jobs and may even lure people back into the job market. But the most important thing is you can't make a living on $4.25 an hour. Now—especially if you have children, even with the working families tax cut we passed last year.

In the past, the minimum wage has been a bipartisan issue and I think it should be again. So I want to challenge you to have honest hearings on this, to get together to find a way to make the minimum wage a living wage.

Members of Congress have been here less than a month but by the end of the week—28 days into the new year—every member of Congress will have earned as much in Congressional salary as a minimum-wage worker makes all year long.

Health Security

Everybody else here, including the President, has something else that too many

Americans do without and that's health care.

Now, last year we almost came to blows over health care, but we didn't do anything. And the cold, hard fact is that since last year—since I was here—another 1.1 million Americans in *working* families have lost their health care. And the cold, hard fact is that many millions more——most of them farmers and small business people and self-employed people—have seen their premiums skyrocket, their co-pays and deductibles go up.

There's a whole bunch of people in this country that in the statistics have health insurance but really what they've got is a piece of paper that says they won't lose their home if they get sick.

Now I still believe our country has got to move toward providing health security for every American family, but—but I know that last year, as the evidence indicates, we bit off more than we could chew.

So I'm asking you that we work together. Let's do it step by step. Let's do whatever we have to do to get something done. Let's at least pass meaningful insurance reform so that no American risks losing coverage for facing skyrocketing prices but that nobody loses their coverage because they face high prices or unavailable insurance when they change jobs or lose a job or a family member gets sick.

I want to work together with all of you who have an interest in this: with the Democrats who worked on it last time, with the Republican leaders like Senator Dole who has a longtime commitment to health care reform and made some constructive proposals in this area last year. We ought to make sure that self-employed people in small businesses can buy insurance at more affordable rates through voluntary purchasing pools. We ought to help families provide long-term care for a sick parent to a disabled child. We can work to help workers who lose their jobs at least keep their health insurance coverage for a year while they look for work, and we can find a way—it may take some time, but we can find a way—to make sure that our children have health care.

You know, I think everybody in this room, without regard to party, can be proud of the fact that our country was rated as having the world's most productive economy for the first time in nearly a decade, but we can't be proud of the fact that we're the only wealthy country in the world that has a smaller percentage of the work force and their children with health insurance today than we did 10 years ago—the last time we were the most productive economy in the world.

So let's work together on this. It is too important for politics as usual.

Foreign Affairs and National Security

Much of what the American people are thinking about tonight is what we've already talked about. A lot of people think that the security concerns of America today are entirely internal to our borders, they relate to the security of our jobs and our homes and our incomes and our children, our streets, our health, and protecting those borders.

Now that the cold war has passed, it's tempting to believe that all the security issues, with the possible exception of trade, reside here at home. But it's not so. Our security still depends on our continued world leadership for peace and freedom and democracy. We still can't be strong at home unless we're strong abroad.

The financial crisis in Mexico is a case in point. I know it's not popular to say it tonight but we have to act, not for the Mexican people but for the sake of the millions of Americans whose livelihoods are tied to Mexico's well-being. If we want to secure American jobs, preserve American exports, safeguard America's borders, then we must pass the stabilization program and help to put Mexico back on track.

Now let me repeat: it's not a loan, it's not foreign aid, it's not a bail-out. We'll be given a guarantee like co-signing a note with good collateral that will cover our risk.

This legislation is the right thing for America. That's why the bipartisan leadership has supported it. And I hope you in Congress will pass it quickly. It is in our interest and we can explain it to the American people, because we're going to do it in the right way.

You know, tonight this is the first State of the Union address ever delivered since the beginning of the cold war when not a single Russian missile is pointed at the children of America.

And along with the Russians, we're on our way to destroying the missiles and the bombers that carry 9,000 nuclear warheads. We've come so far so fast in this post-cold-war world that it's easy to take the decline of the nuclear threat for granted. But it's still there, and we aren't finished yet.

This year, I'll ask the Senate to approve START II to eliminate weapons that carry 5,000 more warheads. The United States will lead the charge to extend indefinitely the Nuclear Nonproliferation Treaty, to enact a comprehensive nuclear test ban, and to eliminate chemical weapons.

To stop and roll back North Korea's potentially deadly nuclear program, we'll continue to implement the agreement we have reached with that nation. It's smart, it's tough, it's a deal based on continuing inspection with safeguards for our allies and ourselves.

This year, I'll submit to Congress comprehensive legislation to strengthen our hand in combating terrorists, whether they strike at home or abroad. As the cowards who bombed the World Trade Center found out, this country will hunt down terrorists and bring them to justice.

Just this week, another horrendous terrorist act in Israel killed 19 and injured scores more. On behalf of the American people and all of you, I send our deepest sympathy to the families of the victims. I know that in the face of such evil, it is hard for the people in the Middle East to go forward. But the terrorists represent the past, not the future. We must and we will pursue a comprehensive peace between Israel and all her neighbors in the Middle East.

Accordingly, last night I signed an executive order that will block the assets in the United States of terrorist organizations that threaten to disrupt the peace process. It prohibits financial transactions with these groups.

And tonight I call on all our allies in peace-loving nations throughout the world to join us with renewed fervor in a global effort to combat terrorism; we cannot permit the future to be marred by terror and fear and paralysis.

The Military

From the day I took the oath of office, I pledged that our nation would maintain the best-equipped, best-trained and best-prepared military on earth. We have and they are. They have managed the dramatic downsizing of our forces after the cold war with remarkable skill and spirit. But to make sure our military is ready for action and to provide the pay and the quality of life the military and their families deserve, I'm asking the Congress to add $25 billion in defense spending over the next six years.

I have visited many bases at home and around the world since I became President. Tonight I repeat that request with renewed conviction. We ask a very great deal of our armed forces. Now that they are smaller in number, we ask more of them. They go out more often to more different places and stay longer. They are called to service in many, many ways, and we must give them and their families what the times demand and what they have earned.

Just think about what our troops have done in the last year, showing America at its best, helping to save hundreds of thousands of people in Rwanda, moving with lightning speed to head off another threat to Kuwait, giving freedom and democracy back to the people of Haiti.

We have proudly supported peace and prosperity and freedom from South Africa to Northern Ireland, from Central and Eastern Europe to Asia, from Latin America to the Middle East. All these endeavors are good in those places but they make our future more confident and more secure.

Well, my fellow Americans, that's my agenda for America's future: expanding opportunity, not bureaucracy, enhancing security at home and abroad, empowering our people to make the most of their own lives.

It's ambitious and achievable. But it's not enough.

We even need more than new ideas for changing the world or equipping Americans to compete in the new economy, more than a Government that's smaller, smarter and wiser, more than all the changes we can make in Government and in the private sector from the outside in.

Values, the Family, and Society

Our fortunes and our prosperity also depend upon our ability to answer some questions from within—from the values and voices that speak to our hearts as well as our heads, voices that tell us we have to do more to accept responsibility for ourselves and our families, for our communities, and yes, for our fellow citizens.

We see our families and our communities all over this country coming apart. And we feel the common ground shifting from under us. The P.T.A., the town hall meeting, the ball park—it's hard for a lot of overworked parents to find the time and space for those things that strengthen the bonds of trust and cooperation.

Too many of our children don't even have parents and grandparents who can give them those experiences that they need to build their own character and their sense of identity. We all know that while we here in this chamber can make a difference on those things, that the real differences will be made by our fellow citizens where they work and where they live.

And it'll be made almost without regard to party. When I used to go to the softball park in Little Rock to watch my daughter's league and people would come up to me—fathers and mothers—and talk to me, I can honestly say I had no idea whether 90 percent of them were Republicans or Democrats.

When I visited the relief centers after the floods in California, Northern California, last week, a woman came up to me and did something that very few of you would do. She hugged me and said, "Mr. President, I'm a Republican, but I'm glad you're here."

Now, why? We can't wait for disasters to act the way we used to act every day. Because as we move into this next century, everybody matters. We don't have a person to waste. And a lot of people are losing a lot of chances to do better.

That means that we need a New Covenant for everybody—for our corporate and business leaders, we're going to work here to keep bringing the deficit down, to expand markets, to support their success in every possible way. But they have an obligation: when they're doing well, to keep jobs in our communities and give their workers a fair share of the prosperity they generate.

For people in the entertainment industry in this country, we applaud your creativity and your worldwide success and we support your freedom of expression but you do have a responsibility to assess the impact of your work and to understand their damage that comes from the incessant, repetitive, mindless violence and irresponsible conduct that permeates our media all the time.

We've got to ask our community leaders and all kinds of organizations to help us stop our most serious social problem; the epidemic of teen pregnancies and births where there is no marriage. I have sent to Congress a plan to target schools all over this country with anti-pregnancy programs that work. But government can only do so much. Tonight, I call on parents and leaders all across this country to join together in a national campaign against teen pregnancy to make a difference. We can do this and we must.

And I would like to say a special word to our religious leaders. You know, I'm proud of the fact that the United States has more houses of worship per capita than any country in the world. These people, who lead our houses of worship, can ignite their congregations to carry their faith into action, can reach out to all of our children, to all of the people in distress, to those who have been savaged by the breakdown of all we hold dear, because so much of what must be done must come from the inside out. And our religious leaders and their congregations can make all the difference. They have a role in the New Covenant as well.

Citizenship

There must be more responsibility for all of our citizens. You know it takes a lot of people to help all the kids in trouble stay off the streets and in school. It takes a lot of people to build the Habitat for Humanity houses that the Speaker celebrates on his lapel pin. It takes a lot of people to provide the people power for all the civic organizations in this country that made our communities mean so much to most of us when we were kids. it takes every parent to teach the children the difference between right and wrong and to encourage them to learn and grow and to say no to the wrong things but also to believe that they can be whatever they want to be.

I know it's hard when you're working harder for less, when you're under great stress, to do these things. A lot of our people don't have the time or the emotional stress they think to do the work of citizenship. Most of us in politics haven't helped very much.

For years, we've mostly treated citizens like they were consumers or spectators, sort of political couch potatoes who were supposed to watch the TV ads—either promise them something for nothing or play on their fears and frustrations. And more and more of our citizens now get most of their information in very negative and aggressive ways that is hardly conducive to honest and open conversations. But the truth is we have got to stop seeing each other as enemies just because we have different views.

If you go back to the beginning of this country, the great strength of America, as de Tocqueville pointed out when he came here a long time ago, has always been our ability to associate with people who were different from ourselves and to work together to find common ground. And in this day everybody has a responsibility to do more of that. We simply cannot wait for a tornado, a fire or a flood to behave like Americans ought to behave in dealing with one another.

Honoring Americans

I want to finish up here by pointing out some folks that are up with the First Lady that represent what I'm trying to talk about. Citizens. I have no idea what their party affiliation is or who they voted for in the last election, but they represent what we ought to be doing.

Cindy Perry teaches second-graders to read in Americorps in rural Kentucky. She gains when she gives. She's a mother of four.

She says that her service inspired her to get her high school equivalency last year. She was married when she was a teen-ager. Stand up, Cindy. She married when she was a teen-ager. She had four children, but she had time to serve other people, to get her high school equivalency and she's going to use her Americorps money to go back to college.

Steven Bishop is the police chief of Kansas City. He's been a national leader—stand up, Steve. He's been a national leader in using more police in community policing and he's worked with Americorps to do it, and the crime rate in Kansas City has gone down as a result of what he did.

Cpl. Gregory Depestre went to Haiti as part of his adopted country's force to help secure democracy in his native land. And I might add we must be the only country in the world that could have gone to Haiti and taken Haitian-Americans there who could speak the language and talk to the people, and he was one of them and we're proud of him.

The next two folks I've had the honor of meeting and getting to know a little bit. The Rev. John and the Rev. Diana Cherry of the A.M.E. Zion Church in Temple Hills, Md. I'd like to ask them to stand. I want to tell you about them. In the early 80's they left Government service and formed a church in a small living room in a small house in the early 80's. Today, that church has 17,000 members. It is one of the three or four biggest churches in the entire United States. It grows by 200 a month.

They do it together. And the special focus of their ministry is keeping families together. They are—Two things they did make a big impression on me. I visited their church once and I learned they were building a new sanctuary closer to the Washington, D.C., line, in a higher-crime, higher-drug-rate area because they thought it was part of their ministry to change the lives of the people who needed them. Second thing I want to say is that once Reverend Cherry was at a meeting at the White House with some other religious leaders and he left early to go back to his church to minister to 150 couples that he had brought back to his church from all over America to convince them to come back together to save their marriages and to raise their kids. This is the kind of work that citizens are doing in America. We need more of it and it ought to be lifted up and supported.

The last person I want to introduce is Jack Lucas from Hattiesburg, Mississippi. Jack, would you stand up. Fifty years ago in the sands of Iwo Jima, Jack Lucas taught and learned the lessons of citizenship. On February the 20th, 1945, he and three of his buddies encountered the enemy and two grenades at their feet. Jack Lucas threw himself on both of them. In that moment he saved the lives of his companions and miraculously in the next instant a medic saved his life. He gained a foothold for freedom and at the age of 17, just a year older than his grandson, who's up there with him today, and his son, who is a West Point graduate and a veteran, at 17, Jack Lucas became the youngest marine in history and the youngest soldier in this century to win the Congressional Medal of Honor. All these years later, yesterday, here's what he said about that day: Didn't matter where you were from or who you were. You relied on one another. You did it for your country. We all gain when we give and we reap what we sow. That's at the heart of this New Covenant. Responsibility, opportunity and citizenship.

More than stale chapters in some remote civic book, they're still the virtue by which we can fulfill ourselves and reach our God-given potential and be like them. And also to fulfill the eternal promise of this country, the enduring dream from that first and most-sacred covenant. I believe every person in this country still believes that we are created equal and given by our creator the right to life, liberty and the pursuit of happiness.

This is a very, very great country and our best days are still to come.

Thank you and God bless you all.

The American Scene

Patrick J. Buchanan
Political commentator;
Candidate for the
1996 Republican
Presidential nomination

1

People feel alienated from Washington and from the turbo-charged, two-tiered go-go global economy. They miss the America they grew up in . . . There are cultural, moral, social crises, plus the sense of economic insecurity. You have to be able to address both the economic and cultural sides of the problem.

Interview, Iowa/
Newsweek,
5-29:45.

Bill Clinton
President of the
United States

2

We must stand up and speak against reckless speech that can push fragile people over the edge beyond the bounds of civilized conduct and take this country into a dark place. I say that no matter where it comes from . . . If people are encouraging conduct that will undermine the fabric of this country, it should be spoken against whether it comes from the left or the right, whether it comes on radio, television or in the movies, whether it comes in the schoolyard or, yes, even on the college campus.

At Iowa State University,
April 25/
The Washington Post,
4-26:(A)14.

3

We should never, ever permit ourselves to get into a position where we forget that almost everybody here [in the U.S.] came from somewhere else and that America is a set of ideas and values and convictions that makes us strong . . . We've done what we could to close the borders and send [illegal immigrants] back. But you know what? This is a nation of immigrants. Most of us do not have ancestors who were born here.

At dedication of
California State University
at Monterey Bay, Sept. 4/
The New York Times,
9-5:(A)1,8.

4

I think if you were betting on which country is likely to be in the strongest shape 20, 30 years from now in the 21st century, you'd have to bet on the United States because of the strength and diversity of our economy and our society.

At press lunch,
Washington, D.C., Sept. 25/
The New York Times,
9-26:(A)13.

5

Americans are getting together around the values that make life worth living. Our country is moving in the right direction and coming back together . . . We have a reassertion of basic values in every community.

Before tourism-industry group,
Washington, D.C., Oct. 30/
Los Angeles Times, 10-31:(A)4.

Robert J. Dole
United States Senator, R-Kansas; Candidate for the 1996 Republican Presidential nomination

1

The keys to our unity are under attack from our government and from intellectual elites who seem embarrassed by America . . . Our diversity requires us to bind ourselves to the American idea in every way we can—by speaking one language, taking pride in our true history and embracing the traditional American values that have guided us from the beginning.

At American Legion convention, Indianapolis, Ind., Sept. 4/ The New York Times, 9-5:(A)8.

Ken Dychtwald
Gerontologist

2

"Never trust anyone under 50!" may become a new rallying cry. In a change reminiscent of the pre-Industrial Age, older people by the year 2020 will dominate everything from business to politics, the culmination of a trend that began in the 1980s.

The Washington Post, 4-26:(A)31.

Newt Gingrich
United States Representative, R-Georgia; Speaker of the House

3

We cannot maintain a civilization with 12-year-olds having babies, 15-year-olds killing each other, 17-year-olds dying of AIDS and 18-year-olds getting diplomas when they can't even read. [Without] bold, dramatic, immediate change, the whole system is going to break down sometime during the next century.

Before National Association of Counties, Washington, D.C., March 7/ USA Today, 3-8:(A)5.

4

If I had one message for this country on this day, it would be a simple message: Idealism is American. To be romantic is American. It's okay to be a skeptic, but don't be a cynic.

Broadcast address to the nation, Washington, D.C., April 7/ The New York Times, 4-8:1.

5

The best of America is romantic realism. It leads us to be permanently frustrated with ourselves because we set an impossibly high ideal.

Interview/ Vanity Fair, September:148.

Phil Gramm
United States Senator, R-Texas; Candidate for the 1996 Republican Presidential nomination

6

My view on life is very much colored by who I am, and where I grew up, and how my people succeeded. And by my wife's story. My wife's grandfather came to this country as an indentured laborer to work in the sugar-cane fields. Her father was the first Asian-

(PHIL GRAMM)

American ever to be an officer of a sugar company. She became chairman of the CFTC [Commodity Future Trading Commission] under [former Presidents Ronald] Reagan and [George] Bush, and regulated sugar-cane futures. That's America in action. Anybody who's gonna try to tell me America doesn't work—they're wasting their breath. It can't be done. I can't be convinced.

The Atlantic Monthly, March:84.

1

We've [the U.S.] gotten off track. It's like a football team. We stopped winning because we stopped doing the things that made us winners. We started to reward people who were doing things that did not represent productive behavior. We started to penalize people who did.

The Atlantic Monthly, March:94.

2

America is not a great and powerful country because the most brilliant and talented people in the world came to live here. It's ordinary people—people who would have been peasants anywhere else—who were able to do extraordinary things.

The Atlantic Monthly, March:84.

Arthur Helton
Authority on immigration, Open Society Institute

3

The U.S. is largely what it is today because of our ability to draw and assimilate new peoples [through immigration]. That has . . . resulted in displacement and conflict from time to time; but without it, we would not be America.

USA Today, 6-30:(A)2.

Buck Henry
Screenwriter

4

Everyone's avocation in America is show business. Television captures the imagination more than anything else in people's lives. The country is somehow held together by celebrities. Celebrity actors. Celebrity talk-show people. Celebrity designers and politicians. It's this jungle of junk. Junk information. Junk misinformation. Half-baked knowledge. Received opinion. It's like a huge orchestra with everyone playing in a different key.

Interview/ The New York Times, 10-10:(B)1.

John Paul II
Pope

5

[On the U.S.]: Your power of example carries with it heavy responsibilities. Use it well, America. Be an example of justice and civic virtue, freedom fulfilled in goodness, at home and abroad . . . It is my prayerful hope that America will persevere in its own best traditions of openness and opportunity. It would indeed be sad if the United States were to turn away from that enterprising spirit which has always sought the most practical and responsible ways of continuing to share with others the blessings God has richly bestowed here.

Newark, N.J., Oct. 4/ Los Angeles Times, 10-5:(A)1,9.

(JOHN PAUL II)

1

For more than 200 years, people of different nations, languages and cultures have come here [to the U.S.], bringing memories and traditions of the old country while at the same time becoming part of a new nation. America has a reputation the world over, a reputation of power, prestige and wealth. But not everyone here is powerful; not everyone here is rich. In fact, America's sometimes-extravagant affluence often conceals much hardship and poverty.

Mass,
Queens, N.Y., Oct. 6/
The New York Times,
10-7:10.

Jack F. Kemp
Former Secretary of Housing and Urban Development of the United States

2

[Saying there are well-off and poor sectors of the U.S. economy]: There's the two Americas: One is macro-democratic and capitalist . . . The other is an economy that is almost a Third World socialist model.

Broadcast interview/
"Meet the Press,"
NBC-TV, 10-8.

Julius Lester
Author;
Professor of Judaic studies, University of Massachusetts, Amherst

3

[Vice President] Al Gore talks about the [computer] Internet as being the information superhighway. But it seems to me it is not information people want, it's a relationship. Millions of people out there are communicating with each other electronically; and what I find that's extraordinary about it is the relationships that are struck up on the Internet. People that I never would have encountered, people who I will probably never meet—yet we have relationships via the computer. In traditional cultures, the storytelling event was a very important component of creating community, bringing people together and giving them a sense of what they had in common. And certainly what we are desperately lacking right now is a sense that we as Americans have anything in common anymore.

Interview/
Booklist,
2-15:1091.

Mike Murphy
Republican Party political strategist

4

People see the whole concept of right and wrong eroding in this country. They see a kind of nihilistic society in which "values" is a dirty word and everything is okay. And that scares them. They want it to change. Politicians are afraid to talk about right and wrong because they are told by the intellectual culture that right and wrong isn't an issue. But voters are demanding that folks start addressing personal responsibility.

Panel discussion,
Washington, D.C./
Harper's,
March:53.

Colin L. Powell
General,
United States Army (Ret.);
Former Chairman,
Joint Chiefs of Staff

1

[In 1991, a black U.S. soldier, when asked if he was afraid because he was being sent into battle in Kuwait, said,] "I am not afraid. And the reason I'm not afraid is that I'm with my family." He looked over his shoulder at the other youngsters in his unit. They were white and black and yellow and every color of the American mosaic. "That's my family. We take care of one another." If we can build a spirit of family into the heart of an 18-year-old black private, send him 8,000 miles away from home, join hundreds of similar teams and have them believe that, can there be any question in your mind or in your heart that we have the capacity as a nation to instill that same sense of family, and all it entails, in every workplace, in every community, in every school, in every home back here in America?

Speech/
Time, 7-10:26.

Ann Richards
Former Governor
of Texas (D)

2

I have a lot of concern that contemporary America has forgotten its roots, has forgotten the reason that the nation was established by immigrants in the first place. The French gave us the Statue of Liberty, which has the inscription "Bring me your poor, your huddled masses," not for a decorative item in New York Harbor, but as a visual reminder to all of us of the tenets on which the nation was founded. And we are, at this day and time, seeming to pull up the gangplank, beginning to turn inward, because contemporary access to the United States is not only changing, but the obligation that we have to those who choose to come here has changed as well. This is not an individual state problem; this is a national issue, and the Federal government has got to determine how they're going to deal with it.

Interview/
"Interview" magazine,
February:28.

Paul E. Tsongas
Co-chairman,
The Concord Coalition;
Former United States Senator,
D-Massachusetts

3

It is my view that people who have inside of them a sense of their own culture and a sense of spirituality are advantaged. What has happened in this country is that we've shied away—particularly Democrats—from acknowledging them. To speak about a God is not what Democrats do. We're not comfortable. And so we leave it to the [conservative] Oliver Norths. There is a hollowness, an emptiness to what we bombard our kids with. The notion of instant gratification. The constant bombardment of sexual innuendo. You end up with a country approaching a 40 percent illegitimacy rate.

Interview,
Boston, Mass./
The Christian Science Monitor,
1-9:19.

Pete Wilson
Governor of California (R); Candidate for the 1996 Republican Presidential nomination

1

To understand America is to see it through [the Statue of Liberty's] eyes. She promises freedom—not a free ride. She promises fairness—not favoritism. She promises unlimited hope—not a guaranteed result.

Opening his campaign for the nomination, New York, N.Y., Aug. 28/ The New York Times, 8-29:(A)6.

Civil Rights • Women's Rights

Madeleine K. Albright
United States Ambassador/
Permanent Representative
to the United Nations

1

[Supporting, against criticism, U.S. First Lady Hillary Clinton's plans to attend a UN women's-rights conference in China, a country with a poor human-rights record]: It just does not make sense, in the name of human rights, to boycott a conference that has as a primary purpose the promotion of human rights.

USA Today,
8-25:(A)5.

Lamar Alexander
Candidate for the 1996
Republican Presidential nomination;
Former Secretary of Education
of the United States

2

I think equal opportunity in this country does not mean treating people as groups. It means treating them as individuals.

New Hampshire,
Feb. 19/
The Washington Post,
2-20:(A)13.

Richard K. Armey
United States Representative,
R-Texas

3

[Criticizing affirmative-action programs]: [Ending discrimination should result from] the fundamental sound goodness of the American people, not what is the bully and guile of the Federal government.

Broadcast interview/
"Face the Nation,"
CBS-TV, 2-26.

Benazir Bhutto
Prime Minister of Pakistan

4

Women who take on tough issues and stake out new territory are often on the receiving end of ignorance.

At luncheon
for visiting U.S.
First Lady
Hillary Rodham Clinton,
Islamabad, Pakistan,
March 26/
The Washington Post,
3-27:(A)13.

Clint Bolick
Litigation director,
Institute for Justice

5

Busing [of schoolchildren for racial balance] has not enjoyed any significant grass-roots support for decades. The only people who support it are the ideologues who continue to occupy leadership positions in the civil-rights establishment. I would be willing to flatly predict that busing for racial balance will disappear from large urban school districts in 10 years or less.

The New York Times,
9-26:(A)1.

Tyrone Brooks
Georgia State Representative (D); Director, Georgia Association of Black Elected Officials

1

[Criticizing the Georgia state flag for still depicting the Confederate battle emblem]: Race relations are not that good [in Georgia]. At one level, I guess people get along well. At another level, I guess they tolerate each other. And then at another level, they're horrible. Black people see this flag as a symbol of the worst part of our history, particularly in the South, and are very much offended by it . . . You see cosmetic change [in the state]. You see black elected officials. You see neighborhoods that are desegregated. You see schools that are desegregated . . . But when you look at the official symbol of the state, it's a racist swastika.

The Washington Post, 8-28:(A)10.

Ronald H. Brown
Secretary of Commerce of the United States

2

We [blacks] have to be more politically involved. It is an absolute disgrace that there are people who shed sweat, tears and blood for the right to vote and we are not participating effectively in the political process. Our rates of voter participation are among the lowest among any identifiable group in the United States population, and that has to stop. We [blacks] have to be full participants in the political process in order to take our destiny in our hands, and we have not done that effectively in the last several elections.

Ebony, February:74.

Charles S. Bullock
Political scientist, University of Georgia

3

[On the Supreme Court's ruling that some of Georgia's Congressional districts were drawn illegally to guarantee the election of blacks to Congress]: Other states are watching this. Because it's certainly not clear where you draw the line between a situation where race is the dominant factor, which the Court says is not Constitutional, and where race is one of several factors, in which case it's acceptable.

The New York Times, 8-15:(A)1.

Charlotte Bunch
Director, Center for Women's Global Leadership, Rutgers University

4

[On women in government]: When you move into the larger policy issues at the regional or national level, women's representation drops dramatically. Women are allowed in the arena of politics that is most close to home—and therefore the more mundane.

Los Angeles Times, 8-24:(A)9.

Robert P. Casey
Former Governor of Pennsylvania (D)

5

I'm a strong Democrat and believe the Party should speak for the powerless. But you can't do that and then endorse abortion on demand.

Interview/ The New York Times, 3-25:8.

Bill Clinton
President of the United States

1

What we have done for women and minorities [through affirmative-action programs] is a good thing. But we must respond to those who feel discriminated against [by those programs] . . . This is a psychologically difficult time for the so-called angry white man.

To California Democrats, April 8/ USA Today, 4-14:(A)9.

2

Our search to find ways to move more quickly to equal opportunity led to the development of what we now call "affirmative action." The purpose of affirmative action is to give our nation a way to finally address the systemic exclusion of individuals of talent, on the basis of their gender or race, from opportunities to develop, perform, achieve and contribute. Affirmative action is an effort to develop a systematic approach to open the doors of education, employment and business-development opportunities to qualified individuals who happen to be members of groups that have experienced longstanding and persistent discrimination . . . [Affirmative action] should be changed now to take care of those things that are wrong [with it], and it should be retired when its job is done. I am resolved that that day will come. But the evidence suggests, indeed screams, that that day has not come. The job of ending discrimination in this country is not over.

At National Archives, Washington, D.C., July 19/ Los Angeles Times, 7-20:(A)12.

3

[Criticizing U.S. Nation of Islam leader Louis Farrakhan, who organized the current "Million Man March" of black males in Washington]: [The marchers should be praised for] standing up for personal responsibility. [But] one million men do not make right one man's message of malice and division. No good house was ever built on a bad foundation. Nothing good ever came of hate.

Speech, Austin, Texas, Oct. 16/ The New York Times, 10-17:(A)13.

Hillary Rodham Clinton
Wife of President of the United States Bill Clinton

4

Investing in the health and education of women and girls is essential to improving local prosperity. Although women comprise 52 percent of the world population, although they are the primary caretakers for children and the aged and are a significant presence in the workforce, they continue to be marginalized in many countries. Worldwide, more than two-thirds of the children who never attended school or who drop out are girls. Of the one billion people who remain illiterate, two-thirds are women. And a disproportionate number of those we call living in absolute poverty are women.

At United Nations World Summit for Social Development, Copenhagen, Denmark, March 7/ The New York Times, 3-8:(A)9.

(HILLARY RODHAM CLINTON)

1

More and more women, particularly the young women I speak with, really see their lives as not having to do everything but doing what is best for them, whatever that might be. There's also the growing recognition that we're all going to live longer. We have many more years of productive, active lives, so the decision you make at 22 doesn't have to be the one you make at 42 or 62. In order for this to come true, though, society has to change. I hope, as we look at the life cycle, that society understands that women today in their 40s and 50s are active and engaged and can be full participants in the workplace. Instead of being discriminated against, women should be welcomed if they raise their children first and then go into the workplace. We are also going to have to do more to support women as parents and workers. We really make it as hard as possible for women to fulfill their dual responsibilities. And so instead of talking about family values, we ought to be thinking of ways to value families.

Interview, Washington, D.C./ Harper's Bazaar, September:382.

Christopher Darden
Deputy District Attorney of Los Angeles County, Calif.

2

All too often, people see me [and] other black professionals and they always want to minimize our accomplishments. Being black always means that you're going to be mistaken for somebody, someone or something you aren't.

Interview/USA Today, 6-5:(A)3.

Robert J. Dole
United States Senator, R-Kansas; Candidate for the 1996 Republican Presidential nomination

3

[On affirmative action]: Has it worked? Has it had an adverse, a reverse reaction? Why did 62 percent of white males vote Republican in 1994? I think it's because of things like this, where sometimes the best-qualified person does not get the job because he or she may be one color. And I'm beginning to believe that may not be the way it should be in America. [In the past in the U.S.,] we did discriminate. We did suppress people. It was wrong. Slavery was wrong. But should future generations have to pay for that? Some would say yes. I think it's a tough question.

Broadcast interview/ "Meet the Press," NBC-TV, 2-5.

4

If affirmative action means remedying proven past discrimination against individuals, then I'm all for it. [But I am not for] quotas, set-asides and other preferences that favor individuals simply because they happen to belong to certain groups. That's where I draw the line.

Before the Senate, Washington, March 17/ The New York Times, 3-18:7.

5

[Criticizing affirmative-action programs]: The policies of preference have grown and grown and grown, pitting individual against

(ROBERT J. DOLE)

individual, group against group, American against American. It is time to stop making government policy by race.

July 27/
USA Today, 7-28:(A)4.

1

[Criticizing U.S. Nation of Islam leader Louis Farrakhan, who organized the recent "Million Man March" of black males in Washington]: Farrakhan is a racist and anti-Semite, unhinged by hate. He has no place in American public life, and all who lead must say so . . . There are probably a lot of well-intentioned people [who came] to Washington. And I like the talk about self-reliance, about picking yourself up, cleaning up our cities and getting kids off drugs. But I don't think Farrakhan should be the leader of the march. He spreads suspicion, separatism and hate wherever he goes. No cloak can cover the ugliness of Farrakhan's purpose.

Speech, New York, N.Y., Oct. 16/
The New York Times,
10-17:(A)12.

Myrlie Evers-Williams
Chairman, National Association for the Advancement of Colored People

2

We can say that hate knows no color. And we can also say that America is not as color-blind as it says it is. It is time for us to check our moral compasses.

Before Consultation on Conscience,
Washington, D.C., May 2/
Los Angeles Times,
5-3:(A)18.

3

We may have thought that we were free of racism and prejudice, but we are finding that it was just sleeping for a while and it's back in full force now.

News conference,
Minneapolis, Minn., July 9/
The Washington Post,
7-10:(A)4.

4

There are isolated cases of racism daily for African-Americans. I am not surprised at anything I see or hear . . . This country is saturated with examples of racism—blatant and subtle—and that is nothing new to African-Americans and it is nothing new to me.

U.S. News & World Report,
10-23:40,41.

Louis Farrakhan
Spiritual leader, Nation of Islam in the United States

5

I don't think we [blacks] can tolerate anymore the injustice that is being heaped on our people. Why should we be asked to be tolerant? That's another name for being an Uncle Tom—you're a tolerant Negro. Hell no. I can't tolerate what's going on in the black community. We can't tolerate black-on-black crime, self-destruction, fratricide. I'm not a tolerant leader. I'm intolerant, and I want the whole black community to rise up and not tolerate what we're doing to ourselves and what others are trying to do to us.

Interview,
Washington, D.C./
U.S. News & World Report,
10-16:60.

(LOUIS FARRAKHAN)

1

Abraham Lincoln was the 16th President of these United States, and he was the man who allegedly freed us [blacks]. Abraham Lincoln saw in his day what [current] President Clinton sees in this day. He saw the great divide between black and white. Abraham Lincoln and Bill Clinton see what the Kerner Commission saw 30 years ago, when they said that this nation was moving toward two Americas, one black, one white, separate and unequal. And the Kerner Commission revisited their findings 25 years later and saw that America was worse today than it was in the time of [the late civil-rights leader] Martin Luther King, Jr. There's still two Americas, one black, one white, separate and unequal.

Speech at "Million Man March," Washington, D.C., Oct. 16/ The New York Times, 10-17:(A)14.

2

White supremacy, when we [blacks] come under it, produces in its wake black inferiority. And black-inferiority thinking always measures success by how close we get to that which we determine is superior. So if you get a big position with *Newsweek* [magazine] or I get one on the Democratic National Committee or something, I have ascended. Why? Because I'm closer to white people, to what they describe as success. That's sick.

Interview, Chicago, Ill./ Newsweek, 10-30:36.

Henry W. Foster, Jr.
Surgeon General-designate of the United States

3

[On the controversy over his having performed abortions]: I abhor abortions. I abhor war. To me, abortion is failure. I don't like failure.

Broadcast interview/ "Nightline," ABC-TV, 2-8.

4

My opponents say that this nomination [for Surgeon General] is about [his support for] abortion. I believe in the right of a woman to choose. And I also support the President's [Clinton] belief that abortions should be safe, legal and rare.

At George Washington University School of Medicine, Feb. 10/ The New York Times, 2-11:8.

Abraham H. Foxman
National director, Anti-Defamation League of B'nai B'rith

5

[On the worldwide "skinhead" movement of neo-Nazi white supremacists]: It is unbelievable that three generations after the Holocaust, we still hear the deadly march of Nazi thugs around the world. Cruel history has taught us that we dare not ignore the first sounds of jackboots. The violent and racist skinhead movement must be countered by government, law enforcement and all decent people.

The New York Times, 6-28:(A)11.

Barney Frank
United States Representative,
D-Massachusetts

1

Gay people have a different role than other minority groups. A lot of minority groups have had to fight for their political rights, but they haven't had to fight as hard as we have for their identity, for having their existence acknowledged. Race has been much more devastating, but there's one physiological factor [that's different]: Very few black kids have ever had to worry about telling their parents that they were black.

Interview,
Washington, D.C./
Mother Jones,
May-June:73.

Newt Gingrich
United States Representative,
R-Georgia;
Speaker of the House

2

[Saying he is against racial quotas]: I want to help people who work hard, who come out of poor neighborhoods, who come out of poor backgrounds, who go to schools in poor counties. I want to see us find ways to reach out and help individuals, but I am against any kind of quota structure or set-aside structure that is based purely and simply on some kind of background, genetic definition. [I would] rather talk about how do we replace group affirmative action with effective help for individuals, rather than just talk about wiping out affirmative action by itself.

Broadcast interview/
"Face the Nation,"
CBS-TV, 4-9.

3

[Arguing against affirmative-action programs]: I believe there is real prejudice in America. I don't believe we live in a color-blind society. But I don't think you can find individual justice by litigation. I think when you try to create that backward-looking grievance system, you teach people exactly the wrong habits. They end up spending their life waiting for the laws to come instead of spending their life seeking opportunity . . . I'm looking for positive models, not ones based on genetic codes that exploit a lawyer-defined system . . . We ended up with a civil-rights movement that was too lawyer-dominated . . . and too dominated by people who thought that there was some way to get fairness of outcome instead of equality of opportunity.

At meeting of black journalists,
Washington, D.C., June 15/
Los Angeles Times,
6-16:(A)31.

Mary Ann Glendon
Professor of law,
Harvard University;
Head of Vatican delegation
to the forthcoming
United Nations Conference
on Women

4

Some of my best friends are radical feminists. These are women of great intelligence and character. [But] the feminist movement of the 1970s is already an old-line sideline movement that has made itself marginal to the concerns of most women. What made it obsolete is loyalty tests, like abortion, and lack of concern with the real problems of American women. The real question is, how do I have a decent family life plus participate in

(MARY ANN GLENDON)

the world of work. For most women, the problem is poverty.

Interview,
Cambridge, Mass./
The New York Times,
8-29:(A)3.

1

[Criticizing abortion]: The whole question about abortion is related to the coarsening of the social fabric. It promotes a certain callousness which has frightening implications for the future.

Interview,
Cambridge, Mass./
The New York Times,
8-29:(A)3.

Al Gore
Vice President
of the United States

2

We [in the Clinton Administration] are opposed to [racial] quotas. We are opposed to ever giving a job to somebody who is unqualified for that job. [But we] are in favor of moving forward to assert diversity as a national value in the interests of the entire country.

Broadcast interview/
"Meet the Press,"
NBC-TV, 4-9.

Phil Gramm
United States Senator, R-Texas;
Candidate for the 1996 Republican
Presidential nomination

3

If I become President, by Executive order I will overturn [racial and gender] quotas, preferences and set-asides. I am for equal and unlimited opportunity in America. But I am for special privilege for no one.

New Hampshire,
Feb. 19/
The Washington Post,
2-20:(A)13.

4

[Saying there isn't a consensus in the country for a Constitutional amendment that would overturn abortion rights, even though such an amendment has been part of the Republican Party platform since the 1980s]: In terms of putting that [Republican anti-abortion plank] into public policy, it's clear we don't have a consensus, [and] there are good Republicans who differ on the issue . . . [But] I'm not going to sign a law that forces taxpayers [through Federally funded abortions] . . . to spend their money on something that they oppose as strongly as abortion on demand.

Broadcast interview/
"Meet the Press,"
NBC-TV, 3-12.

Henry J. Hyde
United States Representative,
R-Illinois

5

[On whether to continue affirmative-action programs]: I never thought much of using discrimination to remedy discrimination. How many hundreds of years must expire before we all are at the starting line? . . . These are very nuanced questions. There are no easy answers and no flip answers.

USA Today,
3-24:(A)4.

(HENRY J. HYDE)

1

[On recent Supreme Court rulings and other anti-affirmative-action moves in Congress and elsewhere, which have been criticized by black leaders]: There obviously is a mood in the country, reflected in Congress and the courts, to restrict [racial] preferences and set-asides. Doing that cannot be described as an assault on civil rights. [Black Congressional Democrats] are not in power anymore, and they really don't like it. They are defensive and in denial right now. And they view every deviation as an assault.

The Washington Post,
7-3:(A)8.

Jesse L. Jackson
Civil-rights leader

2

[Criticizing recent Supreme Court decisions that many have interpreted as being against affirmative-action programs]: The Court has authorized the country to unravel the legal fabric of social justice and inclusion that has been woven together over the last 41 years . . . It is especially painful that a descendant of slaves [black Supreme Court Justice Clarence Thomas], in effect, stabbed [the late civil-rights leader Martin Luther] King . . . in the back, and is paving the way back toward slavery.

USA Today,
6-30:(A)8.

3

[On the "Million Man March" of black males in Washington]: Why are we here today? Because we're [blacks] under attack by the courts, legislatures, mass media. We're despised. Racists attack us for sport to win votes. We're attacked for sport to make money. But I tell you today, rabbit hunting ain't fun when the rabbits stop running and start fighting back . . . We come here today because there is a structural malfunction in America. It was structured in the Constitution, and they referred to us as three-fifths of a human being, legally. There's a structural malfunction. That's why there's a crack in the Liberty Bell. There's a structural malfunction . . . One man standing up, looking down on an apple, sees red and that which is delectable; another man standing on the bottom, looking up, sees rot and sees worms. We all have a right to eat the fruit. None should have the obligation to eat the worms and eat the rot. We want an America for all of us to play on an even playing field, by one set of rules.

Speech at
"Million Man March,"
Washington, D.C., Oct. 16/
The New York Times,
10-17:(A)14.

John Paul II
Pope

4

[Criticizing abortion]: To a great extent, the story of America has been the story of long and difficult struggles to overcome the prejudices which excluded certain categories of people from a full share in the country's life. Sadly, a new class of people is being excluded. When the unborn child—the stranger in the womb—is declared to be beyond the protection of society, not only are America's deepest traditions radically undermined and endangered, but a moral blight is brought upon society . . . The right to life is the first of all rights. It is the foundation of democratic liberties and the keystone of the edifice of civil

(JOHN PAUL II)

society. Both as Americans and as followers of Christ, American Catholics must be committed to the defense of life in all its stages and in every condition.

Mass, East Rutherford, N.J., Oct. 5/ Los Angeles Times, 10-6:(A)26.

Sherry Lansing
Chairman, motion-picture group, Paramount Pictures

1

I remember [actress] Katharine Hepburn saying, "You can't have it all [as a woman]." It's such a profound statement. The most painful thing about the women's movement is that they tell you you *can* have it all. And you will have a nervous breakdown! I believe you can be a wife and a mother and have a career, but then you should be happy being the vice president. You can't be CEO because *something's* gonna give. How do you get to your kid's soccer game? How do you drive him to school and cook? I think you can do two out of the three. You can be married and have a career; you can have a career and have a kid. But you can't do all three and reach your optimum.

Interview, Los Angeles, Calif./ Working Woman, April:39.

John Lewis
United States Representative, D-Georgia

2

[Criticizing recent anti-affirmative-action rulings by the Supreme Court]: Twenty, thirty years ago, we looked to the Supreme Court as a sympathetic referee in the struggle for civil rights and social justice. This [current] court is not a friend of civil rights.

The Washington Post, 7-3:(A)1.

Joseph I. Lieberman
United States Senator, D-Connecticut

3

[Criticizing affirmative-action programs]: You can't defend policies that are based on group preferences as opposed to individual opportunities, which is what America has always been about. When we have such policies, we have the effect of breaking some of those ties in civil society that have held us together, because [those policies are] patently unfair. And those who are the victims of them, and lose out when choices are made based on group preferences as opposed to individual ability, naturally become disaffected from the process.

At National Press Club, Washington, D.C., March 9/ The New York Times, 3-10:(A)8.

Trent Lott
United States Senator, R-Mississippi

4

[Saying affirmative-action programs have outlived their usefulness]: I never thought affirmative action was intended to give, in perpetuity, special preferences and quotas. It was intended to be an encouragement . . . to

(TRENT LOTT)

make sure everyone has an equal opportunity. It is a far stretch from this [today].

USA Today,
3-24:(A)4.

Nelson Mandela
President of South Africa

1

[Comparing racism in the U.S. with the apartheid system that used to exist in South Africa]: What made apartheid a crime against humanity is that the racism was entrenched in the Constitution and the laws of the country. That was never the case in the United States. At least the [U.S.] Constitution prohibited, outlawed racism. It's a vast difference. You do find racism [in the U.S.], but that's a *vast* difference.

Interview, New York, N.Y./
Newsweek, 11-6:51.

Will Marshall
President,
Progressive Policy Institute

2

[On calls for the ending of affirmative-action programs because of their perceived bias against non-minorities]: What's needed is a third way that honors our moral commitments to equal opportunity without further depleting our civic reserves of interracial trust and good-will.

USA Today, 8-4:(A)2.

3

[On the recent trial of black former football star O.J. Simpson, in which the defense used the "race card" in appealing to a predominantly black jury that acquitted Simpson of murdering two whites]: What this episode does is deepen the [black-white] polarization [in the country]. It is really a terrible blow to the idea of a civic culture to which we all owe allegiance that transcends our racial and ethnic identity.

Los Angeles Times,
10-9:(A)5.

Michael D. McCurry
Press Secretary to President
of the United States
Bill Clinton

4

[Saying anti-abortionists have put in doubt the Senate's confirmation of Surgeon General-designate Dr. Henry Foster, who has performed abortions during his career]: The truth is that there are extremists within the right-to-life movement who have now hooked Republicans and Congress by the nose and they're dragging them around.

Press briefing,
Washington, D.C., Feb. 13/
The New York Times,
2-14:(A)8.

Russell Means
American-Indian rights activist

5

[On the American Indian Movement organization]: AIM is an organization I'm very proud of. We were the vanguard of the renaissance of Indian pride and self-dignity. The vanguard. Our primary focus was to fight racism and also to fight for independence, complete independence, and freedom, from the U.S. of A., based upon our treaty law. One of our axioms was self-defense. If we were attacked, we would not turn the other cheek, nor would we bend over to get the other two

(RUSSELL MEANS)

kicked. We fought. Percentage-wise, we suffered more assassinations, governmental pressure, repression and suppression than any other militant organization of that time [the 1960s and '70s]. Yet of all those militant organizations—like the Black Panthers, Weathermen, Brown Berets, Young Lords—we're the only one that survived the '70s.

Interview/Modern Maturity,
Sept.-Oct.:70.

Kate Michelman
President, National Abortion
and Reproductive Rights
Action League

1

[Anti-abortion groups'] goal, however long it takes them, is to make all abortions under all circumstances a crime. They cannot immediately criminalize all abortions under all circumstances, but they have begun to move us step by step down that road . . . Years ago, the whole debate about abortion was about the procedure, about the fetus, and there was never a discussion about the women who faced a crisis pregnancy or the circumstances of their lives. We changed that. But now they are trying to come back to the issue of procedure and sensationalize it to distract people from thinking about the women and the fact that the real issue in the debate is who should decide [whether or not to have an abortion].

The New York Times,
6-19:(A)8.

Carol Moseley-Braun
United States Senator, D-Illinois

2

[On affirmative action]: If there is any objective that should command complete American consensus, it is ensuring that every American has the chance to succeed—and that, in the final analysis, is what affirmative action is all about.

USA Today, 3-24:(A)4.

Karen Nussbaum
Director,
Women's Bureau of Labor,
Department of Labor
of the United States

3

In my generation [she is 45 years old], there wasn't a woman who did not start as a secretary or a waitress, and I did both. If you wanted to sell insurance, you went in as a secretary. There was no other point of entry. Ten years ago, two younger women, right out of college, were in front of me on a plane talking about sales. And I realized, this is different, mostly due to affirmative action and the women's movement and a difference in large part, too, by education and family income. So that a whole group found themselves not starting out as clerical workers. [But] you still find a very large group of women in clerical and low-wage service work, and 75 percent of working women still earn less than $25,000 [a year].

Interview/
The New York Times,
4-27:(A)12.

Alan Parker
Director, Washington office,
(American-Indian)
Tribal Development Association

4

There's a whole mind-set [among American Indians] that has changed in the course of

(ALAN PARKER)

a generation. [It is] a mind-set that says, it may not be easy, but we can gain control of our own destiny . . . We have lately found ways to exploit [our] political rights and to translate them into economic opportunities . . . [and] a competitive edge . . . We have to be [as] economically independent as possible, because . . . it is certainly feasible that any given [U.S.] Congress could pass a law . . . [to] end [the Federal trust] responsibilities the United States has maintained for 150 years. We have to be in a position to protect our interests in the future by having economic success, some sources of income that come back to us so that we're able to have a viable base.

The Washington Post,
9-11:(A)14.

Deval Patrick
Assistant Attorney General,
Civil Rights Division, Department
of Justice of the United States

1

Cases involving employment discrimination against white men are rare, but no less important than cases involving minorities and women . . . The law is the law. When individuals are absolutely precluded from getting a job because of their gender or race, we have an obligation to enforce the law.

March 3/
Los Angeles Times,
3-4:(A)4.

Robert Plotkin
President,
American Civil Liberties Union

2

[Arguing against a proposed curfew for teenagers in Washington, D.C.]: Curfews are a hallmark of non-democratic societies.

U.S. News & World Report,
11-13:38.

Colin L. Powell
General, United States Army (Ret.);
Former Chairman,
Joint Chiefs of Staff

3

How did I [as a black] deal with racism? I beat it. I said, "I am not going to carry this burden of racism. I'm going to destroy your stereotype. I'm proud to be black. *You* carry this burden of racism, because I'm not going to."

Speech/
Time, 7-10:25.

Clement Price
Professor of
African-American history,
Rutgers University

4

The struggle for racial justice and the dignity of all people is enduring; it's part of American society and American culture. The struggle will always be there. It desperately needs people—whites and blacks—with college educations.

At Rutgers University,
Newark, N.J./
The Washington Post,
2-27:(A)1.

Dan Quayle
Former Vice President
of the United States

5

Affirmative action and [racial] quotas are discriminatory and wrong. To accept them is

(DAN QUAYLE)

to take [the late civil-rights leader Martin Luther] King's dream—that Americans be judged "not by the color of their skin but by the content of their character"—and turn it on its head.

USA Today,
2-17:(A)13.

Robert B. Reich
Secretary of Labor of the United States

1

There will be no retreat from the goals of affirmative action. This [Clinton] Administration is absolutely committed to it; the President is committed to it. Now, obviously we have to examine every program. We've got to make sure that affirmative action itself is achieving the goals of overcoming discrimination as effectively and efficiently as possible. But no one should take from the President's decision to review [Federal affirmative-action policies] any retreat from the goals.

Interview/
USA Today, 3-3:(B)4.

Ann Richards
Governor of Texas (D)

2

Little girls are socialized differently from little boys. We [females] are much more likely to try to bring people together than to divide them. We see problem-solving as trying to enlist everyone's ideas. I think the male system is more top-down autocratic. The downside is that women in positions of power and responsibility are still rare. And change is threatening. It doesn't mean the woman is threatening. It just means that making a change is very difficult for people to do. The interesting thing is, once you've made the change, it's no longer a problem. In the jobs I have had, every person who's held the job subsequent to my being there has been female.

Interview, Austin, Texas/
Working Woman,
March:86.

Patricia Schroeder
United States Representative, D-Colorado

3

[Criticizing those who are against Surgeon General nominee Dr. Henry Foster because of his involvement in performing abortions]: We want to say: Stop this nonsense . . . Slow down. We don't believe in lynchings. We don't want to see that kind of goose-stepping over women's rights.

Los Angeles Times,
2-11:(A)4.

John H. Shattuck
Assistant Secretary for Human Rights and Humanitarian Affairs, Department of State of the United States

4

[On civil rights in the U.S.]: Our system is not perfect. But the essential genius of our Founding Fathers lay in their creating a system in and through which injustices . . . could be addressed and rectified, through the will of the people, under the rule of law.

Before International
Human Rights Committee,
United Nations,
New York, March 29/
The Washington Post,
3-30:(A)19.

Theodore M. Shaw
Associate director-counsel,
Legal Defense and Educational Fund,
National Association
for the Advancement
of Colored People

1

[On the increasing criticism of affirmative-action programs]: Certainly the political landscape has changed. The prospect of Congress opening up affirmative-action programs for review is one that is a cause for concern. These issues are very complex and sensitive. The courts have struck a balance that allows affirmative action in limited circumstances. But the political process and the nature of political discourse these days do not insure these issues will be dealt with in a thoughtful and sensitive way.

The New York Times,
2-7:(A)9.

Claude Sitton
Former reporter,
"The New York Times"

2

[On his experiences covering the South for *The New York Times* in the 1950s and '60s]: Everything was clearer [for blacks] then. Going to the back of the bus, drinking out of separate water fountains, going to segregated schools—those are the kinds of things that just hit you right between the eyes.

Newsweek, 6-26:18.

Joshua L. Smith
Chief executive officer,
Maxima Corporation

3

One of the problems that blacks have in this country is an overemphasis on the social side of the equation. I don't say that the concern for social issues is wrong, but the concern for social issues in the absence of an economic base has no future . . . Most Republicans I know care about people. They just recognize that you have to have a foundation before you can build a house.

Ebony,
February:184.

Katherine Spillar
National coordinator,
Feminist Majority
Foundation

4

[Saying opponents of affirmative action don't mention that the elimination of such programs would impact women negatively]: [Those opponents] know affirmative action for women is popular—and they don't dare wake a sleeping giant that is a majority of the American electorate.

The Washington Post,
3-2:(A)9.

Gloria Steinem
Author;
Women's-rights advocate

5

In the backlash against all our work in getting abortion decriminalized here [in the U.S.], the same right-wing forces that say government should get off the backs of corporations are trying to put government into the wombs of women. There's also a big correlation between being anti-abortion and pro-capital punishment, pro-guns and pro-military-spending. The message is that much of the right wing cares less about the sanctity of human life than about who has the power to

(GLORIA STEINEM)

make the decision. If the government or church does, that's okay. If individual citizens do, that's not okay, especially if they're women. That's because in maintaining patriarchy—and maintaining racial "purity" in the long run, and thus racism—you have to control women's bodies as the means of reproduction. That's why this issue goes so deep, and why abortion is opposed with such violence and terrorism, especially now that the right wing has lost by most democratic means [to restrict legal abortions].

Interview/
"Interview" magazine,
June:99.

George C. Wallace
Former Governor
of Alabama (D)

1

[Addressing civil-rights activists on the anniversary of a civil-rights march in Alabama 30 years ago when he was a segregationist Governor]: [I] cannot help but reflect on those days that remain so vivid in my memory. Those were different days and we all in our own ways were different people. We have learned hard and important lessons in the 30 years that have passed between us since the days surrounding your first walk along Highway 80. Those days were filled with passionate convictions and a magnified sense of purpose that imposed a feeling on us all that events of the day were bigger than any one individual. Much has transpired since those days. A great deal has been lost and a great deal has been gained, and here we are. My message to you today is, Welcome to Montgomery. May your message be heard. May your lessons never be forgotten. May our history be always remembered.

Speech,
Montgomery, Alabama,
March 10/
The New York Times,
3-11:8.

Maxine Waters
United States Representative,
D-California

2

[Warning President Clinton and the Democratic Party not to back away from affirmative-action programs]: No party is so important that we [blacks] will belong to it if it undermines us on this issue. No President is so important that [black voters] will belong to him if he undermines us on this issue.

USA Today, 3-24:(A)4.

3

[Criticizing recent Supreme Court rulings and other anti-affirmative-action moves in Congress and elsewhere]: It does not feel good. It feels as if the Supreme Court, legislative bodies, organized right-wing groups have all kind of decided their worst enemy is people of color, and African-Americans specifically . . . Our job is in the streets organizing. Conferences, rallies, protests. We've got to put a face on what is happening to us.

The Washington Post,
7-3:(A)1.

Roger Wilkins
Professor of history
and American culture,
George Mason University

4

[On the NAACP's election of Myrlie

(ROGER WILKINS)

Evers-Williams, a woman, as its new chairman]: Civil-rights organizations have tended to be male-dominated, and that's just got to change . . . I think there may be some men who will be foot-draggers, but I think that there are other men who will rally fiercely to her and will not brook that nonsense.

The Washington Post,
2-20:(A)6.

Pete Wilson
Governor of California (R)

1

[On affirmative-action programs]: I don't think we should be awarding either jobs or places in a graduate-school class based upon race or gender; because if you do, essentially you're talking about a quota system, and I don't think that what we want are quotas. We don't want to deny anybody access, but I don't think you give preferences by virtue of gender or membership in an ethnic group.

Interview/
The Washington Post, 2-4:(A)6.

2

[On criticism that Proposition 187—which California voters passed last year and which bars illegal immigrants in the state from receiving certain public benefits—is racist]: It's not about race at all and it certainly is not anti-immigrant. With all respect, I would have to say to anybody who tries to lecture Californians about racism or about anti-immigrant sentiment—we are a state more than any other, I suspect, that has been built with the courage and sweat of immigrants.

New York, N.Y., March 29/
Los Angeles Times, 3-30:(A)18.

Pete Wilson
Governor of California (R);
Candidate for the
1996 Republican
Presidential nomination

3

[On abortion]: I favor the right of reproductive choice. I think that government has no business making so intensely personal a decision for a woman . . . But I don't think that the taxpayers should necessarily be the ones to pay for it [through Federal funding of abortion for poor women and Federal employees].

Broadcast interview/
"Meet the Press,"
NBC-TV, 8-6.

4

[On his change over the years from a supporter of affirmative-action programs to a critic of them]: I became Mayor of San Diego [in the 1970s] just in time for affirmative-action programs to be applicable to state and local government. There is no question that virtually all Americans, certainly most, felt a sense of guilt, as well we should have, for some two to three centuries of oppression, particularly of African-Americans. There was a desire at that point to engage in compensation . . . But 30 years later, it is impossible to say that we should continue to discriminate against better-qualified applicants in favor of lesser-qualified applicants who have experienced no discrimination, and to penalize those who have practiced no discrimination.

News conference,
Burbank, Calif./
The New York Times,
8-8:(A)6.

William Julius Wilson
Sociologist,
University of Chicago

1

[In periods of economic difficulty, people are] very vulnerable to demagogic messages . . . Instead of associating their economic insecurities and pessimism about the future with economic changes and political changes in the broader society and worldwide . . . they turn on each other, race against race.

Broadcast interview/
"Meet the Press,"
NBC-TV, 2-19.

Commerce • Industry • Finance

Edwin Artzt
Former chief executive officer,
Procter & Gamble Company

1

[On corporations that become bigger through acquisition of other companies]: [Bigger is better,] but only if you retain the advantages you had when you were a smaller company. It's not better if it takes you into businesses that you're not good at . . . When a company gets into a business that is distant from its core strengths, that increases the possibility that down the road they're going to have to get back to basics.

At symposium sponsored by "Business Week" magazine, Sept. 28/USA Today, 9-29:(B)11.

David Asher
U.S. authority on Japan

2

In the early 1990s, the bureaucrats in Japan's Ministry of Finance developed what some rather cynically called a "Lazarus" strategy: They were going to resurrect the Japanese stock market the way Jesus Christ raised Lazarus from the grave. By supporting the market, they thought they could revive economic growth, pulling asset values back up. But the strategy has failed. They've spent trillions of yen pumping air into a dead body, and they're not even eliciting a heart murmur, let alone a brain wave. Valuations of Japanese stocks are absurd. The Nikkei stock index is priced at nearly 105 times earnings. That's the highest in history. U.S. stocks, by contrast, sell for about 17 times earnings. Meanwhile, the Japanese economy's basic problems haven't changed.

Interview/ USA Today, 7-28:(B)10.

John Baldacci
United States Representative,
D-Maine

3

[On his being a small-businessman who ran for Congress]: Small-business people unlock the door in the morning and lock it again at night. That is our life, and no one from Washington can help us. We just don't want them to hurt us.

U.S. News & World Report, 3-27:45.

Anne K. Bingaman
Assistant Attorney General,
Antitrust Division,
Department of Justice
of the United States

4

You see so much in this job because you go to Japan, you go to Europe—the markets [there] are so closed, opportunity is closed off. You have huge, huge companies and tiny little shopkeepers. You don't have this big range of small and medium-sized businesses—people starting their own companies and growing them—that we have in this country. We've got so much more opportunity for average people to start and own their own businesses. We have such lower prices for consumers. Our standard of living is double. And

(ANNE K. BINGAMAN)

we still take it for granted. When you go to these other countries, they look the same; they're industrialized, the people wear suits to work, they drive the cars you know—it looks all the same. But the truth is, what they can buy in stores is limited, the prices are high, they can't start their own businesses, access to the market is limited, it's controlled by a few powerful companies in each industry. We [in the U.S.] have such a dynamic, open and thriving society that helps both businesses and consumers. It really is because for a hundred years we've had this strong, bipartisan support for antitrust enforcement. And it started, of course, under Republicans. Theodore Roosevelt was the original trustbuster. We have such a belief in the importance of open markets and access to markets, and no single company abusing a dominant position in ways that violate the law. It's a powerful, powerful social tool. And the support of average people for that is crucial. And that's what these other countries don't have.

Interview/
The Wall Street Journal,
3-20:(R)23.

Stephen J. Brobeck
Executive director,
Consumer Federation
of America

1

[Bank mergers] don't benefit shareholders as a whole. The merger splurge [is largely due to the] egos of CEOs and management involved, who see bigger as better, and a chance to boost their salaries.

The Christian Science Monitor,
8-30:3.

Ronald H. Brown
Secretary of Commerce
of the United States

2

[Criticizing Republican proposals to eliminate the U.S. Department of Commerce]: [That would be] tantamount to unilateral disarmament in the global battle for competitiveness. [But] in the final analysis, cooler heads will prevail.

To reporters,
Aug. 1/
The Christian Science Monitor,
8-2:4.

Sam Brownback
United States Representative,
R-Kansas

3

To the extent that we can remove the Federal government and get it off [small businesses'] back and out of your pocket, we're going to free you up to allow the genius of America, to allow that individual entrepreneur to grow and prosper.

Nation's Business,
May:21.

Peter Cardillo
Director of research,
Westfalia Investments

4

[On the continuing record rise in the stock market]: This market is like an old soldier that just doesn't give up.

Los Angeles Times,
11-30:(D)3.

James Champy
Management consultant

1

I hardly find a CEO today that doesn't understand the case for major change [in the way companies operate]. Most of them understand that if they don't bring an organization through something—whether you call it re-engineering, transformation or reinvention—you'll either be bought or sold or consolidated into something else. I don't find any manager, senior manager or CEO who doesn't understand that. When I have a one-on-one discussion with them, they often have frustration in their voices, wondering if their immediate managers are the team to bring them through the change.

Interview/
USA Today,
3-31:(B)4.

2

[On the traits of a good company manager]: There's an inclination, what I call being profoundly questioning, that is very important. Always asking the question: "Why do we do this, this way? What is the purpose of the enterprise?" The second characteristic is a willingness to let go of control . . . of being able to understand what is going on in the enterprise without having to control what's going on. Also, an inclination to take reasonable risks . . . and be able to learn from mistakes you've made. The other thing I think you have to be is hopeful.

Interview/
USA Today,
3-31:(B)4.

Hillary Rodham Clinton
Wife of President
of the United States
Bill Clinton

3

There has to be a revision in the minds of many male managers and some female managers about what management styles are appropriate [regarding women in the workplace]. Very often, if you scratch the surface of management decisions that bypass women despite their work, you will find these stereotypes about what a manager should be, how a manager should talk. You will find the stereotypes about whether a woman is tough enough, or whether in fact she is too tough. Now, the same standards are not applied to men and women. You and I have probably experienced and seen this ourselves. You know—the woman who is tough and aggressive and adopts a male management style gets penalized because she's not acting like a "lady"; the woman who adopts a more collegial management style is not thought to be tough enough to move to the highest levels of management. Well, it's a catch-22. In today's world, we need to rethink what group management is and cut the stereotypes back so that women are permitted to be seen as individuals—some are tough, and some are more flexible, and there are as many different management styles among women as there are among men. We should start accepting that.

Interview,
Washington, D.C./
Harper's Bazaar,
September:382.

Michael "Mac" Collins
United States Representative,
R-Georgia

1

Any time you enhance the budget of individuals . . . they have more money to spend on consumer goods or services. And it takes people coming through the door of a business with money in their pockets to enhance that business's cash flow.

Nation's Business,
July:24.

John Costello
Senior executive vice president,
Sears Roebuck & Company

2

For years, marketers were focused on a homogeneous mass market. But with growing appreciation of diversity in society, it's good business to ensure that everyone working on your business reflects it, whether they're within your company or working at your ad agency.

USA Today, 6-12:(B)2.

Alfonse M. D'Amato
United States Senator,
R-New York

3

[Calling for bond brokers to disclose more information to investors about the bonds they're dealing in]: It behooves the industry, which I have been accused of being too protective of, to do something. I don't mean the minimum, but . . . to disclose to the greatest dunderhead what the situation is.

At Senate hearing,
Washington, D.C., Jan. 6/
Los Angeles Times,
1-7:(A)1.

Al Dunlap
Chief executive officer,
Scott Paper Company

4

[On his reputation for being hired to save ailing companies and the methods he uses to cut costs and jobs at those companies]: There's no reason for Al Dunlap to exist if [management] people do their jobs . . . If you keep your eye on shareholder value, you will by definition create the best management, you will have the best factories, you will have the best products, you will have the best balance sheet.

Interview,
Sept. 14/
USA Today, 9-15:(B)2.

Wendell E. Dunn III
Adjunct professor of management,
Wharton School,
and academic director,
Sol C. Snider Entrepreneurial Center,
University of Pennsylvania

5

I'd argue the most common [mistake of start-up small businesses] is simply failing to plan. We like action. We like doing things. Somehow, in planning or thinking about the future, we don't always get a sense of doing things, so there's a tendency sometimes not to plan. And when we do plan, sometimes we think about a document—the business plan—as if *it* were business planning. But they're not the same thing. The important part of business planning [is that] it's a continuing process. It certainly doesn't end with the generation of a business plan . . . I think a common failure is failure to plan for *success.* So many people are concerned about failure, so we plan to avoid failure. But then when we are suc-

(WENDELL E. DUNN III)

cessful in not failing, we discover, sometimes to our horror, that we haven't planned for success. And all of a sudden things take off and they're going like topsy, and you're out of cash, bleeding to death. Everything is going right and nothing is going right.

Interview/
The Wall Street Journal,
5-22:(R)16.

Robert Eaton
Chairman, Chrysler Corporation

1

The nexus of all ethics is truth, and yet a chief executive officer today is constantly being told by his lawyers, his public-relations people and others that "you can't say that!"

U.S. News & World Report,
3-27:62.

Bob Garfield
Advertising critic,
"Advertising Age" magazine

2

[On the controversial ad campaign by fashion designer Calvin Klein, which features young people in sexual poses, and which has now been withdrawn due to criticism]: Calvin Klein has made a career of stepping over the line, shocking consumers to create word-of-mouth. This time he vaulted over the line and beyond the pale—and even he has now discovered there are places you dare not go. Maybe this will put an end to some intentionally outrageous and provocative advertising, and make people think twice about shocking a million people to impress nine.

Aug. 28/
The New York Times, 8-29:(C)6.

Stanley Gault
Chairman,
Goodyear Tire &
Rubber Company

3

[A company's] pursuit of financial results today cannot come at the expense of aid to education, charitable contributions or short-cuts in areas relating to the quality of products or the environment.

U.S. News & World Report,
3-27:62.

Harold Geneen
Former chairman,
ITT Corporation

4

Conglomerates have a lot of value. Take General Electric—they do a good job and haven't been afraid to move out into a number of directions. It's the largest stock holding I have . . . What I know is business. I enjoy business. It's a hell of a lot more interesting than playing slot machines in Reno. I believe opportunity isn't a straitjacket.

Interview/
U.S. News & World Report,
6-26:19.

Alan Greenberg
Chairman,
Bear Stearns Companies

5

[On promoting ethical behavior by company employees]: Trying to change [associates'] ethical behavior is hopeless. The only thing we can do is take them to Sing Sing [prison] so they can see the calculated risk [of breaking rules] isn't worth it.

U.S. News & World Report,
3-20:62.

Lloyd Greif
Investment banker

1

[Saying large institutional investors, not the general public, get to profit most from initial public stock offerings because they can buy IPOs in advance of general trading]: Because they are favored clients of the brokerages, they get the first chance to buy it. And they, of course, get the chance to "flip it" [selling at the moment public trading opens]. Retail [general public] investors are at the end of the queue. By the time it gets handed to them, it's like a time bomb. Each person further down the line who gets it is closer to the fuse.

Los Angeles Times, 8-10:(D)5.

Al Hubbard
Former Executive Director, Council on Competitiveness under then-Vice President of the United States Dan Quayle

2

[Saying the new Republican-controlled Congress should crack down on Federal "pork" for business and industry]: I'm disappointed we haven't moved more aggressively than we have . . . It remains to be seen whether Republicans are going to walk the talk and go after corporate welfare the same way they go after poor-people welfare.

The Christian Science Monitor, 3-22:4.

Robert Iverson
Former chairman, Kiwi Air Lines

3

[On his recently being fired by the employee-run board of Kiwi, an employee-owned company he helped create]: One of the stupidest things I ever did was call everybody owners.

Newsweek, 4-3:19.

Richard Kirshenbaum
Co-chairman and chief creative officer, Kirshenbaum Bond & Partners, advertising

4

[On the controversial ad campaign by fashion designer Calvin Klein, which features young people in sexual poses, and which has now been withdrawn due to criticism]: I've long been a fan of Calvin Klein and his work. His position has always been a sexual one. But I feel he crossed a line in the allusions to children or teenagers and sexuality. And I had problems with that. [Advertisers] should think twice if they do something that smacks of child pornography. At the end of the day, you do have a responsibility.

Aug. 28/ The New York Times, 8-29:(C)6.

Frederick Kobrick
Manager, State Street Research Capital Fund

5

We have endured this bear market for growth stocks for a few primary reasons: a hot economy that took the companies past the point of earnings anticipation; the real economy sucking liquidity out of the financial markets; and funds flowing into foreign securities. Big averages like Dow Jones have not reflected this weakness because they have been held up by large-capitalization stocks that tend to be cyclical and respond well to

(FREDERICK KOBRICK)

recent economic conditions. However, the [interest] rate increases may finally be changing those conditions.

Interview/The Red Herring, February:82.

John P. Kotter
Professor, Harvard Business School

1

[On people who succeed in big companies]: Typically, they were smart in choosing big companies that were showing real signs of change; an example would be a company that was making concrete moves into a new competitive market, introducing products clearly needed by a lot of people at prices that were affordable. They also tended to have a higher tolerance for bureaucracy and politics. Their attitude was: "This is something I'm going to have to put up with for a little bit until we can change it." They also were outstanding leaders. At a big company, they obviously had to lead more people, including people of warring factions, departments that hated each other, a boss who didn't quite understand what they were doing—and then have the capacity to bring them together and motivate them. Most people don't have those leadership skills.

Interview/ U.S. News & World Report, 3-27:63.

Alex Krauer
Chairman and managing director, Ciba-Geigy Corporation (Switzerland)

2

[On his company's strategy]: To have a strong market position is one of the criteria, but it's not the only one. There are two others that are just as important. First: dominate and master the technologies and the innovations. We don't want to be in a business unless we are sure we are at least as good or hopefully better than the most competent competitor. Second: We only want to be in businesses where we can manufacture a certain product with what we call a high value-added. We are not good in mass products.

Interview/ USA Today, 6-9:(B)4.

William Lazer
Marketing consultant

3

In the past, the burgeoning population growth compensated for many marketing miscalculations and provided marketing management with a degree of slack and latitude that will not exist in the future. Growing populations, so characteristic of the past, will not be there to provide a future market cushion . . . The windows of opportunity used to change very slowly, but now companies need to be adaptable and flexible. It's partly because of TV and partly because of changes in consumer lifestyles . . . Small business has to have the twin focus of running a business efficiently and keeping an eye on what the market is doing. Market information is just as much a business asset and just as important as your inventory or the machine you have in the back room.

Nation's Business, July:26.

Arthur Levitt, Jr.
Chairman,
Securities and Exchange
Commission of the United States

1

My greatest worry is that the millions of investors who have expanded into mutual funds in recent years have taken their money in many instances from banks and certificates of deposit. They have never seen a down market and may have inadequate understanding of the relative risks that they will be experiencing.

Interview,
Washington, D.C./
The Wall Street Journal,
7-7:(R)5.

2

U.S. capital markets are the envy of the world because investor confidence in their fairness and integrity promotes the highest market participation at the lowest cost.

July 27/
The New York Times,
7-28:(C)3.

Gary Lynch
Former Director,
Division of Enforcement,
Securities and Exchange
Commission of the United States

3

[On the increase in corporate mergers and acquisitions and the related increase in insider-trading investigations by the SEC): What's happening now is exactly what everyone predicted back in the '80s: that with the number of high-profile cases brought [at that time], the incidence of insider trading would decline for a while, but as memories dulled, insider trading would pick up again. The temptation is too great for people to resist.

Los Angeles Times,
6-24:(D)8.

Peter Lynch
Director,
and former fund manager,
Fidelity Investments

4

The Depression [of the 1930s] affected the [investment] psychology of a lot of Americans. The idea that there were all these people jumping out of windows is an exaggeration; but even so, many retired people have stories about relatives who lost it all and sold apples or pencils, and they're always concerned there might be another one. Understand, these aren't people who run around saying the world is going to end next Thursday—these are normal folks who got hit hard by this rogue wave in the economy . . . [Investors should] take a 20-year view of the [stock] market. You should not be in the stock market if you have a one- or two-year horizon. What the markets are going to do in the next two years is totally random.

Interview/
Modern Maturity,
Jan.-Feb.:60.

William McLucas
Director, Division of Enforcement,
Securities and Exchange
Commission of the United States

5

[On the growing incidence of large corporate mergers and the resultant regulatory investigations of them]: It's a growth industry. In terms of raw numbers, we have as many cases as we've had since the 1980s, when we

(WILLIAM McLUCAS)

were in the heyday of mergers and acquisition activity.

The New York Times,
6-9:(C)1.

Richard Y. Roberts
Commissioner,
Securities and Exchange
Commission of the United States

1

[Saying the recent debacle at Britain's Barings Bank, which resulted from questionable financial tradings by a single employee, indicates the need for strict compliance and oversight of financial institutions]: This event should be another wake-up call for securities firms in the United States. If they are not taking their compliance and risk-management responsibilities seriously, they should. Everyone wants to blame regulators or derivatives. But some of the blame clearly rests on the shoulders of management.

The New York Times,
3-9:(C)1.

Patrick Rooney
Chief executive officer,
Cooper Tire & Rubber Company

2

[On corporations that become bigger through acquisition of other companies]: Growth for growth's sake doesn't work. But being bigger does give you an advantage. We're competing with tire makers all over the world. To compete, you have to be bigger; but the growth must be controlled.

At symposium sponsored by
"Business Week" magazine, Sept. 28/
USA Today, 9-29:(B)11.

David Rowland
Chairman, Lloyd's of London,
insurers (Britain)

3

[On a settlement plan proposed to keep his organization out of bankruptcy]: [If the plan fails,] we haven't got a future. There's no U.S. Cavalry coming over the hill bearing great dollops of money.

Time, 6-5:21.

Robert E. Rubin
Secretary of the Treasury
of the United States

4

Our [international financial] institutions must be as modern as the marketplace. With [the current financial crisis in] Mexico, we have seen how poor policies and markets that lack depth in very short order can destroy a nation's finances and threaten the spread of financial instability.

Before Institute for
Strategic and International Studies,
Washington, D.C./
The New York Times,
6-13:(C)6.

Robert J. Shapiro
Economist, Progressive Policy Institute

5

A serious attack on industry subsidies [from government] will require the President and a majority in Congress to take on much of the Washington establishment. This is a particular challenge to the Republican Party, which thus far has proposed cutting only social programs while leaving benefits for high-income constituencies undisturbed.

The Washington Post,
3-13:(A)13.

John Sidgmore
Chief executive,
UUNET Technologies, Inc.

1

[On recent big increases in the prices of the stocks of his and other computer-related companies]: No one expected to make the kind of money these stocks are being valued at. The figures are so large that it's sort of surrealistic. So I still get up in the morning and take the garbage out, because you never know where stock is going to end up.

The Washington Post,
7-24:(A)10.

Barbara Sinclair
Political scientist,
University of California, Riverside

2

Small-business people tend to think that their reality is the only reality.

U.S. News & World Report,
3-27:45.

Ted Turner
Chairman,
Turner Broadcasting System

3

[On the agreement to merge his company with Time Warner]: I'm tired of being little all the time. I want to see what it's like to be big for a while.

Time, 10-2:32.

Paul A. Volcker
Former Chairman,
Federal Reserve Board

4

[On the weakness of the U.S. dollar against such currencies as the Japanese yen and the German mark]: We have dug ourselves a kind of hole that we can no longer easily get out of because the implicit confidence that everyone had in the dollar, which has been amazing, has eroded and it is a real challenge to restore it. If you think American leadership is important, that erosion is a negative . . . You have all this [U.S.] money out there, in reluctant hands, and $1-billion more going out every business day. And sometimes there are people out there who will buy that many dollars and sometimes there aren't. It gives a constant weak tinge to the dollar.

The New York Times,
5-2:(C)15.

J.C. Watts
United States Representative,
R-Oklahoma

5

Government just cannot replace the millions and millions of decisions that people make in the marketplace on a daily basis. Government is not a good parent, and government is not a good investment adviser. Private industry, risk-takers, entrepreneurs, "Joe Six-Pack" on the street—those are the types of people who make things happen.

Nation's Business, July:22.

Anthony Wright
Coordinator,
Center for Media Education

6

[On the recent spate of giant media-company mergers]: All of these mergers that have been happening in the past few weeks have a real danger of putting too much power in too few hands. This type of concentration is unhealthy for our democracy. We should be very vigilant in making sure that the marketplace of ideas remains in many hands.

Los Angeles Times, 8-31:(D)5.

Crime • Law Enforcement

Joseph M. Arpaio
Sheriff of Maricopa County (Phoenix), Ariz.

1

[On criticism of his policy of cutting back on certain comforts prisoners used to enjoy in his county's jails]: See anybody dying? They're locked up; what am I supposed to be doing with them? So they lost some of their privileges. So what? . . . I want everybody in this county to know that if you commit a crime, you are going into a very bad jail. I want people to say: "I hate that Sheriff; I hate his jails."

Interview/ The New York Times, 3-4:6.

Roscoe G. Bartlett
United States Representative, R-Maryland

2

Much of this firearms legislation [banning private ownership of certain kinds of weapons], no matter how well-intentioned, has simply been distracting and diversionary and gives the illusion that you are doing something about crime, and you are doing nothing about crime. Many of the laws that we have on our books are an infringement of the Second Amendment rights.

The New York Times, 2-14:(A)8.

Sonny Bono
United States Representative, R-California

3

[Criticizing House Judiciary Committee lawyers for haggling over details of a proposed crime bill]: When are we going to stop the games? We get in these [government] buildings, and—with all due respect to lawyers—it's wonderful that you have this intricate knowledge. [But when the police try to do their jobs,] they get hamstrung, then it goes into a court and you do what you're doing now—you break down words to the nth degree, and sometimes I find it rather disgusting, and it goes on and on. And pompously. Let's stop trying to show how brilliant we are here in this room. And if you really want to be brilliant, take a week off, go on a ride-along [with the police]. Go get some experience. And then come back and talk about it.

At House Judiciary Committee hearing, Washington, D.C., Jan. 27/ The New York Times, 1-28:7.

William Bratton
Commissioner of Police of New York, N.Y.

4

[On the drop in murder and other crime rates in his city]: It's not the weather. It's not demographics. It's not economics. What's happening is that you have 38,000 hardworking cops, a Mayor [Rudolph Giuliani] who supports us and a public who is with us.

Time, 7-24:35.

Lee P. Brown
Director, White House Office of National Drug Control Policy

1

[Criticizing a Senate proposal to abolish his Drug Control Policy office]: [Such elimination would do] irreparable damage to the nation's ability to have a coordinated anti-drug strategy among 50 agencies dealing with supply and demand, concerning education, prevention, treatment, enforcement, interdiction, eradication and international cooperation. I think the Senate is acting in a vacuum, not realizing the devastating real impact of cutting the President's ability to coordinate anti-drug efforts.

July 24/ The Washington Post, 7-25:(A)13.

Harvey Burstein
Criminology teacher, Northeastern University; Former agent, Federal Bureau of Investigation

2

[Saying TV programs have caused people to think that complex crimes can be solved quickly]: People have been spoiled. They seem to think that investigations can be wrapped up in 60 minutes with time for commercial breaks.

The Christian Science Monitor, 5-3:3.

Charles T. Canady
United States Representative, R-Florida

3

[Criticizing the ability of prison inmates to go to court to protest certain prison conditions]: They complain about getting only one roll with dinner, having no TV in their room, getting chunky peanut butter rather than creamy peanut butter. One inmate complained that he was suffering cruel and unusual punishment because he was not allowed to smoke but he could look out his window and see other people smoke.

The New York Times, 2-11:8.

Gerald Caplan
Dean, McGeorge Law School, Sacramento, Calif.

4

[On the increasing prison population]: This is part of a general, long-emerging public view that there are no alternatives to prison. Incarceration has increasingly become the acceptable way of handling wrongdoers. Those who argue for leniency are an increasingly smaller crowd.

Los Angeles Times, 12-4:(A)1.

Bill Clinton
President of the United States

5

[Criticizing a possible Republican attempt to repeal last year's legislation banning private ownership of assault weapons]: A lot of people laid down their seats in Congress so that police officers and kids wouldn't have to lay down their lives under a hail of assault-weapon attack, and I will not let that be repealed.

State of the Union address, Washington, D.C., Jan. 24/ The New York Times, 3-18:7.

(BILL CLINTON)

1

[Criticizing U.S. paramilitary groups who may have been responsible for the recent bombing of a Federal Building in Oklahoma City]: They have a right to believe whatever they want; they have a right to say whatever they want; they have a right to keep and bear arms; they have a right to put on uniforms and go out on the weekends. [But] they do not have the right to kill innocent Americans. They do not have the right to violate the laws. And they do not have the right to take the position that if somebody comes to arrest them for violating the law they're perfectly justified in killing them. They are wrong in that.

Broadcast interview/
"60 Minutes," CBS-TV, 4-23.

2

[On the recent bombing of a Federal building in Oklahoma City]: We owe those [the victims] who have sacrificed the duty to purge ourselves of the dark forces which gave rise to this evil. They are forces that threaten our common peace, our freedom, our way of life. Let us teach our children that the God of comfort is also the God of righteousness. Those who trouble their own house will inherit the wind. Justice will prevail. Let us let our own children know that we will stand against the forces of fear. When there is talk of hatred, let us stand up and talk against it. When there is talk of violence, let us stand up and talk against it. In the face of death, let us honor life.

At memorial service for victims of the bombing,
Oklahoma City, Okla., April 23/
The Washington Post,
4-24:(A)10.

3

[Calling for stronger investigative powers for law-enforcement agencies to deal with domestic terrorism]: I take a back seat to no one in my devotion to the Constitution [and the protection it gives citizens against persecution and abridgement of civil liberties]. But we can protect the Constitution and our freedom and be tougher on terrorism in America, and we must.

May 1/
USA Today, 5-4:(A)6.

4

[On his signing legislation that keeps stiff penalties for possession of small amounts of crack cocaine]: We have to send a constant message to our children that drugs are illegal, drugs are dangerous, drugs may cost you your life—and the penalties for dealing drugs are severe. I am not going to let anyone who peddles drugs get the idea that the cost of doing business is going down. Tough penalties for crack trafficking are required because of the effect on individuals and families, related gang activity, turf battles and other violence.

Washington, D.C., Oct. 30/
Los Angeles Times,
10-31:(A)4.

David Cole
Authority on the U.S. Constitution,
Georgetown University

5

[Expressing concern about giving law-enforcement agencies more investigative powers to deal with domestic terrorism]: The FBI has more than enough power to investigate crimes. Our history indicates that even when it's not given the power to investigate

(DAVID COLE)

political activity, it has frequently abused its authority to target political organizations.

USA Today,
5-4:(A)6.

John Conyers, Jr.
United States Representative,
D-Michigan

1

[On a House bill aimed at providing states with more money for prison construction if they meet certain Federal guidelines]: The cumbersome, truth-in-sentencing requirements, in which the Federal government paternalistically tells states how to run their criminal-justice systems, will tie the states up in such knots that they will not be able to qualify.

The New York Times,
2-11:8.

2

[Expressing concern about giving law-enforcement agencies more investigative powers to deal with domestic terrorism]: What I am concerned about is that we will allow Federal authorities to target Americans with a particular [political] belief, and that takes us back to the bad old days.

USA Today,
5-4:(A)6.

Larry E. Craig
United States Senator,
R-Idaho

3

[Saying that, although he opposes gun-control measures aimed at private citizens, he wants to see the disarming of Federal forestry and park officers]: There has always been a healthy suspicion of the Federal agent. Now there is developing a healthy fear, especially if the agent is armed . . . The Second Amendment [allowing gun-ownership] applies to private citizens. We have always controlled and determined who packs a gun as a law-enforcement officer.

Interview,
May 4/
Los Angeles Times,
5-5:(A)19.

Charlie Crist
Florida State Senator (R)

4

[On Florida's revival of the prison chain gang]: What we want to do is tell people that if you commit a crime in Florida, if you're convicted of committing that crime in Florida, Florida will punish you, you will do your time and it will not be pleasant.

Los Angeles Times,
11-22:(A)10.

Mario M. Cuomo
Former Governor
of New York (D)

5

[Criticizing New York Governor George Pataki's signing into law a bill authorizing the death penalty in his state]: This is a step back in what should be a march constantly toward a higher level of civility and intelligence. The argument that the death penalty will deter and reduce crimes has been abandoned almost everywhere.

March 7/
The New York Times,
3-8:(B)12.

Alan M. Dershowitz
Professor of law,
Harvard University

1

[On demands by a police organization that he apologize for saying that police officers are trained to lie on the witness stand]: I will not apologize for telling the truth. Nor will I be coerced by the threatening and intimidating language used by certain police officers . . . Until and unless the police of this country begin to understand that their job of protecting citizens does not include perjury, the liberty of all Americans will be placed in danger.

Interview, March 20/
Los Angeles Times,
3-21:(A)23.

Richard Dieter
Executive director,
Death Penalty
Information Center

2

It used to be that the public generally thought the death penalty was a deterrent to crime. Now favoring it is more of a retribution argument, a life for a life. What is spurring this is the perception that crime is out of control and people want something done.

The Christian Science Monitor,
1-4:2.

John J. DiIulio, Jr.
Professor of politics
and public affairs,
Princeton University

3

I would brace myself for the crime wave that is coming over the next 10 years, secure in the knowledge that virtually nothing we do—including my favorite proposal, more incarceration—is going to make a dramatic difference.

Broadcast discussion/
"Think Tank,"
WETA-TV,
Washington, D.C., 6-3.

4

[On the success of some privately run prisons]: This success comes as a surprise . . . I remain against private prisons for philosophical reasons. People would not be happy with private police or private executions. But I have to concede that the evidence so far is favorable [on private prisons].

The New York Times,
8-19:6.

Robert J. Dole
United States Senator,
R-Kansas;
Candidate for
the 1996 Republican
Presidential nomination

5

[On proposals to give law-enforcement agencies more investigative authority in the wake of recent terrorist attacks in the U.S.): My view is that we better move slowly on the legislation we're considering, make certain we get it right so we can sit here a year from now on this program and say we did the right thing a year ago instead of getting caught up with emotion and going too far and maybe end up trampling on somebody's rights, some innocent group or some innocent person.

Broadcast interview/
"This Week With David Brinkley,"
ABC-TV, 4-30.

Dianne Feinstein
United States Senator,
D-California

1

[Criticizing Senator Robert Dole's push to repeal the ban on personal ownership of assault-type weapons passed by Congress and signed by the President last year]: We [who voted for the ban] won this issue fairly and squarely. We won it because of support of police organizations and the families of victims throughout this nation. Clearly [Dole's move] means the [Senate] Majority Leader has decided to side himself against the police, families and victims and . . . 69 percent of the American people.

News conference, March 17/ Los Angeles Times, 3-18:(A)1.

2

[Criticizing Congressional Republican and NRA attempts to repeal the ban on ownership of assault weapons]: The time has come, particularly for Californians and the people of Los Angeles who are so besieged with violence . . . to stand up and say to the NRA [that] we have had enough of your selfishness. It is reprehensible to try to repeal a law that is just now beginning to work.

Los Angeles Times, 12-6:(A)27.

James Alan Fox
Dean, College of Criminal Justice,
Northeastern University

3

We are in the calm before the crime storm . . . Unless we act now, while our children are still young and impressionable, we may indeed have a blood bath of teen violence by the year 2005.

The New York Times, 5-23:(A)15.

Louis J. Freeh
Director,
Federal Bureau of Investigation

4

[Defending the FBI's handling of the Ruby Ridge incident in 1991, during which civilians were killed by Federal agents at a remote cabin in Idaho]: [The agents] followed the law. They followed the policy. They followed the Constitution, with the objective of protecting the people who were going to kill them.

News conference, Jan. 6/ The Washington Post, 9-4:(A)14.

5

[On the FBI's intelligence-gathering efforts]: Intelligence serves a very useful purpose and helps protect the American people. It should not be considered a dirty word.

Before Senate Judiciary Committee, Washington, D.C., April 27/ The New York Times, 4-28:(A)12.

6

[On criticism that the FBI's monitoring of certain groups it suspects may have criminal intent is politically motivated and violates those groups' civil rights]: Law enforcement is not concerned with a group simply because of its ideology or political philosophy. The fact is we do not need the business.

Before Senate Judiciary Committee, Washington, D.C., April 27/ The New York Times, 4-28:(A)12.

(LOUIS J. FREEH)

1

Police have to police themselves. If you leave policing of a law-enforcement organization to an outside entity exclusively . . . there is more of a tolerance by police commanders and officers to certain kinds of misconduct. What you have to do is ensure oversight . . . [But] it's essential that organizations have the responsibility to police themselves. If you take that away, you take away the accountability and responsibility for assuring professional conduct.

Interview, Aug. 23/ Los Angeles Times, 8-24:(A)21.

James Fyfe
Criminologist,
Temple University

2

[On revelations in recent years of police racism, such as demonstrated in the Rodney King beating and the racial statements of detective Mark Fuhrman in the current murder trial of former football star O.J. Simpson]: The Fuhrman episode has every potential of exceeding the Rodney King beating, two subsequent trials and the [Los Angeles] riots as a mechanism to focus attention on racism within police departments. It underlines in red ink that constant public scrutiny of police is a must.

The Christian Science Monitor, 9-6:4.

Rudolph W. Giuliani
Mayor of New York, N.Y.

3

An arrest is almost a failure. The better way to manage a police department is to prevent crime in the first place and find ways of measuring that [and rewarding police for it].

Time, 7-24:35.

Ira Glasser
Executive director,
American Civil Liberties Union

4

[Arguing against a proposed loosening of standards to permit Federal law-enforcement agencies to investigate organizations they deem to be suspicious or that they think may become involved in criminal activity because of their rhetoric]: Any time you abandon the idea of [an imminent] criminal predicate for an investigation, you have to find something else. What would that be? Maybe national origin, maybe race, maybe political beliefs, maybe militant rhetoric. That's been the history of the FBI, which we have come to deplore. When you don't use a criminal predicate, you must find some other proxy that inevitably tramples on Constitutional principles.

May 3/ The New York Times, 5-4:(A)12.

Gerald H. Goldstein
President,
National Association of
Criminal Defense Lawyers

5

[On Congressional hearings into the FBI's and the ATF's attack on a cult compound in Waco, Texas, in 1993 that resulted in many deaths of cult members]: Even as these subcommittees begin to review the tragic debacle in Waco, ironically both houses of Congress are considering measures to expand still further the powers of the very Federal agencies

(GERALD H. GOLDSTEIN)

responsible for that and other disasters . . . Members of the National Association of Criminal Defense Lawyers are intimately familiar with the growing aggressive, paramilitarization of Federal law enforcement in recent years . . . Election Day rhetoric has given many citizens the misperception that "liberal courts" using "technicalities" regularly loose criminals to prey upon innocent citizens. It is rarely mentioned that these "technicalities" are the first 10 Amendments to our Constitutional bulwark that separates us from those . . . states we so regularly denounce.

Before House Judiciary Subcommittee on Crime, and the Government Reform and Oversight Subcommittee on Criminal Justice, Washington, D.C., July 19/ The Washington Post, 7-27:(A)18.

Frederick K. Goodwin
Director,
Center on Neuroscience,
Behavior and Society,
George Washington University

1

In every fact sheet we have ever sent out, we have said that the National Institute of Mental Health determined years ago that race and crime don't correlate. But that information has never been effectively conveyed, because it takes the punch out of the controversy.

The New York Times, 9-19:(B)9.

Beverly J. Harvard
Chief of Police
of Atlanta, Ga.

2

I'm truly a "prevention" person. I know that in order to prevent [crime], you've got to get the whole community involved with that whole process. We've got to get involved with the community in terms of solving their problems, helping them deal with things that are not necessarily law-enforcement issues at the time. Because if you don't help them address these things at the time, they will ultimately become my issues—law-enforcement issues.

Interview/ Ebony, March:96.

3

The ideal [police] officer, first of all, has to care about people. [Because] if they feel you don't care, they're not going to talk to you. And for everything that happens and goes on out there, there's someone who knows something about it. If people know something about it, then you have to ask the question, "Why aren't they telling the police about it?"

Interview/ Ebony, March:96.

4

[On her desire to involve the community in reducing crime]: If I accomplish anything, it will be that . . . It takes cooperation. Rather than all the finger-pointing and bickering and debating about who's not holding up their end—the police or the communities—we must recognize that we're on the same team and work together.

Interview/ Harper's Bazaar, April:116.

Orrin G. Hatch
United States Senator,
R-Utah

1

[On criticism that, in their anti-terrorist measures, law-enforcement agencies such as the FBI may be infringing on citizens' rights when they investigate extremist groups]: That's ridiculous. We've got to be able to watch some of these extreme groups. And there is a difference between extreme groups and people who are terrorists, but some of the extreme groups have a tendency to become terrorists—and our FBI and our law-enforcement people ought to be involved in going in and making sure that they're on top of these groups.

Broadcast interview/
"Meet the Press,"
NBC-TV,
4-30.

Fred Heineman
United States Representative,
R-North Carolina

2

There's a fire raging on the streets of America today and that fire is crime. Our job is to put that fire out first and then deal with prevention.

USA Today,
1-20:(A)4.

Philip B. Heymann
Former Deputy
Attorney General
of the United States

3

[On Clinton Administration proposals to give law-enforcement agencies more investigative authority in the wake of recent terrorist attacks in the U.S.]: There are some elements of the package that could be quite useful in combating terrorism, such as easing restrictions on access to credit reports of suspects. [But] there are others that have nothing to do with terrorism, like the electronic-surveillance proposal, the proposal to hire 1,000 new agents and prosecutors, and the plan to impose more mandatory minimum prison sentences. They just happened to have been on someone's wish list.

The New York Times,
5-1:(A)10.

Herb Hoelter
Director,
National Center on
Institutions and Alternatives

4

[On the current reinstitution of the chain-gang in Alabama]: It makes for terrific photo ops for people running for office. But it has no correctional application . . . I think it's kind of a miserable thing to do, all in all.

Los Angeles Times,
5-3:(A)5.

Henry J. Hyde
United States Representative,
R-Illinois

5

It is fundamental that if you get violent criminals off the streets, there will be less violent crime. It's always a shock when someone gets a 15-year sentence and then serves only three or four. We're trying to infuse some credibility into the system.

The New York Times,
2-11:1.

(HENRY J. HYDE)

1

[Arguing against a proposed amendment to a crime bill that would permit Federal anti-crime block grants to states to be used to protect abortion clinics from anti-abortion violence]: I would vote against [the amendment]. It is corrosive of, it erodes, the block-grant concept. If abortion clinics are having a problem, they ought to hire guards, like banks do.

The New York Times,
2-11:8.

Jesse L. Jackson
Civil-rights leader

2

[On the recent bombing of a Federal building in Oklahoma City]: Anger leads to hatred, to scapegoats, to violence, to destruction. All the talk—"the Federal government is our enemy, blacks are our enemy, and the President is our enemy"—enough of that talk, plus guns and irrational behavior, leads to an Oklahoma hate bomb.

USA Today,
4-28:(A)13.

Tim Jennings
New Mexico State Senator (D)

3

[On incorrigible criminals and prisoners]: It's my personal belief that if they're not rehabilitated after 15 years, kill 'em.

Newsweek, 2-6:15.

Paul D. Kamenar
Executive legal director,
Washington Legal Foundation

4

You now have what I call "super due process" built into the [legal] system that makes it much harder to get a death penalty. All the laws have safeguards built in, and in some cases, I think, go overboard in making it tough for prosecutors to get capital punishment. People like [mass murderer] Charles Manson, in cases that almost everyone would agree were particularly heinous, may not be eligible for death because they don't fit the strict categories in the state law.

The New York Times,
2-23:(A)13.

Frank A. Keating
Governor of Oklahoma (R)

5

[On the recent bombing of a Federal building in Oklahoma City]: The tragedy of April 19 shocked America. Its unspeakable evil sickened the world. Never in the history of the country have Americans witnessed such senseless barbarism. It has been suggested that those who committed this act of mass murder chose us as their victims because we were supposedly immune, the heartland of America. Well, we *are* the heartland of America. Today, we stand before the world and before our God, our hearts and our hands linked in a solidarity these criminals can never understand.

At memorial service
for victims of the bombing,
Oklahoma City, Okla., April 23/
The Washington Post, 4-24:(A)1.

Bob Kerrey
United States Senator,
D-Nebraska

6

[On the recent bombing of a Federal building in Oklahoma City]: Political appeals

(BOB KERREY)

to white, male gun owners as victims of government oppression can unintentionally provide a silent refuge for right-wing extremists who believe that violence is a reasonable means to reach a justifiable goal.

At National Press Club, Washington, D.C., April 27/ USA Today, 4-28:(A)8.

John Killorin
Spokesman, Bureau of Alcohol, Tobacco and Firearms, Department of the Treasury of the United States

1

We ask the men and women of ATF to do some of the most dangerous jobs in America, and they get the equivalent of spit on, sometimes by elected officials. ATF agents know Congress doesn't love them, and fat-cat lobbyists . . . are doing things that make their jobs harder.

The Washington Post, 7-24:(A)4.

Gary Kleck
Professor of criminology and criminal justice, Florida State University

2

Crime statistics generally stink. Whatever drives the crime rate to be high also produces an overwhelming result: "Why should I bother the police? There are so many crimes that my crime looks petty compared with everyone else's experience."

The Wall Street Journal, 1-5:(A)10.

David Kopel
Research director, Independence Institute

3

[On moves in a number of states to permit citizens to carry concealed weapons in public]: Women and often men are afraid to go into certain neighborhoods, to walk around at night. If this [type of] law gives them that freedom back so the woman says, "Yes, I now feel okay walking three blocks to the 7-Eleven at 9 o'clock to buy some milk I need," that's an important benefit too, even if she never shoots a criminal and even if it doesn't statistically change the armed-robbery rate in that city.

The New York Times, 3-6:(A)11.

Robert Kupperman
Senior adviser, Center for Strategic and International Studies

4

[On terrorist attacks in the U.S.]: The most important thing that has happened is that a line has been crossed [since last month's bombing of an Oklahoma City Federal building]. Terrorism has changed qualitatively . . . With [domestic] paramilitary groups and cults, terrorism has come to the United States.

Los Angeles Times, 5-25:(A)24.

Wayne LaPierre
Executive vice president, National Rifle Association

5

Everywhere I go, people come up to me with a horror story about the [activities of the] ATF. What we find is a drift toward entrap-

(WAYNE LAPIERRE)

ment-type cases and harassment of innocent people. [The NRA doesn't single out the ATF,] they single out themselves.

Interview/
The Washington Post,
4-26:(A)16.

1

[On the NRA's determination to fight gun-control laws]: If there's one thing we've learned over the years, it's that when you feed the alligator, it comes right back for the next bite.

U.S. News & World Report,
5-22:38.

John Lewis
United States Representative,
D-Georgia

2

Increasingly over the past 30 years, crime and violence have been allowed to run virtually unchecked through poor black communities. This widening gyre of destruction first stripped communities of businesses and jobs. It broke down housing. It made schools places of fear, where a quarter of the students might carry weapons for self-defense, and learning was always a casualty. For as life became more dangerous, more subject to hazardous fate, so it became progressively difficult to raise children in the settled peace they require. And more and more the most conspicuous models of success were the racketeer, the pimp and the insidious drug dealer. So more and more children, deprived of reasonable nurture, were sucked into the vortex, to become in their turn the abusers and the destroyers of the children who came after them. It is not only poverty that has caused crime. In a very real sense it is crime that has caused poverty, and is the most powerful cause of poverty today.

Speech/
The Atlantic Monthly,
July:49.

James Lynch
Sociologist, American University

3

[On crime and punishment]: Unlike deterrence and rehabilitation, retribution has the advantage that you don't have to prove it works.

Newsweek, 2-6:24.

Tanya K. Metaksa
Chief lobbyist,
National Rifle Association

4

We have been given assurance for the last few months [by House Republican leaders] that there will be a vote on repealing the [President] Clinton [assault-weapons ownership] ban before the end of the year. Gun owners certainly would view a vote on the repeal of the Clinton gun ban as a nice Christmas present for 1995.

Dec. 5/
Los Angeles Times,
12-6:(A)27.

Norval Morris
Professor of law and
criminology emeritus,
University of Chicago

5

[Criticizing privately run prisons, whose main objective is economic efficiency]: This is simply selling a prisoner into servitude. Obviously, you can build a dungeon and throw

(NORVAL MORRIS)

people in it and throw food down to them very cheaply. The question is what services you provide them.

The New York Times,
8-19:6.

Laura Murphy
Director,
Washington office,
American Civil Liberties Union

1

[On the controversy over the FBI's and the ATF's handling of violent confrontations in Waco, Texas, and Ruby Ridge, Idaho, and possible new counter-terrorism legislation proposed following the bombing of a Federal building in Oklahoma City earlier this year]: Since the Oklahoma City bombing, we've had hearings on Waco and Ruby Ridge which demonstrate the ability of the Federal government to overreach. The thinking, which has crossed party lines, is that if law enforcement can do these things without a counter-terrorist bill, imagine what would happen *with* one.

The New York Times,
10-3:(A)1.

Jay Robert Nash
Crime historian

2

[On the increase in bank robberies]: These are amateurs, often middle-class people in a terrible financial fix, who see the bank as the quickest way to get money. The professional bank robber is a dying breed. It's just too risky. They'd rather steal gems, art work, something with better odds.

The New York Times,
3-28:(A)1.

George E. Pataki
Governor of New York (R)

3

[On his support of capital punishment]: When a society does not express its own horror at the crime of murder by enforcing the ultimate sanction against it, innocent lives are put at risk. Not out of a sense of vindictiveness, then, but a sense of justice—indeed a sense of compassion for those who otherwise might become victims of murder—I will ask the Legislature to pass and I will sign and enforce the death penalty.

Inaugural address,
Albany, N.Y., Jan. 1/
The New York Times,
1-2:9.

4

[Supporting the death penalty, which critics say demeans the state]: What demeans society is when Devorah and David Halberstam can't get justice for their son who was killed by a terrorist because we don't have the death penalty in this state. What demeans society is when too many police officers respond to a call risking their lives to protect us and we as a society don't do everything in our power to protect them and save their lives. This bill [authorizing the death penalty in New York State] is going to save lives.

At signing of death-penalty bill,
Albany, N.Y., March 7/
The New York Times,
3-8:(B)12.

Janet Reno
Attorney General of
the United States

5

[On criticism of her giving the go-ahead

(JANET RENO)

for Federal agents to raid an armed cult barricaded in a compound in Waco, Texas, in 1993, which resulted in more than 80 deaths]: Obviously, I saw what happened [in the raid], and, knowing what happened, I would not do it again. I would say this is going to happen: We are not going to do it again. Our whole purpose [in Waco] was to save human lives . . . I have thought about this almost every single day since April 19th, 1993. It's the single hardest decision I've ever made in my life. The FBI stood back, tried to resolve the situation over 51 days. The whole effort by the FBI was to save human life. They [FBI agents] told me that the conditions were deteriorating inside [the compound]. I was concerned about the safety of the people inside, [and] the behavioral experts were telling me that children [in the compound]—for a siege that could last a year—it would have a lasting effect on them.

Broadcast interview/ "60 Minutes," CBS-TV, 5-14.

Ann Richards
Governor of Texas (D)

1

The public wants to believe there is a way to incarcerate anyone who's committed a crime and keep them there until they won't do it again. Well, that's obviously not true. There are consistent threads that run through people in prison. They are oftentimes the product of abuse as children. They committed their crimes while under the influence of alcohol or drugs. Their education level is insufficient to maintain steady work. And, silly as this sounds, they don't know how to act. Pretty fundamental and basic. They just don't know how to act. It's ridiculous for anybody to think that just keeping them in a cell is in any way going to make society safer once they get out. I believe people deserve punishment. But I believe if you're going to be smart about the criminal-justice system, you have to take advantage of these people while you have them, and focus on what they're going to be like when you release them.

Interview, Austin, Texas/ Working Woman, March:86.

Charles E. Schumer
United States Representative, D-New York

2

[On concerns that proposals to give increased powers of surveillance to Federal law-enforcement agencies in response to the recent bombing of an Oklahoma City Federal building would infringe on the civil rights of Americans]: I think there are two extremes here. One is to say, "Hey, there's an emergency. Let's roll up the civil-liberties carpet." The other is to say, "You can't get tough or it's the beginning of the police state" . . . You have to be aware of the changing world. In wartime, it's different than in peacetime. In terrorism time, it's different from peacetime . . . You can't legislate for the moment.

The Washington Post, 4-25:(A)6.

3

[On current Congressional hearings into the 1993 ATF and FBI siege against a cult compound in Waco, Texas, that resulted in the death of many cult members]: The bad fact of these hearings is you have some really

(CHARLES E. SCHUMER)

crazy and paranoid people out there in America, who want to believe that this was a [government] conspiracy, who want to believe that not only did [Federal authorities] make mistakes of action, but of motivation. That they wanted to kill [cult leader] David Koresh because his religious beliefs were different.

Broadcast interview/ "Meet the Press," NBC-TV, 7-30.

Norman Seabrook
President, New York City Correction Officers Benevolent Association

1

[Arguing against a proposal to privatize New York City's jails]: Privatizing the jails would wreak havoc on the city. You'd be replacing dedicated peace officers with individuals who are paid $7 an hour and would not put their lives on the line to protect the public.

The New York Times, 8-12:16.

Lawrence Sherman
Criminologist, University of Maryland

2

Ironically, the best way to reduce murder may be to make lots of arrests for spitting on the sidewalk, simply as a way to deter criminals from carrying concealed weapons.

Time, 7-24:35.

Howard Snyder
Director of systems research, National Center for Juvenile Justice

3

[Saying the three-year decline in reported serious crimes should not yet be considered a trend]: The figures wiggle from year to year, like the stock market. Crime has been up so high, you'd expect it to go back down.

The New York Times, 5-23:(A)15.

Gerry Spence
Lawyer

4

[On the enmity between the National Rifle Association and the Federal Bureau of Alcohol, Tobacco and Firearms]: The natural enemy of a gopher is a rattlesnake. The natural enemy of the NRA is the ATF.

Time, 7-24:22.

Alan A. Stone
Professor of law and medicine, Harvard University

5

[Criticizing the raid in 1993—which he investigated for the Justice Department—by the ATF and FBI agents on an armed cult in Waco, Texas, which resulted in more than 80 deaths]: There was incredible stupidity, incompetence and provocation by a reckless and overreaching Federal agency.

The Washington Post, 5-15:(A)10.

Victor Streib
Professor of law,
Cleveland State University

1

There are 22,000 homicides a year [in the U.S.], 18,000 arrests and maybe 300 death sentences, leading to maybe 50 or 60 executions. How do you figure out why lightning strikes one defendant and not another? It's been studied for 20 years, and all I can say is, it's not a rational process . . . A key factor is what kind of attorney you can afford, so the death penalty is most commonly imposed on poor people. That often correlates with people who are poorly educated, or people of color; but the issue is really less about race or class than whether they have the resources to pay lawyer fees.

The New York Times,
2-23:(A)1.

Joe Sudbay
Director of state legislation,
Handgun Control, Inc.
(anti-gun lobbying organization)

2

[Criticizing a proposed Oklahoma law permitting citizens to carry concealed weapons]: The same kind of rhetoric you hear from the [private] militia groups [which may have been involved in the recent bombing of an Oklahoma City Federal building] is the kind of stuff you hear from the [pro-] gun lobby. They all say it's safer if everyone has a gun. We think it's clear that Americans are now able to decide whether these are the kind of people they want carrying around concealed weapons.

Los Angeles Times,
5-3:(A)13.

Fred Sunstedt
Chairman,
Special Circumstances Committee,
District Attorney's office of
Los Angeles County, Calif.

3

[On his committee's determining when to seek the death penalty in cases that come before it]: If you have a victim who is a totally innocent child or a totally helpless older person, the jury is more likely to vote for the death penalty. But the major source of cases that come before the committee are hard-core gang shootings, drive-by shootings or drug transactions, and jurors tend to look at victims in those crimes a little differently.

The New York Times,
2-23:(A)13.

Pete Wilson
Governor of California (R)

4

We must reach out to help our kids choose the right path. But if they turn to violence, we will protect the people from them. This is our first responsibility. If that means building more prisons, then we must build them. It's not what we want to do; it's what we must do.

State of the State address,
Sacramento, Calif.,
Jan. 9/
Los Angeles Times,
1-10:(A)15.

5

[On domestic violence or wife-beating]: It is time that we recognize it for what it is: a crime of great seriousness. It is serious when

(PETE WILSON)

you beat someone, particularly when you beat someone you are supposed to love. There is something terribly wrong.

At signing of bill to strengthen domestic-violence laws, Los Angeles, Calif., Oct. 5/ Los Angeles Times, 10-6:(A)3.

Bill Zeliff
United States Representative, R-New Hampshire

1

[On the controversial 1993 raid by the ATF and FBI on a cult compound in Waco, Texas, which resulted in over 80 deaths]: We're trying to establish responsibility at a level higher than [Attorney General] Janet Reno. I don't believe that Janet Reno, all by herself, with [at that time] less than two weeks' experience [as Attorney General], made that decision.

July 31/ The Christian Science Monitor, 8-2:3.

James J. Zogby
President, Arab American Institute

2

[Criticizing proposals to give Federal law-enforcement agencies more power to conduct investigations of groups they consider suspicious): While we need to have some enhanced surveillance [in the wake of the recent bombing of an Oklahoma City Federal building], we cannot give [law enforcement] the free rein they were allowed before. [Historically, the FBI and others] do not go after dangerous groups. They go after unpopular groups.

April 24/The Washington Post, 4-25:(A)6.

Defense • The Military

Boutros Boutros-Ghali
Secretary General
of the United Nations

1

The most safe, sure and swift way to deal with the threat of nuclear arms is to do away with them in every regard. This should be our vision of the future. No more testing. No more production. No more sales or transfers. Reduction and destruction of all nuclear weapons and the means to make them should be humanity's great common cause.

At conference on nuclear weapons, United Nations, New York, April 17/ The New York Times, 4-19:(A)1.

Dennis Boxx
Spokesman for
the Department of Defense
of the United States

2

[Saying the military as a whole should not be tarnished because a former decorated Army sargeant, now a member of a private militia group, has been implicated in the recent bombing of a Federal building in Oklahoma City]: The actions of those individuals who perpetrated [the bombing] are absolutely contrary to everything that the U.S. military stands for and, in fact, has died for. I think the 26 million veterans in this country and the 1.5 million active-duty personnel would take great umbrage at the suggestion that their service in the military in some way was anything other than a benefit to this country and the American way of life.

At news briefing, April 27/ Los Angeles Times, 4-29:(A)18.

Jesse Brown
Secretary of Veterans Affairs
of the United States

3

[On the financial ability of the Department of Veterans Affairs to provide for the medical needs of veteran servicemen and women]: If you lock us into the 1995 spending levels for the next seven years, you make some assumptions almost as though there's nobody out there to treat. A lot of people are behaving as though our veterans are already dead.

Time, 11-13:86.

Patrick J. Buchanan
Political commentator;
Candidate
for the 1996 Republican
Presidential
nomination

4

We need a new foreign policy that ends foreign aid, and pulls up all the trip wires laid down abroad to involve American soldiers in wars that are none of America's business. And we need to demand that rich allies begin paying the full cost of their own defense.

The Christian Science Monitor, 3-3:18.

Bill Clinton
President
of the United States

1

[Saying affirmative-action programs have made the armed forces more representative of the U.S. population]: In education, training, leadership, development, the military is a model. It looks like America, and it works.

News conference,
Ottawa, Canada,
Feb. 24/
The New York Times,
2-25:9.

2

[On suggestions that he may apologize to Japan for the U.S. use of the atom bomb against that country during World War II]: [I am] sensitive [to Japanese feelings,] but that does not mean that [then-President Harry] Truman . . . made the wrong decision [in using the bomb] or that the United States can now apologize for a decision that we did not believe then and I do not believe now was the wrong one.

U.S. News & World Report,
5-1:13.

3

A comprehensive [nuclear-weapons] test ban is the right step as we continue pulling back from the nuclear precipice, a precipice which we began to live with 50 years ago this week. It moves us one step closer to the day when no nuclear weapons are detonated anywhere on the face of the earth . . . American leaders since Presidents [Dwight] Eisenhower and [John] Kennedy have believed a comprehensive test ban would be a major stride toward stopping the proliferation of nuclear weapons. Now, as then, such a treaty would greatly strengthen the security of the United States and nations throughout the world. But now, unlike then, such a treaty is within our reach.

To reporters,
Washington, D.C.,
Aug. 11/
The New York Times,
8-12:1,4.

William E. Colby
Former Director
of Central Intelligence
of the United States

4

[Urging cuts in defense spending]: Our politicians seem to be repeating the mistake usually blamed on Generals: preparing to fight the last war—the Cold War.

U.S. News & World Report,
2-27:29.

Robert J. Dole
United States Senator,
R-Kansas;
Candidate for the
1996 Republican
Presidential nomination

5

When the Smithsonian [Institution] created a display to commemorate the [50th] anniversary of [the U.S. nuclear bombing] of Hiroshima [in World War II], the message was that dropping the bomb was an act of American violence against Japanese culture. [U.S.] veterans groups that complained [about the display] were dismissed as "special interests" who couldn't be objective. Well, if you love

(ROBERT J. DOLE)

this country so much you're willing to die for it, maybe you do belong to a "special interest."

At American Legion convention, Indianapolis, Ind., Sept. 4/ The New York Times, 9-5:(A)8.

Robert K. Dornan
United States Representative, R-California

1

[During the U.S.-Vietnam war of the 1960s and '70s, current U.S. President Clinton] avoided the draft three times and put teenagers in his place . . . Clinton gave aid and comfort to the enemy during the Vietnam war.

Before the House, Washington, D.C., Jan. 25/ Los Angeles Times, 1-26:(A)12.

Newt Gingrich
United States Representative, D-Georgia; Speaker of the House

2

[Supporting development of a U.S. anti-missile system, a scaled-down version of the space-based "Star Wars" project proposed in the 1980s]: One day, mathematically, something bad can happen and you ought to have a minimum screen on a continent-wide basis, and that's doable. And I think compared to the loss of one city, it is clearly a very small investment, although it's a lot of money over time.

To reporters, January/ The New York Times, 2-7:(A)8.

3

[Saying most women are not suited for military combat]: If combat means living in a ditch, females have biological problems staying in a ditch for 30 days because they get infections . . . Males are biologically driven to go out and hunt giraffes.

Newsweek, 1-30:17.

4

[Saying the Republican-controlled Congress may vote to rescind the current policy of allowing homosexuals in the military on a "don't ask, don't tell, don't pursue" basis and go back to an outright ban of homosexuals serving in the armed forces]: The fact is that we're going to probably go back to the rules that existed prior to President Clinton changing them. I'd be very surprised if you don't see a Republican Congress saying that serving in the military has a unique set of requirements, and if the military feels that in fact it's inappropriate [to allow homosexuals in], we're willing to abide by the military's judgment.

Broadcast interview/ "This Week With David Brinkley," ABC-TV, 4-2.

Phil Gramm
United States Senator,
R-Texas;
Candidate for the
1996 Republican
Presidential nomination

1

[Supporting increased spending for the military]: If the lion and the lamb are about to lie down together in the world, it's very important that the United States of America be the lion.

The Atlantic Monthly,
March:84.

Kim R. Holmes
Vice president
and director
of foreign-policy
and defense studies,
Heritage Foundation

2

[On criticism of the large amount of money spent by the U.S. on nuclear weapons since 1945]: I'm not sure what the point [of the criticism] is. If nuclear deterrence worked—and the Clinton Administration is going around saying it still does—it's certainly worth one-third of the [military] budget, even if that's what it costs.

The New York Times,
7-13:(C)18.

John D. Holum
Director, Arms Control
and Disarmament Agency
of the United States

3

[Saying the Non-Proliferation Treaty has worked well in limiting nuclear-weapons in the world]: The NPT has succeeded beyond the wildest dreams of its authors. Non-nuclear has become a global norm.

Newsweek,
7-24:33.

John R. Kasich
United States Representative,
R-Ohio

4

[On the B-2 "Stealth" bomber, which is supposed to be invisible to enemy radar]: If the B-2 is invisible, just announce you've built 100 of them and don't build them.

Newsweek,
7-24:15.

Jon Kyl
United States Senator,
R-Arizona

5

A lot of Republicans believe the ABM Treaty is a relic of the Cold War that is no longer in the interests of either the United States or Russia. It is not more moral to leave yourself open to attack than to be able to defend yourself.

The Washington Post,
3-13:(A)4.

Alexander Lebed
Lieutenant General,
Russian Army (Ret.)

6

[On NATO's airstrikes against Serb positions in the current conflict in the Balkans]: NATO's actions are pushing all the countries of the former Soviet Union—and not only them—to establish a new bloc to protect themselves. Here's the picture that comes to mind

(ALEXANDER LEBED)

[about NATO]: a big, drunk hooligan is in a kindergarten. He is the only grown-up and thinks he can do whatever he wants. The world needs a counterbalance.

Interview,
Moscow, Russia/
U.S. News & World Report,
10-9:60.

1

[On his once meeting U.S. General Colin Powell, then Chairman of the Joint Chiefs of Staff]: We met and we came to the conclusion that we are really a lot alike. Those who experience battle and death inevitably learn to speak plainly. If you don't tell the truth, you can end up with a pile of bodies in a sea of blood.

Interview/
U.S. News & World Report,
10-9:59.

Francois Lecointre
Captain,
French Armed Forces;
Member,
United Nations
peacekeeping forces
in Bosnia-Herzegovina

2

It's against anyone's nature to rush headlong into gunfire. But for the commander it's pride that pushes him. And for his men it's the sight of the commander in front of them. At such moments, you cannot hesitate.

The New York Times,
6-6:(A)1.

Merrill A. McPeak
General (Ret.),
and former Chief of Staff,
United States Air Force

3

[The U.S. military] should walk away from the two-war [capability] strategy. Neither our historical experience nor our common sense leads us to think we need to do this. We've had to fight three major regional contingencies in the past 45 years. One comes along every 15 years or so—[but] two have never come along simultaneously . . . If you come down to 1 million troops, you can do one war, be ready to do it and be modernized to do it.

Time, 6-5:26.

Sam Nunn
United States Senator,
D-Georgia

4

[Criticizing a Republican idea to create a 12-member commission that would review military preparedness, strategy, etc.]: If you did all that, you'd save money because you could abolish the Secretary of Defense, the Joint Chiefs of Staff . . . and all the people in the Pentagon. That's what they do . . . There are some parts of the Republican Contract [with America] on defense and national security I agree with, but I think the commission is a real loser.

Broadcast interview/
"Meet the Press,"
NBC-TV, 1-29.

5

[Expressing concern about President Clinton's proposal to allow the military to become involved in investigating crimes in-

(SAM NUNN)

volving high-explosive, chemical and biological weapons in the U.S.]: [There are reasons] for being very cautious in this area . . . One is that the military is not trained for law enforcement. They are trained to search and destroy using massive military force, not detect and investigate and arrest in accordance with due process and civil procedures . . . Another is, we don't want to have our military so involved in law enforcement that they cannot carry out their primary mission, which is to defend the nation.

Broadcast interview/ "Morning News," Fox-TV, 5-10.

William J. Perry
Secretary of Defense of the United States

1

[On the removal of five pregnant sailors from the *U.S.S. Eisenhower*, the first U.S. warship with women as part of the permanent crew at sea]: Pregnancy is a fact of life, and it will happen a certain percentage of the time. What I am concerned with, what personnel commanders have to be concerned with is, statistically, is it an important problem? Is it causing a significant degradation of readiness and duty? And the answer is: absolutely not.

The Washington Post, 1-30:(A)9.

2

[On Congressional Republicans' plan to establish a commission to evaluate the military's needs]: I cannot support a flawed concept of a commission to decide those matters for both of us [he and Congress]. You are my commission. *I* do not need an independent commission interposing itself between myself and you; and *you* do not need an independent commission interposing itself. You should not dilute the responsibilities of the Secretary of Defense. You should hold me accountable for meeting those responsibilities. And if you find that I'm incapable or unwilling to meet those responsibilities, you should ask me to step down as the Secretary of Defense.

To Republicans on House National Security Committee, Washington, D.C./ The New York Times, 2-4:7.

3

[On the continuing large budget for the U.S. military, almost as much as the rest of the world's armed forces put together, despite the end of the Cold War]: There's no other country that has the requirements we're confronted with. Unless we're willing to back off those requirements and go into an isolationist stance, we will have a uniquely high military budget.

Time, 6-5:26.

John Pike
President, Federation of American Scientists

4

[Supporting the U.S. building a space station in cooperation with the Russians]: As a piece of metal, I'm indifferent to it. As a scientific laboratory, it's worthless. But in terms of defense, it costs 1 percent of what we're

(JOHN PIKE)

spending at the Defense Department. And in terms of making sure the Cold War doesn't come back, that does a lot more than [the Defense Department] does.

Los Angeles Times,
6-19:(A)15.

Alan Sabrosky
Former director of studies,
Strategic Studies Institute,
Army War College

1

[On proposed Congressional legislation that would curb the President from involving U.S. forces in UN peacekeeping missions]: The War Powers Act did not have any effect on [then-Presidents Ronald] Reagan or [George] Bush in Grenada and Panama operations, respectively. [If this new legislation is passed,] it will have no more effect on [President] Clinton or his successors than the War Powers Act has had in the past.

USA Today,
2-17:(A)10.

John M. Shalikashvili
General,
United States Army;
Chairman,
Joint Chiefs of Staff

2

I am of the view . . . that if you use military force, and if you are hesitant and you are timid, you would have all the ill effects of having used military force and probably none—or very few— of the benefits.

Interview/
The New York Times,
7-29:4.

Baker Spring
Analyst,
Heritage Foundation

3

[On a possible revival of the once-proposed space-based missile defense system]: In most likely scenarios, we're talking not about [protection against] the thousands of nuclear weapons of a Soviet nuclear attack, but a handful. [Therefore,] the idea of a complete territorial missile defense becomes much more feasible.

USA Today,
8-28:(A)4.

Ted Taylor
Former Deputy
Scientific Director,
Defense Atomic
Support Agency,
Department of Defense
of the United States

4

We [the U.S.] continue to do something that is insane, which is trying to develop new types of nuclear weapons. We're strongly motivating other countries and terrorists to do the same. The last thing we're doing is deterring the North Koreas of the world. We're saying to them: "We're more secure with nuclear weapons, but you're not." How could that be true? . . . Deterrence doesn't work when you don't know who's launching a nuclear attack. And deterrence doesn't work when the people doing it are interspersed with their own populace, as are terrorists.

Interview/
Mother Jones,
March-April:50.

Strom Thurmond
United States Senator,
R-South Carolina

1

[Supporting development of a U.S. anti-missile system]: Defense of our homeland against direct attack is a priority enshrined in the Constitution, yet it is an aspect of our national defense that has been woefully neglected.

The New York Times,
2-7:(A)8.

2

[Arguing against a nuclear-weapons test ban]: I remain to be convinced that we can monitor the reliability, safety and accuracy of our nuclear weapons without the ability to test them. These weapons are machines, and will break down despite the intense scrutiny they undergo.

Aug. 11/
The New York Times,
8-12:4.

Paul E. Tsongas
Co-chairman,
The Concord Coalition;
Former United States Senator,
D-Massachusetts

3

When the American people hear that we are spending more on defense than the rest of the world put together, they are surprised. Once they hear it, they're not open to the argument that we ought to spend more.

Interview,
Boston, Mass./
The Christian Science Monitor,
1-9:19.

John W. Warner
United States Senator,
R-Virginia

4

[Comparing the relationship between former President George Bush and his Joint Chiefs Chairman Colin Powell, with the relationship between current President Clinton and his Joint Chiefs Chairman John Shalikashvili]: Bush and Powell could relate to each other as military men. Shali [-kashvili] has a greater challenge to work with a President [Clinton] and others in this Administration who have not had military experience.

The New York Times,
7-29:4.

The Economy • Labor

Lamar Alexander
Candidate for the 1996 Republican Presidential nomination; Former Secretary of Education of the United States

1

[Criticizing President Clinton's non-support of the proposed balanced-budget Constitutional amendment]: I think the place where the criticism belongs is President Clinton. If we had a Republican President in Washington, D.C., who understood what we need to do in this country, he'd be out fighting for the balanced-budget amendment in the Senate and it would zip through.

Campaigning in Iowa, March 1/ The Washington Post, 3-2:(A)9.

Maureen Allyn
Chief economist, Scudder Stevens & Clark, investments

2

We see inflation rising to 3% to 3.5% this year and it will be just a shade above 3.5% in '96. I had expected the cyclical peak of inflation to be above 4%, but I just don't think it will get there. A slowing economy will keep a cap on inflation. But it's much more than that. There are structural forces at work that have changed inflation. Globalization has widened the competitive universe.

Interview/ USA Today, 3-8:(B)3.

Bill Archer
United States Representative, R-Texas

3

It's true that Social Security is the biggest entitlement program, but it is separately funded in its own trust fund and we should be looking at it in that [light], not as something that's going to somehow bail us out on the [Federal government's] operating deficit. Social Security is not part of this balanced-budget problem. So how do we [balance the Federal budget]? It just means we're going to have to take a tough look at everything else, and to keep our commitment of no increase in taxes. We're going to have to squeeze and squeeze and squeeze on all fronts.

Interview/ AARP Bulletin, January:7.

4

[On his supporting tax cuts]: The argument [against cutting taxes] goes like this: Congress blew it. Congress spent it. Congress did it. So you, the taxpayer, must suffer. To that I say no way, no how, no chance. Not on my watch.

Before Family Research Council, Washington, D.C., March 9/ The New York Times, 3-10:(A)8.

5

I have lost confidence that we can ever fix the income-tax system. We have to find a new concept . . . It seems clear to me that the

(BILL ARCHER)

only tax that can succeed in achieving [desired] goals is some type of a broad-based consumer tax that completely and totally replaces the present system. [Under such a new system,] there is no tax on savings and investment. You don't pay taxes until you consume.

Nation's Business,
April:22.

1

My economic and tax philosophy reflect what has become a proven fact in the world—that the capitalistic system, which includes the opportunity to move up and to achieve to where everybody does not have the same amount of money, produces in the end the most good for the most people. Our country should be looked at as one of equal opportunity to achieve, not necessarily equal results.

Interview,
Washington, D.C./
The New York Times,
4-4:(A)10.

Richard K. Armey
United States Representative,
R-Texas

2

[Saying an increase in the minimum wage would lead to layoffs and job losses]: I will not hold my nose and vote for something that will be injurious to the least-advantaged people in our labor force, tear the bottom rungs off the occupation ladder away from these people and never allow them to have the dignity of work.

Broadcast interview/
"Meet the Press," NBC-TV, 1-8.

3

A flat-rate tax does everything that you want a tax code to do. It covers individuals' entire earnings—but only taxes them once. It is simple, direct and honest. It would lower the tax burden on virtually all Americans, particularly families with children. And it would create a powerful incentive to save and invest . . . Because of the generous exemptions [in his plan], millions of taxpayers are taken off the rolls entirely, and middle-income Americans receive a tax cut.

Interview/
Nation's Business, April:20.

Jane Armitage
Labor specialist, International Bank
for Reconstruction
and Development (World Bank)

4

There's an extraordinary trend for companies to contract out work, which changes the entire structure of employment. The corps of white-collar jobs is actually shrinking. This trend can be very troubling, as people's relationship with work worldwide has been at the root of deeply held societal arrangements and beliefs. If societies used to the traditional ideas of a job and security suddenly find them eroded, then there's a profound impact on everything from role models to consumer spending patterns.

Los Angeles Times,
3-7:(H)4.

Neil Bernstein
Professor of labor law,
Washington University

5

[On the year-and-a-half labor strike by employees of Caterpillar, Inc., which just

(NEIL BERNSTEIN)

ended with the workers returning to their jobs without winning the concessions they wanted]: The Caterpillar strike is a big balloon that just went poof. If I represent management, and the workers want to organize, I can tell them: "Look what happened at Caterpillar. What good does a union do for you?"

Los Angeles Times,
12-5:(A)5.

Alan S. Blinder
Vice Chairman,
Federal Reserve Board

1

My biggest disagreement with my colleagues at the Fed [-eral Reserve] is over openness. I believe we should talk to society more and say what we are doing and why we think it is right. But the position of this institution has always been to be extremely tight-lipped.

Interview,
Washington, D.C./
The New York Times,
3-18:17.

2

Someone asked me during a recent speech, do I think we can ever achieve zero inflation. I said, "Absolutely, yes." We can get there in only a couple of years if we are willing to pay the price. But I think if you put the quesion to ordinary people—"Would you like right now to have a recession like the one in the early 1990s to get inflation to zero by 1997"—you would be hard put to find a single vote. You can have a more moderate strategy, arriving more slowly with less pain.

Interview,
Washington, D.C./
The New York Times,
3-18:17.

Barbara Boxer
United States Senator,
D-California

3

[Criticizing pending Senate legislation aimed at cutting Federal spending in order to balance the budget by the year 2002]: This budget is the broadest retreat from the American dream I've ever seen in my time as an adult.

Before the Senate,
Washington, D.C.,
May 25/
Los Angeles Times,
5-26:(A)1.

John B. Breaux
United States Senator,
D-Louisiana

4

[Supporting President Clinton's plan for balancing the Federal budget in 10 years, which some Democrats have criticized as moving too close to the Republicans' proposals]: The President did the right thing. He can't just sit back and criticize the way members of Congress can. He must lead. His proposal will make some Democrats mad and some Republicans mad, but in the long run it will be good for the country.

June 14/
Los Angeles Times,
6-15:(A)26.

William Bridges
Management consultant

1

Security today comes from employability, and employability is something in *you*, not the job . . . Just as investment counselors say it's a mistake to invest all your money in one stock, or just in stocks, so is it a mistake to invest all your emotional security "money," or assets, in one job . . . A lot of us grew up with the notion that jobs are part of God's Creation. They aren't . . . We're all going to have a lot of trouble letting go of those expectations and assumptions that were really bred into us by a job-based culture.

Interview,
Mill Valley, Calif./
Los Angeles Times,
5-30:(D)1,2.

Ronald H. Brown
Secretary of Commerce
of the United States

2

[Last year's election victory that put the Republicans in control of Congrcss] rcally puts into danger the economic recovery that is taking place in America. With the creation of over five million new jobs since President Clinton was elected, the approach now seems to be tax breaks for the wealthy, massive budget cuts, except for the military, which is slated under the Republican proposal to have an increased budget. Those policies, in my judgment, will lead us down the same road as the [former Republican President Ronald] Reagan policies of the '80s did, and that was massive budget deficits, which was one of the main causes of our economic recession.

Ebony,
February:74.

Patrick J. Buchanan
Political commentator;
Candidate for the
1996 Republican
Presidential nomination

3

Economics is not the science that sends men to the barricades.

Los Angeles Times,
3-21:(A)17.

4

[On his visits with working people in New Hampshire while campaigning for the Presidential nomination]: This fellow looks in my eyes and says, "Save our jobs." Parts of their paper mill are closing down, and then you go down to Manchester and you read about how the Export-Import Bank is financing a new paper mill in Mexico. And you ask yourself, What are we doing to our fellow countrymen here? . . . You look at those fellows, and you realize they aren't going to be making computers. They're about my age. They're the typc of fcllows I played ball with. And these guys' lives are never going to be as good as they are now.

Time,
11-6:28.

Michael Byrne
Spokesman,
American Federation
of Labor-Congress of
Industrial Organizations

5

[On labor unions' trying to build up their Asian-American membership]: We are a labor movement in dire need of new blood. The fact that we have a large pool of Asian work-

(MICHAEL BYRNE)

ers, and many of them in primitive working conditions, that's a great potential for growth for us.

Los Angeles Times,
5-6:(A)1.

Bill Clinton
President
of the United States

1

[Advocating an increase in the minimum wage]: The only way to grow the middle class and shrink the underclass is to make work pay. Let me say this, too, emphatically: If we're serious about welfare reform, then we have the clear obligation to make work attractive and to reward people who are willing to work hard.

News conference,
Washington, D.C.,
Feb. 3/
The Washington Post,
2-4:(A)5.

2

The country's better off [economically] than it was two years ago. I get tickled, I laugh every time I see one of . . . the Republican [Presidential] aspirants—they have a big fund-raiser and they give them a bunch of money because a lot of them are angry that we raised income taxes on the top 1.2 percent of people to bring the [Federal budget] deficit down. But I'll bet you everybody going to those fund-raisers for those Republicans is doing better under our economic policies in the last two years than they were before . . . This country is doing better, and I am determined to keep fighting for the interest and the values of middle-class people, and I'm going to let [next year's Presidential] election take care of itself, as I believe it will.

News conference,
Washington, D.C.,
March 3/
The New York Times,
3-4:9.

3

Anything we can do to simplify the tax code, consistent with fairness and not exploding the [Federal budget] deficit, we ought to do. The first time I heard about a flat tax, I thought it sounded like a pretty good idea. [But] every analysis that I have seen done indicates that the flat-tax proposals that are out there now will increase the deficit and increase taxes on all Americans with incomes of under $200,000 a year.

Broadcast interview/
The New York Times,
4-18:(A)1.

4

[Criticizing Congressional Republicans for proposing too much in the way of Federal program cuts]: I invite Senators and members of Congress from both parties to join with me in balancing the budget while protecting our common ground. If they refuse, I must continue to act, alone if necessary . . . These priorities are not Democratic or Republican priorities. They are common sense national decisions that have served us very, very well over the last generation. When we ignore the evidence of what has plainly worked in the attempt to fix what is plainly wrong, we pay a terrible price. We mustn't attempt to throw over, in a moment of partisan zeal, the common-sense and bipartisan conclusions of our

(BILL CLINTON)

fathers and mothers, derived from lifetimes of experience.

At Boys Nation conference, Washington, D.C., July 24/ Los Angeles Times, 7-25:(A)15.

1

[On the current budget impasse between himself and the Republican-controlled Congress]: If the American people want the budget that [the Republicans] have proposed to be the law of the land, they're entitled to another President, and that's the only way they're going to get it.

Broadcast interview, Nov. 15/ Los Angeles Times, 11-16:(A)1.

Stanley E. Collender
Authority on the Federal budget, Price Waterhouse, accountants

2

[On the just-passed Senate bill aimed at cutting Federal spending in order to balance the budget by the year 2002]: It's an important first step, but it isn't the final step by any means. Without it, you probably wouldn't get anywhere close to a balanced budget. But with it, there's still no guarantee.

May 25/ Los Angeles Times, 5-26:(A)23.

Kent Conrad
United States Senator, D-North Dakota

3

[Criticizing the proposed balanced-budget Constitutional amendment]: My principal concern is that we not loot the Social Security trust-fund surplus in order to balance the [Federal] budget. As I said last night, only in Washington would people think they're balancing the budget when they're taking trust-fund monies, retirement-fund monies and using it to balance the operating expenses of the government . . . If you read the plain language of the amendment, it is very clear that the Social Security trust-fund surpluses—in the next seven years, $636-billion—will be used, every penny of it. There won't be a trust fund. It will be gone. It will be spent to help balance the operating expenses of the government . . . I think that's wrong.

Broadcast interview/ "Fox Morning News," Fox-TV, 3-1.

Paul Coverdell
United States Senator, R-Georgia

4

[Business organizations especially] have a vital role in this historic moment, because they can serve as educators conveying the balanced-[Federal]-budget message in terms important to business people, to workers and to their families. This generation is being called upon to step up and do the things necessary to give a healthy country to those who come next and not be the first generation in

(PAUL COVERDELL)

our history to hand over a nation crippled by uncontrolled [government] spending and debt.

Interview/
Nation's Business,
July:21.

Thomas A. Daschle
United States Senator,
D-South Dakota

1

[Blaming House Speaker Newt Gingrich for the budget impasse between President Clinton and Congressional Republicans which has resulted in a shutdown of some government agencies and services]: He wants chaos. He wants collapse of the government. And now he's got it.

Nov. 15/
Los Angeles Times,
11-16:(A)16.

David Deferranti
Labor specialist,
International Bank
for Reconstruction
and Development (World Bank)

2

The whole nature of production has changed. It's no longer primarily heavy industry. Manual dexterity and the ability to learn rapidly are critical. Manufacturing often used to favor men. Now it increasingly favors women . . . Job growth is going to be unpredictable, so employers and employees need to be able to switch from what are the slower-growing areas this year to something else next year. They need to recognize where markets are moving and be responsive, quickly. It means a totally different way of thinking and working. So far, most people aren't moving fast enough. [But] through education, people learn how to change or adapt to the environment.

Los Angeles Times,
3-7:(H)4.

Robert J. Dole
United States Senator,
R-Kansas;
Candidate for the
1996 Republican
Presidential nomination

3

[Saying President Clinton shares the blame for the recent defeat in the Senate of a balanced-budget amendment to the Constitution]: The President abdicated his responsibilty on reducing the [Federal budget] deficit. If that's leadership, then there's a new definition for it that I fail to understand.

News conference,
Washington, D.C.,
March 2/
The New York Times,
3-3:(A)10.

4

[Predicting passage of a Senate bill aimed at cutting Federal spending in order to balance the budget by the year 2002]: Today the Senate will make a statement and we'll make history in the process. We will finally begin to speak for the future. And we'll do it with one word: leadership.

Before the Senate,
Washington, D.C.,
May 25/
Los Angeles Times,
5-26:(A)1.

Pete V. Domenici
United States Senator,
R-New Mexico

1

[On the Republicans' Federal budget plan]: I think it's visionary. I think it's necessary. It's visionary because it proposes a very simple but profound proposition that the United States of America should reach a point in time, sooner rather than later, when we pay our bills without borrowing money every year. So from my standpoint, it has been an exhilerating four months getting ready for it. It is probably one of the most pride-filled days of my service to New Mexicans and the nation, because I am absolutely positive—no doubt about it—that I am doing something right for the future of our country and for our children.

Broadcast interview/
"MacNeil-Lehrer NewsHour,"
PBS-TV, 5-9.

2

There is a reward for balancing the [Federal] budget. The reward is a better America, more jobs, more opportunity, lower interest rates, less debt for our children. Add them all up, and every adult leader in America should be willing to stand up and say that is what we really ought to do.

Nation's Business,
July:24.

J. James Exon
United States Senator,
D-Nebraska

3

[Saying he doesn't expect the Democrats' balanced-budget plan will affect the plan of the Republicans, who control Congress]: There is absolutely no way that the minority party is going to influence the majority to go along with any particular plan that we can outline. If we [Democrats] put up a plan, they [Republicans] will shoot it down. They are the majority; they have the obligation to lead.

News conference,
Washington, D.C.,
March 8/
The New York Times,
3-9:(A)8.

Steven Forbes
President and
editor-in-chief,
"Forbes" magazine

4

The [state] income tax seems to have the greatest impact, the most immediate effect on the economy. It's the first thing that any executive looks at in locating in the state. It has a direct impact on business in the state. It is the most direct tax, on work, investment and savings, all the things that make for a vibrant economy.

The Washington Post,
3-2:(A)18.

Rodney Fort
Professor of economics,
Washington State University

5

The rise of [labor] unions in America has always followed the countervailing-power notion. Management with power is eventually confronted by some sort of organized structure . . . The argument boils down to who gets what share.

USA Today,
1-9:(C)2.

Gary A. Franks
United States Representative, R-Connecticut

1

The Republican Party believes that the middle class has been over-taxed to pay for rampant spending of social programming. We believe that we must help those producing jobs in this country to produce more jobs via tax incentives, easing government regulations. We strongly encourage individuals to start their own businesses by making capital more available to budding entrepreneurs . . . African-Americans know that economic development is the key for many of the problems we have in our society today. They know that there's not enough capital in the African-American community for the expansion of business development. Those are the things that the Republican Party believes in, and I [as a black] and other members of the Party are rigorously fighting for.

Ebony, February:74.

Milton Friedman
Economist

2

I have looked at many episodes in the world in which monetary policy went one way and fiscal policy the other, and I have never found a case in which monetary policy did not dominate.

The New York Times, 2-21:(C)9.

John E. Frydenlund
Director, Agriculture Policy Project, Heritage Foundation

3

[Calling for a phasing out of government farm programs and subsidies]: It's time to get rid of the command-and-control features of the agricultural economy. If you eliminate restrictions as you eliminate subsidies, you will get larger production, and incomes will rise . . . What we propose is almost heresy. It's a total departure from the agriculture policy of the last 60 years. We're asking you to look at it a different way.

The Washington Post, 4-25:(A)15.

Richard A. Gephardt
United States Representative, D-Missouri

4

[On the Republicans' Contract With America]: I don't think that what's happened on the Contract has created one job. I don't think it has raised the standard of living or the wages of any American.

The Washington Post, 2-20:(A)10.

5

[Criticizing the Republican Federal budget proposal]: The American people are for balancing the budget, but they are not for balancing it on the backs of senior citizens and middle-income people. I think that if the Republicans insist on doing this and they are able to override Presidential vetoes and implement this budget, it will not go down well with the American people.

The Washington Post, 5-19:(A)4.

6

[On his tax plan, in which 75 percent of taxpayers would pay a 10 percent rate and most deductions would be dropped]: Mine is the only tax-reform plan that is designed en-

(RICHARD A. GEPHARDT)

tirely for working families and the middle class. No lobbyist, no special interest, no corporate contributor will reap special benefits from its passage.

July 6/USA Today, 7-7:(A)6.

Newt Gingrich
United States Representative, R-Georgia; Speaker of the House

1

[Criticizing some Republicans for wanting to cut back on a tax-reduction package the Party has been pushing]: Over this past weekend, I saw some Republicans beginning to backslide, and all I can say is I was there when people told [former] President [George] Bush it was okay to raise taxes. It destroyed his Presidency. I was there when the Establishment of this city [Washington] said it was wonderful that [President] Clinton wanted to raise taxes. It destroyed the [Democatic] majority in the House and the Senate. We [Republicans] gave our word to cut taxes.

At broadcast town meeting sponsored by U.S. Chamber of Commerce, Washington, D.C., March 22/ Los Angeles Times, 3-23:(A)4.

2

Do you think $500 spent by a bureaucrat is better than $500 spent by a parent? That is the core issue on the tax credit for children: Who do you think spends it better?

Nation's Business, May:23.

3

We [Republicans] are building on [our] Contract With America by in effect creating a contract with our children to leave them a balanced [Federal] budget and lower interest rates and lower taxes, and we think that's a very, very important step in the right direction.

To reporters, May 5/ Los Angeles Times, 5-6:(A)12.

Bill Goodling
United States Representative, R-Pennsylvania

4

The right of employees to withhold their labor and the corollary right of management to continue business operations during a strike by hiring permanent replacement workers are the foundation of our system of collective bargaining.

June 14/ Los Angeles Times, 6-15:(D)5.

Robert J. Gordon
Economist, Northwestern University

5

[Saying a dollar that is falling against foreign currencies is not necessarily bad for the U.S. economy]: The dollar fell by one-third between 1985 and 1987 and the result was a very prosperous period for the American economy, with only a modest increase in inflation.

The New York Times, 3-9:(C)1.

Al Gore
Vice President of the United States

1

If we could write a capital-gains tax-reduction bill, of course we could write one that would be good for the country in our view and that we could support. But our opponents in the Congress have made it very clear that the kind they want to pass is aimed at putting a great deal more money in the hands of those making more than $200,000 per year. I don't share that theory, and we will oppose any provision that is designed according to that formula.

Interview, Washinton, D.C., Jan. 6/ Los Angeles Times, 1-7:(A)17.

2

I don't care how hard you tried, if you did try, you could not get President Bill Clinton to shift his attention away from the economy and away from creating jobs and opportunity for the American people. That's his passion. He focuses on that every single day . . . We've got the best economy we've had in a long time. Strong economic growth, historically low inflation, millions of new jobs being created, the first time the deficit has come down three years in a row since Harry Truman was President, and an active effort to reinvent government. Any efforts by the Republicans to prevent that or to turn that around, we'll fight against.

Interview, Washington, D.C., Jan. 6/ Los Angeles Times, 1-7:(A)17.

3

[On a Constitutional amendment mandating a balanced Federal budget as proposed by Republicans]: [The Republicans] tell you they're going to balance the budget without cutting Social Security. But they don't tell you how they're going to do it . . . A balanced budget sounds nice, but only if you know what's going to be done.

Before National Legislative Council of American Association of Retired Persons, Washington, D.C./ AARP Bulletin, March:7.

4

In our view, only the market system unlocks a higher fraction of the human potential than any other form of economic organization, and has the demonstrated potential to create broadly distributed new wealth.

At United Nations conference on social development, Copenhagen, Denmark, March 12/ The Washington Post, 3-13:(A)10.

Slade Gorton
United States Senator, R-Washington

5

[On a Senate appropriations bill that cuts funding of various programs and departments, including the NEA and the Interior Department]: I feel like the Grinch [for supporting the bill]. I'm here managing a bill in which almost every account gets less money than it does for the current year and the argument

(SLADE GORTON)

[in support] of each of the programs taken in isolation is, of course, a persuasive argument.

Washington, D.C., Aug. 9/ Los Angeles Times, 8-10:(A)30.

Phil Gramm
United States Senator, R-Texas; Candidate for the 1996 Republican Presidential nomination

1

[On the 1985 Gramm-Rudman Federal deficit-reduction plan]: The beauty of the Gramm-Rudman idea was that it put the fat in the fire. We could then put out the fire either by raising taxes or by cutting spending. So different people could see it producing different results. And since we had nothing like a majority on this issue, it was necessary that it be viewed as a tool, so that people would think they could do various things with the tool. I thought I could do something. I didn't see it as a gamble. We were losing on defense; we were losing on taxes. No, it wasn't a gamble. At that point it was our best hope.

The Atlantic Monthly, March:89.

2

[Criticizing Democrats for their positions on spending cuts and balancing the budget]: *They* never propose cutting anything. But they can stand up in front of God and everybody else and, oh, they're for a balanced budget . . . It's like [President] Bill Clinton, who "feels our pain" and doesn't share with us that he causes it all the time.

Before the Senate, Washington, May 23/ The New York Times, 5-24:(C)19.

3

[Supporting tax cuts]: How can we be a country that loves jobs and hates the people who create them? Tax cuts are for people who are paying taxes.

Before the Senate, Washington, D.C., May 23/ The New York Times, 5-24:(C)19.

Alan Greenspan
Chairman, Federal Reserve Board

4

[On the dollar's current fall against the Japanese yen and the German mark]: Dollar weakness, while very likely overdone, is unwelcome because it adds to potential inflation pressures in our economy. As I have emphasized numerous times in the past, it is important that we contain such pressures.

Before House Budget Committee, Washington, D.C., March 8/ The New York Times, 3-9:(A)1.

5

We must recognize that the productive potential of the U.S. economy will be shaped significantly by the actions of this Congress regarding the Federal budget deficit . . . Too

(ALAN GREENSPAN)

much of the small pool of national savings goes toward funding the government . . . If we are to sustain the higher levels of investment that are crucial to achieving healthy increases in productivity and to remain a viable competitor in world markets, we must raise the level of domestic saving and reduce our reliance on foreign saving.

Before House Budget Committee, Washington, D.C./ Nation's Business, July:21.

1

I'm not concerned in the slightest that our political system will overdo [Federal budget] deficit reduction. I have been around this town too long to hold that as a deep-seated fear . . . I don't stay up at night worrying about that.

Nations's Business, July:24.

Robert Greenstein
Director, Center on Budget and Policy Priorities

2

[On plans by Republicans in Congress for cutting government spending]: I can't recall any collection of budget cuts from a prior Administration or Congress that was aimed so heavily at the poor.

Feb. 27/ The New York Times, 2-28:(A)11.

Judd Gregg
United States Senator, R-New Hampshire

3

[Supporting a proposed Constitutional amendment mandating a balanced Federal budget]: What's at risk here is our children. Congress has run up a $4.8-trillion deficit, and when you start passing that size of debt onto the next generation, you're essentially making it impossible for the next generation to have a prosperous and worthwhile lifestyle.

Broadcast interview/ "Meet the Press," NBC-TV, 2-26.

Robert Hormats
Vice chairman, Goldman Sachs International; Former Deputy United States Trade Representative

4

[On a new trade agreement between the U.S. and Japan aimed at opening up Japan's market to U.S. auto products]: [U.S. President Clinton may benefit politically at home by] getting an opening in the Japanese market without having to pull the trigger [and impose sanctions]. This really strengthens his claim as the most activist trade President we've had since World War II.

June 28/ Los Angeles Times, 6-29:(A)7.

Jerry Jasinowski
President, National Association of Manufacturers

5

[Government] regulatory decisions are not directly visible to the public, [but] are

(JERRY JASINOWSKI)

passed on to Americans in . . . lower wages, higher prices, increased state and local taxes, slower economic growth and reduced employment opportunities.

Before House Science Committee, Washington, D.C., Feb. 2/ USA Today, 2-3:(A)6.

Nancy L. Johnson
United States Representative, R-Connecticut

1

There is no way America can keep driving itself into debt. We have a lot of work to do reducing the cost of government. [Balancing the Federal budget is] not going to destroy us, but [the debt] will if we don't.

Before National Legislative Council of American Association of Retired Persons, Washinton, D.C./ AARP Bulletin, March:7.

Mickey Kantor
United States Trade Representative

2

Americans have always been very skeptical [about the benefits of foreign trade]. For the first time we're beginning to turn that around . . . But to do that, you've got to build confidence, and to build confidence, you've got to be willing to stand up [and challenge foreign economies that are closed].

Interview, June 9/ The Washington Post, 6-10:(C)6.

3

[In economic terms,] I'm gravely concerned about technology transfer [from the U.S. to other countries]. We recognize that we have an obligation as we open markets and work with other countries to make sure we also produce jobs here at home . . . What we don't want to do is what we did with Airbus [European commercial jetliner] and create a rival, subsidized, state-owned company which Airbus is, which literally took jobs and capital and market share from [U.S. competitor] McDonnell Douglas.

Interview/ Los Angeles Times, 12-2:(A)16.

John R. Kasich
United States Representative, R-Ohio

4

[On his passion for getting to a balanced Federal budget]: I look at this almost like I look at the Vietnam war [of the 1970s]. The [American] people ended the Vietnam war; that's why it ended. And the people are [now] demanding that this [excessive government spending] be ended. And we're [Congress] always behind where the public is.

The New York Times, 3-18:7.

5

[On the Republican economic plan, which is aiming at a balanced Federal budget by 2002]: For the first time in my lifetime, we're trying to make sure the country realizes its destiny.

Washington, D.C., Nov. 17/ Los Angeles Times, 11-18:(A)1.

Nancy Landon Kassebaum
United States Senator,
R-Kansas

1

[On a proposed Constitutional amendment mandating a balanced Federal budget]: [This amendment] may be a bad idea whose time has come . . . [But] I believe that balancing the budget is an enormously important responsibility that we [legislators] have. [The balanced-budget amendment may be worth trying] to get people to realize what it will and will not be able to do.

AARP Bulletin, March:7.

2

[Criticizing President Clinton for signing an order barring Federal agencies from doing business with companies that hire permanent replacement workers during a labor strike]: Congress makes the laws, not the Administration. The Executive Branch should not attempt to use the Federal procurement process to make major changes to our labor laws [which allow the hiring of permanent replacement workers].

March 8/
The New York Times,
3-9:(A)9.

Dirk Kempthorne
United States Senator,
R-Idaho

3

[On unfunded mandates the Federal government puts on states]: If something is truly a national priority, in the best interest of public health or safety, then Congress should be honest and upfront about it and pay for it.

The Washington Post,
1-9:(A)8.

Douglas Kmiec
Professor of law,
University of Notre Dame

4

[Criticizing a proposed Constitutional amendment mandating a balanced Federal budget]: This [new] desire to amend the Constitution is part of the general trend to try to write morality into law. We cannot control our appetite to spend money, so we'll try to control it by writing it into law . . . We have a behavioral problem here on spending, and to think that our behavior will be changed by a few sentences in the document is sad. That's what was sad about Prohibition as well. We can no more stop someone from destroying himself with alcohol than we can control fiscal sanity with an amendment.

The Washington Post,
3-14:(A)1,5.

John P. Kotter
Professor,
Harvard Business School

5

The best way to approach *any* job these days is to say, "This looks like an exciting place where I can learn, where I can make a contribution. And who knows? I might not even be here in five years. But as long as I'm learning, I can always bounce out to something else."

Interview/
U.S. News & World Report,
3-27:63.

Alex Krauer
Chairman and managing director,
Ciba-Geigy Corporation (Switzerland)

6

We watch with some concern [while] two

(ALEX KRAUER)

major players in the world economy, namely the U.S. and Japan, are not handling [their trade] dispute within the spirit and also the formal procedure of [world trade rules]. Europeans in general would prefer to see that dispute shifted to [the WTO].

Interview/ USA Today, 6-9:(B)4.

William Kristol
Chairman, Project for the Republican Future

1

[On the new Republican-controlled Congress]: Part of being the majority is getting to the point where we can go after [spending on] entitlements in a big way. Take [the late President Franklin] Roosevelt as an example. He didn't do everything at once. He phased in most of his big programs. Similarly, we [Republicans] are going to have to be both bold in the vision we hold out for America and somewhat prudent—if I can use a discredited [George] Bush Administration word—and incremental. We need a kind of bold incrementalism that leads people along step by step, so that a year from now they'll be saying, "They really did cut some programs this year, and we like it" . . . People are so distrustful of government right now that we may have crossed some sort of magic threshold where paople are willing to say, "Look, I'll even give up these programs that allegedly help me, because [a] they don't really help me much and [b] I do understand that we have a [Federal budget] deficit and the whole thing is sprawling out of control. I'll give up my chunk of government benefits if everyone else is giving up his."

Panel discussion, Washington, D.C./ Harper's, March:44,46.

Eugene Lehrmann
President, American Association of Retired Persons

2

[On a proposed Constitutional amendment mandating a balanced Federal budget]: Seventy-five percent of all Americans said Congress should spell out which programs will be cut before they pass a balanced-budget amendment . . . Support for this amendment is very shallow. Once the American public comprehends the devastating effects of this amendment, those legislators who supported a balanced-budget amendment may find themselves facing angry constituents.

AARP Bulletin, March:5.

Robert L. Livingston
United States Representative, R-Louisiana

3

[On his being the new Chairman of the House Appropriations Committee, which will be a centerpiece in driving the Republicans' plans to cut government spending]: I have become the Grinch that stole Christmas. But it has its compensation; I have also gone from 18 years in the wilderness to suddenly a center of attraction, for good or bad. I think that about the time we do our job [of cutting spending], it probably will be for bad . . . The [House] Ways and Means [Committee] folks can go out and say, "Oh, look, we cut your

(ROBERT L. LIVINGSTON)

taxes." They can play the role of Santa Claus. And we [on the Appropriations Committee] can play the role of the Grinch . . . [But] I think the American people understand that we must fulfill that commitment [to cut government costs]. I think they are prepared to take cuts in favorite programs in order to assure themselves that they leave their children the long-term health of the United States.

Interview/
The New York Times,
1-14:10.

1

[On Democrats who are expressing alarm at proposed Republican cuts in government spending]: The Chicken Littles, the Democrats, had 40 years [when they controlled Congress] to bring the budget into balance. Folks, if you don't like these cuts, then you aren't going to like the ones to come.

Before the House,
Washington, D.C.,
March 15/
The New York Times,
3-16:(C)23.

2

[On cutting the Federal budget, for which the House Appropriations Committee, which he chairs, bears much of the responsibility]: Everybody is going to feel some of the pain. All of our agricultural people are not happy with the lack of money available; our defense people are unhappy; our labor and health people are unhappy; you name it. But we know what we have to do. We have said the buck stops here, with the Appropriations Committee, and it is time that we acknowledged that.

The New York Times,
6-27:(A)8.

Robert E. Lucas, Jr.
Professor of economics,
University of Chicago;
Winner,
1995 Nobel Prize
in Economics

3

Models that we thought were guiding the fine-tuning of the economy through monetary and fiscal policy are more or less useless. Those models presumed a lot of stupidity on the part of the ordinary citizen.

Los Angeles Times,
10-11:(D)1.

Richard G. Lugar
United States Senator,
R-Indiana;
Candidate for the
1996 Republican
Presidential nomination

4

[On his suggestion that the income tax be replaced by a national sales tax so that people will not have money withheld from their paychecks and be able to spend their income as they wish]: You may save it or spend it, but the paycheck is bigger without the automatic withholding deduction. You need not account for it, report it, or hide it.

The Christian Science Monitor,
4-19:4.

Thomas E. Mann
Director of governmental studies, Brookings Institution

1

The suburban middle-class vote has remained in the Republican Party because they want lower taxes, or so it is believed. But the polls show voters want [Federal budget-] deficit reduction. And a lot of [economic policy] is poll-driven. The question is, what is the Republican priority: lower taxes or reducing the deficit?

The New York Times, 6-19:(A)9.

Dana Mead
Chairman, Tenneco, Inc.

2

We can grow this economy faster than a 2.5 percent [annual rate] without opening the Pandora's box of inflation . . . because of structural changes that have occurred in this economy . . . [And] consumers are damn reluctant to accept price inreases. If you want to stay in business . . . if you want to keep making money . . . you have to find ways to take out costs. American industry has been able to do this, and do it quite successfully.

Interview/ USA Today, 9-29:(B)3.

David Minge
United States Representative, D-Minnesota

3

[Criticizing "pork" delivered by some in Congress to their home districts]: The resolve we have as a nation to accept the sacrifice necessary to balance the [Federal] budget is undermined when certain members of Congress and certain communities get prizes while other people are trying to tighten their belts.

U.S. News & World Report, 7-24:34.

Mike Murphy
Republican political strategist

4

If we [Republicans] do not pass a [Federal] budget that dramatically cuts spending, the kind that *The Washington Post* and *The New York Times* will term a catastrophe, and pay that short-term price, then in the long term we're going to be destroyed, because we will have lied to America. We've got political momentum [now that Republicans control Congress]. If we don't use it right away to make significant cuts, we will be failures.

Panel discussion, Washington, D.C./ Harper's, March:45.

Norman J. Ornstein
Senior fellow, American Enterprise Institute

5

No job is safe anywhere. You're loyal, but you are easily fired. More and more people are working harder than ever, but their basic lives are fraying at the edges. They feel enormous pressures, and they are paying more taxes and getting less for it. There's a sense that Republicans are for the rich and Democrats are for the poor, but who's for the middle class?

The Christian Science Monitor, 10-4:3.

Leon E. Panetta
Chief of Staff
to President
of the United States
Bill Clinton

1

[The Republicans have,] to some extent, painted themselves in a corner by promising what they can't deliver. They have basically promised that they could balance the [Federal] budget by the year 2002, that they could provide tax cuts totaling about $345-billion over 7 years, $600-billion over 10 years. And they are trying to find a way to pay for it. They basically know that they can't deliver on those first two promises without significant cuts in Medicare, along with other programs like Medicaid and education . . . Are they still committed to balancing the budget by 2002? Are they still committed to this huge tax cut for the wealthy? Are they still committed to doing Medicare cuts outside of health-care reform? Where are they at? The only way we can get the answer to that, frankly, is when they present their budget resolution.

Press briefing,
Washington, D.C., May 1/
The New York Times,
5-2:(A)1,13.

2

[Criticizing the Republican idea to balance the Federal budget by the year 2002]: Our approach is we would be willing to agree to a deficit-reduction path that brings us to balance, but we shouldn't just focus on a specific date . . . [The Republicans have] basically grabbed a date out of the air, and now everything has to fit into it. This is a numbers game, as far as the Republicans are concerned. You don't let the date set policy. Policy should set the date.

Broadcast interview/
"Face the Nation,"
CBS-TV, 5-14.

Mike Parker
United States Representative,
D-Mississippi

3

[A balanced Federal budget would eliminate] talk about the next generation not having a higher standard of living than the previous generation. All of a sudden people would have hope again, people would be in a situation where they could look forward to things, where they could look forward to having a future and be able to have a career, have a family and have a home, have retirement, and have a higher standard of living than their parents.

Nation's Business, July:24.

Peter Peek
Economist,
International
Labor Organization

4

The world's job market is undergoing an historic transformation at an unprecedented pace. And it's not over. We're only somewhere in the middle of the process . . . Globalization is bringing about a new division of labor whereby the north must specialize in products and services requiring expensive use of high technology or skilled workers in which it has a comparative edge over the south. It can't compete with China in producing shirts anymore.

Los Angeles Times,
3-7:(H)1,4.

James P. Pinkerton
Lecturer, Graduate School of Political Management, George Washington University; Former Deputy Assistant for Policy Planning to the President of the United States (George Bush)

1

In some areas of Republican ideology, there is a sense that the highest value is not work but just making money. We have to say that's wrong, that there is more merit to a person getting up every morning and going to work than someone just inheriting a fortune.

Panel discussion, Washington, D.C./ Harper's, March:49.

Robert B. Reich
Secretary of Labor of the United States

2

We're going to fight very hard for [a] minimum-wage increase because it's just, it's right, it's necessary, it doesn't cost jobs, and we want to make work pay for the average American.

Press briefing, Washington, D.C., Feb. 3/ The Washington Post, 2-4:(A)5.

3

Getting people into work and getting them prepared for work has got to become a national passion. It's got to become the primary goal of the public. People ask me, what's a way to solve our social ills? I give you three ways of solving the major social problems of this country: They're jobs, jobs and jobs.

Interview/ USA Today, 3-3:(B)4.

4

The surest way to profits and productivity is [for companies] to treat employees as assets to be developed rather than costs to be cut.

News conference, June 5/ Los Angeles Times, 6-6:(D)1.

5

[When the automobile caused buggy-whip manufacturers to go out of business,] no one foresaw the number of manufacturing jobs that would be created because no one could foresee the assembly line. Entire categories of jobs will be eliminated [in the future], just like buggy-whip manufacturers and horseshoers. But that doesn't mean there won't be a lot of categories of jobs emerging over the next 10 years that we don't even have names for [today].

USA Today, 7-28:(B)2.

6

[Criticizing employers]: If companies have responsibilities, don't they have a responsibility to provide decent wages to their employees? Corporate profits are setting record levels; the stock market is surging. [And] don't they have a responsibility to hire disadvantaged teenagers for the summer? And what about the responsibility of companies to train their workers and upgrade their skills? . . . [There is] a major shift from earned to

(ROBERT B. REICH)

unearned income [among executives], from paychecks to dividends and capital gains . . . This is the clearest evidence yet of the effects of "trickle-down economics." How can anyone with a straight face propose a capital-gains tax cut when owners of capital are running off with these gains from workers?

At National Baptist Convention, San Diego, Calif./ The Wall Street Journal, 8-24:(A)16.

1

There are substantial numbers of workers who are not now unionized who are ripe for the picking [by unions]. What I hear again and again, what people tell me, is that they have no bargaining leverage [with employers], and they feel treated badly by employers, and they feel the old implicit employment contract has been breached.

Interview/ Los Angeles Times, 10-26:(A)14.

Andrew Reschovsky
Economist, University of Wisconsin

2

The supply-side arguments about state income taxes are largely overblown. I don't think there is a lot of good empirical evidence that suggests that tax rates affect economic growth rates . . . I think most economists believe that taxes play some role but it's only on the margin.

The Washington Post, 3-2:(A)18.

Bill Richardson
United States Representative, D-New Mexico

3

The hottest political issue [right now] is how much you can cut [government spending]. It's how you prove your political mettle.

USA Today, 6-29:(A)6.

Robert E. Rubin
Secretary of the Treasury of the United States

4

It's a new economy; it's a global economy. And we have to somehow or other . . . increase public understanding of what a global economy really means, because we don't have the predicate right now for doing the kinds of things that need to be done if we're going to get done that which is in the self-interest of this country to get done.

Speech, Feb. 1/ The Washington Post, 3-14:(A)7.

5

We [the Clinton Administration] do not comment with respect to the [actions of the] Federal Reserve Board, and we believe strongly that any comments with respect to the Federal Reserve Board may be counter productive. The independence of the Federal Reserve is very important to the credibility of our markets and how those markets are viewed around the world.

Interview, June 12/ The New York Times, 6-13:(C)18.

(ROBERT E. RUBIN)

1

[Criticizing Congressman Richard Armey's proposal for a "flat" income tax]: The more people looked at it, the more they became troubled by it. Our estimates are that it has a very substantial . . . shortfall in terms of deficit neutrality. To get back to deficit-neutral under its construct, you'd have to raise [a flat-tax rate] to about 23 percent. At 23 percent most people would pay more than they do [under today's graduated income tax].

To reporters,
Aug. 9/
Los Angeles Times,
8-10:(A)17.

2

[On the current shutdown of some government agencies and services due to a budget crisis between President Clinton and Congressional Republicans]: I have taken actions to prevent a default for the first time in our history on the full faith and credit of the United States. This is no way for a great nation to manage its financial affairs.

Nov. 15/
Los Angeles Times,
11-16:(A)16.

Martin Olav Sabo
United States Representative,
D-Minnesota

3

[Criticizing the Republican economic plan, which is aiming at a balanced Federal budget by 2002]: [The plan] represents a one-sided attack on lower- and middle-income citizens who will see the doors of opportunity closed as chances to better themselves disappear. Under this budget, millions of low-income families will see the safety net that ensures them adequate food, shelter and medical care shredded.

Los Angeles Times,
11-18:(A)16.

Jeffrey Sachs
Professor
of international trade,
Harvard University

4

The American economy and the American people are more used to change than any other economy in the world.

U.S. News & World Report,
9-18:24.

Joe Scarborough
United States Representative,
R-Florida

5

[Saying his Party should specify plans for cutting Federal spending before, not after, cutting taxes]: Some of the more conservative members [of Congress] believe you're either for tax cuts unequivocally or you're a traitor to the conservative cause. I just don't believe that, and I won't be cowed. It is financially irresponsible to pass a significant tax cut before you have any idea if Congress is going to have the political will to pass the spending cuts that are necessary . . . I'm not going to be party to anything that repeats the mistakes of the '80s when we cut taxes without paying for it. If they want to cut taxes, we say show us your spending cuts . . . Haven't seen 'em yet.

USA Today,
4-3:(A)10.

Charles E. Schumer
United States Representative, D-New York

1

[Criticizing proposed Republican cuts in Federal spending]: The [Speaker of the House Newt] Gingrich-GOP cuts are not fair; they are not evenhanded. These cuts come down like a ton of bricks on cities across the country. Housing will be gutted. Heating for the elderly, gone. Drug-free schools, cut. AIDS prevention, forget it.

March 15/ Los Angeles Times, 3-16:(A)15.

Gerald B. Solomon
United States Representative, R-New York

2

[On criticism of Republican plans to cut the Federal budget, which would affect welfare and social programs]: We've heard the same rhetoric about [how Republicans lack] compassion. [But] if we don't make these cuts and more, we're going to add another trillion dollars to our four-and-a-half trillion dollar national debt. What, I ask, is so compassionate about saddling our children and grandchildren with such staggering debt?

March 16/ The New York Times, 3-17:(A)1.

Fortney H. "Pete" Stark
United States Representative, D-California

3

[Criticizing President Clinton for announcing a plan to balance the Federal budget in 10 years, instead of the Republicans' plan of seven years, which in some ways, such as Medicare funding, resembles what Republicans have been proposing]: [The President] did a dumb thing Tuesday night. The politics of this are his call, but his Medicare policy is just as bad as the Republicans' . . . The only difference is that his policy will be bad for 10 years while theirs will be bad for only seven.

June 14/ Los Angeles Times, 6-15:(A)26.

Herbert G. Stein
Former Chairman, Council of Economic Advisers to the President of the United States (Richard M. Nixon)

4

[Criticizing a proposal by some House Republicans to abolish the President's Council of Economic Advisers]: I think it's a stupid idea. [The Council is] the only group of economists in the government that doesn't have some agency ax to grind. It has a budget of $3.4-million. The President is making decisions about a $7-trillion economy. I think we can afford to give him the best possible advice . . . The main thing the Council does is give the President a view of his options. Even if he disagrees, he makes a better decision because he has seen what the options are.

The New York Times, 6-28:(C)2.

George Stephanopoulos
Senior Adviser to President of the United States Bill Clinton

5

[Criticizing the Republicans' Federal budget plans]: They are prisoners of [their]

(GEORGE STEPHANOPOULOS)

"Contract With America." [Speaker of the House] Newt [Gingrich] is the ultimate Frankenstein and the Contract is his monster. The freshman [Republicans in Congress] can't go for a [compromise budget] deal. Absent a financial crisis, I can't see how there's going to be a deal.

Interview, Nov. 2/
Los Angeles Times,
11-3:(A)25.

James A. Traficant, Jr.
United States Representative,
D-Ohio

1

[On the Federal Reserve Board's increasing interest rates for the seventh time in a year]: I say it's very simple. [Fed Chairman] Alan Greenspan is simply giving America the finger.

Newsweek,
2-13:21.

Paul E. Tsongas
Co-chairman,
The Concord Coalition;
Former United States Senator,
D-Massachusetts

2

[Supporting a proposed Constitutional amendment mandating a balanced Federal budget]: The balanced-budget amendment is not a thing of beauty. It is an overdue act of contrition by a generation that has compromised the future of its own children. It is a quest for redemption by elected officials of both parties who have unfailingly placed their own re-election above the sacredness of their generational responsibility . . . It is a sorry and undignified awareness that our political leaders need the imposition of discipline from without.

At Senate hearing,
Washington, D.C., Jan. 5/
The Christian Science Monitor,
1-9:19.

3

We were told that [President Clinton] would take the moral high ground against the Republicans [in cutting government spending] . . . Instead, he took Social Security off the table [of possible cuts] the week before the [1994 Congressional] election by raising it as a campaign theme against the Republicans. And then [he made his] speech on the middle-class tax cut and the commitment to more defense spending. Then you have [House Speaker Newt Gingrich] doing the same thing. More defense spending, more tax cuts . . . no Social Security [reform]. It's a clash of the "pander bears."

Interview,
Boston, Mass./
The Christian Science Monitor,
1-9:19.

Laura D'Andrea Tyson
Chairman,
National Economic Council

4

The problem is not that some Americans are getting richer. The problem is that most Americans are getting nowhere. This is a problem for a market-based system and a democracy.

To construction executives,
Washington, D.C./
USA Today, 5-3:(B)2.

Maxine Waters
United States Representative,
D-California

1

[Criticizing the Republican stance against raising the minimum wage]: You cannot have a society where goods and services increase [in price] and wages are suppressed. We'll have a disagreement on that until hell freezes over.

Los Angeles Times,
11-6:(A)17.

J. C. Watts
United States Representative,
R-Oklahoma

2

[I] know that when we reward families that break up more than we reward families that stay together, we are going to create problems. And I know that when we reward the drug dealer on the street more than we reward black businessmen who risk their capital to create employment, we're going to create poverty. When we create policies that penalize rather than reward, discourage rather than encourage, when we create policies that will weaken the link between effort and reward, we're destined to failure.

Ebony,
February:72.

3

If you raise the minimum wage, what happens is the little person ends up being the person that's laid off and out of a job.

Los Angeles Times,
11-6:(A)17.

John C. Wells
Director,
Federal Mediation
and Conciliation Service

4

[Employee] co-ownership [of companies] is one arena of worker participation that is growing and is power-sharing at the highest level. It is happening at an accelerating rate. The most recent example is at United Airlines, with the pilots and machinists. I stand in admiration of that. The employees own 55 percent of that corporation, and that invests them not only with greater power and authority but also with greater responsibility to make the enterprise succeed. It provides a more mature level of relationship between labor and management. I would like to see more of that as we evolve our labor relations in the future.

Interview/
Los Angeles Times,
2-19:(M)3.

Robert A. White
Senior vice president,
Standard Chartered Bank,
New York, N.Y.

5

[On the continued slide of the U.S. dollar against foreign currencies]: It's pandemonium, isn't it? It's shocking to a lot of us old-timers in the market to see the dollar ostensibly removed as the reserve currency of the world . . . There's a complete lack of faith in the Fed [-eral Reserve], the [Clinton] Administration and in Congress to get the [Federal] budget in order, to get the trade balance in order.

Los Angeles Times,
3-8:(A)18.

Janet L. Yellen
Governor,
Federal Reserve Board

1

I believe the classic mistake of Fed [-eral Reserve] policy is to not look far enough ahead and to overreact. You have to guard against a possibility that we could say, "Let's clobber the economy [with high interest rates] because it has not slowed down enough yet."

The New York Times,
3-18:30.

Education

Lamar Alexander
Candidate
for the
1996 Republican
Presidential nomination;
Former Secretary
of Education
of the United States

1

[Supporting Republican plans to eliminate the U.S. Department of Education and instead give block grants to the states]: I just don't think we need a U.S. Department of Education. It operates on the assumption that teachers and principals are too stupid to make decisions for themselves.

Interview,
Nashville, Tenn./
Los Angeles Times,
5-25:(A)18.

Herman Badillo
Trustee,
City University
of New York

2

[Criticizing the policy of CUNY that guarantees admission to any student who graduates from New York City's public high schools]: Open access to college without standards is really a hoax. These kids are not going to make it. Remedial education should be in high school or junior high school, not in college.

Los Angeles Times,
5-30:(A)5.

Terrel H. Bell
Former Secretary
of Education
of the United States

3

[On suggestions that the U.S. Department of Education be eliminated in favor of the states taking more responsibility]: We talk about giving more responsibility to the states and I think we should. But we shouldn't do it because of their record in education. It's been terrible.

The New York Times,
2-21:(A)10.

William J. Bennett
Former Secretary
of Education
of the United States

4

People were always asking me if I thought we even needed the [U.S.] Department [of Education]. I often told them, "No."

The New York Times,
2-21:(A)10.

Ernest L. Boyer
President,
Carnegie Foundation
for the Advancement
of Teaching

5

[On his organization's new recommendations for the improvement of public-school systems]: Many of those other ideas, such as charter schools, are fine. But the fact is that for some time ahead the vast majority of our students are still going to go to traditional

(ERNEST L. BOYER)

neighborhood schools. I don't see a model replacing that. We have to work on the schools we have.

The Washington Post,
4-10:(A)11.

Amanda Broun
Director,
center for policy
and programs,
Public Education
Fund Network

1

[Expressing concern about private-foundations' funding of public schools]: There aren't enough private dollars to go around, and you end up increasing disparities by giving more to some [schools] and none to others. Second, you lose accountability—private resources aren't subject to public scrutiny, and the donor can change his or her mind, leaving the school in a lurch. And finally, you have let the public off the hook; if the public sees the foundation can pay for the art teacher, why should they tax themselves to pay the art teacher?

The Washington Post,
8-28:(A)8.

Michael Casserly
Director,
Council of
Great City Schools

2

[Criticizing Republican plans to abolish the U.S. Department of Education and instead give block grants to the states]: At least for the major cities, a block grant is the same thing as a cut. People at the state level have so many political forces pulling and tugging that the state's reaction is to spread the money out as thinly as possible. It does some good everywhere, but it doesn't get the bang for the buck that it ought to get because it does not reach the places it's needed the most in great enough magnitude.

Los Angeles Times,
5-25:(A)18.

Steve Chabot
United States Representative,
R-Ohio

3

[Supporting Republican plans to abolish the U.S. Department of Education and instead give block grants to the states]: There's a revolution going on in Washington, and this is part of it. This is about taking power from Washington and giving it to local communities. I'm very pro-education, but the Federal government has done a lousy job since it's injected itself into schools.

Interview/
Los Angeles Times,
5-25:(A)18.

Bill Clinton
President
of the United States

4

[Criticizing what he says is a Republican Party plan to cut education spending]: [We must reduce] unnecessary, wasteful, bloated government [in Washington. But cutting education spending] will be just as dangerous as it would have been for us to disarm in the middle of the Cold War. This is not rocket science. This is basic and this is America's future . . . You should say to all of us [in government]—get that deficit down, get this

(BILL CLINTON)

economy going. Be fair to American taxpayers. But do not cut education. Yes, we have to get things under control in Washington. But we dare not in the information age believe that the answer to America's growing insecurity about jobs and income is to undermine the very thing [education] that will take us into the 21st century still the strongest country in the world.

At Arkansas State University,
Jonesboro, Ark., April 3/
The Washington Post,
4-4:(A)7.

1

[Calling for more Federal spending on education]: The unmistakable fault line in America over who makes it and who doesn't, today more than ever before, is education. So as we go back to school and the Congress goes back to work, the question is, will your country continue to help those who want to help themselves?

At Southern Illinois University,
Sept. 11/
The New York Times,
9-12:(A)10.

Hillary Rodham Clinton
Wife of President
of the United States
Bill Clinton

2

No single factor contributes to the long-term health and prosperity of a developing nation or any nation more than investing in education for girls and women. In countries where governments have invested in primary and secondary schooling for girls and women, the investment has been repaid many times, through higher economic productivity, greater participation of women in the modern labor sector, lower infant and maternal mortality rates, improved child nutrition and family health, longer life expectancy, lower birth-rates, and stronger families and communities.

At United Nations
World Summit
for Social Development,
Copenhagen, Denmark,
March 7/
Los Angeles Times,
3-9:(A)12.

Ward Connerly
Member, Board of Regents,
University of California

3

The whole culture of academia is such that we are probably the most race-conscious institution in America, because of the principle that we want to be diverse [in the make-up of the student body], which is a commendable principle. But I think that we have built in a whole system of race-consciousness . . . There are some of us who say that we ought to be re-examining that.

June 15/
Los Angeles Times,
6-16:(A)35.

Catheryn Cotten
International adviser,
Duke University Medical Center

4

[Criticizing a U.S. law which tends to limit the number of foreign nationals hired by U.S. universities in the science and medical research fields]: If you want to make sure there are enough Americans in these fields,

(CATHERYN COTTEN)

you have to start when kids are in kindergarten and first grade and let them know science and research and math are wonderful, fascinating fields. You don't solve [the problem] today by saying we stop hiring foreign nationals and start hiring Americans who are less-qualified just for the sake of hiring Americans. Or stop doing the research because there's not enough Americans to do it.

The Washington Post,
7-3:(A)7.

Alexis Crow
Legal coordinator,
Rutherford Institute

1

[On home-schooling]: Some mainstream home-schoolers are now saying, "Don't send your kid to college." [But] our view has always been to get into the best [colleges], get into the power centers, and affect the culture positively. You just can't run out and hide in the hills.

Christianity Today,
7-17:52.

Irene Dandridge
President,
Baltimore (Md.)
Teachers Union

2

[On Baltimore's non-renewal of its contract with a private organization to run its public schools]: It just couldn't work. I don't think we've learned anything except to be wary of people who make money off education.

Los Angeles Times,
11-24:(A)34.

Robert J. Dole
United States Senator,
R-Kansas;
Candidate for the
1996 Republican
Presidential nomination

3

[Arguing against bilingual education in the U.S.]: With all the divisive forces tearing at our country, we need the glue of language to help hold us together. If we want to ensure that all our children have the same opportunities in life, alternative-language education should stop and English should be acknowledged once and for all as the official language of the United States.

Before American Legion,
Indianapolis, Ind..,
Sept. 4/
Los Angeles Times,
10-31:(A)13.

Newt Gingrich
United States
Representative,
R-Georgia;
Speaker of the House

4

[Encouraging students to finish high school in less than four years]: We're subsidizing dating. We're maintaining a fabric of education within which they can pursue their social life.

U.S. News & World Report,
2-20:24.

5

Spending [Federal] money on education is a fiasco . . . People do not believe that turn-

(NEWT GINGRICH)

ing more money over to unionized public bureaucracies gets you *anything*.

Interview, Washington, D.C., July 25/ The Christian Science Monitor, 7-26:4.

1

[Arguing against bilingual education in the U.S.]: Allowing bilingualism to continue to grow is very dangerous. We should insist on English as a common language . . . That's what binds us together.

At Georgia Institute of Technology, Oct. 30/ Los Angeles Times, 10-31:(A)13.

John Golle
Chairman,
Education Alternatives, Inc.

2

[On criticism that school systems that have privatized their functions using his company have failed to improve]: The press is making this out as Waterloo. I don't think so at all. School reform is a freight train moving down the track . . . There are a whole bunch of people who like [government-run schooling] just the way it is and would prefer that people believe that we've not been successful—when in fact we have.

Time, 11-13:88.

Carol A. Gresser
President,
Board of Education
of New York, N.Y.

3

[Criticizing New York Mayor Rudolph Giuliani for saying private Catholic schools do a better job of educating students than the city's public schools]: Comparing our public schools to our Catholic schools is like comparing a city pool to a private beach club—both have water to swim in, but they are not the same. Certainly, our Catholic schools are very fine schools. But did the Mayor mention the little matter of tuition?

Aug. 14/ The New York Times, 8-15:(A)16.

Steve Gunderson
United States Representative,
R-Wisconsin

4

[Criticizing Republican plans to eliminate the U.S. Department of Education and instead give block grants to the states]: Abolishing the Department and scattering the programs creates chaos . . . In a high-tech global economy, there is a legitimate national interest in having a high-skilled workforce.

Los Angeles Times, 5-25:(A)18.

Margaret Heisel
Director of outreach,
admissions and student affairs,
president's office
of the University of California

5

[On the University of California Board of Regents' decision to eliminate race as a

(MARGARET HEISEL)

criterion for student admission]: [A recent study shows] that if you take out race in the admission criteria and rely exclusively on socioeconomic factors, a great amount of ethnic diversity disappears. African-American are reduced by 40 to 50 percent, Chicano-Latino by 5 to 15 percent, Asians make a gain and whites remain constant.

The New York Times,
7-22:9.

Douglas Jones
Philosopher,
New Saint Andrews College

1

We've often bought the modern lie that children will only learn if the subject is fun and thrilling. But education is a discipline, and it should involve hard work.

Christianity Today,
7-17:51.

Paul Krouse
Publisher,
"Who's Who
Among American
High School Students"

2

Today's teenagers are being forced into adulthood at a very young age. Schools have changed so much in the past 25 years that it's like comparing *The Brady Bunch* to *the Wild Bunch.*

U.S. News & World Report,
6-26:20.

David Lavin
Professor,
Lehman College,
City University
of New York

3

When there's enough funding, liberal [college-admission] policies are more politically successful. In times of scarcity, then questions are raised: Is higher education an entitlement or a privilege? It's about abundance and scarcity.

Los Angeles Times,
5-30:(A)5.

Patricia Lines
Policy analyst,
Department of Education
of the United States

4

[On home-schooling vs. learning in schools]: For a determined [home-schooling] family, there's really nothing they can't accomplish. We certify [public-school] teachers to learn how to establish discipline and how to teach to a group. I've seen no evidence that a teaching certificate [requirement] would enhance a one-on-one situation [in the home].

Christianity Today,
7-17:51.

Camille Paglia
Author, Critic

5

[Criticizing suggestions that, in this computer age, encyclopedias are becoming irrelevant]: More than ever, encyclopedias are crucial. It is intellectual laziness and postmodernist navel-gazing and just lack of I.Q. that would make any humanities people say, Oh, it's just impossible to have a general

(CAMILLE PAGLIA)

encyclopedia. We need *world* encyclopedias.

Newsweek, 5-29:61.

Leon E. Panetta
Chief of Staff to President of the United States Bill Clinton

1

[Criticizing the recent decision by the Regents of the University of California to stop using race-based criteria in hiring and student-admission decisions]: It is a major retreat, in terms of a university and a state that has always been on the leading edge of moving forward in terms of education and research and in equal justice. I think it's divisive, and I think it's really going to set that state back.

Broadcast interview/ "Face the Nation," CBS-TV, 7-23.

Robert Peterkin
Director, urban superintendents program, Harvard University

2

[Criticizing a trend toward hiring economic and management types, rather than educators, as city school superintendents]: Education is not like any other business. The leader needs to have more than a trivial knowledge of schools.

Newsweek, 8-7:52.

Dang Pham
Acting Director, Office of Bilingual Education, Department of Education of the United States

3

[Criticizing the suggestion that bilingual education in the U.S. can lead to problems such as those being experienced by Canada and its French-speaking province of Quebec]: I think comparing [bilingualism] in Canada and the United States is like comparing apples and oranges, [because in the U.S. English is the national language and in Canada both English and French are official]. Besides, in the United States language is not the true bond. The true bonds are our shared values of freedom, democracy and human rights. That is truly the glue that helps people stick together.

Los Angeles Times, 10-31:(A)13.

Lawrence O. Picus
Director, Center for Education Finance, University of Southern California

4

[On financing of school systems]: We really need to look at broad-based taxes, most likely property taxes, to generate the kind of revenues over time that it will take to make our graduates competitive with those in other countries.

Los Angeles Times, 11-27:(A)3.

Peter Powers
Deputy Mayor
of New York, N.Y.

1

[Saying his and other cities are looking more for economic and management types, rather than educators, to run their school systems]: Educators have controlled this system since its inception, and no one is happy with the results. We need someone who can cut fat and ruffle the establishment's feathers—make them upset.

Newsweek,
8-7:52.

W. Ann Reynolds
Chancellor,
City University
of New York

2

[Criticizing proposals in Congress to limit Federal aid for college students who are legal immigrants]: There really has been the thought out there that those who can pay more should, and we'll have ways the poor, talented students can go to school. Now we are taking away the support for that poor talented student. We are simply knocking that poor, talented, energetic student out of college with this.

The New York Times,
10-21:10.

Richard W. Riley
Secretary of Education
of the United States

3

[On suggestions that the U.S. Department of Education be eliminated]: I didn't come here to fight for the bureaucracy. That's not my nature. But it hits me that to do away with the Department of Education at this particular moment in history would be like doing away with the Department of the Army in the middle of World War II.

The New York Times,
2-21:(A)10.

4

[Supporting U.S. bilingual education programs]: Obviously, English is our national language. New immigrants are clamoring to learn it as fast as they can. All over America, people are standing in lines and placing their names on waiting lists to take English and literacy classes . . . It would be sheer folly to deny millions of school children the opportunity to learn English at a time when the need is greatest. Unfortunately, these efforts to make English the "official" language and to eliminate programs that teach English are more about politics than improving education.

Los Angeles Times,
10-31:(A)13.

Joe Scarborough
United States Representative,
R-Florida

5

[On Republican plans to eliminate the U.S. Department of Education and instead give block grants to the states]: This is a serious effort to give back to teachers, parents and communities the dominant role in education that they have had historically.

Washington, D.C.,
May 24/
Los Angeles Times,
5-25:(A)18.

Jose Scheinkman
Chairman,
department of economics,
University of Chicago

1

[On his school's professors winning Nobel Prizes in Economics five out of the past six years]: For me, the fear is that things cannot get any better. [Becoming department chairman now] is a little like becoming President of a country that is [already] booming.

Interview/Time,
10-23:32.

Franklin L. Smith
Superintendent of Schools
of the District of Columbia

2

The reality is that we have not taught until students have learned. And if students are not learning, the performance of teachers and administrators is not satisfactory.

The Washington Post,
8-28:(A)1.

August Steinhilber
General counsel,
National School Boards Association

3

[On home-schooling]: Most parents are qualified [to teach their children] because they know what's best for their children. The only drawback is when the parent doesn't take the responsibility seriously.

Christianity Today,
7-17:51.

Charles E. Young
Chancellor,
University of California,
Los Angeles

4

[Defending his university's affirmative-action program for admitting students]: I don't think we ought to discriminate against people because they're white, because they're rich, because they are males. [But] we ought to work hard to enlarge the pool of people who can participate from under-represented groups. The programs that we operate have not brought people into the university who are not qualified.

Interview,
Los Angeles, Calif.,
March 1/
Los Angeles Times,
3-3:(A)28.

The Environment • Energy

Bruce Babbitt
Secretary of the Interior of the United States

1

[Supporting the Clinton Administration's proposal to exempt owners of fewer than five acres of land from the restrictions of the Endangered Species Act]: These principles . . . reduce the conservation burden on small landowners and show the Administration is serious in its efforts to balance the rights of individual landowners with the community's right to a healthy environment.

March 6/ Los Angeles Times, 3-7:(A)3.

2

Habitat conservation is the best single means to counter [species] extinction.

June 29/ USA Today, 6-30:(A)8.

Ann Belkov
Superintendent, Statue of Liberty/ Ellis Island National Monument

3

"Marketing" has been a dirty word among us [National] Park Service purists. [But] we need to find a way to sell ourselves, make deals, take in partners and raise money.

U.S. News & World Report, 6-19:36.

Carol M. Browner
Administrator, Environmental Protection Agency of the United States

4

[On proposals for moderating the pollution reductions contained in the Clean Air Act]: I do not think the standards should be weakened. And I do not think the timeliness should be changed. The American people were told they would have clean air. We are making significant progress in that direction . . . We have protected millions of Americans from cancer, heart disease and premature death. But more still needs to be done.

Before House Commerce Subcommittee, Washington, D.C./ The New York Times, 2-14:(C)19.

5

[Criticizing a bill sponsored by Senator Robert Dole that would allow review of a myriad of government environmental rules and regulations]: Mr. Dole has managed to go even further than the House in providing relief for the special interests, the polluters and their lawyers. This does not represent rational reform or refinement; this is a continuation of the frontal assault [on] our ability to do our job.

The New York Times, 4-28:(A)9.

Kevin Buckley
Superintendent,
Gateway National
Recreation Area,
New York, N.Y.

1

[Arguing against cutting funding for urban recreational parks such as his]: For a few hours or for a day or two, [poor city children] are literally in another world [at Gateway]. Isn't that what a national park is supposed to be all about?

U.S. News & World Report,
6-19:28.

Gino Casasa
Director
of Antarctic programs,
University of Magallanes,
Punta Arenas, Chile

2

[On worries about an "ozone hole" above the city of Punta Arenas, Chile]: Everybody agrees that ozone is a big concern, but the problem I see is that the population doesn't understand that there's no scientific data showing any impact on biological life here. People are spreading myths about rabbits and buying expensive eyeglasses and creams without any basis.

The New York Times,
3-3:(A)4.

Bill Clinton
President
of the United States

3

There is an effort in Congress to cut the budget in a way that could have forced the closure of 200 of these [National Park Service] parks. That's wrong. There are some who say we ought to just sell some of our natural treasures off to the highest bidder, and that's wrong . . . We have a big stake in what you see around here at Yellowstone. It's part of what I call our common ground, and we should not do anything this year—anything—to weaken our ability to protect the quality of our land, our water, our food, the diversity of our wildlife and the sanctity of our natural treasures. We can balance the [Federal] budget without doing any of that.

At Yellowstone
National Park, Wyo.,
Aug. 25/
The New York Times,
8-26:7.

Sheila Copps
Deputy Prime Minister,
and Minister for
the Environment,
of Canada

4

[Criticizing proposals before the U.S. Congress which she says would have negative effects on Canada's environment]: We don't want to interfere in domestic affairs in the United States. The problem is that actions being debated in the Congress . . . affect the air that flows freely over our undefended border . . . They affect the health of over 30 million Americans and Canadians living in the Great Lakes Basin . . . [The proposals would] gut [laws on] industrial pollution, sewage, storm-water controls, wetlands, agricultural runoffs, water quality and air quality.

July 24/
The Washington Post,
7-25:(A)10.

Douglas W. Dockery
Harvard University researcher and author of a comprehensive study on air-particle pollution

1

When you compare the effect of [air-particle pollution] to smoking cigarettes, this is a fairly low level of hazard. For example, smoking might reduce your life expectancy by 10 years or more, and particle pollution might reduce your life span by a year or so. [But] there is an increased mortality rate of 15 percent or so that we can see between the cleanest cities and the dirtiest cities. Even an average city that is in compliance with Federal air-pollution standards will have a mortality that is 3 percent to 8 percent higher than the cleanest cities.

The New York Times, 3-10:(A)9.

Mike Dombeck
Acting Director, Federal Bureau of Land Management

2

[Criticizing proposed legislation that would give ranchers more control of Federal lands they now use for livestock grazing]: The grazing bill focuses public rangeland management on the single use of livestock grazing—de-emphasizing other uses and values of the public lands such as mining, hunting, recreation and wildlife. The bill would severely limit public involvement in the management of the public lands.

Congressional testimony, Washington, D.C./ The Christian Science Monitor, 8-16:4.

Thomas Eisner
Biologist, Cornell University; Chairman, Endangered Species Coalition

3

Nature is a vast unknown. The most valuable data in the bank is as yet untapped. The irony of the Endangered Species Act is that most species can't be listed on it because they have no name yet.

News conference, Washington, D.C./ The New York Times, 3-7:(B)7.

Denis P. Galvin
Associate Director, National Park Service of the United States

4

Politicians love adding new parks and [park] visitor centers, but nobody wants to cut the ribbon on a new sewage-treatment plant.

U.S. News & World Report, 6-19:26.

Newt Gingrich
United States Representative, R-Georgia; Speaker of the House

5

[On a House bill that would cut back on Federal environmental regulations]: What you'll find, I think, as we negotiate with the Senate and as this thing goes to hearings in the Senate, is we'll find a common ground which will create more respect for private property while still maintaining the vast bulk of the government's powers to save the envi-

(NEWT GINGRICH)

ronment and to insure public safety and public health.

March 3/ The New York Times, 3-4:1.

Al Gore
Vice President of the United States

1

[On dangerous chemicals that find their way into the world's oceans]: [The problem is] one that all nations share in, not just because of the dangerous consequences in areas close to their use and production, but also because we have seen these compounds migrate far from their source.

At United Nations Environment Program conference, Washington, D.C., Nov. 1/ Los Angeles Times, 11-2:(A)6.

Slade Gorton
United States Senator, R-Washington

2

[On the cost involved in saving certain endangered species]: There is a cost beyond which you just have to say very regrettably [that] we have to let species or subspecies go extinct.

The Christian Science Monitor, 1-25:2.

3

[Criticizing a Supreme Court ruling that strengthens the legality of the Endangered Species Act that permits government to regulate private lands in order to protect such species]: The need to reform the law is more urgent than ever. The ruling gives the [Clinton] Administration exactly what it wanted: a green light for the wholesale regulation of private property and private actions.

June 29/ USA Today, 6-30:(A)8.

James V. Hansen
United States Representative, R-Utah

4

[Saying, in his capacity as Chairman of the House National Parks Subcommittee, that there are too many small, unnecessary and inappropriate projects in the National Park Service system, considering the limited funds available to operate and maintain them]: I work with 534 guys [in Congress], and every damned one of them has a "great idea" for a park in his district. I get so tired of hearing the phrase "national treasure." There is not one snowball in hell's chance of the Park Service getting more money [from Congress].

U.S. News & World Report, 6-19:30.

Joel Hefley
United States Representative, R-Oklahoma

5

[On his proposal to create a Federal commission to review which properties administered by the National Park Service should be turned over to other, non-Federal, entities because of the cost of maintaining them]: I grew up in Oklahoma. I didn't grow up in a wealthy family. Each summer, what we did

(JOEL HEFLEY)

was load up the station wagon to go to the national parks. I became a great lover of the national parks . . . [But] if there is something that shouldn't be [in the system, the commission] can say so. Somewhere along the line, I'm beginning to hear [critics] say it is a thinly veiled attempt by Republicans to sell off our national parks. [But] there's nothing sinister; there's nothing thinly veiled. My goal is to have better parks, significant parks [by being selective in what the Park Service administers].

Interview/
Los Angeles Times,
11-24:(A)31.

Fran Hunt
Environmentalist,
Wilderness Society

1

We cannot create wilderness. We can only protect what we have, or it's lost forever.

U.S. News & World Report,
9-18:55.

Kay Bailey Hutchison
United States Senator,
R-Texas

2

Environmental enforcement has become overly zealous, threatening the Constitutional principle that ensures private property shall not be taken for public use without just compensation, a principle enshrined in our Bill of Rights.

The Christian Science Monitor,
1-25:2.

Frank R. Lautenberg
United States Senator,
D-New Jersey

3

Under the guise of balancing the [Federal] budget, [the Republicans in Congress] have systematically savaged the Environmental Protection Agency budget, not so much to balance the budget but to serve the special interests by crippling the Agency's ability to enforce our environmental laws.

News conference, Nov. 29/
Los Angeles Times,
11-30:(A)16.

Nathaniel Lawrence
Senior attorney,
Natural Resources
Defense Council

4

[Criticizing the Clinton Administration's proposal to exempt owners of fewer than five acres of land from the restrictions of the Endangered Species Act]: It shows that this Administration would rather shoot craps with [species] extinction than stand up to the alarmists and extremists in Congress that want to gut the Act. I wonder what other laws this Administration is willing to suspend for people who are only going to trash five acres of the environment at a time.

March 6/
Los Angeles Times,
3-7:(A)3.

Jerry Lewis
United States Representative,
R-California

5

There's little question . . . Uncle Sam has gone much too far [in imposing environmen-

(JERRY LEWIS)

tal regulations]. There is no doubt government has a role to play. But excessive regulation . . . is undermining public support for environmental concerns.

Before the House, Washington, D.C., Nov. 2/ Los Angeles Times, 11-3:(A)23.

Jim Lyons
Assistant Secretary for Natural Resources and Environment, Department of Agriculture of the United States

1

Our role [in administering national forests] is not to favor one industry over the other. [And] we cannot manage the national forests by threat from either industry or environmentalists.

The New York Times, 9-12:(A)8.

Bedrich Magas
Professor of electrical engineering, University of Magallanes, Punta Arenas, Chile

2

[Warning about dangers from an "ozone hole" above the city of Punta Arenas, Chile]: Why shouldn't we speak as loudly and as accurately as possible about this problem that will have a tremendous impact on the earth. I have been careful not to create a panic over the ozone hole, but people are hard-headed and you have to constantly hit them over the head again and again for them to fully realize the ramifications of the situation.

The New York Times, 3-3:(A)4.

Richard Moe
President, National Trust for Historic Preservation

3

[Criticizing large chain stores for contributing to commercial sprawl]: In too many instances, the stores are located in strip malls and suck the life out of downtown areas. It's very hard to find a sense of community in a strip mall.

U .S. News & World Report, 10-2:19.

Frank Murkowski
United States Senator, R-Alaska

4

[Supporting a proposal to open part of Alaska's Arctic National Wildlife Refuge to oil and gas exploration, despite environmentalists' objections]: [Opponents] sell America short. American ingenuity and technology is up to the job of opening up [the Refuge] safely, creating thousands of new jobs and reducing our dependency on imported oil. Let's keep our jobs and dollars here at home.

USA Today, 9-21:(A)9.

Gaylord Nelson
Former United States Senator, D-Wisconsin

5

When experts are asked to list the most critical environmental problems, they are

(GAYLORD NELSON)

practically unanimous in ranking at the top of the list the calamitous consequences of continued exponential population growth. Since 1916, U.S. population has rapidly expanded from 98 million to 260 million . . . The numbers boggle the mind: a net increase in world population of 95 million per year—260,000 a day or 10,800 an hour. The question is this: Do we have the wit clearly to perceive the long-term implications and ramifications of continued exponential population growth soon enough effectively to address that issue within our own borders? Indications are that, as of now, the answer is no.

Speech/
The Washington Post,
4-12:(A)24.

Robert Priddle
Executive Director,
International Energy Agency

1

[Saying the world must use less and less of fuels that create "greenhouse gases" which lead to global warming]: What our figures show is that unless there are new policy interventions, that won't happen. Those greenhouse gases are going to be higher by about 10 percent by the year 2000 and by perhaps 40 percent by the year 2010. And a greater part of that increase is going to come from the less-developed world—the part of the world which has not given commitments under the Rio Convention [of 1992] . . . [Third World and non-OECD countries] will consume an ever-increasing share of the world's crude oil, from about one-third today to almost one-half by 2010. OECD countries will become increasingly aware that they are operating in a world market that they no longer dominate.

April 24/
The Washington Post,
4-25:(A)3.

James Ridenour
Director,
Eppley Institute
for Parks and Public Lands,
Indiana University;
Former Director,
National Park Service
of the United States

2

[Saying the U.S. can't afford to continue to administer many Park Service properties that may not be sufficiently important to remain under Federal jurisdiction]: I'm not sure how nationally significant are the beaches of New York City. And the Santa Monicas [mountains in California] are nice, but they're not the Rockies. They are not a nationally significant range.

Los Angeles Times,
11-24:(A)30.

Juan Roederer
Professor emeritus
of geophysics,
University of Alaska

3

[On the decline in funding of scientific research on the environment]: The danger is to choose a billion-dollar solution for just a million-dollar problem, and face economic disaster; or to select a million-dollar solution for a billion-dollar problem, and face environmental disaster.

Los Angeles Times,
10-11:(D)5.

Ismail Serageldin
Chairman,
Consultative Group
on International
Agricultural Research

1

[On feeding the world's continuingly expanding population]: We are in a race with time. [The] nightmarish pressure of population growth against limited resources [means that the increasing need] cannot be met exclusively by [crop-] yield increases. It can't be done without expansion of agricultural land and irrigation.

The Washington Post,
2-13:(A)3.

John Shlaes
Executive director,
Global Climate Coalition

2

[Saying the government should beware of imposing too strict environmental regulations on U.S. businesses]: We live in a very competitive world. What are presented as environmental issues are really economic and trade issues we do not yet fully understand.

The New York Times,
8-22:(C)2.

Rick Steiner
Marine adviser for
Prince William Sound,
University of Alaska

3

[On the decision to export Alaskan oil to foreign markets such as the Far East]: Now a lot of the tankers heading out of [Alaska's] Prince William Sound are going to be heading right, past Kodiak Island and past the Aleutian Island chain, heading to Japan, Korea, the markets. It will expose the entire thousand-mile coastline to the eventuality of tanker spills for the first time.

Los Angeles Times,
3-2:(A)7.

David A. Summers
Director,
High Pressure
Waterjet Laboratory,
University of Missouri, Rolla

4

[Calling for more mining research]: We need energy, and oil supplies are declining. Nuclear is going nowhere, and the prospects of renewable resources are uncertain. We'll need energy from the ground for a while, but we're in danger of losing our mining expertise in a few years.

Interview,
Rolla, Mo./
The New York Times,
1-10:(B)9.

Steve Trombulak
Biologist,
Middlebury College

5

One of the things conservation biology tells us is that you don't need all *that* much land set aside for biotic integrity. Species are pretty widely distributed, so you only need to set aside about half the landscape for nature. Now, a lot of people hear that and say it's ridiculous—there's no way we can set aside half for nature. I don't see it that way. That's about what it's like in the Adirondacks. More than half of Maine is for sale by the paper companies. Here in Vermont we've got the Green Mountains. Half leaves so much for humans

(STEVE TROMBULAK)

to do with what they will, so long as they don't create havoc with the air and the water.

Interview,
Vermont/
The Atlantic Monthly,
April:75.

Robert S. Walker
United States Representative,
R-Pennsylvania

1

[Supporting proposals to make it more difficult for government agencies to impose environmental, health and safety regulations]: We will usher in a new era of rationality in the imposition of regulations. This bill will require the use of sound science and sound economic principles to determine if there is a rational basis for imposing new and costly regulations.

Feb. 27/
The New York Times,
2-28:(A)10.

Henry A. Waxman
United States Representative,
D-California

2

[Criticizing proposals to make it more difficult for government agencies to impose environmental, health and safety regulations]: This [proposal] is a fraud. These are tools that are used now, wisely. They are very helpful in deciding what regulations are appropriate. But what they in fact do in this bill is create so many hurdles, to regulatory actions that Federal agencies will simply be unable to protect the public health and the environment anymore.

Feb. 27/
The New York Times,
2-28:(A)10.

Edward O. Wilson
Biologist,
Museum of
Comparative Zoology,
Harvard University

3

A healthy ecosystem gives us soil that stays arable, freshens the water, and manufactures the very air we breathe. If we start reducing the diversity of life and the amount and coverage of natural environments around the world, we're changing the planet and the climate in ways that are far likelier to be unhealthy for human beings than to be healthy . . . The environmentalist movement, unfortunately, from Earth Day on, took on a negative image because it stressed consistently the need for constraints, for using less, for expecting less. And this is uncongenial to the American spirit in particular. No doubt we still have to think in these essentially constricting terms. We have to slow down some of our activities, especially those that are extinguishing life forms. But beyond that, the living environment gives us an almost unending potential for exploration, the discovery of new species, the rediscovery of rare and endangered species, and the means to improve not just our material existence but our health and psychological well-being.

Interview,
Cambridge, Mass./
American Way,
1-15:55,57.

Don Young
United States Representative,
R-Alaska

1

[Criticizing environmentalists]: I am not an elitist. [But] the average salary of most of the members of the Sierra Club is $70,000 a year. Is that a person who is in the ghetto? Is that the working person? No. The environmentalists think nothing about taking jobs away from the working American [through job-depleting environmental regulations].

Los Angeles Times,
3-18:(A)1.

Government

Spencer Abraham
United States Senator,
R-Michigan

1

[Calling for the elimination of the U.S. Departments of Energy, Commerce, Education, and Housing and Urban Development]: These four departments alone employ more than 74,000 bureaucrats and have combined budgets of $70-billion, 133 times more than the entire Federal government spent in Theodore Roosevelt's era. While some programs within these departments are useful, we don't need huge bureaucracies to oversee them.

Before Senate Governmental Affairs Committee, Washington, D.C., May 18/ The Washington Post, 5-19:(A)23.

Jerry Abramson
Mayor of
Louisville, Ky.

2

We're [Mayors] the ones who have the most credibility with our constituents. We have to decide when and where to expend funds. And we're very uncomfortable with politicians in Washington who have been far removed from the local street level for many years determining what's in our local interest.

The Christian Science Monitor, 9-6:3.

Lamar Alexander
Former Secretary
of Education
of the United States

3

[On the sweeping Republican victory in last fall's Congressional elections]: The key issue in the last election was the arrogance of Washington, D.C. The job of the Republicans is to reverse a century of centralism and shift responsibility from Washington back to where it ought to be—states, local governments, schools and neighborhoods.

USA Today, 1-5:(A)3.

Wright Andrews
President,
American League of Lobbyists

4

[Supporting legislation that would place certain restrictions and registration requirements on those who lobby Congress]: Because the average person doesn't understand the valuable work that lobbyists do, they often have a very negative stereotype of what they do. People would feel a little better about us if they understood who is paying us to do what we are doing. We don't have a problem with that.

Los Angeles Times, 11-30:(A)17.

Richard K. Armey
United States Representative,
R-Texas

5

Because we've (Congressmen) been working so hard in Washington, we get too

(RICHARD K. ARMEY)

many of our members spending too much of the time in Washington and allow them too little of the time back in America, where we talk to real people.

Broadcast town meeting sponsored by U.S. Chamber of Commerce, Washington, D.C., March 22/ Los Angeles Times, 3-23:(A)4.

Nan Aron
Director,
Alliance for Justice

1

[Saying lobbyists fill a legitimate need]: The fact is that you'll have a hard time getting your calls answered on Capitol Hill if you call up and say, "I'm Jane Doe and I want to bring this to your attention." And more non-profits are realizing that they can't afford to sit on the sidelines while Congress acts on, or doesn't act on, issues that affect them.

The Washington Post, 7-10:(A)6.

Haley Barbour
Chairman,
Republican National Committee

2

Government is too big for its britches, and we're not getting our money's worth for our tax dollars. That's part of what's happened to the American dream. It's been undermined by huge [Federal budget] deficits and debt.

Nation's Business, May:18.

Paul Begala
Political Adviser
to President
of the United States
Bill Clinton

3

[On Senator Phil Gramm, who is a candidate for the 1996 Republican Presidential nomination]: He is a man who has never drawn a breath that the government didn't pay for. He has had his snout in the trough for 50-some-odd years . . . Gramm is pretty ripe for the argument "If government is so bad, why don't you get the hell off it? If government-run health care is so bad, why have you had it since a government-paid doctor slapped your butt in a government-run hospital?"

Vanity Fair, May:168.

Alex Benes
Managing director,
Center for Public Integrity

4

[On Washington]: What rules in this town is power and access to power.

Los Angeles Times, 1-5:(A)14.

John A. Boehner
United States Representative,
R-Ohio

5

Congress does whatever the American people demand—nothing less, nothing more. This institution truly does reflect the will of the American people. If they really want to have an impact, they should contact their members of Congress through meetings or by sending personal letters themselves.

Nation's Business, July:17.

J. Christian Bollwage
Mayor of Elizabeth, N.J.

1

The philosophy espoused by state and national leaders that urban areas just throw [state and Federal aid] money away is not true, and I challenge anyone who believes it to come to Elizabeth and see that it is not true.

March 6/ The New York Times, 3-7:(A)8.

Bill Bradley
United States Senator, D-New Jersey

2

The politicians can't see beyond themselves. We think that all answers to public life will come through politics. And we just narrow our possibilities by thinking of them through that rat-a-tat-tat.

U.S. News & World Report, 6-19:39.

3

We live in a time when, on a basic level, politics is broken. In growing numbers, people have lost faith in the political process and don't see how it can help their threatened circumstances.

Announcing his decision not to seek re-election next year, Newark, N.J., Aug. 16/ Los Angeles Times, 8-17:(A)27.

John B. Breaux
United States Senator, D-Louisiana

4

[On the current shutdown of many Federal government agencies and services, except essential services, due to the budget impasse between President Clinton and Congress]: Everybody loses if we try to bring the government to a standstill. We're so busy trying to score political points, I think some people in Louisiana believe even we in Congress are not "essential" employees who should report to work tomorrow.

Nov. 13/ Los Angeles Times, 11-14:(A)14.

Sam Brownback
United States Representative, R-Kansas

5

[On being a freshman Congressman]: My only surprise since coming to Washington is that I wasn't harsh enough in my anti-Washington rhetoric. This is a self-serving place that had become incredibly ossified.

The Washington Post, 7-10:(A)6.

John Bryant
United States Representative, D-Texas

6

[Supporting legislation that would ban members of Congress from accepting gifts from lobbyists and would require lobbyists to register with Congress]: This goes to the concern of the American people that unseen forces [influence Congress]. Congress will no

(JOHN BRYANT)

longer be wined and dined, and these forces will no longer be unseen.

Los Angeles Times, 11-30:(A)17.

Robert C. Byrd
United States Senator, D-West Virginia

1

George Washington warned us in his farewell address against factions, against parties. He should be living today. My gosh, he would be so astonished, so depressed, so disappointed! That seems to be the only goal of some in this Senate: party! It doesn't make any difference how many political corpses you trample on or walk over to get your party on top. The object is to win the next election. The object is to be able to say . . . "Our party will be in control." When I came here, there was partisanship. Everett Dirksen was a partisan. Mike Mansfield was a partisan. But they were not bitter partisans. There was civility in the Senate.

Interview, Washington, D.C./ Los Angeles Times, 1-29:(M)3.

Charles T. Canady
United States Representative, R-Florida

2

[Supporting term limits for members of Congress]: Congress has become too much like a permanent class of professional legislators. Term limits will break the power of entrenched incumbency.

Los Angeles Times, 3-30:(A)14.

Warren Christopher
Secretary of State of the United States

3

[Saying the State Department's technological capability needs updating]: Our telephone system is so outdated that when we needed repairs the other day in our vital 24-hour operations center, the AT&T repairman who came to do the work had to consult with Bell Labs to find out how to repair the antiquated system.

To Senate subcommittee, Washington, D.C., March 1/ The New York Times, 3-6:(A)5.

William F. Clinger, Jr.
United States Representative, R-Pennsylvania

4

Before we sort of sell off the government and go to privatization, we really ought to see if we can't make substantial headway by elimination of regulations and the streamlining of procurement rules. When you look at the corporization of the Post Office department, I don't see the enormous advantages that have accrued from that.

Interview, Washington, D.C./ The Washington Post, 2-27:(A)17.

Bill Clinton
President of the United States

5

I believe the purpose of government is not to expand bureaucracy but to expand oppor-

(BILL CLINTON)

tunity. I do not believe government is inherently good or bad.

Interview/ The New York Times, 1-2:7.

1

Being President is like running a cemetery: You've got a lot of people under you and nobody's listening.

Speech, Galesburg, Ill./ U.S. News & World Report, 1-23:23.

2

[On the investigations going on of top officials in his Administration]: We live in a time now where the first thing people call for is a special counsel [to investigate government officials]. I mean, we really have to ask ourselves whether we are creating a climate here in which a lot of people will be reluctant to serve [in government].

News conference, Washington, D.C., March 3/ Los Angeles Times, 3-4:(A)16.

3

The old Washington view, I think it's fair to say, is that the Federal government could provide solutions to America's problems. The Republican Contract [With America] view reflects in many cases an outright hostility to governmental action, although in some cases a curious willingness to increase the Federal government's control over our daily lives. My view, what has loosely been called the New Democratic view or the New Covenant view, is to be skeptical of government but to recognize that it has a role in our lives and a partnership role to play.

News conference, Washington, D.C., March 3/ The New York Times, 3-4:9.

4

It used to be the prevailing theory was there was a big-government solution for every problem. Now the prevailing theory is that government would mess up a one-car parade and, if it didn't exist, America wouldn't have any problems. Both theories are wrong.

At White House-sponsored Southern Economic Regional Conference, Emory University, March 29/ Los Angeles Times, 3-30:(A)11.

5

I watched from afar when I was a [state] Governor and a citizen for 12 years while people here [in Washington] walked away from problem after problem. And I sustained, as President, an amazing experience when large numbers of people walked away from problems that I asked them to face, for short-term political gain.

At White House Conference on Aging, Washington, D.C., May 3/ The New York Times, 5-4:(A)14.

(BILL CLINTON)

1

[Criticizing private militias' anti-government stance]: How dare you [militias] suggest that we in the freest nation on earth live in tyranny? How dare you call yourself patriots and heroes? If you appropriate our sacred symbols for paranoid purposes and compare yourselves to Colonial militias who fought for democracy you now rail against, you are wrong.

At Michigan State University commencement, May 5/ Los Angeles Times, 5-6:(A)1.

2

We have cultural problems and economic and political challenges in this country, and we should not permit Washington to be divided over what is essentially a phony choice. Keep in mind, often when we talk about cultural problems up here, we're looking for an excuse not to do our part and assume our responsibility.

At swearing-in of police officers, Washington, D. C./ Los Angeles Times, 6-19:(A)10.

3

You couldn't run a family, a business, a university, a church, a civic organization, you couldn't run anything in this country the way people try to run politics in Washington, where talking is more important than doing.

At dedication of California State University at Monterey Bay, Sept. 4/ The New York Times, 9-5:(A)8.

4

The first two years [of his Administration] I knew exactly [the things] I wanted to do and I went about doing them. And I was obsessed with doing them . . . And I would have been better-served, I think, and the country probably would have been better-served . . . if we had done slightly less, if people had understood the big picture more. And the President, in a way, has to impart the big picture.

Interview aboard Air Force One/ U.S. News & World Report, 10-9:44.

Kathleen Connell
State Controller of California

5

[On business people who decide to work in government]: Business people need to mellow out a little bit. You have to be willing to listen to views that aren't as well-formed as they would be in the corporate sector, because this is an open process. There is a tremendous value in this.

Los Angeles Times, 8-10:(A)22.

John Conyers, Jr.
United States Representative,
D-Michigan

1

[Arguing against term limits for members of Congress]: American voters . . . already have the power to impose term limits [through elections]. I do not think it is a good idea to deny these voters the right to elect the person they think best represents their interests.

Washington, D.C.,
March 29/
The Washington Post,
3-30:(A)7.

Paul Coverdell
United States Senator,
R-Georgia

2

Washington wonks tend to over-intellectualize, to deal in murky details. They lose contact with people who don't live and breathe this sort of thing every day.

Interview/
Nation's Business,
July:21.

Gray Davis
Lieutenant Governor
of California (D)

3

There shouldn't be any sacred cows in public policy, and all of us should have the courage to re-examine policies, no matter how noble, to make sure they're still wanted.

To political writers,
Los Angeles, Calif.,
Feb. 1/
Los Angeles Times,
2-2:(A)3.

Thomas M. Davis III
United States Representative,
R-Virginia

4

[On Washington, D.C.'s fiscal crisis]: Washington, D.C., is coming apart at the seams . . . It has more than adequate revenue, [but] it tries to fund everything it wants instead of trying to fund the things it needs. Generosity became indulgence. We see before us a broken city.

Washington, D.C.,
April 3/
The Washington Post,
4-4:(A)16.

John D. Dingell
United States Representative,
D-Michigan

5

[Criticizing the power and influence that new House Speaker Newt Gingrich has over House business]: It depends on what you want: good legislation or an efficient functioning machine. The result of this is that bad legislation is being written every day.

USA Today,
3-8:(A)5.

Robert J. Dole
United States Senator,
R-Kansas;
Candidate
for the 1996
Republican
Presidential nomination

6

[On the new Republican-controlled Congress]: We will roll back Federal programs,

(ROBERT J. DOLE)

laws and regulations from A to Z—from Amtrak to zoological studies.

Before the Senate,
Washington, D.C.,
Jan. 4/
The New York Times,
1-5:(A)1.

1

Reining in our [Federal] government will be my mandate [as new Senate Majority Leader], and I hope it will be the purpose and principal accomplishment of the [new] 104th Congress . . . If I have one goal for the 104th Congress, it is this: that we will dust off the 10th Amendment [to the U.S. Constitution, which deals with the responsibilities of the states vs. the Federal government] and restore it to its rightful place in our Constitution.

Before the Senate,
Washington, D.C.,
Jan. 4/
The New York Times,
1-5:(A)10.

2

[Saying that, if nominated for President, he would consider pledging to stay for one term only]: If [I] decided to serve one term [as President], it would be sort of get in, get it done and get out. I mean, on the theory the American people want somebody with no special interests go in and do it in four years and then get out and move on to something else.

Broadcast interview/
"This Week With David Brinkley,"
ABC-TV, 2-19.

3

[Urging passage of a constitutional amendment mandating a balanced federal budget, which would have to be approved by state legislatures before such an amendment could become law]: Return power to the people; return power to the states. That's what this debate is all about. The answer is democracy. Democracy. The answer is to trust the people.

Before the Senate,
Washington, D.C.,
March 2/
Los Angeles Times,
3-3:(A)24.

4

[Supporting the elimination of the U.S. Departments of Education, Housing and Urban Development, Energy and Commerce]: The best thing we could do is turn out the lights [at those Departments], lock the doors and send the workers home . . . When they were created, they were supposed to be the answer to our challenges in education, poverty, energy and economic opportunity. Instead . . . they have caused more problems than they have solved.

Before National
Newspaper Association,
Washington, D.C.,
March 10/
Los Angeles Times,
3-11:(A)18.

Dennis E. Eckart
Former United States Representative,
D-Ohio

5

The generation that fought World War II and then expanded America saw government

(DENNIS E. ECKART)

as a partner in their lives. [But] the children of that generation, standing on their parents' shoulders, don't see government as a necessary force for them.

U.S. News & World Report, 11-6:35.

Henry Ernsthal
Former director, association management program, George Washington University

1

[On polls that show Americans think Washington lobbyists have too much influence]: It's fairly typical for Americans. People love their doctor, but don't like doctors; they love their member of Congress, but don't like politicians; the groups that represent our interest aren't special interest, it's the other guy.

The Washington Post, 7-10:(A)6.

Mark Foley
United States Representative, R-Florida

2

[On becoming a Congressman after working in blue-collar jobs]: No job is beneath me.

Newsweek, 4-10:19.

Thomas S. Foley
Former United States Representative, D-Washington; Former Speaker of the House

3

[On a recent Supreme Court ruling that blocks the setting of term limits for members of Congress]: Term limits is dead. [But] I think [supporters of term limits] are going to push very hard to try to keep this ill-considered movement alive. And they'll spend a lot of money—they have great private resources—and they'll try to make it a political issue in the next [election] campaign. I think it's against the interests of voters of both parties . . . You're going to hear a great deal of chest-beating and threats and very boastful talk from the term-limit community. It's deeply angered by this [Supreme Court] decision, which they should have seen coming.

May 22/ The New York Times, 5-23:(A)11.

Steven Forbes
President and editor-in-chief, "Forbes" magazine

4

[On the possibility of his running for the 1996 Republican Presidential nomination]: I've worked for years with people on the staffs of think tanks. I could [as President] immediately staff not just the top level of government, but the second and third and fourth level. As you know, personnel is policy.

Interview/ The Washington Post, 8-7:(A)9.

Tillie Fowler
United States Representative, R-Florida

5

[On term limits for members of Congress]: [Term limits would make Congress] closer to the people [and] reduce the power of [Congressional] staff, since the most pow-

(TILLIE FOWLER)

erful staffers are always those who work for the most senior members.

Washington, D.C.,
March 29/
The Washington Post,
3-30:(A)7.

Barney Frank
United States Representative,
D-Massachusetts

1

[Arguing against term limits for members of Congress]: [I believe] in representative democracy untrammeled, unrestricted, unrestrained. Democracy is not simply what a given majority in a public-opinion poll thinks at a given time.

Los Angeles Times,
3-30:(A)14.

David Frum
Political columnist;
Commentator,
"Morning Edition,"
National Public Radio

2

What I hope we'll see is a government whose social-welfare functions are essentially confined to insuring people against the uninsurable catastrophic risks of ordinary life—catastrophic illness, short periods of unemployment, indigence. I also hope that we will have gotten government out of the business of monkeying around in the private economy, which means that virtually all of the Department of Commerce and the Department of Energy will be gone, as well as a lot of the Department of Transportation . . . Instead of cutting incrementally—a little here, a little there—I would say that on a single day this summer we eliminate 300 programs, each one costing a billion dollars or less. Maybe these cuts won't make a big deal of difference, but, boy, do they make a point. And you can do them right away, because, unlike Medicare, Medicaid and welfare, they're not intellectually challenging.

Panel discussion,
Washington, D.C./
Harper's, March:45.

Mitch Geasler
Special Assistant
to Deputy Secretary
of Agriculture
of the United States
Richard E. Rominger

3

[On the Agriculture Department's downsizing, which will involve staff cuts of 13,000 over five years]: You go through all the same stages [of mourning a death]. You get angry—why did this happen? You get through the emotional stress, and you finally come around to the point where you realize the person had a great life. We have all stages going on in the Department at the same time.

The Washington Post,
4-3:(A)12.

Richard A. Gephardt
United States Representative,
D-Missouri

4

[Addressing Newt Gingrich, who has become Speaker of the House as a result of the sweeping Republican victory in last fall's Congressional elections]: As you might imagine, this is not a moment that I had been waiting for . . . We may not all agree with today's

(RICHARD A. GEPHARDT)

changing of the guard [from a Democrat- to a Republican-controlled Congress]. We may not all like it. But we enact the people's will with dignity and honor and pride. And in that endeavor, Mr. Speaker, there can be no losers and there can be no defeat. Of course, in the 104th Congress there will be conflict and compromise. Agreements will not always be easy. Agreement sometimes is not even possible. But while we may not agree on matters of party and principle, we all abide with the will of the people. That is reason enough to place our good faith and our best hopes in your able hands. I speak from the bottom of my heart when I say that I wish you the best in these coming two years. For when this gavel passes into your hands, so do the futures and fortunes of millions of Americans.

At opening of 104th Congress, Washington, D.C., Jan. 4/ The New York Times, 1-5:(A)13.

1

There are days on which I feel like the House is the staff for the Senate. We send over rough drafts [of legislation], and they try to figure it out.

Washington, D.C., March 8/ The New York Times, 3-9:(A)9.

Newt Gingrich
United States Representative, R-Georgia; Speaker of the House

2

We're starting the 104th Congress . . . And I don't care what your ethnic background, what your ideology; I don't care whether you're younger or older; I don't care whether you were born in America or you're a naturalized citizen—every one of the 435 people [in Congress] have equal standing because their citizens freely sent them, and their voice should be heard, and they should have a right to participate.

Accepting the Speakership, before the House, Washington, D.C., Jan. 4/ Los Angeles Times, 1-5:(A)15.

3

If each of us [in the new Congress] will reach out prayerfully and try to genuinely understand the other, if we'll recognize that in this building we symbolize America writ small, that we have an obligation to talk with each other, then I think a year from now we can look on the 104th [Congress] as a truly amazing institution, and without regard to party, without regard to ideology, we can say here America comes to work.

Accepting the Speakership, before the House, Washington, D.C., Jan. 4/ The New York Times, 1-5:(A)10.

4

[Saying he is reversing long-standing policy and will allow House members to live in their offices]: I don't think members should be made homeless . . . Unless it becomes a health hazard, I don't think I [as Speaker] want to micromanage the personal lives of mem-

(NEWT GINGRICH)

bers. I realize some people believe in the nanny state, but I think the idea of the Speaker chatting with members about where they sleep, you know, whatever you may think about my level of influence in the House, that just went beyond.

Jan. 27/
The Washington Post,
1-30:(A)13.

1

It doesn't say anywhere in the Declaration of Independence or the Constitution that anybody is entitled to anything except the right to pursue happiness.

At town meeting,
Marietta, Ga.,
Feb. 18/
The Washington Post,
2-20:(A)11.

2

The [Republicans'] Contract With America is only a beginning. It is the preliminary skirmish to the big battles yet to come. The big battles will deal with how we remake the government of the United States.

Broadcast address
to the nation,
Washington, D.C.,
April 7/
The New York Times,
4-8:1.

3

[On the increasing power of Congress]: We are going back to a pre-Woodrow Wilson era, where the Presidencies are important, but they're not decisive. What you're going to see is the emergence of the President as first among equals.

Interview/
Time, 6-5:25.

4

[On President Clinton's possible veto of Republican legislation that would cut spending and reduce government operations, such a veto leading to a possible shut down of the government for lack of a spending agreement]: He can run the parts of government that are left [after the Republican cuts], or he can run no government. Which of the two of us do you think worries more about the government not showing up?

Interview/
Time, 6-5:23.

5

[Contrasting his views with those of President Clinton]: This is a great country filled with good people, and our job is to educate, empower and liberate good people. The President seems to believe this is a great government that hires good bureaucrats.

To group
of conservatives,
New Hampshire,
June 12/
USA Today,
6-13:(A)1.

6

[Advising the public to be wary of politicians]: Don't trust anyone you loan power.

At conference
of United We Stand America,
Dallas, Texas/
The Washington Post,
8-14:(A)17.

(NEWT GINGRICH)

1

[Arguing against independents running for political office]: This country is a party country. You run the House and Senate with parties. You appoint Cabinets out of parties. There is no magic independence of people who are just able to stand up and magically produce a government.

Broadcast interview/ "Meet the Press," NBC-TV, 9-10.

2

In this city [Washington], you either act decisively and get things done, or you hang around long enough for all the various special-interest groups to mount a big enough lobbying campaign to stop it.

USA Today, 9-21:(A)5.

Stephen Gold
Director, Center for the Study of the States

3

We're in a period of fend-for-yourself Federalism. The Federal government is putting more responsibility on state government, and state governments are putting more responsibility on local governments. If all of this goes too far, we're going to have a property-tax explosion. It's like a rubber band that is getting tighter and tighter and tighter.

The Washington Post, 3-2:(A)18.

Doris Kearns Goodwin
Historian, Biographer

4

[On the influence of private money in government]: Money gets the individuals into the door. Money revises legislation. Money restrains the enforcement of laws. Money has a direct impact on the substance of almost every piece of legislation. Politicians know the system stinks, [but there is a] fatal addiction that prevents anything from turning it around.

At Presidential news briefing, Washington, D.C., Aug. 4/ The New York Times, 8-5:9.

Charles E. Grassley
United States Senator, R-Iowa

5

[On Federal-state relations]: We should start with the presumption that states can do it. We should have no inhibitions as to the ingenuity and ambition of Governors to solve their [own] problems.

USA Today, 1-27:(A)11.

Tom Harkin
United States Senator, D-Iowa

6

[Proposing a simple majority vote in the Senate to end a filibuster, rather than the three-fifths required now]: The filibuster is nothing short of legislative piracy. Now that the tables are turned [with Republicans in the majority in the Senate], the temptation is great

(TOM HARKIN)

to do unto them as they did unto us [Democrats]. But we cannot allow the filibuster to bring Congress to a grinding halt. So today I start a drive to do away with a dinosaur—the filibuster rule.

Jan. 4/
The New York Times,
1-5:(A)10.

Howell T. Heflin
United States Senator,
D-Alabama

1

My service on the [Senate] Ethics Committee can be described with many adjectives, none of which include "enjoyable." [But the Senate has] made great strides [in its ethical behavior]. While there is still room for much improvement, I am, nevertheless, convinced that the Senators now serving are the most ethical in the history of the Senate.

Before the Senate,
Washington, D.C.,
March 29/
The Washington Post,
3-30:(A)5.

Henry J. Hyde
United States Representative,
D-Illinois

2

[Arguing against the current calls for term-limit legislation for members of Congress]: America needs leaders. It needs statesmen. It needs giants. And you do not get them out of the phone book. New is always better? What in the world is conservative about that? Have we nothing to learn from the past, tradition, history, institutional memory? Do they not count? . . . This [call for term limits] is not conservative. It is radical distrust of democracy. It is cynical. It is pessimistic, devoid of the hope and the optimism that built this country . . . "Career politician" [has become] an epithet. [Pass term limits] and professionals, my friends, will run this government. Only they will not be elected; they will be the faceless, nameless, try-to-get-them-on-the-phone, unaccountable permanent bureaucracy.

Before the House,
Washington, D.C.,
March 29/
The Washington Post,
4-5:(A)19.

Gary Jacobson
Professor of political science,
University of California,
San Diego

3

[On ballot initiatives that are approved by voters and then overturned by courts]: When you vote for something and it doesn't happen because the courts stop it, that's not fun . . . When the voters put themselves in a position to make policy, they will run into the same kind of barriers that legislators do. When the Constitution is not on your side, you lose.

Los Angeles Times,
11-22:(A)27.

Nancy L. Johnson
United States Representative,
R-Connecticut

4

[On the House Ethics Committee, which she chairs and which investigates possible

(NANCY L. JOHNSON)

ethics breaches by House members]: Any action [by the Committee], particularly on a hard case, ought to be an action that the Committee on the whole agrees with. Good decisions should have far broader support than simply the allegiance of a member to one party . . . The goal of the Committee is to come to not necessarily 100 percent agreement, but to come to consensus on issues.

Interview/
The Washington Post,
4-3:(A)17.

Roger W. Johnson
Administrator,
General Services
Administration
of the United States

1

[On the downsizing of the Federal government]: The fact is, this whole government is in a shrinking mode. The question is just to what degree.

The Washington Post,
4-3:(A)1.

Charles O. Jones
Visiting fellow,
Brookings Institution

2

[On the position of U. S. Senate Majority Leader]: The Senate is essentially an institution that can't be led. Leading the unleadable is a tough task.

The New York Times,
3-3:(A)10.

Bruce Josten
Senior vice president
for membership policy,
United States
Chamber of Commerce

3

The underlying theme of the [Republican Party's] Contract [With America] is to shrink, change and question every function of government. It seeks to end what I call betterment through bureaucracy.

Nation's Business, May:20.

John R. Kasich
United States Representative,
R-Ohio

4

Our [Republican] vision for the 21st century is taking power and money and control and influence from [Washington] and giving it back to men and women all across the country. Frankly, the power of bureaucracy and red tape and misplaced compassion . . . in some respects takes away the incentives for the individual to fly.

May 18/
The Washington Post,
5-19:(A)1.

Edward M. Kennedy
United States Senator,
D-Massachusetts

5

[Arguing against a proposed Constitutional amendment to make desecrating the American flag a crime]: The Constitution is the enduring charter of our nation and our liberties. It should not be treated as a billboard on which to plaster the bumper-sticker slogan of the moment.

USA Today, 6-29:(A)6.

Donald F. Kettl
Professor,
University of Wisconsin, Madison

1

The tough thing now for the [Clinton] Administration is to engage Republicans in downsizing [government] without sacrificing the basic performance of government. How do you create a government that costs even less but works well?

The Washington Post,
1-30:(A)13.

James B. King
Director, Federal Office
of Personnel Management

2

[Warning against cuts in pensions for long-time Federal workers]: It makes no sense to make retirement less attractive, or worse yet to create insecurity, about the system, at a time when we want to reduce the [Federal] payroll through voluntary retirement . . . We must remember that Federal retirement is an earned benefit. [Those who have spent their lives in public service] deserve a final chapter of dignity and security, not uncertainty, sacrifice and fear.

Before National Association
of Retired Federal Employees,
Washington, D.C., March 13/
The Washington Post,
3-14:(A)15.

Lane Kirkland
President,
American Federation
of Labor-Congress
of Industrial Organizations

3

The more fiercely the current debate rages about the appropriate role of the Federal government in our society, the more clearly I remember a lot of things about our country before there was such a role. There were county poorhouses out on the edge of town. That's where people went when they became too old or too sick to work. Then Social Security came and tore those poorhouses down. The rivers of my state ran brick-red from the erosion of farms, and the topsoil of the Great Plains literally blew away—turning thousands upon thousands of farm families into homeless nomads. Then came the tree-planting of the CCC and the farm programs of the New Deal. Today, those rivers run black and clear. Free enterprises such as the paper, forest-products and agri-business industries shared abundantly in those government initiatives. I remember when rural homes were lit by kerosene, before the REA electrified and humanized them, bridging the cultural gap between town and country—creating new markets for the appliance industry. I am proud to acknowledge that I am a child of [the late President] Franklin Roosevelt's New Deal. But then, every person alive today, regardless of age or previous condition, is an heir of the works of that great period in our nation's life. I do not and cannot forget those roots in the past. So today, if asked whether the label "liberal" or "conservative" or "misanthrope" fits, I can only respond that I am a New Dealer, pure and simple and unreconstructed.

At ceremony
marking 50th anniversary
of the death
of Franklin Roosevelt,
Warm Springs, Ga.,
April 11/
The Washington Post,
4-19:(A)22.

Sergei A. Kovalev
Former Commissioner of Human Rights of Russia

1

We need to make those in power understand that they are supposed to listen to the people. A civil society can never be built by orders from above.

At seminar, Moscow, Russia, Dec. 5/ Los Angeles Times, 12-6:(A)14.

Aleksander Kwasniewski
Candidate for President of Poland

2

The role of ex-Presidents in the United States is very impressive; I would like to study such examples. Ex-Presidents can be very useful, and sometimes an ex-President is much more useful than when he was President.

To reporters/ Los Angeles Times, 11-21:(A)1.

Tom Latham
United States Representative, R-Iowa

3

[On his being a small-businessman who ran for Congress]: I had seen the stifling effect government has on small business . . . Too many people in government have no idea what it is like to make a living in the real world.

U.S. News & World Report, 3-27:42.

Richard L. Lesher
President, United States Chamber of Commerce

4

The whole country is going through a reinvention and downsizing. Most large American companies have gone through it; state and local governments have gone through it. Even academic institutions are going through it. The last one to go through it is the one that caused all the problems: Uncle Sam.

Nation's Business, May:21.

Robert L. Livingston
United States Representative, R-Louisiana

5

[On new House Speaker Newt Gingrich's tight reign on House committee chairmen, most of whom he appointed]: It is no longer a feudal system. It's a federation. It enhances cohesion—cohesion, not coercion.

USA Today, 3-8:(A)5.

Burdett Loomis
Professor of political science, University of Kansas

6

[On Senator Nancy Landon Kassebaum's decision not to seek re-election next year]: Kassebaum's departure is one large chunk out of the foundations of civility in the Senate. The Senate becomes a different kind of body [with her departure]. There's less room for deliberation and honest debate. It becomes more like the House. If you have the votes, you cram it down someone's throat.

Nov. 20/Los Angeles Times, 11-21:(A)18.

Theodore Lowi
Professor of government,
Cornell University

1

[On recent Congresses]: What happened is that as the quality of the legislature went up, its performance went down. These people [in Congress today] are much more individual entrepreneurs; they have far less respect for party institutions and hierarchy . . . They don't have the party to hide behind anymore. Because they're more individually accountable, they feel much more vulnerable and they react accordingly [to changeable public opinion].

The Atlantic Monthly,
May:94,96.

Frank Luntz
Republican Party
public-opinion analyst

2

In our polling, we find very different priorities in the white and the non-white communities. The black community has become very dependent on the government to provide services, and it expects government to get involved and fix America's ills. At the same time, the white community has become particularly hostile about the government and the services it provides.

Panel discussion,
Washington, D.C./
Harper's, March:50.

Carolyn B. Maloney
United States Representative,
D-New York

3

[Calling for the Federal government to be more aggressive in collecting money owed to it from loans, penalties, etc.]: I know these numbers look boring, but if we manage [debt collection] better, it could be very exciting. I think it's very liberal. If you run your government better, you have more money for [such programs as] AmeriCorps [and] school lunches.

The Washington Post,
7-31:(A)19.

David Mason
Congressional analyst,
Heritage Foundation

4

People are fed up with a [Federal] government that has become too big, too intrusive and too much of a busybody for them to tolerate. They want a less-centralized, more-responsive government.

USA Today, 1-5:(A)3.

Robert McClure
Political scientist,
Syracuse University

5

[On the changes envisioned by the new Republican-controlled Congress]: In some symbolic, historic and policy sense, the New Deal is ended as a basis from which we think about how we're going to do things in the future.

USA Today, 1-5:(A)3.

Daniel Patrick Moynihan
United States Senator,
D-New York

6

The House of Representatives gets carried away with great enthusiasm. They go this way, they go that way, they have two-year

(DANIEL PATRICK MOYNIHAN)

elections . . . Things come over to the Senate and cool off.

USA Today,
1-9:(A)4.

Sam Nunn
United States Senator,
D-Georgia

1

[The Republicans, who now control Congress, are] heading down the right road by recognizing there's too much Federal government . . . But there are a lot of red lights and caution lights up there and they're ignoring them. Changes need to be made [with] sensitivity and with prudence. If they don't do that . . . their "Contract With America" will be a renewable lease with voters rather than a permanent lease.

News conference
announcing his retirement
from the Senate
next year,
Atlanta, Ga., Oct. 9/
Los Angeles Times,
10-10:(A)14.

David R. Obey
United States Representative,
D-Wisconsin

2

The most fundamental threat to the long-term liberty of this country lies in the unchecked use of Executive [Presidential] power.

Before the House,
Washington, D.C./
The New York Times,
2-7:(A)1.

3

[Criticizing the power and influence that new House Speaker Newt Gingrich has over House business]: You have one man making all the decisions. These guys [Republican committee chairmen] are simply carrying out their marching orders, and woe be to anyone who has an independent thought.

USA Today,
3-8:(A)5.

June O'Neill
Director,
Congressional
Budget Office

4

I think everybody at CBO is particularly distressed at attacks that seem to question our credibility or impartiality . . . Congress makes policies. We're essentially a number-crunching operation.

Interview/
Los Angeles Times,
12-11:(A)16.

Bruce I. Oppenheimer
Professor
of political science,
Vanderbilt University

5

The [increase] in work load has affected the way Congress acts, which in turn has affected public perceptions. In a time-constrained environment, the opposition gains power. The filibuster wasn't used much before 1970, because it wasn't a very effective weapon. Who cared [then] if you wasted time? Congress never ran out of time.

The Atlantic Monthly,
May:104.

Bob Packwood
United States Senator,
R-Oregon

1

In my experience in life, small things are better-administered than big things. It doesn't matter if it's government or industry, which is why a lot of small, sharp entrepreneurs are beating the socks off of corporate behemoths. Many of the things we administer at the Federal level, we just don't do very well. I'm afraid it is inherent in the bigness of centralization. Does that guarantee that the states will do better? No. There is no guarantee. But is it worth a try? Yes.

Washington, D.C,
March 27/
The New York Times,
3-28:(A)10.

Leon E. Panetta
Chief of Staff
to President
of the United States
Bill Clinton

2

[On the problems involved with Presidential nominations to fill Federal vacancies]: You want to move to fill a vacancy. [But] at the same time, you know full well that you're looking at about a two- or three-month FBI check [of the nominee], which is standard now in these situations, and that something may come out of that check . . . So it becomes a Catch-22 [when people criticize the President for taking too much time to fill vacancies]. The unfortunate thing is that it can really hurt people in the nomination process.

Broadcast interview/
"Face the Nation,"
CBS-TV, 3-12.

George E. Pataki
Governor of New York (R)

3

When government accepts responsibility for people, then people no longer take responsibility for themselves. Individual responsibility and personal freedom are inevitably linked.

Inaugural address,
Albany, N.Y.,
Jan. 1/
The New York Times,
1-2:9.

Ronald Peters
Director,
Carl Albert
Congressional Research
and Studies Center,
University of Oklahoma

4

Sure, Congress has changed, but so has the country. Things have become less hierarchical than they once were almost everywhere. Part of this is generational, but a lot of it is just the way we've changed as a people. Legislators are more autonomous, but so is everyone else in the culture. [Congress] may be more professional, but all disciplines are becoming more professionalized. This is all part of a larger pattern, which in one sense couldn't be more representative.

The Atlantic Monthly,
May:96.

Scott Rassmussen
Chairman,
Term Limits
Leadership Council

5

It's clear that Congress has no interest in

(SCOTT RASSMUSSEN)

term limits [for themselves]. For them, it's a conflict of interest.

The New York Times,
9-19:(A)10.

Ralph Reed
Executive director,
Christian Coalition

1

You can't be part of a movement for limited government without accepting limits to what government can do. That's one of the things that I think separates conservatives from liberals. We [conservatives] genuinely believe that some of the greatest work, the most productive and fruitful work that will be done in society to improve people's lives, will be done by institutions other than the government.

Panel discussion,
Washington, D.C./
Harper's, March:53.

Robert B. Reich
Secretary of Labor
of the United States

2

[On the public's desire for a smaller, more efficient government and the fact that he is 4-feet 10-inches tall]: I defy anyone to come up with a smaller, more efficient Labor Secretary. I can get by on 800 calories a day.

U.S. News & World Report,
1-9:22.

Ann Richards
Governor of Texas (D)

3

There are lots of rewards to public service; but to be good at this, you almost have to have a missionary zeal.

Interview,
Austin, Texas/
Working Woman,
March:85.

Robert E. Rubin
Secretary
of the Treasury
of the United States

4

I'm not as good at prioritization as people should be. I find everything sort of interesting. I think all of us should try to work on a lot of different fronts at the same time.

Interview,
Washington, D.C./
The Washington Post,
3-14:(A)7.

Mark Sanford
United States Representative,
R-South Carolina

5

[Supporting term limits for members of Congress]: There is a direct correlation between length of time in office and a propensity to spend Federal dollars. The sum total of votes [by old-guard Congressmen] is a $4.8-trillion debt . . . It's not like we're dealing with brain surgery. Probably there's a six-month learning curve, and even after a year, you don't have it down pat. But over time, you begin to erode your sense of the outside world. And at some point, you begin to think that it's absolutely essential to the nation that you stay in office.

The Washington Post,
3-30:(A)7.

Barbara Sinclair
Political scientist,
University of California,
Riverside

1

The Republicans want government out of the way. Democrats say that is fine, but some of us are in wheelchairs and others of us are Olympic athletes . . . The Republicans are trying, in a sense, to push the line of tough love: "We're doing this for your own good." Maybe they believe that. But in a sense, they think that a lot of people's problems are their own, and the poor will always be with us [no matter what government does].

The Christian Science Monitor,
1-25:4.

Darry Sragow
Consultant to
the Democratic Party

2

Voters are sufficiently cynical to suspect that politicians' behavior is going to be less than perfect. They think all politicians are self-serving, rule-bending opportunists . . . [But] they want [government] to be fixed, and they vote for whomever they think will fix it.

Los Angeles Times,
5-5:(A)26.

Al Swift
Former United States Representative,
D-Washington

3

[Criticizing the increasing independence of members of Congress]: We'd be better off with four hundred and ten followers and twenty-five leaders than the other way around.

The Atlantic Monthly,
May:94.

Fred Thompson
United States Senator,
R-Tennessee

4

[On his being a freshman Senator]: I've still got a lot to learn about Washington. Why, yesterday I accidentally spent some of my own money.

At Salute
to Congress dinner,
Washington Press Club,
Washington, D.C./
Newsweek,
2-6:15.

James T. Walsh
United States Representative,
R-New York

5

[Criticizing Washington Mayor Marion Barry's asking for Federal aid to help with his city's $722-million budget deficit]: You made your bed; you ought to lie in it.

U.S. News & World Report,
3-6:30.

Henry A. Waxman
United States Representative,
D-California

6

I think a lot of people take a lot of government programs and services for granted. If the Republicans say "reform regulations," it sounds good; but what they're really doing is rolling back government's ability to guarantee safe drinking water and food and drugs. It has to be pointed out what's really going on.

U.S. News & World Report,
1-9:26.

Fred Wertheimer
President, Common Cause

1

There is no way in the world you can change the way Washington operates without changing the influence-money system that pervades Congress. To argue that you want to eliminate the double standard for Congress but hold on to your freebies from lobbyists is a fraud.

The New York Times, 1-3:(A)8.

2

[Criticizing recent calls for Constitutional amendments to address various problems]: Got a problem? Let's have a Constitutional amendment. There is an attitude out there that shows a total lack of perspective on the role the Constitution is supposed to play. Either the Constitution is one of the most important documents in civilization or it's a piece of paper that you change when you don't like something.

The Washington Post, 3-14:(A)5.

James Q. Wilson
Professor of management and public policy, University of California, Los Angeles

3

Several things happen when the government gets into these areas [such as education, crime, welfare, etc.]. First, no one really knows how to solve these problems. Second, the public itself is deeply conflicted about most of these issues; you rarely have a consensus from which to act. Third, these issues tend to be so complex that they overwhelm the process. And finally, when these measures fail to do much to solve something like crime—which is what inevitably happens—they greatly reinforce the general disillusionment with government. There's something to be said for sticking with what you know how to do.

The Atlantic Monthly, May:101.

Pete Wilson
Governor of California (R); Candidate for the 1996 Republican Presidential nomination

4

Members of Congress can abstain from voting [on issues], but [state] Governors can't abstain from leadership.

Opening his campaign for the nomination, New York, N.Y., Aug. 28/ The New York Times, 8-29:(A)6.

Jonathan D. Asher
Executive director,
Legal Aid Society
of Metropolitan Denver

1

[On Federal cuts in spending on legal aid for the poor]: The only thing less popular than a poor person these days is a poor person with a lawyer.

The New York Times,
9-5:(A)1.

Edward W. Beglin
Head Judge,
Superior Court
of New Jersey
for Union County

2

[Criticizing the fact that New Jersey's Superior Court judges have not had a salary increase since 1991]: You can't operate a system forever without increasing the compensation for the principals in the system. No one wants to come if they view it as static. The system will tend to suffer in quality after a while. We run the risk of losing people who just have to go back to [private law] practice to get the last two kids' education.

The New York Times,
2-23:(C)18.

William J. Brennan
Former Associate Justice,
Supreme Court
of the United States

3

[Expressing his unhappiness with the conservative tilt of the Supreme Court since he retired, especially the number of 5-4 conservative decisions]: I've regretted [retiring] every minute since I did . . . God, when I see some of the decisions, I think, "Jeez, if only I were there."

Interview/
Los Angeles Times,
6-15:(A)5.

Steven Brill
President,
Court TV

4

[Supporting Judge Lance Ito on his handling of the controversial murder trial of former football star O. J. Simpson]: Let's remember that Judge Ito is the person in charge of the action in the longest-running live television event in history. Imagine yourself being called on to make dozens of decisions, many of them spontaneous and just as highly complicated, every day for months before a live audience.

Before
Southern California
chapter of American
Civil Liberties Union,
May 24/
Los Angeles Times,
5-25:(A)27.

5

[Defending the use of TV cameras in the courtroom]: The camera is the antidote to the media circus. [Lawyers will] "showboat" even without cameras.

Time, 7-24:38.

Carol Chase
Professor of law,
Pepperdine University

1

[On what some see as Judge Lance Ito's loss of control of the high-profile murder trial of former football star O. J. Simpson]: I think circumstances have taken control of the courtroom, and I'm not sure there's anything that Judge Ito could have done about that. He has relied on the attorneys to behave ethically and honestly, and we have seen attorneys take advantage of that. The criminal-justice system begins to fall apart when attorneys play it like a game that has to be won.

The Washington Post,
4-25:(A)3.

Erwin Chemerinsky
Professor of law,
University of Southern California

2

[On the recent controversial murder trial of former football star O. J. Simpson]: For years to come, people will view the justice system through the prism of the O. J. Simpson case, and it is a very distorting lens. There is nothing typical about this case. But it has become so much a part of our shared culture that it's going to have profound effects.

U.S. News & World Report,
10-9:47.

Bill Clinton
President
of the United States

3

I do believe that the *habeas corpus* provisions of the Federal law, which permit [death-penalty] appeals sometimes to be delayed seven, eight, nine years, should be changed. I have advocated that. I tried to pass it last year. I hope the Congress will pass a review and a reform of the *habeas corpus* provisions, because it should not take eight or nine years and three trips to the Supreme Court to finalize whether a person, in fact, was properly convicted or not.

Broadcast
interview/
"60 Minutes,"
CBS-TV, 4-23.

4

[Criticizing a proposal to put a cap on civil law-suit damage awards]: [Such a cap would be protection for the deeds of] drunk drivers, murderers, rapists . . . despoilers of our environment, like the Exxon Valdez [oil spill], and perpetrators of terrorist acts and hate crimes.

USA Today,
5-5:(A)1.

L. Gordon Crovitz
Writer
on legal affairs

5

[The proliferation of lawsuits, large settlements and the ever-litigious nature of the system] makes U. S. law the subject of endless fascination and horror, especially to foreigners.

U.S. News & World Report,
5-22:24.

Alfonse M. D'Amato
United States Senator,
R-New York

6

[Supporting legislation intended to limit securities- and stock-fraud lawsuits]: [It is aimed at] specious lawsuits that are not well-

(ALFONSE M. D'AMATO)

grounded and only designed to shake down businesses, shake down insurance, shake down people. That is wrong and we have got to stop it. [The] fact of the matter is we are paying millions of dollars out because we've allowed this practice to continue and it has become a very sophisticated art form.

The New York Times,
6-27:(A)10.

Christopher Darden
Assistant District Attorney
of Los Angeles County, Calif.

1

[On the current controversial murder trial of former football star O. J. Simpson, in which he is one of the prosecutors]: Everybody who has to sit or witness these proceedings, or listen to the details of this crime or these accusations—we're all tarnished. I don't know if I ever want to try another case . . . It has shaken my faith in a system . . . Frankly, I'm ashamed to be part of this case.

Interview/
U.S. News & World Report,
6-19:39.

Alan M. Dershowitz
Professor of law,
Harvard University

2

[As a lawyer,] I have three rules: I never believe what the prosecutor or the police say; I never believe what the media say; and I never believe what my client says.

The New York Times,
6-2:(B)16.

Jo-Ellan Dimitrius
Trial consultant

3

[On trial juries]: What happens is the courtroom becomes their home. They know everybody who walks in and out of that door. They notice not only what you have on but how all the people in the courtroom interact with one another, not just the defendant and the attorneys, but the reporters, the judge, the bailiff and the people in the audience. Trials get to be monotonous, so [the jurors] look around the courtroom for reactions . . . We all look for validation. [But] how do you do that when you're sitting in the jury box and you're told you cannot talk about the case or anything having to do with the case? The validation you get is through the body language of everybody in that courtroom. That's a very important part of the process.

Los Angeles Times,
3-15:(A)16.

Susan Estrich
Professor of law,
University of Southern California

4

[Criticizing the defense's use of race in pleading its case to an almost all-black jury in the current controversial murder trial of former football star O. J. Simpson]: It will be terrible for the criminal-justice system if [the race card] works [and Simpson is freed]. The jury is being asked [by defense attorney Johnnie Cochran] to do politics, and it's a recipe for disaster. Juries have to realize they're not political leaders and they're not an audience on [TV's] *Oprah* [Winfrey show]. The most you can ask a jury to do is to pass judgment on who did what to whom. We have to understand that you cannot and should not

(SUSAN ESTRICH)

solve social problems in criminal juries.

Forum sponsored by "Time" magazine/ Time, 10-9:36.

Henry A. Freedman
Executive director, Center on Social Welfare Policy and Law

1

[Criticizing cuts in Federal spending on legal aid for the poor]: With such new discretion in the states, many poor families will face termination or denial of desperately needed aid because of policies or practices that raise important Constitutional questions. If equal justice under law means anything, these families should be provided legal representation so they can get their day in court.

The New York Times, 9-5:(A)9.

Stephen Gillers
Professor of legal ethics, New York University Law School

2

[On the current controversial murder trial of former football star O. J. Simpson]: Once again, we are reminded of the uncomfortably close relationship between justice and money. If Simpson were middle-class or merely rich, good defense lawyers confronting the mass of scientific evidence and police testimony against him would have pressed for a plea bargain. Although the Simpson trial is to trials like Mount Everest is to a child's sand castle, unrealistic defendants may not appreciate that their court-appointed or bargain-basement lawyers lack both the talent of a Johnnie Cochran [one of Simpson's team of lawyers] and the investigative resources of an [enormously wealthy] O. J. Simpson. An acquittal in the Simpson case will give other defendants false hopes that their cases can be beat as well.

Forum sponsored by "Time" magazine/ Time, 10-9:37.

Charles E. Grassley
United States Senator, R-Iowa

3

[Saying recent legislation requiring Congress to abide by national labor and anti-discrimination laws in its hiring of employees should also apply to the Federal Judiciary]: We are pursuing this based on the principle that employees of the Judiciary ought to have the same protections of private-sector employees. The principle that applied to the reform of Congress should apply to the reform of the Judiciary. Judges should feel the impact of laws they interpret just as Congress should feel the impact of laws they pass.

Interview/ The Washington Post, 2-13:(A)19.

Orrin G. Hatch
United States Senator, R-Utah

4

[Saying, as Chairman of the Judiciary Committee, that the Senate, even though controlled by Republicans now, will be fair in dealing with the confirmation of President Clinton's judicial nominations]: As long as [the nominees] are qualified, in good health

(ORRIN G. HATCH)

and understand the role of judges, they'll get through.

The Washington Post,
2-13:(A)7.

Henry J. Hyde
United States Representative,
R-Illinois

1

Lawsuit abuse saps our economy, eliminates jobs, pits neighbor against neighbor and injures our country's global competitiveness.

The New York Times,
3-10:(A)8.

Lance A. Ito
Judge, Superior Court,
Los Angeles, Calif.

2

[On the controversial murder trial of former football star O. J. Simpson, in which Ito is judge and which is now entering its sixth month]: I would like to finish this case sometime in this lifetime.

Newsweek,
7-10:15.

Joel I. Klein
Deputy Assistant
Attorney General,
Antitrust Division,
Department of Justice
of the United States

3

[On the Justice Department's push to have the ABA change its accreditation procedures for law schools, which the Department says drives up tuition costs and gives law professors too much power]: I hope today's action has consequences throughout the accreditation community, so that people take a hard look at their process to make sure that the legitimate pro-competitive quality concerns remain the purpose of accreditation, and that guild and other impermissible considerations do not enter into it.

June 27/
The New York Times,
6-28:(A)1.

Adam Kurland
Professor of law,
Harvard University

4

[On the current controversial murder trial of former football star O. J. Simpson]: The prosecution seems to have a very strong case . . . [But] you see how difficult a time they're having when their resources are matched [by the defendant's being able to afford a team of top lawyers]. Think what would happen . . . if every defendant had the presumption of innocence and roughly equal resources. It would lead to a crumbling of the justice system.

USA Today,
6-12:(A)4.

Abner J. Mikva
Counsel to President
of the United States
Bill Clinton

5

The [Presidential] nomination and [Senate] confirmation of judges is a political process. If we find that objections are raised [about particular nominees] that mean [those nominees] won't get hearings or that we will end up with a fight that looks like it won't go

(ABNER J. MIKVA)

anywhcrc, [thc Administration will look for other persons to nominate]. [But] we're still looking for the best people we can get.

Feb. 10/
The Washington Post,
2-13:(A)7.

1

[Criticizing a Republican bill that would, among other things, limit punitive-damage awards in civil cases and make the loser pay legal costs of the winner in lawsuits]: When I look at bills like these, I can believe that [Republican House Speaker Newt] Gingrich means what he says when he describes himself as a revolutionary.

Interview/
The New York Times,
3-6:(A)1.

Andrew P. Napolitano
Judge,
Superior Court
of New Jersey

2

[Saying he is leaving the Court to join a law firm because of New Jersey's ban on its judges having income other than their salaries]: I can live on a judicial salary, but I don't want to die on it . . . A lot of superstar lawyers out there would be very fine judges. [But] they don't even consider the bench because of the extraordinary diminution of income that they and their families would have to suffer from.

The New York Times,
2-23:(C)18.

Ron Packard
United States Representative,
R-California

3

The Legal Services Corporation is more focused on advancing grand social causes than on helping the poor with ordinary legal problems.

The New York Times,
9-5:(A)1.

Leon E. Panetta
Chief of Staff
to President
of the United States
Bill Clinton

4

[Criticizing Republican proposals to, among other things, put Federal limits on civil lawsuit damage awards]: [President Clinton] for a long time has felt that the states ought to have jurisdiction over these issues . . . [Republicans are] talking about giving the states greater flexibility on welfare, they're talking about sending school nutrition programs back to the states; but when it comes to . . . tort laws and protecting consumers, they're willing to have the Federal government tell the states what to do.

Broadcast interview/
"This Week With David Brinkley,"
ABC-TV, 3-5.

Wade Ricks
Field producer,
Cable News Network

5

[Defending the use of TV cameras in the courtroom]: Trials can be handled in a

(WADE RICKS)

thoughtful manner so that they instruct, enlighten and entertain [viewers].

Time,
7-24:38.

Gerry Spence
Lawyer

1

[On the public spectacle being made of the current controversial murder trial of former football star O. J. Simpson]: It's already too late. Bring on Barnum and Bailey. It has become infected with the need of the public to watch, and the need of the participants to *be* watched—an ugly, voyeuristic display.

USA Today,
1-20:(A)2.

Shelby Steele
Professor of English,
San Jose State University

2

[On the current controversial murder trial of black former football star O. J. Simpson, who is accused of killing two white people, for which the majority of the white population say he is guilty and the majority of the black population say he is innocent]: They are looking at it through two different moral prisms. Blacks view it through the moral prism of history, where blacks have been the victims of America's legal corruptions for centuries. Their standard of evidence has to do with history. For whites, it is just this one case: Did he kill these people or not?

USA Today,
9-29:(A)2.

Gerald F. Uelmen
Professor of law,
University of Santa Clara

3

[Criticizing proposed changes in the jury system as a result of public dissatisfaction with the not-guilty verdict in the recent murder trial of former football star O. J. Simpson]: Doing this as some sort of response to the O. J. verdict really sets the stage, I think, for over-emphasizing the public reaction to that verdict. The worst mistake we could make would be to reform the system based on the kind of skewed experience of this one case.

Los Angeles Times,
10-31:(A)15.

Robert Weisberg
Professor of law,
Stanford University

4

[On the controversial murder trial of former football star O. J. Simpson]: The trial has become a bizarre spectacle. The criminal justice system has been overtaken by the psychopathology of pop culture.

Newsweek,
4-17:26.

John Shepard Wiley, Jr.
Professor of law,
University of California,
Los Angeles;
Former prosecutor

5

[On eyewitness testimony in trials]: It is the most theatrical moment in the trial when the witness points the finger at the defendant and says, "He did it." Everybody in the jury box looks at the witness, looks at the finger

(JOHN SHEPARD WILEY, JR.)

and follows thc linc right to thc dcfcndant. And just about every defendant squirms.

Los Angeles Times,
2-11:(A)1.

Pete Wilson
Governor of California

1

[Saying excessive and unnecessary lawsuits increase insurance premiums even for companies not involved in the suits]: The costs of lawsuit abuse are monumental. Those costs are not just absorbed . . . [It] translates into an increased cost for a Toyota and an increased cost for a condominium . . . It is an unfairly high cost that Californians are paying.

Van Nuys, Calif.,
March 10/
Los Angeles Times,
3-11:(A)25.

John Alexander
Historian,
University of Cincinnati

1

Normally, the shape of a Presidential election campaign develops over a fairly long period. But sometimes a series of concrete events, packed into a short span of time, become the potentially defining moment for a whole campaign.

Los Angeles Times,
11-21:(A)17.

Lamar Alexander
Candidate for the
1996 Republican
Presidential nomination;
Former Secretary
of Education
of the United States

2

[Saying one of his opponents for the Presidential nomination, U.S. Senator Robert Dole, is not part of the younger generation that the Presidency requires]: I think the 1992 elections and the 1994 elections were generation elections. We've moved into a telecommunications age, a different time. We have the greatest respect for the people of every generation, particularly the World War II generation. But I think it's time to move on, and my assumption is that most Republican voters, by the time we get down to the caucuses and primaries, will think the same thing . . . If the people of Iowa and this country want our most senior and experienced Washington-based leader, then Bob Dole will probably be nominated. But almost never do we take a United States Senator and make him President of the United States . . . I'm going to try to persuade the people of Iowa that Bob Dole is an excellent [Senate] Majority Leader and that he can make his greatest contribution to the country right where he is.

Campaigning,
Waterloo, Iowa,
March 1/
The Washington Post,
3-2:(A)9.

3

I'm a more temperate person than, say, some others. [Republican activist and former Education Secretary] Bill Bennett could stand up and say, "Have a nice day," and everybody would say, "What a great, fiery conservative speech." And I could say, "Let's hang 'em by their toes and cut out their entrails," and they'd say, "What a pleasant person he is." So it's a matter of style.

Interview/
Vogue,
September:606.

4

[Saying his being a Washington outsider is a plus for him over other Presidential candidates who are Senators or Congressmen]: It is hard to change the culture of Washington if you *are* the culture of Washington.

At Republican Presidential
candidates' debate,
Manchester, N.H.,
Oct. 11/
Los Angeles Times,
10-12:(A)14.

John B. Anderson
Former
United States
Representative,
R-Illinois

1

[Saying an independent may have a real chance to win the Presidency in next year's elections]: This is not just fanciful speculation. Anybody who thinks it's in the bag for either the Republican nominee or the Democratic nominee is whistling up the wrong alley. There's a huge degree of flux in the political situation in this country, and we could have some very surprising results.

The New York Times,
6-6:(A)13.

Wright Andrews
President,
American League
of Lobbyists

2

[Criticizing the decision by House Republicans to end the practice of allowing lobbyists access to the Capitol after hours and to non-public areas of the building, thus trying to rebuild public confidence in Congress by not seeming to give special privileges]: What that will do is give very selective access. People will work out regular arrangements with certain members [of Congress] or staff. People who are allowed in may be some of the lobbyists who can make the biggest [political] contributions. When you ask people for favors, it would not be unprecedented for them to ask for favors in return.

May 24/
Los Angeles Times,
5-25:(A)20.

Bill Archer
United States Representative,
R-Texas

3

[On the current shutdown of many Federal government agencies and services due to the budget impasse between President Clinton and Congress]: Mr. President, will you get with us and get tough and get this nation going? President Clinton uses welfare reform [which is part of the budget impasse] just like he used tax cuts—as an election device. The very man who pledged to get things done is now the man who stands in the way.

Nov. 13/Los Angeles Times,
11-14:(A)15.

Don Argue
President-elect,
National Association
of Evangelicals

4

[On religion and political activism]: To wrap ourselves in the flag of any one particular party is very dangerous. And there has been quite a movement that has identified evangelicals as part of the Republicans and part of the extreme right. Although evangelicals may hold some of these same positions, they are very, very . . . [averse] to being identified with one particular party or one particular ideology.

The Washington Post,
3-27:(A)1.

Ross Baker
Political scientist,
Rutgers University

5

[On whether President Clinton's handling so far of the recent bombing of an Oklahoma

(ROSS BAKER)

City Federal building will help him politically]: Clinton may have found a common foe he can use to do what Americans elect Presidents to do: unify and lead them in a righteous battle against forces that threaten their homeland.

The Washington Post, 4-24:(A)10.

Haley Barbour
Chairman, Republican National Committee

1

I try not to answer questions about things I don't know anything about, unless I see a political advantage.

To reporters/ Los Angeles Times, 1-26:(A)5.

2

[On the Republican Party's effective use of electronic communications to reach the public]: I came in here with the idea [that] we had to learn how to take advantage of every potential avenue to reach the voters. The big change is that the telecommunications revolution has given power to the recipient of news . . . He can hear it unfiltered.

The Washington Post, 4-24:(A)4.

3

[On criticism that there is too much tension among Republican candidates for the Presidential nomination next year]: We shouldn't expect a campaign to go to its conclusion without understanding where Candidate A and Candidate B differ on issues. That's what politics is all about.

At Republican Party summer meeting, Philadelphia, Pa., July 13/ The New York Times, 7-15:8.

4

[On the forthcoming 1996 national elections]: In 1994, the Republicans won the greatest midterm majority sweep [in the Congressional elections] of the 20th century because we ran a national issue campaign that offered the voters a positive alternative agenda. We'll do the same thing in 1996 . . . The greatest danger for us would be if we stop short of delivering on the mandate of 1994's election. We need to act boldly but speak temperately.

USA Today, 8-11:(A)4.

5

We recognize there is a significant constituency available to the Republican Party among African-American voters. The polls show 25 to 45 percent of African-American voters consider themselves conservative. I think the biggest single reason we [Republicans] have not done better [among blacks] is lack of effort.

U.S. News & World Report, 10-16:50.

6

[On the number of Democratic law-makers who have switched to the Republican Party]: Democrats are running away from their own Party like scalded dogs.

U.S. News & World Report, 10-23:38.

(HALEY BARBOUR)

1

[On criticism within the Republican Party of former Joint Chiefs of Staff Chairman Colin Powell, who may run for the 1996 Republican Presidential nomination]: The idea that General Powell is not welcome, or that he's out of the mainstream of the Party, is silly.

U.S. News & World Report, 11-13:42.

Bob Beckel
Democratic Party consultant

2

[On the list of candidates for the 1996 Republican Presidential nomination]: With the exception of [Senator] Bob Dole, to borrow a baseball analogy, these are replacement players.

U.S. News & World Report, 3-6:30.

Paul Begala
Political Adviser to President of the United States Bill Clinton

3

[Former President] Ronald Reagan certainly had his flaws, but the American people knew what he stood for—lower taxes, less government and a strong defense. [Even when he compromised and] raised taxes, his staff always said they had to drag the old man kicking and screaming into accepting the deal.

U.S. News & World Report, 1-9:26.

Robert F. Bennett
United States Senator, R-Utah

4

[On the new crop of Republicans who swept into Congress after last fall's elections]: Every single freshman [in the Senate] is more conservative than the Senators they replaced. Moving the Senate that much to the right has had an enormous impact, even if they had done nothing else.

The Washington Post, 7-10:(A)6.

Joseph R. Biden, Jr.
United States Senator, D-Delaware

5

[On the controversial nomination of Dr. Henry Foster to be Surgeon General]: I'm not going to vote for a nominee where no deep thought was given [by the Clinton Administration] before the nomination was sent up. It was a political blunder in the extreme.

Washington, D.C., Feb. 10/ The New York Times, 2-11:8.

Merle Black
Political scientist, Emory University

6

It's the worst picture for the Democrats in the South that I've seen for 30 years . . . A lot of Southern whites looked at [President] Clinton and thought he wasn't being straight with them. They decided he doesn't have the kind of moral stature they expected in a President. They think he is really a liberal, and

(MERLE BLACK)

when he takes conservative positions they say he's a phony.

Los Angeles Times, 6-19:(A)10.

1

This is the first time since Reconstruction that a majority of [state] Governors, U.S. House members and Senators from the 11 states in the South are Republican . . . Among the younger whites in the south, the overwhelming majority are Republicans. There is a very strong racial polarization. Since whites make up large majorities in every Southern state, the politicians who come out of that see the Republicans as the party of the future.

The New York Times, 10-7:8.

Ken Blackwell
State Treasurer of Ohio

2

There is a growing belief in the black community that they need to get out of an untenable political situation—the Democrats take them for granted and the Republicans write them off.

U.S. News & World Report, 10-16:50.

Tony Blankley
Spokesman for Speaker of the U.S. House of Representatives Newt Gingrich

3

[Saying Congressional Democrats are not yet used to the fact that the Republicans now control the House and Senate]: They have not accepted, in a psychological sense, [last year's] election results. They don't really see Dick Armey as Majority Leader and Newt Gingrich as Speaker. They know Dick and Newt are in those roles, but they think fate has put them in a parallel universe where the real reality doesn't exist. Until they come to grips with the reality, they won't start using their minority status as effectively as they could.

The New York Times, 2-23:(A)11.

Sherwood Boehlert
United States Representative, R-New York

4

I am convinced Republicans will be in control of Congress for the next generation, if we soften some of our hard edges.

U.S. News & World Report, 11-13:45.

John A. Boehner
United States Representative, R-Ohio

5

[On Republican Speaker of the House Newt Gingrich]: He is always ahead of us [other Republicans when it comes to formulating policy]. The last six weeks [that] we were working on the [Republican] Contract [With America], he spent 75 percent of his time thinking through the budget issues. And since May, he has been working on the Medicare problems we'll face in September.

The Washington Post, 7-17:(A)12.

(JOHN A. BOEHNER)

1

Presidents never really stop campaigning, and re-election is always being factored into whatever they do.

USA Today,
6-30:(A)5.

David E. Bonior
United States Representative,
D-Michigan

2

[On his becoming the Democrats' chief critic of Republican policies since the Republicans took control of Congress this year]: There are huge risks for me. They'll be coming at me like a freight train. [But] there are people out there who don't want us [Democrats] just to walk away. We put too much of our heart and soul and energies and convictions into what we believe . . . And so I felt the need to not let them [Republicans] take advantage of us when we were vulnerable—psychologically.

Interview/
The Washington Post,
1-9:(A)4.

3

[Criticizing now-House Speaker Newt Gingrich for stating in a House speech last year the phone number to call to order cassettes of a college course he teaches]: This isn't the Home Shopping Network. This is the House of Representatives. And Newt Gingrich has no business using a 1-800 number to hawk videotapes on the House floor . . . Newt Gingrich knows full well that you cannot use the *Congressional Record* [which prints the proceedings of the House and Senate] to advertise or promote the work of an outside organization. As with so many of the other activities the Speaker is involved with, this doesn't pass the smell test.

News conference,
Washington, D.C., March 8/
Los Angeles Times,
3-9:(A)14.

4

[Criticizing the Republicans, who now control Congress]: We've heard a lot of talk [from the Republicans] about revolution the past eight months. If [House Speaker] Newt Gingrich says the Republicans are revolting, who are we to disagree? This is the most hard-hearted, short-sighted, suck-up-to-the-rich and soak-the-middle-class Congress in American history. And we believe the worst is yet to come.

Washington, D.C., Aug. 4/
The New York Times,
8-5:8.

Barbara Boxer
United States Senator,
D-California

5

[Calling for public hearings on sexual harassment charges against Senator Bob Packwood]: Here you have people—Republicans—who want to clear the air on Whitewater [the scandal that might involve President Clinton] . . . want to clear the air on Waco [the controversial decision by the Clinton Administration's Justice Department to attack a cult compound in Texas]. But they don't want to clear the air on [their fellow Republican] Bob Packwood; they want to shut the doors [and have closed hearings] . . . In my view, that's hypocritical, at the least. At

(BARBARA BOXER)

the most, maybe they're just protecting one of their own . . . It reminds me of a trial where only one side is heard; a miscarriage of justice, any way you slice it.

Los Angeles Times,
8-3:(A)19,17.

Bill Bradley
United States Senator,
D-New Jersey

1

A larger segment of the middle class—more than ever before—finds itself not only vulnerable but powerless. There is more ferment in the political system today than any time I've been in politics. People are uncertain . . . and they're not going to believe any politician until their own circumstances change.

The Christian Science Monitor,
10-4:3.

John B. Breaux
United States Senator,
D-Louisiana

2

[Comparing Democrats in the Senate and in the House, both of which Republicans now control following last year's elections]: We're [Senators] in a different mode [than Democrats in the House]. We're not setting the agenda anymore, [and] we respond to their [Republicans'] agenda with our proposals. [But] we're in the same position as the last Congress in the sense that neither side [in the Senate] has [enough votes to end a filibuster or override a Presidential veto]. I think you'll [therefore] find more working together and common ground between the Democrats in the Senate working with Republicans. [By contrast,] the Republicans in the House all of a sudden have all the keys to all the locks. You'll be seeing them assert their power in a way that says, "We don't need Democrats. We'll do it ourselves."

The Washington Post National Weekly,
1-9:15.

Ronald H. Brown
Secretary of Commerce
of the United States

3

It seems to me that it is a kind of mean-spirited approach that has been taken by at least some of the new Republican leadership [in Congress]. It puts in grave danger the kind of direction the Clinton Administration has set and that was a direction of inclusion and involvement and participation as well as a focus on policies that have a very positive impact on those that have not yet had the opportunity to fully participate in our economic system through programs like Headstart—programs that the Administration has been committed to full funding but that Republicans seem to have the ax poised to chop.

Ebony,
February:74.

Willie Brown
Candidate for Mayor
of San Francisco, Calif.;
Former Speaker
of the California Assembly (D)

4

[On his running for Mayor]: In San Francisco, politics is a contact sport. All my campaigns added together haven't been this hard. You have to personally shake hands with ev-

(WILLIE BROWN)

ery single person in this city. And if you don't, they're insulted!

Time,
11-6:42.

John Bryant
United States Representative,
D-Texas

1

[Saying Democrats will become more aggressive in their criticism of Republicans now that the Republicans control Congress]: Frankly, the fact that it was not done by our leadership for so many years when [new Republican Speaker of the House] Newt Gingrich was allowed to say the wildest and most improbable things about us, is ultimately why we lost [control of Congress in last year's election]. We not only had no offense, we had a piddling defense.

The Washington Post,
1-9:(A)4.

Bay Buchanan
Chairman of
Patrick Buchanan's campaign
for the 1996 Republican
Presidential nomination

2

Pat [Buchanan] represents an element of the [Republican] Party that is presently unrepresented by other candidates [for the Presidential nomination]. He is an economic nationalist and believes our trade policies and economic policies should help Americans. He is also a strong social conservative, and other candidates are waffling on these issues.

Interview/
Los Angeles Times, 3-21:(A)17.

Patrick J. Buchanan
Political commentator;
Candidate for
the 1996 Republican
Presidential nomination

3

Our [American] people [are] not realizing the fruit of their labor [because] we have a government . . . that is too busy taking phone calls from lobbyists for foreign countries and the corporate contributors of the Fortune 500 . . . When I walk into the Oval Office [as President], we start looking out for America first.

Announcing his candidacy
for the nomination,
Manchester, N.H.,
March 20/
Los Angeles Times,
3-21:(A)17.

4

[Saying his Presidential campaign, as a conservative Republican, in having an effect on other Republican candidates, as he travels and campaigns in his van]: All the candidates are responding to it. These moderate Republicans can't go in the direction they want to go because of our campaign. We are setting the agenda for the Party and, I think, to a degree, for the country. Right from this van . . . This is what gets me about my Republican friends: It's not just that they disparage me. They will not even recognize what is going on in their own country.

Time, 11-6:27,28.

5

[Criticizing Senator and Presidential hopeful Robert Dole for not being conservative enough for Republican nomination]: His record is not the record of a conservative. It's

(PATRICK BUCHANAN)

the record of a practitioner of the politics of compromise.

*Concord, N.H./
Los Angeles Times,
12-11:(A)18.*

Charles S. Bullock
*Political scientist,
University of Georgia*

1

There used to be a fire wall [in the South] separating national [political] offices from state offices. Whatever infection Southerners saw in the Democratic Party at the national level, it didn't touch local races. You'd vote for good old [Democrat] Bob [for local office] because he wasn't like [Democratic U.S. Senator Walter] Mondale or [Democratic Presidential candidate Michael] Dukakis. You'd hunted and fished together [with Bob]. But voters are no longer making that kind of distinction. They're just seeing Democrats and they don't like what they see.

*Los Angeles Times,
11-1:(A)5.*

2

Democrats still have a strong black base, but the white base is slipping through their hands like sand.

*U.S. News & World Report,
11-6:37.*

Robert C. Byrd
*United States Senator,
D-West Virginia*

3

[On the Republicans' Contract With America, on which they ran successfully in taking control of Congress in last year's elections]: There is something called a "Contract With America." I have not read it. I have not signed it. I had no part in formulating it. I've read about it. I've heard about it. Also, I've heard that the desire was, on the part of the new majority in both houses, to ram this thing through, to get it enacted quickly—someone said something about 100 days. That may come to pass, I don't know. But I was re-elected in this last election also—for my seventh term. The people of West Virginia did not re-elect me to roll over and play dead for the new majority in the Senate. They did not re-elect me on the basis of my support of a so-called "Contract With America," because that wasn't discussed in my campaign. The people of West Virginia expect me to do my best to uphold the Constitution and to carefully study legislation that comes before the Senate, to vote for it or against it based on the facts as I see them.

*Interview,
Washington, D.C./
Los Angeles Times,
1-29:(M)3.*

Ben Nighthorse Campbell
*United States Senator,
R-Colorado*

4

[Announcing his leaving the Democratic Party to become a Republican]: I can no longer represent the agenda that is put forth by the [Democratic] Party, although I certainly agree with many of the things that Democrats stand for . . . I've always been considered a moderate, to the consternation of the left wing of the Democratic Party. I imagine my

(BEN NIGHTHORSE CAMPBELL)

moderacy will be now to the consternation of the right wing of the Republican Party.

News conference,
Washington, D.C., March 3/
The New York Times,
3-4:8.

Jimmy Carter
Former President
of the United States

1

[On criticism of him from the time he was President to his activities today]: I think I understand where some of it comes from. Go back and look at the [newspaper] cartoons when I became President. My family's depicted as hillbillies with straw sticking out of our ears, our eyes crossed, saying *sho'nuf.* I didn't dwell on it, but it represents a bias that still exists in this country, an underestimation of Southerners. I don't feel I have any need for redemption. I don't feel I failed as President. They write about me like I'm a different person now. As a matter of fact, I haven't changed.

Interview/
Life, November:106.

John H. Chafee
United States Senator,
R-Rhode Island

2

[On Senators who think about running for the Presidency]: They see the President, and as in most things, they say to themselves, "Hey, I can do that job, and do it better." It's only crossed the minds of maybe 98 [out of 100] Senators.

The New York Times, 2-18:1.

Bill Clinton
President
of the United States

3

This idea that there's some battle for my [political] soul is the biggest bunch of hooey I ever saw. I know who I am. I know what I believe.

Interview/
The New York Times,
1-2:7.

4

[On his dealings with the new Republican-controlled Congress]: My job is not to stand in the way and be an obstructionist force. My job is to work with [Republicans] to try to help build this country . . . I do not want to see a series of partisan battles . . . I think the people are sick, literally sick, of seeing all this partisan infighting up here. I just showed up here two years ago, and I was bewildered by it . . . And I was revolted by it. And I think the American people are, too.

Washington, D.C.,
Jan. 5/
USA Today, 1-6:(A)4.

5

[On his relations with the incoming Republican-controlled Congress]: There will be divisions; there will be differences; there will be fights. There ought to be . . . I can assure you there will be.

Newsweek,
1-9:17.

6

[On polls that indicate the public to be uncertain of his willingness to stand on his convictions]: [It's] a problem of perception

(BILL CLINTON)

rather than reality . . . It's clear that, A, I'll take on unpopular things; B, I'll make enemies; and C, I'll fight until I win.

Broadcast interview/
USA Today,
1-27:(A)11.

1

[Saying he has been like a dentist because of his politically unpopular actions]: I had a drill to the tooth of America for the last two years.

U.S. News & World Report,
2-13:30.

2

I don't think it's . . . so good for the country to have people [politically] polarized. I think it's okay for people to feel passionately about their political positions, and it's okay for them to say they think they have to do it because they think it's the right thing to do. But I believe that Lincoln was right, and we should have malice toward none and charity for all.

Broadcast interview/
"This Morning," CBS-TV, 2-20.

3

[On suggestions that, now that both houses of Congress are Republican-controlled, his Presidency has lost most of its clout]: I don't consider myself a titular head of state, and until there is some evidence to the contrary, you shouldn't either.

News conference,
Ottawa, Canada, Feb. 24/
The New York Times,
2-25:1.

4

I love the euphemisms we all use around Washington. Now that the Republicans are in power [in Congress], they use the same sort of tortured language we Democrats used to . . . They say, "We're not slashing the budget, we're making 'recisions.'" The problem is that the Republicans are making cruel, painful cuts. I think we should call those "circum-recisions."

At Gridiron Club dinner,
Washington, D.C., March 25/
The Washington Post,
3-27:(D)5.

5

[Kiddingly suggesting how to improve his image among the male population]: We want to combine the Bureau of Alcohol, Tobacco and Firearms with both the Bureau of Fisheries and the Interstate Trucking Commission. We're going to call it the Department of Guys.

U.S. News & World Report,
3-27:20.

6

The old labels of liberal and conservative, spender and cutter, even Democrat and Republican, are not what matter most anymore. What matters most is finding practical, pragmatic solutions based on what we know works in our lives and our shared experiences so that we can go forward together as a nation. Ideological purity is for partisan extremists. Practical solution[s] based on real experience, hard evidence and common sense—that's what this country needs.

Before American Society
of Newspaper Editors,
Dallas, Texas, April 7/
The New York Times, 4-8:9.

(BILL CLINTON)

1

[On the criticism of his nomination of Dr. Henry Foster to be U.S. Surgeon General]: Now you know how easy it is to make something big little, something little big, something straight twisted, something good look wrong.

The Christian Science Monitor, 5-3:2.

2

[On the difficulty in getting out a positive image of himself with the public]: One of the most frustrating things about being President is, with 260 million people in this country and so many intermediaries between you and the White House and the people out where they live, it's hard to know sometimes. I mean, look, half the time when I see the evening news, *I* wouldn't be for me, either.

At Montana State University, May 30/ The New York Times, 6-2:(A)10.

3

If you want us [Democrats and Republicans] to work together, instead of figuring out who's got the best 30-second attack on the other, you need to really hammer [this] home, you need to tell all of us [this]: Be clear about your differences, but don't divide the country.

To the public, at debate with House Speaker Newt Gingrich, Claremont, N.H., June 11/ The Washington Post, 6-12:(A)8.

4

[On "family values" as a political idea]: Families do not eat and breathe and sleep political slogans. Most families couldn't tell you for the life of them whether I'm up or down in the polls this week, and they couldn't care less. They just know whether they're up or down in their real-life struggle this week. And that's what we ought to think about . . . We don't have to have a partisan, divisive fight about family values. And we don't have to argue whether we need improvement in personal conduct or political policies and economic policies. The truth is, we need a whole bunch of both.

Before American Federation of Teachers, Washington, D.C., July 28/ The New York Times, 7-29:9.

Hillary Rodham Clinton
Wife of President of the United States Bill Clinton

5

I am surprised at the way people seem to perceive me. And sometimes I read stories and hear things about me and I go, "Ugh. I wouldn't like her, either." It's so unlike what I think I am or what my friends think I am. So I can only guess that people are getting perceptions about me from things I am saying or doing in ways that don't correspond with things I am trying to get across. I didn't get this whole image-creation thing. I see what it can do but I'm not sure I get it. I have let other people define me.

Interview, Washington, D.C., Jan. 9/ The New York Times, 1-10:(A)1.

William S. Cohen
United States Senator,
R-Maine

1

[On the new crop of Republicans who swept into Congress after last fall's elections]: It's far too early to tell what the impact will be, but the dynamism they've injected into the system is probably their most notable achievement. There's a real sense of mission ... They want to change the status quo, break out of the mold.

The Washington Post,
7-10:(A)6.

John Conyers, Jr.
United States Representative,
D-Michigan

2

[Criticizing the new Republican majority in Congress]: We're [Democrats] furious that programs going as far back as the New Deal are being overturned with the briefest of scrutiny.

USA Today,
3-31:(A)8.

Charles Cook
Political analyst

3

My theory is that an incumbent [President] will always be fully funded [for his re-election campaign]. The question is how much work and how much time does it take to get there. Having a President who has stepped on a lot of toes of party constituencies is likely to make it harder.

Los Angeles Times,
6-22:(A)16.

Mary Crawford
Spokesman,
Republican
National Committee

4

[On the increase in small-donor financial support for the Republican Party]: Giving a financial contribution is kind of the ultimate expression of support. It's the ultimate participation in building the Party. That's not "access" money. That's "belief" money.

The New York Times,
4-29:6.

Randy (Duke) Cunningham
United States Representative,
R-California

5

[Saying House Republicans are overworked trying to pass legislation and live up to their Contract With America in the first 100 days of the new Congress]: I've had three hearings today. I've got constituents waiting for me. I've got calls like yours and votes on the floor. I'm not getting to sleep until 2 a.m. It's crazy.

Interview,
Washington, D.C./
The New York Times,
3-9:(A)9.

Alfonse M. D'Amato
United States Senator,
R-New York

6

[On criticism of the $225,000 publishing deal for his new autobiography]: What are we talking about? I didn't know that because people are in office they don't have a right to

(ALFONSE M. D'AMATO)

be heard, to publish. I mean, that is ridiculous. I worked for two years to put this book out. Two years! And if people like it, they'll buy it. If they don't like it, they won't buy it.

Interview, Washington, D.C./ Los Angeles Times, 8-17:(E)1.

Thomas A. Daschle
United States Senator, D-South Dakota

1

[Saying the Republicans are well ahead of the Democrats in the use of electronic communications to reach the public]: They really are years ahead. I wouldn't want anybody to think that in a matter of months or one session of Congress we can catch up . . . It might cost [the Democrats] $50-million between now and the end of the decade to get [their own electronic-communications system] up and running. We've come to the realization that if we don't do it, we're never going to be able to compete. It's inevitable, or equally inevitable that we won't win.

The Washington Post, 4-24:(A)4.

Richard Davis
President, Washington (State) Research Council

2

Politicians are great at stealing good ideas. It's one of the things they do best.

The Christian Science Monitor, 2-1:4.

Christopher J. Dodd
United States Senator, D-Connecticut; Chairman, Democratic National Committee

3

[On last fall's elections, in which the Republicans took control of both houses of Congress]: A lot of Democrats want to deny what people were saying last fall, but I don't. [The message of the voters was:] "Democrats don't have their priorities straight. They used to be the Party that talked about jobs, financial security, personal security. They were more likely to be on my side. But I don't feel that any longer."

U.S. News & World Report, 11-6:35.

Robert J. Dole
United States Senator, R-Kansas; Candidate for the 1996 Republican Presidential nomination

4

[On whether, if he becomes the 1996 Republican Presidential nominee, he would reject an abortion-rights supporter as his Vice-Presidential running mate]: [That's] like saying you are not going to have anybody who is left-handed or right-handed.

U.S. News & World Report, 2-27:29.

5

[On how to find new conservative Congressman Sonny Bono's office]: He's in the right wing of the Capitol. But to get there you gotta take a right, then you take another far

(ROBERT J. DOLE)

right, and then you go to the extreme right, and he should be right there.

Newsweek, 3-6:23.

1

[Saying leading Senators have a special role to play in supporting legislation the majority of their party is backing]: I think everybody [agrees] that you can't have a litmus test with every vote. But you do have a responsibility. If you're going to be a leader, you pay a price.

Washington, D.C.,
March 8/
The New York Times,
3-9:(A)9.

2

[On why he is suited to be President]: I think I fit the job description. People want someone who's been tested. I'm still close to people in my home state, my hometown. They hope I haven't lost my compass around here. Conservative. Right-wing conservative. But hopefully, sensitive to the needs of some people who are never going to make it.

Interview,
Washington, D.C./
Esquire, April:67.

3

[On suggestions that, at 72, he may be too old to run against the much-younger Bill Clinton in next year's Presidential election]: My cholesterol's lower than Clinton's, my blood pressure's lower than Clinton's, my weight is less than Clinton's. I am not going to make health an issue.

Newsweek, 8-14:19.

4

[Humorously commenting on the possibility of former Joint Chiefs of Staff Chairman Colin Powell running for the 1996 Republican Presidential nomination]: If he gets in [the race], we'll go out to Iowa and talk target prices, hog prices, corn prices—a lot of the things he talked about at the Pentagon.

U.S. News & World Report,
11-13:38.

Robert K. Dornan
United States Representative,
R-California;
Candidate for
the 1996 Republican
Presidential nomination

5

[On his acerbic style of politics]: On the floor of the House, in the well, yes, I've been tough—tough as Patrick Henry yelling, "Give me liberty or give me death." I apologize for nothing where I was indignant over my years in the House. But I will tell you that if someone is not publicly indignant about the bankrupt policies of this, the richest country ever, destroying the American dream economically, and if somebody is not publicly indignant and saying, "Stop this," with our cultural meltdown and moral decline, then I'll show you somebody who doesn't understand the facts. I'll show you somebody who's a bystander watching the destruction of their country.

Announcing
his candidacy for
the Presidential nomination,
Washington, D.C.,
April 13/
The New York Times,
4-4:(A)7.

Stephen Entin
Tax specialist,
Institute for the Research
of the Economics
of Taxation

1

[On the Republican Party's Contract With America]: The Contract is not as carefully drawn as it should have been. It's not as coherent as the agenda we had during the early [then-President Ronald] Reagan years. Frankly, the Contract is kind of a grab bag.

Los Angeles Times,
4-5:(A)16.

J. James Exon
United States Senator,
D-Nebraska

2

[Saying he will not run for re-election]: The ever-increasing vicious polarization of the electorate . . . the us-against-them mentality, has all but swept aside the former preponderance of reasonable discussions of the pros and cons of the many legitimate issues. [If not for that,] the old fire horse within me wanted to answer the bell for another race.

At meeting with
friends and family,
Lincoln, Neb.,
March 17/
Los Angeles Times,
3-18:(A)27.

Louis Farrakhan
Spiritual leader,
Nation of Islam
in the United States

3

We are advocating no more party loyalty. We intend to create a Third Force or a Third Power out of Republicans, Democrats and independents. We're not going to vote for anybody because he talks like Kennedy—no, no, no, no! That's all over with.

Interview,
Chicago, Ill./
Newsweek,
10-30:36.

Richard Fenno
Political scientist,
University of Rochester

4

[On the fall of Senator Bob Packwood, resulting from revelations concerning his sexual harassment of women and questionable financial dealings]: I don't regard sexual harassment as one of the great problems of the American political system. I do regard the relationship between members [of Congress] and people with money as one of the greatest problems.

U.S. News & World Report,
9-18:49.

Kellyanne Fitzpatrick
Public-opinion analyst,
Luntz Associates

5

In a political environment where moral, religious and family issues have moved to the center, this [new Republican-controlled] Congress cannot ignore such issues. America looks first at its pocketbook. But there are other heartstring issues out there. Don't be surprised if you have a [Republican] Contract With America Part II.

The Christian Science Monitor,
1-4:1.

Marlin Fitzwater
Former Press Secretary
to former Presidents
of the United States
Ronald Reagan
and George Bush

1

It sounds like [President Clinton is] returning to the campaign mode that was successful for him in the past. It is what he does best—the town meeting, the moving around the country, the talking with groups informally. A lot of people would say he's never done as well since he was inaugurated as he did in the campaign [for President in 1992].

Interview/
The New York Times,
1-5:(A)13.

Steven Forbes
President and
editor-in-chief,
"Forbes" magazine

2

My grandfather used to say that you can learn more about the prospects of a company by looking at the headknocker—what we'd call the CEO—than at the balance sheet. The same holds true in public life.

Interview/
The Washington Post,
8-7:(A)9.

Don Fowler
Chairman,
Democratic National Committee

3

[On the large number of members of Congress and state legislatures switching from the Democratic to the Republican Party]: Generally, they are doing it for reasons that relate to their own ambition . . . If you're that cavalier about what you believe, in terms of issues, you don't do the party any good by staying . . . I'm not suggesting that all is sweetness and light with us Democrats. We have a lot of work to do, but we're doing it, and it's paying dividends by the turnaround in the polls. We've started paying better attention to our politics.

The New York Times,
10-7:8.

Barney Frank
United States Representative,
D-Massachusetts

4

[New Republican House Speaker Newt] Gingrich is a clever man, and energetic, but you do not identify him with any legislative positions. That's why he says so many wrong things. He doesn't know a lot of about substance. He half-reads some future-oriented books, and out of that comes a gabble that's not terribly coherent. In all of his past years in Congress, he was not identified with abortion, or foreign policy, or defense policy. He's a mechanic of power. He's very good at it. He understands that the way to get power is to delegitimize the opposition. He made his reputation in part by helping other Republicans learn how to be vituperative. He's always said these things that were wildly irresponsible and often quite abusive of people, and he had the luxury of irrelevance, which is a great advantage. We didn't take him seriously enough.

Interview,
Washington, D.C./
Mother Jones,
May-June:72.

(BARNEY FRANK)

1

The Republican Party in the House now is the first ideologically disciplined national political party we've had. The reason we haven't had discipline in American politics is you couldn't defeat people. The open-primary system undercuts party discipline because no matter how mad people get at you here in Washington, if you can go home and win the primary, then to hell with them. There's very little they can do to punish you. The last person the Democrats punished, in fact, was on the Budget Committee. He was misbehaving, so we kicked him off the Committee . . . But now Republicans have overcome this problem: [New Republican House Speaker] Newt Gingrich and his allies have established nomination control. The [conservative commentators] Rush Limbaugh, Pat Robertson, etc., influence is very strong, so that those who don't agree with Gingrich and the [Republican] Contract With America are afraid that if they break with them, they'll lose the primary. That's what gives Gingrich discipline: fear. We don't have any similar kind of fear on the Democratic side.

Interview,
Washington, D.C./
Mother Jones, May-June:70.

2

[On the recent Congressional hearings on the Whitewater scandal, which allegedly may involve President Clinton and his wife]: I think the general impression the public got is the Clintons were sloppy as citizens with their private finances, but that all of this is greatly overblown.

The Washington Post, 8-14:(A)6.

Al From
President,
Democratic Leadership Council

3

[On President Clinton]: The problem for us *and* him is that Clinton promised to be different. He's been that a bit, but the whole is less than the sum of the parts. The fundamental change he pledged hasn't come. We've been consistent in articulating the ideas he won on, but he hasn't been consistent in advancing them. We were at this before Clinton, and we'll be at it after he's gone—because a long-term majority will never be created around the interests represented by [civil-rights leader] Jesse [Jackson] and the labor unions. Most people are politically homeless now. They're our target. We'll work to get Clinton to pursue us, but we're damn sure going to make it hard for him to catch us.

Time, 7-10:31.

4

[On the increasing liberal bent of the Democratic Party]: At the very time when most of the country is interested in sensible, centrist candidates, in the Democratic Party the center is falling out. The President [Clinton] in many ways will run alone as he runs to the center.

Oct. 9/
Los Angeles Times,
10-10:(A)14.

5

If anybody believes Republican mistakes are going to be the basis of a new Democratic majority, we are kidding ourselves . . . [The electorate] may think the Republicans are moving too hard and too fast, but they don't

(AL FROM)

want to go back to the old Democratic status quo.

At Democratic Leadership Council meeting, Washington, D.C., Nov. 13/ Los Angeles Times, 11-14:(A)21.

John Kenneth Galbraith
Economist

1

[Urging President Clinton to become an activist like the late President Franklin Roosevelt]: F.D.R. enjoyed his enemies.

U.S. News & World Report, 4-24:24.

Curtis B. Gans
Director, Committee for the Study of the American Electorate

2

In every year since 1964, the Republican vote for House seats [in the South] has been going up and the Democratic vote has been going down. That trend climaxed in the last [1994] election, and it essentially took the perception of an unpopular and failed President [Clinton] for it to happen.

Los Angeles Times, 6-19:(A)10.

John W. Gardner
Founder, Common Cause; Former Secretary of Health, Education and Welfare of the United States

3

[Criticizing the current system of private contributions to candidates' election campaigns]: [The system is] a cancer eating at the vitals of government. Americans have always believed in the consent of the governed. It now looks as though we're talking about consent of the donors.

At Presidential news briefing, Washington, D.C., Aug. 4/ The New York Times, 8-5:9.

Richard A. Gephardt
United States Representative, D-Missouri

4

[Criticizing Republicans on the 50th day of their planned 100-day time-frame to get the provisions of their Contract With America voted on]: The fact is, the Contract With America does absolutely nothing to address the problems most Americans face in their daily lives—good jobs, affordable health care, access to quality education, and a rising standard of living. Halfway to nowhere is still nowhere.

Feb. 22/ The New York Times, 2-23:(A)10.

Newt Gingrich
United States Representative, R-Georgia; Speaker of the House

5

[On the reaction of Democrats to the Republicans taking control of the new Congress]: I've heard rumors that imply that [the Democrats are now] just into sort of a fairly stupid strategy of cheap and nasty. To have the Party which has run this House like a machine, which was defeated [by the Repub-

(NEWT GINGRICH)

licans in last year's Congressional elections] after 40 years, which has been repudiated, to have the same gang [of Democrats] in charge come back now—and I saw one of them, I understand he was on TV this morning—saying, oh, we're [Republicans] not being fair, we're not for real reform! It does at times make one wonder just how dumb they think the American people are.

News conference,
Washington, D.C., Jan. 4/
The New York Times,
1-5:(A)10.

1

[On Democratic Party critics of the Republicans, who now control both houses of Congress]: If we just methodically keep moving forward, they [the Democrats] can scream as the parade goes by . . . I am a genuine revolutionary. They are the genuine reactionaries. We [Republicans] are going to change their world. They will do anything to stop us. They will use any tool. There is no grotesquerie, no distortion, no dishonesty too great for them to come after us.

Before Republican
National Committee,
Washington, D.C., Jan. 20/
The New York Times,
1-21:1,8.

2

[On Democratic Party criticism of his being offered a $4.5-million advance by the publisher of his forthcoming book]: I want to remind all of you I turned down [the] $4.5-million. And I'll be glad to debate any Democrat who has turned down $4.5-million about ethics. This is the amount of the advance: $1 . . . I'm going to write a book. I don't know if it's going to be a good book or a bad book . . . If people want to buy it, [his wife] Marianne and I will probably do pretty well. If people don't want to buy it, we probably won't do very well. This is a system called free enterprise. The socialists in the Democratic Party don't quite get it.

Before Republican
National Committee,
Washington, D.C., Jan. 20/
The New York Times,
1-20:8.

3

[Saying he will not run for President next year]: People who want to get involved in the Presidential race ought to get involved. People who want to help us in Congress pass the [Republicans'] Contract With America and work on renewing American civilization and replacing the welfare state will have to focus on that. We'll work on that for the next year and a half, and we'll let the other folks go out and run for President.

To reporters,
Marietta, Ga., Feb. 13/
The New York Times,
2-14:(A)8.

4

[Responding to Congressman David Bonior's criticism that Gingrich violated House rules last year by stating in a House speech the phone number for ordering cassettes of a college course he teaches]: [The Democrats] have these daily strategy meetings to see how they can smear me and apparently this was the latest gimmick. [And the press helps to] fan a piece of nonsense into a

(NEWT GINGRICH)

serious story. [The Constitution protects a House member's right] to say virtually anything on the House floor . . . I didn't "sell" [the cassettes by giving the phone number]. I just told members how they could get a copy if they wanted them.

News conference, Washington, D.C., March 8/ Los Angeles Times, 3-9:(A)14.

1

[On the Republican Party's Contract With America]: While we've done a lot, this Contract has never been about curing all the ills of the nation. One hundred days [of Republican control of Congress] cannot overturn the neglect of decades.

Broadcast address to the nation, April 7/ Nation's Business, May:18.

2

A third-party candidate [in next year's Presidential election] is a total disaster [for the Republican nominee] and is the only way [President] Bill Clinton will get re-elected.

The New York Times, 6-6:(A)13.

3

[Saying he does not plan to run for President next year]: There were an awful lot of people [during his current trip to New Hampshire] saying, "Don't run"—not because they were opposed to what we were doing [in changing government] but because they are so much in favor of what we're doing. They think it's very helpful to shift power out of the White House back to the Congress . . . I don't have any great need to be President. I have a great need to help set the tone of the national dialogue. [My] interest is in leading the country, as opposed to holding a particular office . . . You could be a leader in your country without necessarily sitting in the White House being surrounded by Secret Service.

News conference, Manchester, N.H., June 12/ The New York Times, 6-13:(A)11.

4

[On the Clinton Administration]: We have the least competent, least adult, least structured and least disciplined and least reasonable Administration, I think, probably in our country's history. [But] if the 1996 [Presidential] election is about personality, there is a fair chance that Bill Clinton will get re-elected. I do not know in our lifetime of any political figure with a greater capacity to make you feel good for 30 seconds.

At Republican Party summer meeting, Philadelphia, Pa., July 14/ The New York Times, 7-15:8.

5

[On the Whitewater scandal, which might involve President Clinton]: There is substantial ground to wonder how this case has been handled from opening minutes of its discovery, and it verges on the bizarre.

Interview, Washington, D.C., July 25/ The Christian Science Monitor, 7-26:4.

(NEWT GINGRICH)

1

If I have one disappointment this summer, it has been the sort of unending left-wing rhetoric and sort of negative partisanship [from Congressional Democrats]. We've seen a sort of [Democratic Congressman David] Bonior-dominated, left-wing faction in the House that has been, I mean, unendingly uncooperative. I'm a partisan and I like partisan debates. But this hasn't been a debate because they've had no ideas to debate, and it's been just remarkably lacking in any kind of cooperation.

News conference,
Washington, D.C., Aug. 4/
The New York Times,
8-5:8.

2

[On demonstrators who try to disrupt his public speeches]: One of the major impediments to reform in America is the capacity of very small groups to get together and chant mindlessly in the hope they will be able to block something from happening.

To reporters,
Atlanta, Ga., Aug. 7/
The New York Times,
8-8:(A)8.

3

[On the difficulty the new Republican-controlled Congress is having in getting its legislation through as quickly as it would like]: If we're only an aberration, then this is a crisis. But if we're the beginning of a long period of center-right power, then you take 80 percent this year, and you come back again in January. You come back in '97, you come back in '98, and every year, inexorably, you get a little more.

Interview/
The Christian Science Monitor,
9-20:1.

4

[Criticizing the Democrats for their campaign against Republican plans to reform Medicare]: Think about a Party whose last stand is to frighten 85-year-olds, and you'll understand how totally morally bankrupt the modern Democratic Party is.

U.S. News & World Report,
9-25:36.

5

One of the great myths of modern politics is that [election] campaigns are too expensive. The political process, in fact, is under-funded. It is not over-funded.

At House hearing
on campaign-finance reform,
Washington, D.C., Nov. 2/
Los Angeles Times,
11-3:(A)25.

6

If you're a conservative [in an election campaign], you spend more money undoing the damage done [to you] by [the] media then you spend defeating your opponent.

Before Association
of Opinion Page Editors,
Atlanta, Ga., Nov. 3/
Los Angeles Times,
11-4:(A)27.

7

[On whether Republican Senator and Presidential hopeful Robert Dole is up to be-

(NEWT GINGRICH)

ing the leader of the "Republican revolution"]: I think he's effective at it. Whether he's comfortable, you'd have to ask him; but he's certainly effective . . . There seems to be a relaxed, comfortable effectiveness, which is very real. Now, whether or not, inside himself, that fits his zeitgeist, I haven't a clue.

Interview/
Time, 11-13:79.

Lindsey Graham
United States Representative,
R-South Carolina

1

[On Labor Secretary Robert Reich, whose Democratic Party claims the loyalty of the average working American]: [During Congressional testimony, Reich] used the words "working stiff" 21 times. I wrote it down every time he said it. Well, the working stiff, the little guy, elected *me* [a Republican conservative in an area where the average income is below $14,000]. The picked *me*!

The Washington Post,
7-24:(A)9.

Phil Gramm
United States Senator,
R-Texas;
Candidate for the 1996
Republican Presidential nomination

2

There are only two issues when running against an incumbent: [his] record, and I'm not a kook. Forget the feel-good stuff. Say, "This is *[his]* record; this is what *I'm* for." If a subject can't get you elected, don't talk about it.

The Atlantic Monthly, March:82.

3

[Saying it will cost more than $44-million to run for the Presidency in 1996]: That's a lot of money to raise when somebody can give you only a thousand dollars. I think management and organization are things that are greatly undervalued in politics. The question is, who can put together this forty-four-million-dollar corporate entity? Who can set up a structure to manage it? No one running for office has ever had to do what you're going to have to do in this election to win the nomination, and that is you're going to have to raise all this money early, you're going to have to run in 15 or 20 states at the same time, without being the Party nominee, without having every political operative in the Party working for you—which they will after you get the nomination.

The Atlantic Monthly,
March:94.

4

There's an effort to knock me out [of the race for President next year] because I'm the real conservative in this race. See, people are for me and against me for exactly the same reasons. They know what I stand for. I'm not gonna reinvent myself to run for President—I don't have to do a 180 on [racial] quotas like [fellow Republican Senator who is running for the nomination] Bob Dole, or change my views every couple of months like the President [Clinton]. I am who I am.

Interview,
Oklahoma City, Okla./
Newsweek, 6-19:41.

5

[On political commentator Pat Buchanan, who is also a candidate for the Republican

(PHIL GRAMM)

Presidential nomination]: The idea that Pat Buchanan wants to engage me on economic issues is laughable. I never duel with unarmed men.

U.S. News & World Report,
7-24:22.

John Green
Director,
Ray C. Bliss Institute
of Applied Politics,
University of Akron

1

[On religion and political activism]: We're going to hear the criticism more and more as we go into [the] '96 [Presidential elections], because the real political groups among evangelicals have only had their appetites whetted. And they're going to be big players in '96, win, lose or draw.

The Washington Post,
3-27:(A)10.

Tom Harkin
United States Senator,
D-Iowa

2

[President Clinton] has to use the bully pulpit of the Presidency . . . to draw a contrast and to accurately portray what [new Republican House Speaker] Newt Gingrich's agenda really is. Gingrich's agenda is to destroy the underpinnings of any compassion or caring [about people].

USA Today,
1-6:(A)4.

Peter Hart
Democratic Party
public-opinion analyst

3

Voting for a legislator, we say, "I've got problems with him on this or that issue." But voting for a President, we say, "What kind of a leader will this person be? Do I trust this person? Does he have the toughness to govern?"

Time,
7-10:26.

Michael Huffington
Former United States
Representative, R-California

4

[Saying the Democratic Party committed fraud in last year's election in which he was defeated for the U.S. Senate by Democratic Senator Dianne Feinstein]: If an election is worth winning, it's worth stealing. We have people who registered after they died and then voted . . . I am not at all surprised to find more Democrats who are dead and voting. I have no idea if [Feinstein] knew [about the alleged fraud], but I know a dead person can't vote without somebody actively getting their ballot.

Washington, D.C.,
Jan. 4/
Los Angeles Times,
1-5:(A)3,10.

5

[On the possibility that former Joint Chiefs of Staff Chairman Colin Powell will run for the 1996 Republican Presidential nomination]: He has character, he's clean, he's a leader and he wouldn't be caught up in the issue du jour. Republicans aren't excited about

(MICHAEL HUFFINGTON)

[Senator and Presidential hopeful] Phil Gramm. But Powell is exciting.

Interview,
Palm Desert, Calif./
Los Angeles Times,
10-9:(A)3.

Henry J. Hyde
United States Representative,
R-Illinois

1

[Blaming Democrats for what he says is too much bickering in the House]: I've never seen generalized incivility like this. They start every day off with personal attacks, and then it goes downhill.

USA Today,
3-31:(A)8.

Harold M. Ickes
Deputy Chief of Staff
to President
of the United States
Bill Clinton

2

That's one of the problems with so-called liberal Democrats: They are continually looking for perfection. There is no perfection.

Newsweek,
6-19:39.

Gary Jacobson
Professor of political science,
University of California,
San Diego

3

[On California Governor, and candidate for the 1996 Republican Presidential nomination, Pete Wilson]: He knows better than most politicians how to aggressively ride a hot issue. And so, more than most, he tends to get into these timeless tugs between good governing and getting elected. What can get you elected often has little to do with good governing. But he's also shown that he'll do the responsible thing, too, even if it can hurt him, like raising taxes because the state has to have the money.

The New York Times,
8-8:(A)6.

4

You get third parties when there's a lot of discontent out there and neither of the two major parties can pose as the vehicle for taking care of that discontent. From time to time, [third parties] get on the ballot. But they rarely go anywhere.

Los Angeles Times,
10-27:(A)1.

Charles O. Jones
Presidential scholar,
University of Wisconsin

5

[On whether President Clinton's handling so far of the recent bombing of an Oklahoma City Federal building will help him politically]: Clinton's handling of this meets the public expectation of what Presidents ought to do. In my judgment, he has gone out of his way the past two years to look un-Presidential. This [current crisis] has emphasized his Presidential-ness rather than that image as boy-President. [But in the long run,] it meets expectations, and so I don't think [it] will make that great a difference [to him politically].

The Washington Post,
4-24:(A)10.

Elaine Kamarck
Former fellow,
Progressive Policy Institute

1

The DLC worries about dying off if [President Clinton is] defeated [for re-election next year]. The battle for the [Democratic] Party's soul will continue even if he wins. But if he loses, the liberals will claim that the DLC's centrist views were responsible and should be tossed aside entirely. The counter-argument will be that just because the messenger proved imperfect, doesn't mean the message itself should be junked.

Time, 7-10:31.

Nancy Landon Kassebaum
United States Senator,
R-Kansas

2

Politics has never been a revered profession in America. We all like to joke about or sneer at Congress, and all too often there is a good cause for that. But politics is nothing more or less than the working out of our competing interests and priorities as a nation. Politics is, in fact, the lifeblood of democracy, not a spectator sport.

News conference announcing her decision not to seek re-election next year, Topeka, Kansas, Nov. 20/ Los Angeles Times, 11-21:(A)18.

David Keene
President,
American Conservative Union

3

[On the possibility that former Joint Chiefs of Staff Chairman Colin Powell will run for the Presidency next year]: One of the reasons people talk about him is that they can look at him and see him as a President. That's a very important quality, and he's got it, no question about it. It's one of those necessary-but-not-sufficient things that go into the mix.

Vanity Fair, October:230.

Jack F. Kemp
Former Secretary of Housing and Urban Development of the United States ;
Former United States Representative, R-New York

4

[Saying he has decided not to run for President in 1996, mostly because he dislikes the process of fund-raising]: My passion for ideas is not matched with a passion for partisan or electoral politics . . . There are a lot of grotesqueries in politics, not the least of which is the fund-raising side. You end up talking more about why you should vote for somebody or support somebody and less about what he or she should be supporting, what their ideas are. [At fund-raising events,] I don't seem to be talking about the things that the fund-raising people want me to talk about.

To reporters, Washington, D.C., Jan. 30/ The New York Times, 1-31:(A)6.

Edward M. Kennedy
United States Senator,
D-Massachusetts

5

If [we] Democrats run for [political] cover, if [after last year's sweeping Republi-

(EDWARD M. KENNEDY)

can election victories in the House and Senate] we become pale carbon copies of the opposition and try to act like Republicans, we will lose—and deserve to lose. Democrats must be more than warmed-over Republicans . . . My fundamental recommendation to the President [Clinton] is that he stay the course of change and do what he thinks is right. My advice to my fellow Democrats is that we work with the President for change—instead of seeking to change our principles, or distance ourselves from him.

At National Press Club, Washington, D.C., Jan. 11/ Los Angeles Times, 1-12:(A)15.

Bob Kerrey
United States Senator, D-Nebraska

1

We [Democrats] may not be qualified to recapture the majority [in Congress] until we've given Americans a clear sense of our purpose and what it is that we intend to do with the power that we would have if we controlled the Congress once more . . . We're going to fight the battles that we believe are important. And if, in winning those battles, we win the majority, so much the better.

At National Press Club, Washington, D.C., April 27/ USA Today, 4-28:(A)8.

Alan Keyes
Candidate for the 1996 Republican Presidential nomination; Former Assistant Secretary for International Organization Affairs, Department of State of the United States

2

In politics, the heart eventually wins. [Some of the other Republican Presidential candidates] don't realize that the Party's present and future are now being decided at the grass roots and not in their councils of power in Washington.

Interview, Raleigh, N.C., Sept. 14/ USA Today, 9-15:(A)7.

Andrew Kohut
Director, Times Mirror Center for the People and the Press

3

[On the possibility that former Joint Chiefs of Staff Chairman Colin Powell will run for the Presidency next year]: At a time when distrust of politicians is at a record high, he is an example of personal integrity and trust. The downside is that people don't know a damned thing about what he stands for.

Vanity Fair, October:230.

4

One of the most striking findings [of a new public-opinion poll conducted by his organization] is the extent to which President Clinton escapes blame for the public's dissatisfaction [with the way the country is head-

(ANDREW KOHUT)

ing]. Only 7 percent blame him for what's wrong. He looks better today because he's not one of those Republicans [who now control] Congress.

Nov. 13/
Los Angeles Times,
11-14:(A)20.

William Kristol
Chairman, Project for the Republican Future

1

[On Senator and Presidential candidate Robert Dole]: If I were writing the Dole script [for running for the 1996 Republican Presidential nomination], it would be, "In a revolutionary age, you need an old pro to make it work." He's got to be the old pro who signed onto a new agenda. [What he should not be] is Bob Dole, legislative tactician and compromiser who's bogged down in the messy process in Washington, vs. Phil Gramm [another Senator running for the Republican Presidential nomination], new leader of the [former President Ronald] Reagan coalition.

The New York Times,
2-18:8.

2

The interesting thing about the 1994 election [in which the Republicans were victorious in taking over control of Congress] is that by conventional analysis, it shouldn't have happened. It was an old-fashioned party election. It looked like elections from the 1890s, for god's sake. Maybe it's an aberration; maybe it can't last. Maybe a year from now we'll be back into chaos and into Perot squared. But maybe it really was a decisive moment, and successful governance by the Republican majority will move us toward a generational realignment. At this point, I think those are basically the two alternatives: Republican success or political chaos.

Panel discussion,
Washington, D.C./
Harper's,
March:53.

3

[President Clinton] totally lacks credibility with the American people . . . With a new candidate [in the 1996 Presidential election], the Democrats could get 43 percent of the vote again. And if it's a three- or four-way race in 1996, that could lead to a Democratic victory. I don't think any of us discounts that possibility. In fact, I think Clinton has made a mistake by conceding so many of our [Republicans'] premises. I mean, all be's doing now is cutting taxes and cutting spending. He's been harsher on public-housing programs than any conservative I can think of, which is a terrible concession for him to have made. He may have created room for some liberal to stand up and say, "Look, liberalism does have an honorable tradition. [Franklin] Roosevelt helped people. [Lyndon] Johnson helped people. We're for civil rights. The Republicans are rich and mean-spirited. I'm going to defend these Federal programs." Within the Democratic primary process, that would be a very attractive message from a fresh liberal face. I think it's a message that would defeat Bill Clinton in [the] 1996 [Democratic primary].

Panel discussion,
Washington, D.C./
Harper's,
March:51.

(WILLIAM KRISTOL)

1

It's terribly important that [the 1994 sweeping Republican Congressional election victories] be followed by a Republican victory in [the Presidential election in] 1996. You can't really realign our politics or our public policy without the White House. You can make a start with Congress, but you need the White House.

Nation's Business,
May:20.

2

[On the possibility of former Joint Chiefs of Staff Chairman Colin Powell running for the 1996 Republican Presidential nomination]: 1994 was a big breakthrough, a possible watershed for conservatives [when Republicans took over control of Congress]. But there are lots of moderates and independents out there who voted Republican in 1994, who are well-disposed toward the Republican agenda, but need to be reassured . . . Powell offers that possibility.

Los Angeles Times,
10-26:(A)16.

Bill Lacey
Deputy chairman of
U.S. Senator Robert J. Dole's
campaign for the 1996 Republican
Presidential nomination

3

Generally in politics, when you focus on details you can gain tactical advantage in the short run; but strategic advantage goes to the candidate with the broad-brush ideas.

Los Angeles Times,
11-21:(A)17.

Celinda Lake
Democratic Party
public-opinion analyst

4

Polls now show that Democrats rank behind Republicans on keeping America prosperous. If Democrats are not good for your jobs and pocketbooks, what good is having Democrats?

USA Today,
8-18:(A)5.

Jim Leach
United States Representative,
R-Iowa

5

[On the Whitewater scandal, which allegedly may involve President Clinton and his wife, and the recent House Whitewater hearings, which he chaired]: It's my view that the issues of illegality [in Whitewater] are the proper province of the Independent Counsel. Issues of public ethics, however, and implications for public policy are the proper province of Congress. [In the hearings,] I think we've laid forth a case study of excesses [in Whitewater] in a government circumstance that will be a reminder to many people.

The Washington Post,
8-14:(A)6.

Joseph I. Lieberman
United States Senator,
D-Connecticut

6

While it is true that many Americans worry today that Congressional Republicans are going too far, it is also true that they believe Republicans are at least headed in the right direction and have at least embraced the

(JOSEPH I. LIEBERMAN)

concept of "change," and that too many Democrats simply have not.

At Democratic Leadership Council meeting, Washington, D.C., Nov. 13/ Los Angeles Times, 11-14:(A)21.

1

[On the current budget impasse between President Clinton and Congressional Republicans]: In negotiations, people naturally start out expressing a strong position and expect to compromise later. The danger is that, as you state your position as strongly as you can, it makes it harder to compromise on it. The Administration doesn't want Republicans to feel that the President can be rolled. But I worry a little bit that both sides might have gone too far.

Los Angeles Times, 11-16:(A)23.

Rush Limbaugh
Radio and television talk-show host

2

[On criticism that the rhetoric of conservative talk-show hosts such as himself is partly to blame for the recent bombing of an Oklahoma City Federal building]: Make no mistake about it: Liberals intend to use this tragedy for their own political gain. Many in the mainstream media [are guilty] of irresponsible attempts to categorize and demonize those who had nothing to do with this . . . There is absolutely no connection between these nuts [who were involved in the bombing] and mainstream conservatism in America today.

April 24/ The Washington Post, 4-25:(A)1.

Nita M. Lowey
United States Representative, D-New York

3

[Saying the religious right helped elect a Republican-controlled Congress in 1994 and is now expecting to be paid back in favorable legislation]: The religious right's bill has come due. They handed the new majority an agenda and the Republicans are ticking off the items.

The New York Times, 7-22:7.

Theodore Lowi
Professor of government, Cornell University

4

[On industrialist Ross Perot's bid to form a third party]: The times have never been so favorable for a third-party movement . . . [But] Perot's problem is not lack of imagination, it's lack of patience . . . It won't work unless he sees his party as an investment that pays off two, four, six years from now. He shouldn't seek immediate payoff.

USA Today, 9-29:(A)5.

Richard G. Lugar
United States Senator, R-Indiana; Candidate for the 1996 Republican Presidential nomination

5

[Saying he will run for the 1996 Republi-

(RICHARD G. LUGAR)

can Presidential nomination even though he may not be able to raise as much campaign money as his opponents]: I've rejected the idea that there should be an entry fee of [$20-million to $25-million] to even be considered for President of the United States. I think the public will find that obnoxious and will reject what amounts to really a competition for raising money.

March 3/ Los Angeles Times, 3-4:(A)12.

1

[In election campaigns,] there's often a rivalry to appear to be the sternest, most mean-spirited candidate in the field—really pounding down into the pavement almost everyone who doesn't seem to fit. Once again, that's a loser.

At Republican Party summer meeting, Philadelphia, Pa., July 14/ The New York Times, 7-15:8.

Brian Lunde
Democratic Party consultant

2

[President Clinton's] political history is that he never takes any election for granted and he's willing to do whatever it takes to get re-elected.

USA Today, 6-30:(A)5.

Frank Luntz
Republican Party public-opinion analyst

3

[The Republican Party's Contract With America] is a document that takes us from 1994 to 2004. If we succeed, we may hold the government for a decade or more.

Los Angeles Times, 1-5:(A)15.

4

[For the Republican Party,] the black community is not ripe for picking. The black community's policies and beliefs are actually very closely aligned with the Democratic Party. Blacks are making a rational decision by voting Democratic. If the black community thinks it's better off and the country's better off with a Democratic Administration, then its members should vote that way. The rest of America doesn't think so.

Panel discussion, Washington, D.C./ Harper's, March:50.

Eddie Mahe, Jr.
Republican Party consultant

5

[On President Clinton's chances for re-election next year]: By and large, he tends to be a likable person. That quality can carry some water. He's also protected by a Republican Congress; anything bad he can blame on them. And since you can't pin him down on philosophy, wrestling with him is like wrestling with Jell-O. If you can't get hold of him, you can't throw him out of the ring.

USA Today, 3-7:(A)11.

(EDDIE MAHE, JR.)

1

[On former Joint Chiefs of Staff Chairman Colin Powell, who may run for the 1996 Republican Presidential nomination]: [If he were President and] presented with a new issue, it would seem that his natural reaction is going to be a moderate, midstream, middle-American type of reaction. That's not where the country should be going.

U.S. News & World Report, 11-13:42.

2

We [Republicans] can't win a [public-opinion] fight [with President Clinton] over 24-hour [spending] resolutions. Clinton just goes into the White House press room and beats us every time . . . But once we pass a balanced budget, the burden will be on him . . . Clearly we're deep in a hole [in public opinion] because we're playing with volatile issues like Medicare. But six months from now, we will be able to point out that we promised and we delivered.

Los Angeles Times, 11-16:(A)23.

Thomas E. Mann
Director of governmental studies, Brookings Institution

3

[As a result of the sweeping Republican victory in last fall's Congressional elections,] Democrats are perforce in a defensive mode, the President [Clinton] as well as the Congressional Democrats. I don't think there's a silver bullet that's called "economic populism," or crying about the rules [that the Democrats should try]. Republicans did that for decades, and it didn't work.

The New York Times, 1-5:(A)13.

4

[On Connecticut, Maine, Massachusetts, Rhode Island and Vermont moving their 1996 Presidential primaries to the same earlier date in order to gain more clout]: It makes good sense for a regional group of relatively small states to band together early in the process. But we've got to remember that candidates are confronting an unbelievably compressed [campaign] schedule. It's going to be a heavily media-oriented campaign once it moves past New Hampshire, and one shouldn't overestimate the amount of candidate time you'll get [in that bloc of states].

The New York Times, 6-6:(A)13.

5

[On U.S. Senator Bill Bradley's decision not to seek re-election next year]: He has failed to live up to his promise as a national political star. What Democrats saw in him was the perfect resume: The athlete, the Rhodes scholar, the fine human being. All of it seemed absolutely ideal. They saw him as the Democrats' salvation. It didn't develop. Perhaps he didn't have the fire in the belly.

Aug. 16/ Los Angeles Times, 8-17:(A)27.

Marjorie Margolies-Mezvinsky
Former United States Representative, D-Pennsylvania

6

[On the "year of the woman" election of

(MARJORIE MARGOLIES-MEZVINSKY)

1992]: We knew something was different here when we started to talk about our pollsters the way we used to talk about our gynecologists.

At Forum for
Women State Legislators,
Coronado, Calif./
Los Angeles Times,
11-24:(A)3.

Will Marshall
President,
Progressive Policy Institute

1

The Republicans are foolish if they think the verdict of 1994 [the sweeping Republican victory in that year's Congressional elections] was anything but a provisional one. Bashing the old liberal programs doesn't do it. People want to know what you are going to do for them, not just that you identify with their critique of ultra-liberalism and big government. The [Republicans'] Contract [With America] looks back at the Republican argument with Democratic Party liberalism, not ahead to the Republican vision for governing America in a post-New Deal era.

Nation's Business,
May:20.

Robert T. Matsui
United States Representative,
D-California

2

[On the Republicans gaining control of the House in last year's elections and the effect of that on Democrats]: [House Democrats are] really into control. We always want to be in charge and we have been in charge, and when you lose control you do become very impatient and anxious. I think we really have to have a personality transplant in some respects.

The Washington Post National Weekly,
1-9:15.

Ann McBride
President,
Common Cause

3

[Criticizing so-called "soft money," corporate contributions made to political organizations that are not subject to the legal limits of contributions given to specific candidates]: [Such soft-money contributions are] infecting the political system, influencing legislation and really undermining our system of government. The soft-money system is a rotten system no matter who the money goes to; but what we see is now that the Republicans are in control [in Congress], there's a huge flood into the coffers of the Republicans.

April 5/
The Washington Post,
4-6:(A)19.

Michael D. McCurry
Press Secretary to President
of the United States Bill Clinton

4

[On Democrats who have criticized President Clinton for cooperating with, or not taking a harder stand against, Republicans]: We would say to House Democrats that we understand your anger, we understand your desire to score political points at the expense of the Republicans; but the President lives in a different house.

U.S. News & World Report,
6-26:11.

Jim McDermott
United States Representative,
D-Washington

1

[Saying Democratic members of Congress are finding it hard to cope with being a minority now that Republicans control Congress]: You find people in all of these stages [denial, apathy, anger and resolution]. There are people still denying. They are crafting legislation that they actually think will pass. That's denial. But you can't go through a loss without going through these stages.

The New York Times,
2-23:(A)1.

Cynthia McKinney
United States Representative,
D-Georgia

2

[Criticizing the Supreme Court's ruling that drawing Congressional districts so as to guarantee the election of blacks is un-Constitutional]: I fear the ultimate bleaching of the U.S. Congress.

Newsweek,
7-10:15.

Mark Mellman
Democratic Party
public-opinion analyst

3

People are unwilling to believe the best about a politician or a party, but they're very willing to believe the worst.

U.S. News & World Report,
11-13:41.

Kweisi Mfume
United States Representative,
D-Maryland

4

[On the possibility of former Joint Chiefs of Staff Chairman Colin Powell, a black, running for the 1996 Republican Presidential nomination]: African-Americans should be in every political party and we should be independents. Clearly, if ever there was in infusion of racial balance needed, the Republican Party needs it. Colin Powell in that respect helps the Republican Party with its perception problems.

U.S. News & World Report,
10-16:51.

George Miller
United States Representative,
D-California

5

[Criticizing President Clinton for not backing Democratic Party and liberal stands on various issues]: He thinks we [Congressional Democrats] are like abused children who will come back and ask him to love us again. We won't. We do better in our own districts than he does.

U.S. News & World Report,
6-26:11.

James Moore
Professor of political science,
University of Portland (Ore.)

6

[On Senator Bob Packwood, who is resigning under Senate Ethics Committee fire for his alleged sexual harassment of women]: He was a procedural master, brilliant in many ways. But what did him in with the Senate was the same thing that got him in trouble

(JAMES MOORE)

with the women—he couldn't read human nature. It wasn't that he doesn't "get it" on women's issues. He doesn't "get it" on people.

The New York Times,
9-9:8.

John Morgan
Republican Party consultant

1

[On the large number of members of state legislatures, especially in the South, switching from the Democratic to the Republican Party]: Once these chambers go Republican, the Democrats aren't coming back. The Democrats have been propped up by Congressional and legislative gerrymanders that have been broken at the Congressional level and will be broken at the legislative level once the Republicans get the pen. There aren't any conservative Southern Democrats to speak of anymore.

The New York Times,
10-7:8.

Milton Morris
Vice president, Joint Center for Political and Economic Studies

2

Blacks, like others, have been looking around and express their uneasiness in a variety of ways. There is a very substantial degree of cynicism right now and discomfort with the Democratic Party leadership. The problem for blacks is that when everything is said and done, they do not seem to find viable alternatives. In short, everything else out there is more threatening to their interests.

U.S. News & World Report,
10-16:50.

Mike Murphy
Republican Party political strategist

3

The media hates us [Republicans]. We just won a huge victory [in 1994's Congressional elections], but [new Republican Speaker of the House Newt Gingrich's] numbers are 20 to 28 fave/unfave because he gets smeared every day in the press. Today I saw my third newsweekly cover photo of Gingrich, like, strangling a kid. It's amazing. [Libyan leader Muammar] Qaddafi gets better press. The point is that we can do all this strategic [political] stuff, we can hold great photo ops and all that, and the folks who write the CBS national news are still going to say, "Meet Mrs. X. She's dying tonight because of the Republican [economic] plan. If [we Republicans] lose it and freak and stampede, then we're going to blow the whole thing.

Panel discussion,
Washington, D.C./
Harper's, March:50.

Tom Murphy
Speaker of the House of Representatives of Georgia

4

You can't take the politics out of politics, I don't think.

U.S. News & World Report,
8-28:35.

Grover Norquist
President, Americans for Tax Reform

5

[On the tactics of conservatives, such as himself, fighting liberal causes]: In an analogy with the Soviet Union, you are talking

(GROVER NORQUIST)

about the [former U.S. President Ronald] Reagan doctrine of going to the other team's territory and challenging them for it, fighting in Afghanistan, Nicaragua, Angola. [Today, conservatives are] going after Americorps, legal services and the National Endowment for the Arts, going after the weakest parts of the [liberal] empire . . . [Conservative House Speaker Newt Gingrich's] argument [is] that you go out and fight all the time; you wake up every morning and say, "What can I do to move things forward?" I [want] to play with guys who work like that . . . How do you expect to gain allies [if what you say is]. "I'm standing in the train tracks and the train is going to run me over, but the right and virtuous thing for you to do is stand with me while we lose"? I think you run up 100 yards and blow [up] the train tracks and then see what the train thinks about that.

The Washington Post,
9-4:(A)8.

Sam Nunn
United States Senator,
D-Georgia

1

The ability to raise big money and buy saturation television ads have become the dominant theme of our political races. Too often the tactics of obsessive polling, negative and cynical campaigns, and horse-race media coverage overwhelm substantive debate.

News conference announcing
his retirement from the Senate
next year, Atlanta, Ga., Oct. 9/
The New York Times,
10-10:(A)13.

2

[The voices of common sense in Congress are being] drowned out by the extremes in both parties who are usually wrong but never in doubt.

U.S. News & World Report,
10-23:20.

Bernard Nussbaum
Former Counsel
to President
of the United States
Bill Clinton

3

[On criticism that White House officials restricted access of investigators to the files of White House aide Vincent Foster after he committed suicide in 1993]: Nothing was destroyed. Everything was preserved. [Ultimately,] everything that law-enforcement officials asked for was turned over to them . . . I did not, nor to my knowledge did anyone else in the White House, destroy, mishandle or misappropriate any document in Vincent Foster's office.

Before Senate
Whitewater Committee,
Washington, D.C., Aug. 9/
Los Angeles Times,
8-10:(A)29.

David R. Obey
United States Representative,
D-Wisconsin

4

I think most of us learned some time ago that if you don't like [President Clinton's] position on a particular issue, you simply need to wait a few weeks.

Newsweek,
6-26:15.

Thomas P. O'Neill III
Lieutenant Governor
of Massachusetts (D)

1

[Saying President Clinton's current trip to Europe, during which he talked about peace in such places as Northern Ireland and Bosnia, may help his poll ratings at home]: My father [the late Speaker of the House Thomas P. O'Neill, Jr.] used to say that all politics is local. Now we'll add: All politics must be peacemaking.

Los Angeles Times,
12-4:(A)8.

Norman J. Ornstein
Senior fellow,
American Enterprise Institute

2

Today's populist Republicans are suspicious of anything big, including big business.

U.S. News & World Report,
3-27:43.

Bob Packwood
United States Senator,
R-Oregon

3

[On charges that, over the years, he has sexually harassed women]: In most cases, I cannot remember the person who is complaining, and I cannot remember the incident. I'd like to be of more help to the Ethics Committee, but I just have no memory. I think part of the reason—you can see it in the depositions of the women—is that I was drunk. That is not an excuse for conduct, but it probably may account for loss of memory . . . If you are going to allege a pattern of conduct, what does "pattern" mean? How far back do you go in somebody's life—a quarter of a century?

Time,
8-21:30.

George E. Pataki
Governor
of New York (R)

4

[On why, in his first year as Governor, he has already begun raising funds for his 1998 re-election campaign]: The longer period of time we can do the fund-raising over, the broader the base, the broader the number of people we can reach out to. We're looking to not have a frenzied last six months, but to have an orderly process over the four years.

News conference,
Saratoga Springs, N.Y.,
Aug. 18/
The New York Times,
8-19:11.

William Paxon
United States Representative,
R-New York

5

[On the Republican Party's Contract With America]: The items in the Contract had to be doable, and they had to be things that would have resonance with the American people. That's why school prayer and other items were left out. Teams put the proposed legislation together, but [new House Speaker] Newt [Gingrich] made the decisions.

Mother Jones,
March-April:58.

Ross Perot
Industrialist;
1992 independent
Presidential candidate

1

If an independent party or a third party emerges [in next year's Presidential election], it is because the [Democratic and Republican] candidates didn't face the problems. If candidates continue to run their campaigns based on what people want to hear, then that will intensify our country's problems.

Interview, June 2/
The New York Times,
6-6:(A)13.

Pete Peterson
United States Representative,
D-Florida

2

[On his efforts as a bridge-builder between Republicans and Democrats in Congress]: Unfortunately, the current political climate on Capitol Hill and throughout the nation has rendered this approach ineffective. I have found that it's very difficult to function as a moderate in Congress today.

Announcing
his retirement next year/
U.S. News & World Report,
9-25:30.

James P. Pinkerton
Lecturer, Graduate School
of Political Management,
George Washington University;
Former Deputy Assistant
for Policy Planning to the President
of the United States (George Bush)

3

[On the possibility of a third-party candidate entering the 1996 Presidential race and splitting the Republican vote]: It's a more difficult challenge for the Republicans than simply doing a good job [running Congress]. Because in an era of post-party factionalization, there is not a lot stopping some ambitious egomaniac with a billion dollars from saying, "I don't care if I have any issues or not, I just want to be President." I think we're going to see a whole slew of them: [industrialist] Ross Perot/[Italian Prime Minister] Silvio Berlusconi types, out there running just for the hell of it. This is how all our [Republican] plans for coalitions and cleverness come crashing down.

Panel discussion,
Washington, D.C./
Harper's, March:53.

Nelson Polsby
Political scientist,
University of California, Berkeley

4

[On the possibility of a third party in next year's Presidential elections because of public anger at the Republicans and Democrats]: We've always had public angst. We've never had successful third parties.

USA Today,
9-29:(A)5.

Colin L. Powell
General,
United States Army (Ret.);
Former Chairman,
Joint Chiefs of Staff

5

[On whether he would run as a Republican or a Democrat if he chooses to enter next year's Presidential race]: I don't find yet that I fit neatly into either party. I have very strong

(COLIN L. POWELL)

Republican leanings on economic matters and international-affairs matters. [But] I'm still a New Deal kid [on other matters].

To mutual-fund executives, May 18/ The Washington Post, 5-19:(A)6.

1

[On whether he will run for President next year]: Even after working two years in the West Wing [of the White House], there isn't a single one of my White House friends from those days who could tell you whether they think I'm a Republican or a Democrat. That was part of the code I lived with. Now I'm no longer protected by my uniform. As I go around the country, I'm trying to develop a political philosophy, just to be a good citizen, not necessarily to run for office. I want to keep the option of elective office open because I think I should do that. Why close off possibilities? I want to be of some service to the nation in the future. I just don't know if it will be an appointed office, charitable work, educational work . . . I don't find a passion for politics. I don't find that I have that calling for politics. But I want to keep the option open.

Speech, San Diego, Calif./ Time, 7-10:24.

Ralph Reed
Executive director, Christian Coalition

2

[Urging the Republican Party to have an anti-abortion stance in the 1996 elections]: Pro-life and pro-family voters, a third of the electorate, will not support a party that retreats from its noble and historic defense of traditional values and which has a national ticket or a platform that does not share [former President]Ronald Reagan's belief in the sanctity of innocent human life . . . To economic conservatives who may be liberal on social issues: We stood with you in victory; we stood with you in defeat. We've been willing and we are willing now to be patient on our own agenda so that we can assist you in realizing our broader agenda together. [But] we will require of those who desire to be our leaders and our President, that they stand firm on the values of work, of faith, of responsibility, of self-reliance, of a need for values and of respect for human life.

At Conservative Political Action Conference, Washington, D.C., Feb. 10/ The New York Times, 2-11:1,9.

3

The most important thing for the Republicans [who now control Congress] to do right now, in order to rebuild the trust of the electorate, is simply to do what they said they would do. What they said they would do is honor the Contract With America. The Republicans have got to resist every temptation to get off that message. The great temptation right now, in the euphoria and giddiness after the [1994 Congressional] election, is to begin to think of lots of other ideas, to begin to raise expectations even higher and try to do many other things that weren't in that Con-

(RALPH REED)

tract. If the Contract is successfully redeemed, then we will have built an enormous reservoir of political capital that we can carry into these other battles. So let's concentrate on the Contract for now.

Panel discussion,
Washington, D.C./
Harper's,
March:45.

1

The Christian Coalition is not and never has claimed to be a church or a ministry. It is an explicitly grass-roots lobbying organization representing people of faith and seeking family-friendly public policy . . . I don't think anyone is operating under the false assumption that the church is a wholly owned subsidiary of the Republican Party, particularly when you have the Catholic bishops criticizing Republican welfare proposals, Marian Wright Edelman [head of the liberal Children's Defense Fund] quoting from the Bible, and the National Council of Churches condemning the [Republican-sponsored] balanced-budget amendment . . . There is a diversity of religious voices out there.

The Washington Post,
3-27:(A)10.

2

As religious conservatives, we have finally gained what we have always sought: a place at the table, a sense of legitimacy, and a voice in the conversation that we call democracy. This is not a Christian agenda. It is not a Republican [Party] agenda. It is not a special-interest agenda . . . Our purpose is not to legislate family values. It is to ensure that Washington values families.

Introducing his organization's
Contract With the American Family,
Washington, D.C., May 17/
Christianity Today, 7-17:54.

3

[Saying his organization is more interested in supporting local government officials who share its views than it is in influencing Presidential nominations]: I would rather have a thousand school-board members and 2,000 state legislators than a single President . . . If we so chose, we could exercise a tremendous amount of influence over the selection of the [1996] Republican [Presidential] nominee. [But] if we are smart . . . we will not exercise that option. It sounds a little crazy to say you're more ambitious than winning the White House; but what we want is to see people who share our values . . . sitting in mayoralties, city-council seats, county commissioners, state legislatures and Congress.

Interview/
USA Today, 9-8:(A)6.

Robert B. Reich
Secretary of Labor
of the United States

4

Loyalty to party as party is probably less today than at any time in recent memory.

U.S. News & World Report,
11-6:35.

Ann Richards
Former Governor of Texas (D)

5

So often what is done in politics is done because it's less trouble to put people you

(ANN RICHARDS)

know on a board, for example. It's a whole lot less trouble to name your old roommate in college that you've known all your life than it is to reach out and search for qualified candidates who come from entirely different backgrounds.

Interview/ "Interview" magazine, February:31.

Charles "Buddy" Roemer
Former Governor of Louisiana (D)

1

[On Senator Phil Gramm, who is a candidate for the 1996 Republican Presidential nomination]: Voters vote for people they like. Now, Phil, I know his mother likes him; I know [his wife] Wendy likes him. I think his dog likes him. And I like him. I've named four. Can that move out across the country? I honestly don't know . . . Politics is a funny kind of thing. Phil could be a great candidate, or he could be a total bust.

Vanity Fair, May:170.

Sal Russo
Republican Party consultant

2

[On the possibility that former Joint Chiefs of Staff Chairman Colin Powell will run for the 1996 Republican Presidential nomination]: There are five things people are looking for in a President: a leader, a vision, a non-insider, an ability to make change, and character. Powell passes four of those tests. He's not scoring on "vision" now, but he can get there. Powell's race [black] is a plus because there are more whites who want to prove they're open-minded by voting for a black than there are people who would not vote for one.

Los Angeles Times, 10-9:(A)3.

Larry J. Sabato
Professor of government, University of Virginia

3

[Saying Senator Robert Dole's age, 72, could be a handicap in his run for the Presidency in 1996]: [Every time he gets a cold,] his political opponents will be fitting him for a coffin. It's crass. It's wrong. But it's true.

USA Today, 7-21:(A)2.

Bernard Sanders
United States Representative, I-Vermont

4

[Criticizing current Congressional hearings into the Whitewater scandal]: Sixty-one percent of the American people did not vote. If we don't talk about issues of far more enormous consequence [than Whitewater], we're going to have fewer and fewer people voting and only make a cynical country more cynical.

At House Banking Committee hearing on Whitewater, Washington, D.C., Aug. 7/ The New York Times, 8-8:(A)12.

William Schneider
Political analyst, American Enterprise Institute

5

[On the race for the 1996 Republican

(WILLIAM SCHNEIDER)

Presidential nomination]: This is a simple story. The Republican race consists of [Senator] Bob Dole and a bunch of other guys. Dole has dominated the polls and continues to. The guy who dominates the early field always wins the Republican nomination. Always.

Los Angeles Times,
6-5:(A)3.

Charles E. Schumer
United States Representative,
D-New York

1

[On the disagreements within the Democratic Party following last year's sweeping Republican Congressional election victory]: At both the Congressional and Presidential level, our Party has received a real kick. Anybody who thinks we're going to all have agreement and know what to do isn't realistic. For the next six months, as Republicans learn how hard governing is, and we rethink where we're going, the theory ought to be, "Let 1,000 flowers bloom."

The New York Times,
1-17:(A)1.

Alan Secrest
Democratic
Party consultant

2

[On the Democratic Party, which lost control of Congress in last year's elections]: You had a Party suffering from the arrogance of power, a Party that refused to reassess its message for years, even when the corrosion within was becoming evident.

U.S. News & World Report,
11-6:36.

F. James Sensenbrenner, Jr.
United States Representative,
R-Wisconsin

3

If we Republicans do not prove ourselves in the next two years, having been given this majority [in the House and Senate in last year's elections], I think both political parties are going to be so discredited that we may very well see a third political party arise. The stakes, in my opinion, are as great as the survival of the Republican Party. We know we're going to have to deliver.

The New York Times,
1-17:(A)8.

Robert Shrum
Democratic Party consultant

4

[On Speaker of the House Newt Gingrich]: As a politician, he's permanently in heat. If Newt Gingrich climbed Mount Everest, his first question would be, "Isn't there another mountain even higher?"

Newsweek, 6-19:34.

Don Sipple
Media adviser
to California Governor
and candidate for the
1996 Republican
Presidential nomination,
Pete Wilson

5

Wilson is sometimes a polarizing figure and takes on controversial issues. But at least he goes where others fear to tread. Issue positions are the prism through which people see character.

The New York Times,
8-25:(A)8.

David E. Skaggs
United States Representative,
D-Colorado

1

It is remarkable to me how many Democrats, if you pushed them, would agree with the notion that it was much more interesting to listen to [new Republican House Speaker] Newt Gingrich than it was to listen to ourselves over the last few months [since the Republicans took control of Congress]. We were not fully represented on the battlefield of ideas.

The Washington Post National Weekly,
1-9:15.

Gene Sperling
Deputy Assistant to President
of the United States Bill Clinton
for Economic Policy

2

[On House Speaker Newt Gingrich and Senator Robert Dole, both Republicans, inviting President Clinton to meet with them to discuss Medicare-budget problems]: You have to admire their chutzpah. They have a tactic a day, a gimmick a day, to avoid their basic obligation to tell the American people the specifics of their budget for the Contract With America, the contract they ran on, brag about and gloat over every chance they get.

May 2/
The New York Times,
5-3:(A)1.

Gloria Steinem
Author;
Women's-rights advocate

3

We [the U.S.] are currently the least participatory democracy in the world. Thirty-nine percent of eligible voters in this nation vote . . . Meanwhile, right-wing groups are voting—they say—a very high percentage of their membership, and I have no reason to disbelieve them. They had a massive grass-roots mobilization campaign [in last fall's Congressional election], and we [liberals] didn't. I'm not being dramatic about the electoral system. I never think for a moment that change starts in the electoral system; it doesn't. It starts in the streets. But it can be stopped by the electoral system. So it seems to me that the 1996 election is more crucial than any election in my memory.

Interview/
Mother Jones,
Nov.-Dec.:24.

Ted Stevens
United States Senator,
R-Alaska

4

It is not a healthy concept to think everyone has to fit through the same keyhole to belong to the Republican Party.

Los Angeles Times,
3-9:(A)18.

Duane Tananbaum
Historian,
Lehman College,
City University of New York

5

[In politics,] if you're waging a holy war, you can't compromise with the devil. And we are getting closer to that. The danger of the firebrands has become clearer.

Los Angeles Times,
11-21:(A)17.

W. J. "Billy" Tauzin
United States
Representative,
D-Louisiana

1

President [Clinton] could have led. He could have led on welfare reform; he could have passed a sensible health-care bill; he could have done a lot of things. He could have led the country, but he chose not to, and he's made himself irrelevant. He talked during the [1994 Presidential election] campaign as if he believed in a new, more conservative Democratic agenda, then abdicated it the minute he got into office. He has ruined the DLC by completely destroying our credibility.

The New York Times,
4-29:6.

2

[On conservative Democrats in Congress such as himself]: We've got the most endangered political status on the planet. We hold seats the Republicans want and cherish as conservative, and we represent a philosophy the Democrats [as a whole] don't like.

The New York Times,
7-13:(A)13.

Joe Trippi
Political consultant

3

[On President Clinton's penchant for changing positions on issues]: He's a very smart kid with 100 different cookie jars.

U.S. News & World Report,
1-30:22.

Paul E. Tsongas
Co-chairman,
The Concord Coalition;
Former United States Senator,
D-Massachusetts

4

There is a [political] center in this country—whether you call it the passionate center, the radical center, the sensible center—that is basically socially inclusive, fiscally conservative, pro-environment, pro-[election]-campaign reform. And those people feel rather disenfranchised at this point.

Broadcast interview,
Nov. 26/
Los Angeles Times,
11-27:(A)11.

Herbert Valentine
Chairman,
Interfaith Alliance

5

[On the conservative, politically oriented Christian Coalition]: For the Christian Coalition to claim the ideological and spiritual endorsement of 40 million Christians is not only ludicrous, it is inexcusable.

Christianity Today,
7-17:54.

Rex Waite
Chairman,
Republican Party
of Pima County
(Tucson), Arizona

6

[On the 1996 Presidential election]: [President] Clinton is Mr. Excitement. We [Republicans] don't have anyone who can rival him as a politician.

USA Today, 6-5:(A)6.

Enid Waldholtz
United States Representative,
R-Utah

1

[On the new crop of Republicans, such as herself, who swept into Congress after last fall's elections]: We don't look to politics as a career path. It gives us a real focus about getting things done in a hurry, and a real willingness to take some risks.

The Washington Post,
7-10:(A)6.

Robert S. Walker
United States Representative,
R-Pennsylvania

2

[On Democrats who are using House rules and speeches to criticize Speaker Newt Gingrich's recent $4.5-million advance from a book publisher, which he subsequently decided to forgo]: They [Democrats] are starting to act more and more like a minority every day. These are clearly disruptive tactics that are aimed at preventing the [Republicans'] Contract [With America] from getting voted . . . The Democrats have decided they cannot speak to the ideas agenda, so they have gone on the [personal political] attack. And they will go so far as to disrupt the workings of the House.

Los Angeles Times,
1-19:(A)6.

Faye Wattleton
Women's-rights advocate;
Former president,
Planned Parenthood

3

[On right-wing religious extremists]: There seems to be a nerve that's touched in the hearts of more progressive people that maybe these people have a right to work for something they believe in. My view is—not quite. There are limits to what we ought to be willing to tolerate in the name of what people believe in.

Mother Jones,
Nov.-Dec.:42.

Lowell P. Weicker, Jr.
Former Governor
of Connecticut (I);
Former United States Senator,
D-Connecticut

4

The American people are fed up with party labels. They've come to know that that's relatively meaningless. What is the purpose of a party platform? Nobody lives up to it. It says the most inane things.

At political forum,
Washington, D.C./
The New York Times,
6-6:(A)13.

David Welch
Republican
Party consultant

5

If we Republicans want to elect a President, the more centrist we are, the better off we are.

U.S. News & World Report,
11-13:41.

William F. Weld
Governor of Massachusetts (R)

6

[Saying he will not run for the 1996 Republican Presidential nomination]: It may be possible to be a Governor, a father and a Presi-

(WILLIAM F. WELD)

dential candidate all at the same time, but I think at least one of those roles would suffer. Probably all three.

Interview,
Boston, Mass., Feb. 27/
The New York Times,
2-28:(C)19.

Paul M. Weyrich
Chairman,
Free Congress Foundation

1

[Saying former Joint Chiefs of Staff Chairman Colin Powell is not conservative enough to run for the 1996 Republican Presidential nomination]: Colin Powell is the Trojan horse of the Establishment. The ongoing conservative revolution in this country is a revolution against the Nelson Rockefellers and Colin Powells of the world. [We] Americans who are working for that revolution are finished forever with politicians and would-be politicians who want to be something but stand for nothing.

At National Press Club,
Washington, D.C., Nov. 2/
Los Angeles Times,
11-3:(A)19.

Charles Wilson
United States Representative,
D-Texas

2

[On being a Democrat in the new Republican-controlled Congress]: I don't know if it's paranoia or not, but the doorkeepers and the elevator operators look at you differently.

USA Today,
1-5:(A)2.

Pete Wilson
Governor of California (R);
Candidate for
the 1996 Republican
Presidential nomination

3

[On his pledge, during last year's Gubernatorial election, that he would not run for President if re-elected Governor of California]: Last fall I meant it . . . [But other Republican Presidential candidates] got out. People were suddenly confronted with a choice between [U.S. Senator Bob]Dole and [U. S. Senator Phil] Gramm [for the 1996 Republican Presidential nomination] and a lot of people came to me and said, "We don't think they're going to beat [incumbent Democratic President] Bill Clinton. We think you can." I am the candidate the [Clinton] White House fears most. Objectively, it has reason to . . . I've been tested as a chief executive . . . given leadership on some tough issues . . . [Dole and Gramm] have been sitting there [in the Senate] talking, holding hearings.

Interview/
Los Angeles Times,
6-19:(A)3.

4

I am guided by four fundamental principles: Individuals should be responsible and accountable for their actions; individuals should be rewarded on the basis of merit; government should be limited to safeguard freedom and opportunity; and we should value family as the foundation of our society.

Presidential campaign
TV ad/
The New York Times,
8-25:(A)8.

(PETE WILSON)

1

I have habitually, through life, been underestimated by my opponents. It's been a great advantage.

Interview,
Sacramento, Calif./
USA Today, 8-28:(A)6.

Paul D. Wolfowitz
Former Under Secretary
of Defense
of the United States

2

[On former Joint Chiefs Chairman Colin Powell, who may run for President next year]: He has that rapport good politicians have with people. A lot of them go through the motions very well and convince people that they care. Then there are the gifted ones who are really connecting. He does that, and I think it's related to the fact that there are things he cares deeply about. There is an intensely human quality about Powell that I think is exceptional.

Time, 7-10:25.

Daniel Yankelovich
Public-opinion analyst

3

I am not by temperament a political partisan. But I believe it is bad for the nation to have liberalism boxed into a corner where it can no longer exercise an influence for the good.

Mother Jones,
Nov.-Dec.:30.

Social Welfare

Eloise Anderson
Director,
California Department
of Social Services

1

[On welfare]: [We] ought to develop a safety system so that when people are unemployed—and that happens to a lot of us now and then—there's some place they can go temporarily until they find another job. But [welfare] shouldn't be viewed as a lifestyle. It shouldn't be viewed as "that's something I'm going to do until the kid is 18." It shouldn't be viewed as "that's my income" . . . It's got to be temporary. And the question is *how* temporary.

Interview/
Los Angeles Times,
2-5:(M)3.

Bill Archer
United States Representative,
R-Texas

2

I am very, very opposed to means-testing Social Security benefits . . . It is not a welfare program.

Before American Association
of Retired Persons,
Washington, D.C., Feb. 3/
The Washington Post,
2-4:(A)5.

3

Social Security shouldn't be on the table for balancing the [Federal] budget. Social Security is not the problem keeping us from getting to a balanced budget in the next seven years. [But the solvency of Social Security] is a problem for the long term that we cannot ignore.

Before
National Legislative Council
of American Association
of Retired Persons,
Washington, D.C./
AARP Bulletin,
March:8.

Gary L. Bauer
President,
Family Research Council

4

The welfare culture we have established has increased both abortion and illegitimacy. The only way we're going to turn that around is to deconstruct that welfare culture.

Christianity Today,
3-6:44.

William J. Bennett
Former Secretary
of Education
of the United States

5

[Supporting the idea of cutting welfare payments to unmarried women under 18 who have children out of wedlock]: Welfare may not cause illegitimacy, but it does make it economically viable. It sustains it and subsidizes it. And what you subsidize, you get more of.

Before House Ways
and Means Committee,
Washington, D.C.,Jan. 20/
The New York Times,
1-21:9.

Gordon Berlin
Senior vice president,
Manpower Demonstration
Research Corporation

1

[On the effects of cutting welfare programs, as is contemplated by New York's Mayor Rudolph Giuliani]: The cream of the crop [of welfare recipients] can figure out a new system. But the people who are barely coping now probably won't negotiate the new barriers, and they're also the people more likely to slip into homelessness or whose poverty ends up causing them to neglect their children.

The New York Times,
5-1:(A)1.

Rebecca M. Blank
Professor of economics,
Northwestern University

2

There is little relationship between welfare-payment levels and rising problems of out-of-wedlock births. It is hard to understand how [as some critics charge] the recent rapid increase in unwed motherhood can be fueled by public-assistance payments, [since the purchasing power of those payments has been declining].

Before House Ways
and Means Committee,
Washington, D.C., Jan. 20/
The New York Times,
1-21:9.

John B. Breaux
United States Senator,
D-Louisiana

3

[Criticizing proposals to turn over the welfare system from Federal to state control]: We are saying with this approach [that] we [at the Federal level] don't have either the intelligence or the courage . . . to solve the problem of welfare. We have an obligation to do something rather than just ship the problem to the states.

May 26/
Los Angeles Times,
5-27:(A)20.

David Camp
United States Representative,
R-Michigan

4

The Democrats have taken a walk on welfare reform. The President [Clinton] left it out of his budget and he hasn't introduced his own bill. They've had 40 years to correct the welfare system and they have not done it. They have allowed it to fester and cause untold harm to children and families.

Feb. 10/
Los Angeles Times,
2-11:(A)18.

Henry G. Cisneros
Secretary of Housing
and Urban Development
of the United States

5

[Criticizing plans by Republicans in Congress to cut over $7-billion from HUD's budget]: For the first time since the election [of 1994, in which the Republicans took control of Congress], people are going to be hurt, and hurt soon . . . We just cannot afford to have women and children on the streets in this country.

The New York Times,
2-28:(A)11.

(HENRY G. CISNEROS)

1

[On his plan to overhaul HUD's housing programs]: Our fight is not about HUD. Our fight is about American's cities. The nation cannot treat entire cities as if they were disposable, as if they were rusty junk cars or used-up machinery. The cities are America too.

Announcing the plan, Washington, D.C., March 20/ Los Angeles Times, 3-21:(A)21.

Bill Clinton
President of the United States

2

[Criticizing a Republican proposal to turn the Federal school-lunch program over to the states in the form of block grants]: An old conservative adage used to be, if it ain't broke, don't fix it. Here's a program that isn't broke, that's done a world of good for millions and millions of children of all races and backgrounds all across our country. And I think it would be a terrible mistake to put an end to it, to gut it, to undermine it.

To Congressional Democrats, Washington, D.C., Feb. 22/ Los Angeles Times, 2-23:(A)23.

3

The Republicans now have proposed to cut education, nutritional help for mothers and schoolchildren, anti-drug efforts in our schools, and other things which to me appear to target children, in order to pay for tax cuts for upper-income Americans. I do not believe that that is consistent with our interests as we build America into the 21st century and we move into this new global economy.

News conference, Washington, D.C., March 3/ The New York Times, 3-4:9.

4

I don't think we should let budget-cutting be wrapped in a cloak of welfare reform. Let's reform welfare. Let's cut the [Federal budget] deficit. But let's don't mix up the two and pretend that one is the other.

Before National Association of Counties, Washington, D.C., March 7/ The New York Times, 3-8:(A)12.

5

[Criticizing the Republican plan to turn over the school-lunch program to the states]: You cannot make me believe [that] with all the poor kids in this world today who show up hungry to school every day, whose only decent meal occurs in school, you cannot make me believe that we cannot find a way to eliminate unnecessary spending from the [Federal] budget without cutting the school-lunch program.

Before League of Cities, Washington, D.C., March 13/ The Washington Post, 3-14:(A)6.

6

Both the Republican Contract [With America] and my New Covenant have focused

(BILL CLINTON)

heavily on welfare reform. What do we agree on? That there ought to be a limit to welfare, that there ought to be flexibility for the states, that we ought to have the toughest possible child-support enforcement and that people have to take more responsibility for their own lives and for children they bring into this world.

Before American Society of Newspaper Editors, Dallas, Texas, April 7/ The New York Times, 4-8:9.

1

I am opposed to welfare reform that is just really just a mask for Congressional budget-cutting, which would send you [in the states a block-grant] check with no incentives or requirements on states to maintain their own funding support for poor children and child care and work. And I do believe honestly that there is a danger that some states will get involved in a "race to the bottom." But not, as some have implied, because I don't have confidence in you, not because I think you want to do that, not because I think you would do it anyway if you could avoid it, but because I have been a Governor [of Arkansas] for 12 years in all different kinds of times. And I know what kind of decisions you are about to face if the range of alternatives I see coming toward you develop . . . My experience is that the poor-children's lobby is a poor match for most of those forces in most state legislatures in the country. Not because anybody wants to do the wrong thing, but because those [other] people [making claims on funds] are deserving too, and they will have a very strong case to make.

Before National Governors' Association, Burlington, Vt., July 31/ The New York Times, 8-1:(A)8.

2

[Criticizing Republican proposals to limit the earned-income tax credit]: If there are problems in the administration of the program, let's fix those. But let's don't raise taxes on working people while we're lowering taxes on everybody else in the country. It just does not make sense, and it is inconsistent with rewarding work and responsibility and strengthening families. It's inconsistent with those basic bedrock values this country should be standing for now . . . I think [limiting the credit] will substantially undermine our ability to move people from welfare to work. And more importantly, it will make a statement that we're backing off of this value that we want people to succeed as workers and as parents, that if they're willing to work, no matter how meager their incomes, we want to lift them above poverty, if they work full time.

Interview, Washington, D.C., Sept. 18/ The New York Times, 9-19:(A)12.

Howard Dean
Governor of Vermont (D);
Chairman,
National Governors' Association

3

[The Republicans' welfare-reform plan is] to starve children and kick old people out of their homes . . . I think some of them think

(HOWARD DEAN)

they've got a mandate to starve children, and they don't . . . We've given up on them. They talk to us [Democrats] and say, "yes, yes, yes," and then they get intoxicated when [new House Speaker Newt] Gingrich gets them in the room.

Interview, Jan. 8/
The Washington Post,
1-9:(A)6.

1

[Saying there should be national standards for the welfare of children]: I think America has a national interest in its children, and the same benefits and strength and support that a child from Minnesota deserves [are] the same benefits and strength and support that a child from Alabama deserves.

The Christian Science Monitor,
3-3:5.

E. "Kika" de la Garza
United States Representative,
D-Texas

2

We have a responsibility as a nation and as a people, a moral responsibility, to see that in this, the greatest nation in the world, there is no hunger.

The New York Times,
3-8:(A)12.

Robert J. Dole
United States Senator,
R-Kansas;
Candidate for the 1996
Republican Presidential nomination

3

[Supporting continuing Federal control of the school-lunch program]: In my own view, I would not block-grant [to the states] the school lunch program. It works pretty well as it is.

Washington, D.C.,
June 14/
Los Angeles Times,
6-15:(A)23.

4

The most graphic failure of the Federal government is welfare. It is a point where liberal rhetoric meets reality, and for a long, long time—and I've been there, maybe I've voted that way from time to time—you [think if you] just spend a little more money on welfare, start a new program and wait for a few more years, our welfare system will start to work. But our welfare system doesn't work, and the American people know it. It doesn't work because it's not based on the classic, proven American formula for escaping poverty: a job, a strong family, a good education, saving money to buy a home. Instead, our welfare system undermines almost every value and virtue that leads to self-reliance and success. It discourages work; it penalizes marriage and traps people in government-owned housing. The fact is, there are more people living in poverty today than before the Great Society [program] was started. There can be no escaping the conclusion that the current system has failed. It's failed. It doesn't work. And it will keep failing until we change it.

Before National
Governors' Association,
Burlington, Vt.,
July 31/
The New York Times,
8-1:(A)8.

Bill Emerson
United States Representative,
R-Maryland

1

[Supporting a proposed reform and retrenching of the food-stamp program]: There is no intention to punish anyone for anything, but to have a tight program that helps real people who need real help and to eliminate fraud, abuse and trafficking.

USA Today,
3-10:(A)11.

John Engler
Governor
of Michigan (R)

2

[Saying states should be allowed to allocate welfare funds as they see fit, with a minimum of Federal regulation]: Conservative micromanagement [by the Feds] is just as bad as liberal micromanagement. States must have the freedom, with no strings attached, to implement change. Washington had 60 years to tackle the welfare problem. It's time to give the states a chance.

Before House Ways
and Means Committee,
Washington, D.C.,
Jan. 13/
The New York Times,
1-14:10.

Myrlie Evers-Williams
Chairman,
National Association
for the Advancement
of Colored People

3

Imagine the monstrous consequences if [Speaker of the House] Newt [Gingrich] succeeds in making starvation public policy in a society where the poor are heavily armed.

Before Consultation
on Conscience,
Washington, D.C., May 2/
Los Angeles Times,
5-3:(A)18.

Robert J. Fersh
President, Food Research
and Action Center

4

[Criticizing proposed Federal block grants to states for food and nutrition programs rather than having the Federal government run them]: A block grant cannot keep up with the real needs of real people. It's almost impossible to devise a formula that responds to changing circumstances like population growth, recession, migration, unemployment and natural disasters.

The New York Times,
2-18:1.

David Frum
Political columnist;
Commentator, "Morning Edition,"
National Public Radio

5

People's attitudes about the poor have changed significantly in the last decade. People are tired of the constant moaning they hear about the poor. A lot of middle-class taxpayers feel that they're paying more and more for the poor and that the poor are behaving worse and worse. And people are not sure that they're as sympathetic as they used to be. I don't think we [Republicans] should go out of our way to be callous. But there is no way that the Republican Party is going to be able to remain true to its principles without being

(DAVID FRUM)

accused of being callous. In the current environment, being accused of callousness might even be to our advantage. [Former HUD Secretary] Jack Kemp spent a lot of time trying to come up with ideas that would both be conservative and avoid these accusations, and he failed.

Panel discussion,
Washington, D.C./
Harper's, March:50.

Richard A. Gephardt
United States Representative,
D-Missouri

1

The proposal that the Republicans are passing off as welfare reform—the proposal that they say will replace welfare with work—does absolutely nothing to accomplish that goal . . . They're just playing around with the process—trying to slash the [Federal] budget to pay for a capital-gains tax for wealthy investors and a "Star Wars" [missile] defense disaster that does nothing for struggling families.

News conference,
Washington, D.C., Feb. 10/
Los Angeles Times,
2-11:(A)1.

Newt Gingrich
United States Representative,
R-Georgia;
Speaker of the House-designate

2

I think eventually you can re-examine Social Security [to fix its economic problems], in six to eight years. But I think that the current generation of politicians does not have the moral standing, doesn't have the trust [of the people], to open up the largest trust fund and the largest social-insurance program in the country. And I think if you'd try to do it, you'd just get into a brutal, nasty, mean fight, and you'd lose.

Broadcast interview/
C-SPAN, 1-2.

Newt Gingrich
United States Representative,
R-Georgia;
Speaker of the House

3

The answer to aging is to design expert systems, decentralize care and the ability of families to take care of their own, and to live as long as possible with a sense of independence and involvement . . . But the current system says, "We're not really going to help you till you get sick enough that we put you away, and so we're going to maximize a program which maximizes your costs and minimizes your quality of life." Now, we should redesign that from the ground up, and we'll not only save money, but we'll save lives and improve the quality of care.

Before National
Hospital Association,
Washington, D.C.,
Jan. 30/
The New York Times,
1-31:(A)8.

4

I'm sure you've all heard the dire cries that we [Republicans] are going to take food out of the mouths of schoolchildren. The fact of the matter is that all we did was to vote to increase school-lunch [program] money 4 1/2 percent every year for the next five years

(NEWT GINGRICH)

and give money to the states [in block grants] to spend.

Broadcast address to the nation, April 7/ Nation's Business, May:20.

1

I'm prepared to say to the poor, you have to learn new habits. The habits of being poor don't work. In this country in 1996, if you work twice as hard, you're going to succeed.

At meeting of black journalists, Washington, D.C., June 15/ Los Angeles Times, 6-16:(A)31.

Phil Gramm
United States Senator, R-Texas; Candidate for the 1996 Republican Presidential nomination

2

I've never had [an election] campaign that I didn't have an opponent who was rich, and who had rich parents, telling me about poor people. I'm not going to be cowed by people who want to accuse me of being anti-poor. I'm not going to be swayed by people who say, "You have no compassion." I have great compassion. I think of the unwed mother who is working as a cook in a little restaurant, working 10 or 11 hours a day. She is barely making ends meet. It is wrong that people who aren't working are getting more money than she is. I think she ought to get to keep more of what she earns. I don't think it's fair that because she is working, she gets no medical coverage, or has difficulty getting it, and somebody who doesn't work gets the best in the world.

The Atlantic Monthly, March:83.

3

[Supporting a proposal to deny cash benefits to teenage women who have children out of wedlock]: I don't think we can deal with welfare in this country without dealing with illegitimacy. This problem has reached crisis proportions. We've got to eliminate financial incentives for people to have babies out of wedlock.

Interview/ Los Angeles Times, 8-3:(A)14.

4

We can't fool around with marginal changes [in the welfare system]. We're either going to dramatically change welfare and break this cycle, or we're going to end up losing America as we know it.

Broadcast interview/ "Face the Nation," CBS-TV, 8-6.

Robert Greenstein
Executive director, Center on Budget and Policy Priorities

5

[On the welfare-reform proposals being developed by Congress and the Administration]: Any fair analysis is going to find that this bill is harsh on children and increases child poverty. One would have to jump

(ROBERT GREENSTEIN)

through hoops to twist an analysis around to suggest that it would not.

Los Angeles Times,
10-27:(A)14.

James C. Greenwood
United States Representative,
R-Pennsylvania

1

[On criticism that Republican budget plans cut Federal spending for the school-lunch program]: What is indisputable is that we are not proposing a cut of one penny in the school-lunch program. The President [Clinton], in this year's budget proposal—the President of the United States, the one who went to visit the schoolchildren in Maryland for lunch—he proposed a 3.6 percent increase this year. And we [Republicans] proposed 4.5 percent.

March 22/
The New York Times,
3-25:8.

Jesse L. Jackson
Civil-rights leader

2

As a people, we [blacks] must fight to end welfare as we know it. We know it to be demeaning and intrusive. Welfare is the caboose of the train. We must fight to be in the engine, where capital is created, where land is controlled and developed. We must fight, therefore, for a community-investment act to end redlining of our banks and our insurance companies and mortgage companies. We must fight for capital formation, economic development and wealth first, and gainful work benefits second. And if that fails, then [we should use] welfare as an assistance in our struggle to get to the engine where dignity and development lie.

Ebony,
February:74.

Carlton Jenkins
Chairman,
Founders National Bank,
Los Angeles, Calif.

3

[Addressing President Clinton]: The same energy [that has gone into welfare reform and gun control] needs to be focused on the whole issue of the urban community and the inner city. The biggest problem is the perception that these are risky places to lend money. Changing that perception can start with *you.*

At Portland
State University/
Los Angeles Times,
6-28:(A)17.

Avis LaVelle
Assistant Secretary of Health
and Human Services
of the United States

4

There is a re-evaluation going on throughout [HHS] as to the whole concept of entitlement programs. It's just not smart for us to take an advocacy position one way or the other. The ground is shifting under our feet.

The New York Times,
1-2:7.

Rick Lazio
United States Representative,
R-New York

5

[Criticizing HUD's just-announced plan

(RICK LAZIO)

to overhaul its housing programs]: This latest incarnation of reinvention retains a fundamental, longstanding HUD flaw; HUD insists on micro-managing every neighborhood in America.

March 20/
Los Angeles Times,
3-21:(A)21.

Lawrence M. Mead
Visiting professor
of public policy,
Princeton University

1

[On welfare policy]: There has been a certain reversal in party positions. At the behest of the [state] Governors, Republicans de-emphasized work requirements. Democrats now claim to be the party of work requirements [for welfare], which they never were. The threat of time limits and other restrictions on [welfare] benefits by Republicans has forced the Democrats to emphasize work requirements for the first time. They see work requirements as an alternative to more drastic action by Republicans.

March 6/
The New York Times,
3-7:(C)18.

Barbara A. Mikulski
United States Senator,
D-Maryland

2

The [state] Governors . . . want maximum state flexibility [to handle their own welfare programs. But] we want to be clear there are core national standards. A transfer of responsibility [from the Federal government] to the states should not mean an abdication of responsibility,

USA Today,
1-27:(A)11.

Wally N'Dow
Secretary General,
United Nations Center
for Human Settlements

3

The most pressing global environmental, economic and social issues that we will face in the next century will be in cities. Homelessness and poor housing conditions are at the root of all these problems. Urban areas have the resources to solve housing problems, but waste and mismanagement of urban resources cripples the effort . . . The bottom line is that the 21st century will be the first urban century. The problem is that we are woefully unprepared for it. That means the United States as well as my country, The Gambia.

Interview,
Nov. 5/
Los Angeles Times,
11-6:(A)6.

Bob Packwood
United States Senator,
R-Oregon

4

Welfare started as a substitute for a deceased breadwinner. But it became a lifetime support system for someone who never had a breadwinner.

Before the Senate,
Washington, D.C.,
Aug. 7/
The New York Times,
8-8:(A)8.

Leon E. Panetta
Chief of Staff
to President
of the United States
Bill Clinton

1

[Criticizing the proposed Republican House welfare-reform bill]: There are places where we [in the Administration] are going to draw lines . . . [The bill is] weak on work requirements and very tough on children. We want to basically reverse those priorities . . . If they intend to block-grant [to states] the school-lunch program, and the school-breakfast program, and the food-stamp program and programs that we think are necessary in order to assist nutrition for children, then there is no question that the President would object to those proposals.

Broadcast interview/
"Meet the Press,"
NBC-TV, 3-26.

James P. Pinkerton
Lecturer, Graduate School
of Political Management,
George Washington University;
Former Deputy Assistant
for Policy Planning
to the President
of the United States
(George Bush)

2

I can't imagine a [Republican] welfare plan that doesn't involve us saying, "If you can work, you have to work. there's no more welfare." But in order to be successful, we're going to have to create some sort of program like [the late President Franklin] Roosevelt's Civilian Conservation Corps to guarantee that, although nobody gets a check for doing nothing, nobody is starving . . . The Republican message has to be totally clear: Nobody is going to starve. Everybody's going to make it. Everybody is going to work. I'm all for devolving education and housing and transportation and road-building to the states. I just think that on this one issue of welfare, you need a Federal guarantee.

Panel discussion,
Washington, D.C./
Harper's, March:49.

Robert Rector
Senior policy analyst,
Heritage Foundation

3

[On the controversy over how to parcel out Federal block grants to states as part of a welfare-reform program]: I think the real issue in welfare reform is saving the marriage and saving the family and thereby saving society. So I'm a little distressed when the debate shifts off to how to divvy up the spoils of the welfare system.

The New York Times,
6-28:(A)8.

Ralph Reed
Executive director,
Christian Coalition

4

According to our polling data, the first thing people want Congress to do is to reform welfare. So if you go out there early and pass a tough and strong and dramatic welfare-reform bill that encourages work and marriage and discourages out-of-wedlock birth, then rhetorically you can say, "Look, we've asked the least among us to sacrifice so that we can have a smaller government, so that we can have a more civil society, so that we don't

(RALPH REED)

have this spiraling [Federal] debt. We can't ask the least among us to get out of the wagon and start pulling unless you get out, too." That's my argument on [cutting Federal funds for] the NEA and the National Endowment for the Humanities. How can you go to a single mother in the inner city and say, "You're going to have to start carrying more weight," if you don't also go to the tuxedo-and-evening-gown crowd and say, "You're going to have to start paying for your own symphony." By starting with welfare, we can turn these cuts into a populist program that will actually work to our advantage.

Panel discussion, Washington, D.C./ Harper's, March:47.

Edward Rendell
Mayor of Philadelphia, Pa.

1

[Criticizing Congress for proposals he said would cut funding for services that cities provide]: In the best-case scenario, we're getting ravaged. It's both geographic and demographic. Cities have huge portions of the nation's poor. They gravitate to cities because that's where the services are.

USA Today, 7-28:(A)4.

Robert E. Rubin
Secretary of the Treasury of the United States

2

[Criticizing Republican proposals to reduce the earned-income tax credit]: It's a bad idea to increase taxes on lower-income working families as a means of reducing the [Federal budget] deficit . . . If you increase the taxes on the lowest-income working families, there is less incentive to work and a greater number will be pushed back on welfare rolls—the exact opposite of what you want to accomplish in welfare reform.

Interview, Aug. 16/ Los Angeles Times, 8-17:(A)11.

Charles E. Schumer
United States Representative, D-New York

3

[Criticizing Republican proposals that would turn over welfare responsibility to the states in the form of Federal block grants]: The welfare system is in drastic need of overhaul, but the Republicans punted. They said, "Okay, states, here's some money. Do what you want with it." But we get less money.

The New York Times, 3-28:(A)10.

Richard J. Schwartz
Senior Adviser to New York Mayor Rudolph W. Giuliani

4

[On New York City's plan to crack down on welfare fraud]: This is not an effort to deny benefits to anyone. It is an aggressive effort to insure that people who receive benefits are eligible, and those who are not eligible don't. That's a revolutionary thought for most of the people in the advocacy world, but the fact is that most of the people who are eligible and belong in the system are tired of being stigmatized by individuals defrauding the system.

The New York Times, 8-8:(A)13.

E. Clay Shaw, Jr.
United States Representative,
R-Florida

1

[On the idea of a Federal emergency fund as part of a reform of the welfare system which could give more control to the states]: Right now, the concept is in my head. But we could model the program after the unemployment-compensation system. We pay into an unemployment fund every year, and states can draw it down in times of high unemployment. We could set up a similar welfare fund that would be triggered in times of economic downturn.

Interview/
The Washington Post,
1-30:(A)8.

Christopher Shays
United States Representative,
R-Connecticut

2

We have to get [entitlement] programs off auto-pilot. They should be subject to annual appropriations. Entitlements have taken away the power of the people, through Congress, to decide where money is spent each year.

The New York Times,
1-2:7.

Freya L. Sorenstein
Director,
Population Studies Center,
Urban Institute

3

We have a family-planning system set up for women in terms of how to choose contraception. But there is nothing for men. Public policy holds men's feet to the fire in terms of increasing child support, but we haven't done anything on the other side in terms of trying to reach them before that point.

The New York Times,
5-23:(A)7.

James M. Talent
United States Representative,
R-Missouri

4

[The current welfare system, although] trying to give people material wealth and lift them out of poverty, is luring them into a kind of spiritual poverty by destroying their families and their incentives to work.

March 24/
The New York Times,
3-25:1.

Maxine Waters
United States Representative,
D-California

5

[Criticizing the idea of having volunteers, charities and the church take over many welfare services for the poor now provided by government]: That's crazy. That's absolutely nuts. Volunteers are great. But volunteers cannot be relied on. Anybody who wants to run a real business does not say: I'm going to run this business with volunteers. You can't get housing by having [former President] Jimmy Carter and his volunteers come and build 15 houses in Watts. It's cute. It's good. I like it. I'm not against it. But it's not real public policy.

Los Angeles Times,
11-6:(A)17.

J. C. Watts
United States Representative, R-Oklahoma

1

I think for the last 35 to 40 years, we have measured compassion not by how few people are on food stamps and public housing, but by how many. I think we should measure it by how few are there because we have given them the means to climb the ladder to economic opportunities.

Ebony, February:72.

Christine Todd Whitman
Governor of New Jersey (R)

2

[Saying she does not understand Democrats who are reluctant to have states take over welfare programs from the Federal Government]: I am very puzzled by the premise that you can't trust states and Governors to look out for their neediest citizens. I don't know any Governor who is going to abandon children.

Washington, D.C., Jan. 30/ The New York Times, 1-31:(A)8.

3

For our urban strategy to truly succeed, we are calling on everyone—community groups, businesses, clergy, educators, local officials, police and charitable foundations—to work together. The power that comes from these partnerships will revitalize our cities neighborhood by neighborhood.

Speech, Trenton, N.J., March 6/ The New York Times, 3-7:(A)8.

James Q. Wilson
Professor of management and public policy, University of California, Los Angeles

4

Throughout the world, we have seen a fundamental shift in attitude toward the importance of marital commitment. It is not a peculiar defect in the United States . . . I don't believe that taking welfare benefits away from children [born out of wedlock] would cause the problem to go away. [But it may be common sense that] if people cannot get more money for having more children, they are less likely to have more kids.

Before House Ways and Means Committee, Washington, D.C., Jan. 20/ The New York Times, 1-21:9.

Pete Wilson
Governor of California (R)

5

We will insist the father pay child support. We've got a message for deadbeat dads: Your child is your responsibility, not the taxpayers'. We hold you accountable for the children you father. But being a father means more than just sending a check. It means giving the love and discipline, the nurturing and guidance that young children—especially young boys—need to keep them from becoming young thugs.

State of the State address, Sacramento, Calif., Jan. 9/ Los Angeles Times, 1-10:(A)15.

Pete Wilson

Governor of California (R);
Candidate for the 1996 Republican Presidential nomination

1

It's unfair for a young couple . . . who cannot afford a child [to] pay taxes to provide a greater stipend to a woman on welfare who continues to have one child after another out of wedlock.

Broadcast interview/
"Meet the Press,"
NBC-TV, 8-6.

2

[Criticizing President Clinton for not living up to his 1992 election-campaign promise to "end welfare as we know it"]: Every day that Bill Clinton sits in the Oval Office, he is not ending welfare as we know it. He is extending welfare, and he knows it.

Before
Heritage Foundation,
Washington, D.C.,
Sept. 6/
Los Angeles Times,
9-7:(A)16.

Transportation

Thomas Accardi
Director
of Flight Standards Service,
Federal Aviation Administration

1

[Saying FAA inspectors can never do a complete safety monitoring of all airlines]: We believe safety is a shared responsibility [among the FAA and the airlines]. We don't think you can just inspect it in . . . We will never have an inspector in every cockpit or a maintenance expert in every airplane.

U.S. News & World Report,
6-26:37.

Bill Clinton
President
of the United States

2

[On a new agreement between U.S. and Canada allowing their airlines to fly freely to and from points between the two countries]: The only bad news is for those of you with frequent-flyer accounts. It means you'll earn fewer miles because it will be so much easier and quicker to get back and forth.

To business leaders,
Ottawa, Canada,
Feb. 24/
The New York Times,
2-25:1.

David R. Hinson
Administrator,
Federal Aviation Administration

3

Over the past 15 years, flying has become so commonplace and accidents so rare that people now seem to believe that the system is essentially 100 percent risk-free. Expectations are so high that when an aviation accident does occur, it can dramatically distort the public's view of aviation safety. There has always been an attitude [that] we can almost get to zero accidents. But somebody will always have an accident. I think we need to dispense with that attitude.

At airline safety conference,
Washington, D.C.,
Jan. 9/
The New York Times,
1-10:(A)7.

4

From a safety and reliability standpoint, and a passenger comfort standpoint, an anxiety standpoint . . . the [air-traffic-control] system is more reliable statistically than it has ever been.

Sept. 14/
USA Today,
9-15:(A)3.

David Morris
Co-founder, Institute for
Local Self-Reliance

5

The production of automobiles is the world's number 1 industry. The number 2 industry supplies their fuel. Six of America's 10 largest industrial corporations are either oil or auto companies . . . A recent British estimate concludes that half of the world's earnings may be auto- or truck-related.

The Atlantic Monthly,
January:83.

Federico F. Pena
Secretary of Transportation of the United States

1

[On his Department's proposed new rules that would require small commuter aircraft to meet many of the standards required for large aircraft operated by the major airlines]: The rules being issued today are just a step toward insuring that the public can be confident that no matter what type of aircraft they fly on—from a 400-plus seat Boeing 747 to a 19-seat Beech 1900—they can be certain that each aircraft is subject to the same level of safety.

March 24/
The New York Times,
3-25:1.

Nick Joe Rahall II
United States Representative, D-West Virginia

2

[Arguing against repeal of the Federal 55-m.p.h. speed limit by giving the states the right to set their own limits]: [Eliminating the 55 limit would] turn our nation's highways into killing fields. This is not a matter of states' rights. It's a matter of human rights.

USA Today,
9-21:(A)1.

Michael Replogle
Former Transit Coordinator, Montgomery County, Md.

3

Transportation and land-use problems are a failure of the market. We have allowed large hidden subsidies to dictate land-use and development patterns. Traffic engineers have destroyed grids and funneled roads into major arteries, which limit walking. Separating land uses into nothing but houses or nothing but shops, so that the vast majority of people have no option but to use a car, hurts small-business formation by not allowing business near neighborhoods.

The Atlantic Monthly,
January:93.

Vincent Scully
Art historian

4

One principle is certainly the control of the automobile. This goes right to the heart of the American experience, because along with the single-family house, the other thing that everybody was taught to believe he has a right to was the automobile. It is still, I think, to be decided in history whether the automobile and civilization as we know it—by which we mean the culture of cities—can coexist. Because the automobile has shown us that if we design only for the automobile, we smash every kind of decent urban grouping that there is, whether it's in the center of the city or in the suburbs . . . The car, you know, has strange psychological effects on us. One of the major ones is that in a car, we don't feel that we have any community responsibility at all. We feel free. We feel alone . . . [In a car,] you're all by yourself in a perfectly controlled environment, but all sense of community is lost. We forget that if the community didn't build roads and provide police and signage and everything, we couldn't move around in the car at all.

Interview/
Humanities,
May-June:47.

PART TWO

International Affairs

Foreign Affairs

Gary L. Ackerman
United States Representative,
D-New York

1

This is a different era [with the new Republican-controlled U.S. Congress], probably one of the most partisan over foreign-policy decisions. [Congressional Republicans] are trying to tear down and destroy [foreign-policy initiatives with] xenophobic, anti-UN stands. What the Republicans are trying to do is to steal foreign policy from the President's bailiwick and put it in the Congress.

USA Today, 5-25:(A)8.

Lamar Alexander
Candidate for the 1996
Republican Presidential nomination;
Former Secretary of Education
of the United States

2

After two years of [U.S.] President Clinton, we find ourselves in the midst of what might be called "a new world disorder" . . . When the U.S. is not strong and certain in its course, the rest of the world becomes . . . more dangerous.

USA Today, 1-27:(A)11.

Les Aspin
Chairman, Presidential commission
evaluating the role of
intelligence services today;
Former Secretary of Defense
of the United States

3

[On the role today of intelligence services such as the CIA]: What does it all mean now? What are the targets now? What are you trying to do? How do you organize it? And at what costs? If the cost can't be sold politically, then what are we going to collect?

Interview/
The New York Times,
3-18:7.

J. Brian Atwood
Administrator,
Agency for
International Development
of the United States

4

[On the Republican-controlled U.S. Congress' inclination to cut foreign aid]: We've had a bipartisan consensus supporting foreign-aid programs over the years, but this time the debate at the philosophical level will be deep. The debate will be more about the premise than the details of foreign aid.

The Christian Science Monitor,
2-22:4.

5

[Criticizing those who want to merge his agency into the State Department and to cut its aid programs for Third World countries]: I didn't take this job because I wanted to identify myself with a bureaucracy . . . I think what our opponents have done is perpetuate the notion that this is just a big bureaucratic battle with personalities and constituencies and politics involved and that there is no principle or vital U.S. interest at stake . . . What is being proposed on the [Capitol] Hill is being done to find cost savings, not to improve the way

(J. BRIAN ATWOOD)

we do business. The programs they want to eliminate are the development programs.

Interview/ The Washington Post, 3-2:(A)19.

1

[On U.S. foreign aid]: Foreign assistance is not just the province of do-gooders. It is a primary tool of foreign policy.

Los Angeles Times, 12-4:(A)10.

James A. Baker III
Former Secretary of State of the United States

2

Words matter. Words really matter in foreign policy. Even empty words matter in foreign policy . . . Broken promises, policy flip-flops debase the currency of American credibility . . . It's very, very hard to get people to follow if they think you might change course at any time.

Before International Republican Institute/ USA Today, 6-26:(A)11.

Joseph R. Biden, Jr.
United States Senator, D-Delaware

3

[On increasing Congressional Republican criticism of U.S. President Clinton's handling of foreign policy): The Republicans want to have a foreign policy on the cheap. When the Republicans were in the White House, they kept on saying, "Don't micromanage foreign policy." But [now that Republicans control Congress,] they have turned out to be the biggest micromanaging, tinkering fools around.

The Washington Post, 6-26:(A)4.

Christian Bonte-Friedheim
Former official, United Nations Food and Agriculture Organization

4

[On the Food and Agriculture Organization]: It's the same problem everywhere in the United Nations. The agency is accountable to no one but its member nations, and they have no focus.

USA Today, 6-26:(A)4.

Boutros Boutros-Ghali
Secretary General of the United Nations

5

[Saying the UN's peacekeeping operations have overshadowed other areas where the organization should direct its attention]: The problems of the environment, of under-development, of the demographic explosion and illegal immigration are long-term problems . . . [But] because of the peacekeeping operations, we have not paid attention to this dimension of the United Nations, and there is a distortion in the system. We hope that through this year of celebration [of the UN's 50th anniversary] we will be able to project a new image of the United Nations after the end of the Cold War, dealing with the problems of tomorrow.

Interview, United Nations, New York/ The New York Times, 1-3:(A)4.

(BOUTROS BOUTROS-GHALI)

1

I agree that the United States is the most important member [of the UN] and the main actor. But we must avoid projecting the image that the United Nations is a subcontractor of the [U.S.] State Department. That is not in the interests of the United States and not in the interest of the United Nations.

Interview,
United Nations,
New York/
The New York Times,
1-3:(A)4.

2

Absolute poverty, hunger, disease and illiteracy are the lot of one-fifth of the world's population. There can be no more urgent task for development than to attack both the causes and the symptoms of these ills.

At United Nations
World Summit
for Social Development,
Copenhagen, Denmark,
March 5/
Los Angeles Times,
3-6:(A)4.

3

States are suffering from a kind of fatigue. They thought that once the Cold War was won, they could rest easy. They are discovering instead that the Cold War masked some 30 little wars that we are facing only today. It is hard to gain support for intervention.

Interview/
World Press Review,
June:14.

4

[On the negative attitude toward the UN from the new Republican-controlled U.S. Congress]: The new majority in Congress is isolationist. It is up to us to talk to members of Congress and try to explain that it will cost them less to intervene [internationally] by peacekeeping operations through the UN system than to go it alone. And we must remind them of the material interest the U.S. has in having the UN on American soil. The U.S. is the world's most powerful nation, but there are 184 other countries that do want the UN. Of the peacekeeping operations underway, there are a dozen in which the U.S. has not participated—Mozambique, Angola and Cambodia, and even in a country as important to the U.S. as El Salvador. If worse comes to worst, if the U.S. completely loses interest in the UN, the organization could continue with the aid of the international community. It might decide to create another organization. But for the moment, there is only one international forum: the UN. Everyone has a stake in strengthening the organization. Everyone has occasion to use it. The U.S. itself was able to intervene in Iraq only after approval from the [UN] Security Council. The same goes for action in Haiti. The UN represents a political and moral force that should not be underestimated.

Interview/
World Press Review,
June:12.

5

[On working conditions at the UN]: To work here you have to be cuckoo—like me.

Newsweek,
10-30:27.

Patrick J. Buchanan
Political commentator;
Candidate for the
1996 Republican
Presidential nomination

1

This President of the United States [Clinton] has to stop thinking about some utopian New World Order and start thinking about America first. Read my [Presidential-candidate] announcement speech in 1992. I attacked [then-President] George Bush's "New World Order"—globalism, the surrendering of American sovereignty to international institutions.

Campaigning,
Coralville, Iowa/
Newsweek,
5-29:45.

Michael P.C. Carns
Director-designate
of Central Intelligence
of the United States

2

[On the continuing importance of the CIA even in today's post-Cold War period]: The Cold War may have passed into history, but regional instability, terrorism, drug trafficking, crime and the proliferation of nuclear weapons all loom large as threats to our interests and to our people . . . Reinvention and downsizing [of the CIA] will be major factors, even as we continue to produce high-quality intelligence. We will be leaner, but at the same time we will do more of the more important things.

Washington, D.C.,
Feb. 8/
Los Angeles Times,
2-9:(A)26.

Hodding Carter III
Political commentator;
Former Spokesman
for the Department of State
of the United States

3

[Criticizing U.S. President Clinton's changeable foreign policies]: The problem is inconsistency. This is a situation where the public is up for grabs, but it requires you to sustain a steady conversation about foreign policy, even though you may be taking considerable heat. But Clinton gets spooked by events or by poll results and pulls the plug on his own policy.

Los Angeles Times,
6-6:(A)8.

Jimmy Carter
Former President
of the United States

4

[On his negotiations in recent years with foreign dictators who are causing problems in the world]: The people who cause human-rights abuses are the same ones who can stop them, and if no one else will talk to them, I will. It's not only an opportunity, it's a *responsibility.* Whenever I go on a peacekeeping mission, it's with the full permission of our President. There's no doubt there's more respect for me overseas [than in the U.S., where there is criticism of him for engaging in such negotiations]. Americans are much more likely to see things in black and white: We and our friends are angels and our enemies are devils; so we will not communicate with them; we will not acknowledge their legitimate grievances or needs or ambitions or fears.

Interview/Life, November:106.

Fidel Castro
President of Cuba

1

Ultra-rightist sectors seem to be gaining considerable political terrain within the United States. That was the way the dreams of world domination rose up in Nazi Germany. Except that [Nazi leader Adolf] Hitler did not possess such gigantic power [as the U.S. does today].

At summit meeting of non-aligned nations, Cartagena, Colombia, Oct. 18/ Los Angeles Times, 10-19:(A)4.

Jacques Chirac
President of France

2

I will not hide the fact I am very worried about the isolationism of the current American Congress. I hope [U.S.] President Clinton will react against this alarming tendency toward a sort of isolationism that is very dangerous for the whole world.

Los Angeles Times, 12-2:(A)10.

Warren Christopher
Secretary of State of the United States

3

[Arguing against cutting the U.S. foreign-aid budget]: The resources that we are requesting are the rock-bottom minimum that we need to defend and advance America's interests. Last November's elections [which resulted in the Republican Party taking control of both houses of Congress] certainly changed many things; but they were not a license to lose sight of our global interests or to walk away from our commitments around the world.

Press briefing, Washington, D.C., Feb. 6/ The New York Times, 2-7:(A)4.

4

[Arguing against a proposal in the U.S. Congress to cut foreign aid and eliminate some foreign-affairs agencies]:[The bill] wages an extraordinary assault on the President's Constitutional authority to manage foreign policy . . . We cannot support our nation's foreign policy on the cheap. We cannot protect our interests as the world's most powerful nation if we do not marshal the resources to stand by our commitments.

Before Council of the Americas, May 22/ The New York Times, 5-23:(A)6.

5

The reality of Japan, Hong Kong, South Korea and Thailand tells us that the rule of law and accountable government are the bedrock of stability and prosperity. The reality of Burma and North Korea tells us that repression entrenches poverty.

To students, Hanoi, Vietnam, Aug. 6/ The Washington Post, 8-7:(A)12.

Bill Clinton
President of the United States

6

[The] new isolationists [of the Republican Party would] eliminate any meaningful

(BILL CLINTON)

role for the United Nations . . . would deny resources to peacekeepers and even to our [own] troops, and squander them on "Star Wars" [an anti-missile system]. And they would refuse aid to fledgling democracies. New isolationists, some of them being hypocritical, say we must trumpet the rhetoric of American strength but then argue against the resources we need to bring stability to the Persian Gulf, restore democracy to Haiti, control the spread of drugs and organized crime, and meet our most elemental obligations to United Nations peacekeeping. We must not let the ripple of isolationism they have generated build into a tidal wave. If we withdraw from the world today, we will have to contend with the consequences of our neglect tomorrow and tomorrow and tomorrow.

At Nixon Center for Peace and Freedom, Washington, D.C., March 1/ The Washington Post, 3-2:(A)13.

1

At the end of the Cold War, in this country and I sense throughout Europe perhaps, there are forces arguing for kind of an inward-looking approach [to foreign policy] . . . and there are others who believe we must still continue to broaden the frontiers of relationships, to expand trade in order to support democracy and prosperity. I am in that latter group.

News conference, Washington D.C., April 4/ Los Angeles Times, 4-5:(A)6.

2

[Criticizing U.S. Congressional proposals to cut foreign aid and some foreign-affairs agencies]: Under the cover of budget-cutting, back-door isolationists on the left and the right want to cut the legs off of our leadership. We did not win the Cold War to walk away and blow the peace on foolish penny-wise-pound-foolish budgeting.

Speech/ The New York Times, 5-23:(A)6.

3

[Criticizing the Republican-controlled U.S. Congress for its proposals to cut foreign aid and reduce the President's foreign policy authority]:[These are] the most isolationist proposals to come before the United States Congress in the last 50 years . . . Taken together, these constraints represent nothing less than a frontal assault on the authority of the President to conduct the foreign policy of the United States, and on our nation's ability to respond rapidly and effectively to threats to our security. [The proposals] would compromise our efforts to stop North Korea's nuclear program, impose conditions that could derail our support for democratic reform in Russia, and restrict the President's ability to prevent illegal immigration [to the U.S.] . . . While I hope it doesn't happen any time soon, someday there will be a Republican President here again and this is about the Presidency. The Presidency cannot be hamstrung [in foreign policy].

To reporters, Washington, D.C., May 23/ Los Angeles Times, 5-24:(A)1, 18.

(BILL CLINTON)

1

Over the years, [the UN] has grown too bloated, too often encouraging duplication, and spending resources on meetings rather than results. As its board of directors, all of us—we the member states—must create a UN that is more flexible, that operates more rapidly, that wastes less and produces more, and more importantly, that inspires confidence among our governments and our people.

At ceremony marking 50th anniversary of the United Nations, San Francisco, Calif., June 26/ The New York Times, 6-27:(A)5.

2

[International] peacekeeping [operations] can only succeed when the parties to a conflict understand they cannot profit from war. We have too often asked our peacekeepers to work miracles while denying them the military and political support required and the modern command-and-control systems they need to do their job as safely and effectively as possible.

At ceremony marking 50th anniversary of the United Nations, San Francisco, Calif., June 26/ The New York Times, 6-27:(A)5.

3

This isolationist backlash [in the U.S.], which is present in both [political] parties, is very real. And if you look at it from the point of view of people who feel threatened by the changes in the world, it is even completely understandable. So it is important that we not simply condemn it, it is even more important that we explain the way the world is working . . . There are people who say . . . "What we need is for America to stand up alone. We'll decide what the right thing to do is and do it; let the rest of the world like it or lump it. That's what it means to be the world's only superpower." [But] that also is a disguised form of isolationism. Unilateralism in the world that we live in is not a viable option. When our vital interests are at stake, of course, we might have to act alone. But we need the wisdom to work with the United Nations.

Before Freedom House, Washington, D.C., Oct. 6/ The New York Times, 10-7:1,5.

4

Does the United Nations need to be reformed? Has a lot of our money and everybody else's money been wasted? Of course. Is that an argument for taking a dive on the United Nations? No.

Before Freedom House, Washington, D.C., Oct. 6/ Los Angeles Times, 10-7:(A)6.

5

There are those who say . . . we can afford to relax now behind our secure borders. These are the siren songs of myth. They once lured the United States into isolationism after World War I. They counseled appeasement to Britain on the very brink of World War II. We have gone down that road before. We must

(BILL CLINTON)

never go down that road again . . . Though the Cold War is over, the forces of destruction challenge us still . . . In their variety, these forces of disintegration are waging guerrilla wars against humanity. Like Communism and Fascism . . . they will be defeated only because free nations join against them in common cause. We will prevail again if and only if our people support the mission.

Before British Parliament, London, Nov. 29/ Los Angeles Times, 11-30:(A)1,6.

1

I think the American people should know that we have a unique responsibility at this moment in history. After the Cold War, the United States was left with a certain superpower status and a certain economic standing that imposes on us great responsibilities along with the opportunities we have.

News conference, Madrid, Spain, Dec. 3/ Los Angeles Times, 12-4:(A)1.

Joseph E. Connor
Under Secretary General of the United Nations for Administration and Management

2

[Saying the UN must operate on a leaner budget]: Governments are downsizing, outsourcing, innovating, and we have to be the same way. It's imperative that all international organizations realize that they don't work for themselves; they represent the member states. They've got to justify what they produce.

Interview, United Nations, New York/ The New York Times, 4-28:(A)7.

John M. Deutch
Director of Central Intelligence of the United States

3

[On the effect on CIA intelligence-gathering operations of the Aldrich Ames double-agent spy scandal]: The Ames damage assessment, in all its detail, does nothing to shake my conviction that we need a clandestine service. Of all the intelligence disciplines, human intelligence is the most subject to human frailty, but it also brings human intuition, ingenuity and courage into play.

To reporters, Washington, D.C., Oct. 31/ Los Angeles Times, 11-1:(A)12.

Anatoly Dobrynin
Former Soviet Ambassador to the United States

4

Nowadays, Presidents like to speak directly to one another on the phone. On the one hand, that's a big plus, since after all they are the ones who make the final decisions. But Presidents still need good support teams to work out how to implement decisions. You can't discuss everything only on the highest level. Presidents are busy people; they don't know—or need to know—all the details.

Interview, Washington D.C./ U.S. News & World Report, 11-13:70.

Elton Gallegly
United States Representative,
R-California

1

[On proposals in the House to enact stiff penalties for illegal immigrants in the U.S.]: I don't think anybody should construe what we're doing as not being compassionate. We have a limit as to how generous we as a country can be.

Los Angeles Times,
6-29:(A)1.

Norbert Garrett
Former Station Chief,
Central Intelligence Agency
of the United States

2

[On whether the CIA should be used for "economic espionage" to help U.S. companies in foreign countries now that the Cold War is over]: The Agency for [the] last five years or so has been wrestling with the question of whether it has a role in support of American industry. It may sound crazy, using an intelligence apparatus to find out the French position on how many American movies [the French want to] import. But if it was of sufficient importance to the American side in the trade negotiations, you could make a case that there's a role.

The New York Times,
2-23:(A)4.

Leslie Gelb
President, Council on
Foreign Relations,
(United States)

3

The main strategic challenge for the United States [in the post-Cold War era is to] develop plans . . . to stem [foreign] civil wars . . . [They are] the new core problem in post-Cold War politics. Democracies have a large practical as well as moral stake in finding reasonable responses [to such conflicts].

The Atlantic Monthly,
May:58,67.

Benjamin A. Gilman
United States Representative,
R-New York

4

[On a House bill to cut foreign-aid spending and put more reins on how it is spent]: This bill charts a new and positive direction for the conduct of U.S. foreign policy. It scrapes away 50 years' worth of barnacles and cobwebs that have accumulated during the Cold War.

June 8/
The New York Times,
6-9:(A)7.

Newt Gingrich
United States Representative,
R-Georgia;
Speaker of the House

5

[Criticizing those who say conservatives such as himself who are wary of U.S. foreign interventions are isolationist]: I'm always curious when there is some presumption we are in any way isolationist . . . My commitment to the international cause of freedom is pretty overwhelming.

March 1/
Los Angeles Times,
3-2:(A)7.

(NEWT GINGRICH)

1

[On U.S. foreign policy]: We're now married to the world. But we keep acting like we're on a big date.

Newsweek,
7-31:19.

Patrick Glynn
Resident scholar,
American Enterprise Institute

2

[Saying the big powers may not want to get involved in major foreign-policy issues for a while]: You have domestically beleaguered [big-power] governments, you have a messy world in which there's not a lot of agreement, and you have a lot of countries with unclear definitions of what their vital interests are.

The Christian Science Monitor,
2-1:7.

Phil Gramm
United States Senator,
R-Texas;
Candidate for the
1996 Republican
Presidential nomination

3

[Criticizing U.S. President Clinton's handling of foreign affairs]: There is no isolationism in my heart and no protectionism. But part of being a great power is understanding when to use power. And the President treats foreign policy like social work. He sees something on television and [it] looks like there is some good to be done, and he makes commitments without thinking through the ramifications of it.

Interview/
Los Angeles Times,
3-6:(A)8.

4

Foreign policy is not social work. You don't look around the world for things you could do to make things better.

Broadcast interview/
"This Week With David Brinkley,"
ABC-TV, 11-26.

Jesse Helms
United States Senator,
R-North Carolina

5

[Proposing the elimination of a number of U.S. foreign-policy-oriented agencies by merging them into the State Department]: Our foreign-policy institutions are a complete mess. Over the past four decades, key foreign-policy functions have been spun off into a constellation of money-absorbing, incoherent satellites, each with its own entrenched, growing bureaucracies and its own bureaucratic interest. The result has been an incoherent mishmash which no one policy-maker can control.

News conference,
Washington D.C., March 15/
The New York Times,
3-16:(A)3.

6

If the whole concept of giving foreign aid seems foreign to many Americans, it should, because it doesn't make any sense.

USA Today,
5-25:(A)8.

Bruce Hoffman
Co-director,
Center for the
Study of Terrorism
and Political Violence,
St. Andrews University
(Scotland)

1

[On the recent terrorist attack using poison gas in the Tokyo subway]: We've definitely crossed a threshold. This is the cutting edge of high-tech terrorism for the year 2000 and beyond. It's the nightmare scenario that people have quietly talked about for years coming true.

Los Angeles Times,
3-21:(A)1.

Sut Jhalloy
Professor of communications,
University of Massachusetts,
Amherst (United States)

2

[Expressing concern about the international nature of the new mass media and their influence on foreign cultures]: I don't think it's bad by itself, a culture changing—many are very repressive toward women—but where does the change come from and who's in control? My perspective is that it's always dangerous when a culture gives up control of its cultural space to outside influences, because you cannot control them, whether they be good or bad, regardless of their intention. I worry about a global culture that is becoming driven by a few giant corporations who don't care about culture, who only care about selling.

The Christian Science Monitor,
3-22:8.

John Paul II
Pope

3

Unhappily, the world has yet to learn how to live with diversity, as recent [conflicts] in the Balkans and Central Africa have painfully reminded us. Amplified by historic grievances and exacerbated by the manipulations of the unscrupulous, the fear of "difference" can lead to a denial of the very humanity of "the other," with the result that people fall into a cycle of violence in which no one is spared, not even the children.

At United Nations,
New York, Oct. 5/
Los Angeles Times,
10-6:(A)27.

Chalmers Johnson
Professor of economics,
University of California, San Diego;
President, Japan Policy
Research Institute (United States)

4

[On a new U.S. trade agreement with Japan aimed at opening up Japan's market for U.S. auto products]: This was a total Japanese victory. [U.S.] President Clinton has managed to demonstrate that the only thing he knows and is good at is [domestic] politics.

USA Today,
6-29:(B)3.

Ahmad Kamal
Pakistani Ambassador/
Permanent Representative
to the United Nations

5

[Criticizing proposals aimed at reforming the UN's financial affairs]: The objective

(AHMAD KAMAL)

of the developed world is to create a kind of stockade it can live behind. The developed world says to the developing world, "You're not using well the money we're giving you." But it's a subterfuge to preserve the stockade. The developing countries want more money from the developed countries, and they see [financial] reform [proposals] as a cover-up for an even further decline.

Time,
10-23:76.

Samuel Kernell
Presidential scholar,
University of California,
San Diego

1

Foreign-policy successes don't help Presidents win re-election. But foreign-policy failures can hurt them.

Los Angeles Times,
11-28:(A)8.

Robert M. Kimmitt
Former Under Secretary
for Political Affairs,
Department of State
of the United States

2

[Warning against the U.S. turning too inward in its foreign policy]: [Following World War II,] the natural tendency was to return to our problems at home. But we had a group of people who realized that we must be strong and successful abroad. My sense is that we're slipping back into a sort of zero-sum analysis—the kind that can give you trouble.

Los Angeles Times,
5-3:(A)10.

Anthony Lake
Assistant to President
of the United States
Bill Clinton
for National Security Affairs

3

[Criticizing an increasing sentiment in the U.S. for isolationism and cutbacks in foreign-policy funding]: Our policy of engagement in world affairs is under siege, and American leadership is in peril . . . These back-door isolationists and unilateralists cast themselves as the true guardians of American power. But through their actions, they could become the agents of American retreat. They champion American leadership, but they want it the one way you can't have it: on the cheap . . . Defeating [foreign] threats requires persistent engagement and hands-on policies. Defeating them demands resources. Throwing money at problems won't make them go away—but we also cannot solve problems without money. The measure of American leadership is not only the strength and attraction of our values, but what we bring to the table to solve the hard issues before us.

Before
Woodrow Wilson Center,
Washington, D.C., April 27/
The New York Times,
4-28:(A)7.

Lee Teng-hui
President of Taiwan

4

We believe that international relations should not be solely seen in terms of formal operations regulated by international law and international organizations. We say so because there also are semi-official and unofficial rules that bind the international activities of nations.

(LEE TENG-HUI)

This being so, we submit that a nation's substantive contribution to the international community has to be appreciated in light of such non-official activities as well.

At Cornell University, June 9/ Nation's Business, October:60.

David Little
Scholar, U.S. Peace Institute

1

[On the recent assassination of Israeli Prime Minister Yitzhak Rabin, who was killed by an Israeli religious extremist]: Groups that think their spiritual destinies are in jeopardy often turn to extreme means to protect themselves when they believe no one else will listen or protect the values they believe in. Because of the current global upheaval that is threatening the fundamental way of life in many parts of the world, no doubt we'll see more of this [violent behavior] in the future.

Los Angeles Times, 11-6:(A)12.

Robert L. Livingston
United States Representative, R-Louisiana

2

[Saying the U.S. has become involved in too many foreign military and peacekeeping missions in recent years]: Sooner or later, we have to say, "Look, we gave at the office." And the rest of these countries are going to have to pony up. They've got to pay their share. I think the [1994 U.S.] elections [said] . . . scale it back . . . our international presence—but most importantly our being looked upon as Uncle Sucker.

The Washington Post, 1-23:(A)14.

Edward Luck
President-emeritus, United Nations Association of the United States

3

It's really quite remarkable that there would even be an attempt to put the UN in the middle of a [civil war in a] place like Bosnia or Somalia. It's no picnic to be in these places. Much of the humanitarian and peacekeeping work that's been done is really quite heroic . . . Yes, the track record is mixed, but isn't that better than having no track record at all? The rest of us are sitting on the sidelines—carping.

The Christian Science Monitor, 1-4:6.

Nelson Mandela
President of South Africa

4

[The developing world believes] the United Nations should be restructured so as to reflect the main forms of civilization in the world. And there should be no monopoly by the Western powers on the permanent seats at the Security Council. That is what is being raised, and I think it is a very fair argument. The developing countries are also saying that we must examine the distribution of resources; it is hunger, poverty and disease that make people rebel. At the same time, we must not dismiss the Western powers' concerns—they carry the financial burden.

Interview, New York, N.Y./ Newsweek, 11-6:51.

Charles William Maynes
Editor,
"Foreign Policy" magazine

1

[Former Secretary of State Henry] Kissinger changed the job description for Secretary of State. To be considered good, it's now become one of the requirements of the job to dominate the media or manipulate it.

Newsweek,
6-26:33.

John McCain
United States Senator,
R-Arizona

2

[Criticizing U.S. President Clinton's handling of foreign affairs]: I have always respected the foreign-policy prerogatives of the Commander-in-Chief. But I must say, at times, my fidelity to that principle has been tested by the frustration I have experienced as I have seen threats left unanswered and opportunities left unexploited by a foreign policy that has—as far as I can determine—no conceptual framework to guide it.

At conference sponsored
by Nixon Center
for Peace and Justice,
Washington, D.C.,
March 2/
The New York Times,
3-3:(A)5.

Mitch McConnell
United States Senator,
R-Kentucky

3

If we have a mandate [from the people] to shrink the [U.S.] government, foreign aid is certainly not going to be exempt from that. And so the issue becomes: What do you do with a shrinking [foreign-aid] pie? My view is you have a sort of laser-like focus on where American interests lie. And the principal criteria for expenditure of tax dollars abroad ought to be what is in our national-security interest . . . We ought not to be spending money on anything abroad we wouldn't be spending it on at home. Sort of the "smell test" for foreign aid . . . I'm an internationalist. I believe in foreign aid as a tool . . . There are others who don't think we ought to have it at all . . . But I do think that aid ought to be married up with interest.

Interview,
Washington, D.C./
Los Angeles Times,
1-8:(M)3.

Michael D. McCurry
Press Secretary
to President
of the United States
Bill Clinton

4

[On growing Congressional criticism of President Clinton's handling of foreign policy]: I can't think of another time when there has been such controversy [over the conduct of foreign policy] between the Executive and Legislative branches. Foreign policy is playing the kind of role in national politics that it played in 1973 and 1974, in the aftermath of Vietnam and Cambodia. Once again, we are seeing foreign policy being used as a device by the President's opponents to define themselves politically.

Interview/
The Washington Post,
6-26:(A)4.

Hosni Mubarak
President
of Egypt

1

Democracy in the United States can't work in Saudi Arabia. It can't work here or there. Each country has its special tradition, it's special way of dealing. So you can't ask all countries to have the same democracy. It will never work. What's happening in Africa because of democracy and freedom? Every day, there is a coup, a coup, a coup—because of democracy. In some countries, [there are] tribal systems. Do you want them to have democratic systems? Look at what happened in Rwanda and Burundi.

Interview,
Washington, D.C./
Los Angeles Times,
4-9:(M)3.

Sadako Ogata
United Nations
High Commissioner
for Refugees

2

[On the UN's refugee operations]: It is our job to carry on with our work no matter what. This is painful because we cannot solve problems unless there are political solutions. But since the political solutions don't come, we have to carry on a lot of the alibi work. Under the beautiful name "humanitarian," there is a lot of non-action.

Interview,
Geneva, Switzerland/
Vogue,
September:388.

Shah Pakash
Ambassador/
Permanent Representative
to the United Nations
from India

3

The East-West [Cold War] has ended, but the North-South [divide between the developed and the developing nations] has not ended. While political issues receded into the background because of the end of the Cold War, there are still many non-political issues that are unresolved.

At summit meeting
of non-aligned nations,
Cartagena, Colombia, Oct. 18/
Los Angeles Times,
10-19:(A)4.

Karl Paschke
Under Secretary General
of the United Nations
for Internal Oversight Services

4

After seven months on [this] job, I think the UN is a good example of waste and inefficiency.

Time, 10-23:75.

Shimon Peres
Foreign Minister of Israel

5

What we are trying to do [today] is define a new character of a border. Instead of making the border a dividing line, and having to fortify it with fences and mines, we want to make the whole border an occasion for economic cooperation.

Interview/
"Interview" magazine,
July:88.

William J. Perry
Secretary of Defense
of the United States

1

We do not envision any major NATO operations being conducted . . . without the U.S. It has to do with U.S. leadership as much as anything.

Sept. 14/
USA Today, 9-15:(A)2.

Thomas Polgar
Former Bonn (Germany) and
Saigon (Vietnam) Station Chief,
Central Intelligence Agency
of the United States

2

[On the CIA's role in the post-Cold War world]: That is the real crisis of American intelligence: What is the clandestine service supposed to be doing these days? Learning the intentions and capabilities of the enemy had a potential impact on the national security of the United States. The question of whether or not the French allow fewer Disney movies into their country [which the CIA has allegedly been secretly investigating] does not affect the national security of the United States . . . Maybe there are economic issues that are important [and that the CIA may be involved in covertly investigating]. But the question is, what can the CIA do about them that the rest of the American government cannot?

The New York Times,
2-23:(A)4.

Poul Nyrup Rasmussen
Prime Minister
of Denmark

3

Europe has now lived through a period where thousands and thousands and thousands of refugees are coming from various parts of the world. I feel that ordinary people now recognize more and more [what] the global situation is. You don't have the Cold War. You don't have a well-defined enemy. But you have a hot peace, in the way that you see new ethnic conflicts, new social conflicts. We have a good argument now, a very concrete one, for ordinary people, which is, if you don't help the Third World, if you don't help northern Africa, if you don't help eastern and central Europe with a little part of your welfare, then you will have these poor people in our society.

Interview,
Copenhagen, Denmark/
The New York Times,
3-10:(A)5.

Jeremy Rosner
Scholar,
Carnegie Endowment
for International Peace
(United States)

4

[On increasing Congressional criticism of U.S. President Clinton's handling of foreign policy]: Peace on Earth usually means less peace down the length of Pennsylvania Avenue. If there is a benign security environment, it is more or less inevitable that Congress will be more assertive, no matter who controls it.

The Washington Post,
6-26:(A)4.

5

[On the large number of new, Republican members of the U.S. Congress]: These are not people who came to Congress to work

(JEREMY ROSNER)

on foreign policy. If some of them are more extreme than other Congressmen about [cutting] foreign aid, it's because they came to town to shrink the [Federal budget] deficit. If some of them are more extreme about reorganizing the State Department, it's because they came to town to shrink the size of the Federal government. Everyone's looking for the new strategic doctrine for foreign policy that will replace [Cold War] containment [of the Soviet Union]. Well, I think we've got a new doctrine. It's called deficit reduction.

Los Angeles Times,
12-2:(A)12.

Joseph Rotblat
Founder, Pugwash Conferences on Science and World Affairs

1

[On the 1995 Nobel Peace Prize being awarded to him and his Pugwash Conferences, which have argued for decades against nuclear weapons]: I see this honor not for me personally, but rather for the small group of scientists who have been working for 40 years to try to save the world, often against the world's wish.

Time, 10-23:84.

Wayne Rychak
Director, Office of Physical Security Programs, Department of State of the United States

2

There's now a realization that there's not a budget big enough to continue to build [U.S. diplomatic] missions throughout the world with total risk-avoidance [against terrorist attacks]. As budgets shrink, the money spent on building fortresses can't be justified when you don't even have the funds for ordinary diplomacy.

Los Angeles Times,
11-14:(A)10.

Chris Sale
Deputy Director, Immigration and Naturalization Service of the United States

3

[On illegal immigration to the U.S.]: Until it is understood that if you attempt to enter illegally, you will be stopped; until it is understood that if you are here illegally, you will be found and processed for removal; until it is understood that if you have exhausted your opportunity for consideration under the law, you will be removed, we will not achieve the fundamental objective of public confidence in the immigration system, which we hope will then guarantee our commitment to legal immigration.

At briefing at USIA Foreign Press Center, Washington, D.C., Feb. 15/
The Washington Post,
2-16:(A)22.

Ephraim Sneh
Minister of Health of Israel

4

The processes that dominate the world now are of national separation and economic integration. People think they have to have their own flag, passport and identity, but they want to erase borders when it comes to trade.

Los Angeles Times,
10-26:(A)11.

Stephen J. Solarz
Former United States Representative, D-New York

1

[Foreign policy in the U.S. Congress this year] is characterized neither by internationalism nor isolationism, but by indifference. There's a feeling [in Congress] now that with the end of the Cold War, there are not many vital American interests anywhere in the world.

Los Angeles Times, 12-2:(A)10.

Dick Thornburgh
Former Attorney General of the United States

2

[On the UN]: The potential is there and the talent is there, but first you've got to clear away 45 years of debris. The United Nations is being asked to be the world's 911 emergency number, and it can't handle it.

USA Today, 6-26:(A)4.

Paul E. Tsongas
Co-chairman, The Concord Coalition (United States); Former United States Senator, D-Massachusetts

3

Nuclear terrorism is *the* foreign-policy threat. It is somebody who has access to a nuclear weapon who has a hatred. This idea of leaving behind all these people who have a hatred of the United States because we have indifference to their plight will inevitably lead to one of them pulling it off. The notion that you can have a foreign policy that is morality-free is an illusion. The notion that you can be safe because there is an Atlantic and a Pacific Ocean is also an illusion in a nuclear age. We have all this nuclear weaponry floating around in black-market circumstances.

Interview, Boston, Mass./The Christian Science Monitor, 1-19:19.

Brian Urquhart
Scholar-in-residence, Ford Foundation (United States); Former Under Secretary General for Special Political Affairs of the United Nations

4

[On the UN]: What's there now is probably just enough to prevent the worst from happening [in the world]. But there's not a hope in hell it can make a dent in the really big problems: conflicts, poverty, environment, women's rights, unemployment.

USA Today, 6-26:(A)4.

Thomas Weiss
Authority on peacekeeping operations, Brown University (United States)

5

[On the increase in UN-sanctioned, but not UN-controlled, foreign military operations by various countries]: I do think these kinds of [UN] subcontracts . . . are probably the wave of the future, and we might as well recognize it. Peacekeeping operations are becoming more and more military. The UN is an over-developed political animal and an under-developed military one.

The Christian Science Monitor, 1-4:6.

Charles Wheeler
Director,
National Immigration
Law Center
(United States)

1

[Criticizing proposals in the House to enact stiff penalties for illegal immigrants in the U.S.]: This eclipses [California's] Proposition 187 in its severity and mean-spiritedness. These are probably the most extreme measures one could take. It's the equivalent of killing a mosquito with a neutron bomb.

Los Angeles Times,
6-29:(A)16.

Philip C. Wilcox
Coordinator
for Counterterrorism,
Department of State
of the United States

2

[Saying more countries today are willing to fight terrorism]: There's less ambivalence in the world today that terrorism is simply a crime, whereas in the past there was often a tendency to tolerate terrorism, to look the other way, because of the political motivation of the terrorists.

News conference, April 28/
The New York Times,
4-29:5.

Africa

Ahmedou Ould Abdallah
United Nations
Special Representative
in Burundi

1

[On trying to prevent ethnic conflict in Burundi]: All we do is postpone short-term [disasters]. Here, long term is the day after tomorrow . . . [and] the future is immediate survival . . . Whatever you do, with the population doubling every 15 years . . . Burundi will explode every five or 10 years. Burundi's second-largest city is a refugee camp; 60 percent of the population is under 20, and there are no prospects for work abroad.

Interview,
Bujumbura, Burundi/
The Washington Post,
4-10:(A)12.

Sully Abu
Former editor,
"African Guardian"
magazine (Nigeria)

2

[On government repression in Nigeria]: There's such a pall of helplessness over the place that people feel like things can only get worse [without international intervention]. These people [in the military government] don't care about public opinion here. If you don't agree with them, they blow your brains out or throw you in jail.

The Washington Post,
4-3:(A)1,16.

Sharaf-el-Din Ibrahim Bannaga
Minister of Housing,
Khartoum State,
Sudan

3

[On the criticism of the Muslim Sudanese government's bulldozing of residential areas where predominantly non-Arab, non-Islamic people live]: Is bulldozing only done in Sudan? There is bulldozing going on everywhere—in Europe, South America. Wherever you have illegal building, you have to demolish them because you cannot leave anyone to grab a piece of land.

The Christian Science Monitor,
7-26:7.

Mustapha Bouhade
National secretary,
Front for Socialist Forces
(Algeria)

4

[Saying the Algerian government is wrong in using force to stop Islamic fundamentalists from taking over the country]: The only way to control armed groups is by allowing their political leadership to play a political role. I don't fear Islamists if I have to combat them democratically. What the government is doing, instead, is getting us used to a certain level of violence as they proceed under the notion of eradicating Islamists. It won't work. Neither the Army nor the Islamists can settle this by force.

The New York Times,
6-6:(A)6.

Boutros Boutros-Ghali
Secretary General of the United Nations

1

[On the inability of the UN to prevent genocide in Rwanda]: This is, after all, the result of a certain indifference with regard to a certain continent. I knocked on the doors of 35 African heads of state, looking for involvement by their troops. But they didn't budge. It took the publication of photographs in the press to finally rally public opinion [in the world] . . . I swear to you that we could have stopped the genocide in Rwanda with 400 paratroopers.

Interview/ World Press Review, June:14.

Jimmy Carter
Former President of the United States

2

[On the civil war in Sudan, for which he just negotiated a cease-fire]: [This war has] been going on for 12 years. One of the major reasons is the efforts [by the Sudanese government] to impose Islamic laws in the entire country. This includes the southern region, where most people are either Christian or non-Muslim. This is one of the issues that will have to be solved—whether or not the Islamic law will apply over people who are not Muslims.

Interview, Plains, Ga., March 30/ USA Today, 3-31:(A)13.

John Chipman
Director, International Institute for Strategic Studies (Britain)

3

In the early 1990s, [now-French President Jacques] Chirac said that Africa was not ready for democracy, warming the hearts of a number of scoundrels. But a certain number of issues have been resolved for Chirac before his arrival in power, and my impression is that a lot of these views will be modernized.

The New York Times, 7-22:5.

Alex de Waal
Co-director, Africa Rights (Britain)

4

[On the Sudanese government's alleged efforts to oust non-Arab, non-Islamic residents]: Some international organizations say this government can't be criticized because [it is] Muslim and [it] should be allowed to be different. But the vast majority of Sudanese detest what is going on.

The Christian Science Monitor, 7-26:7.

Elizabeth II
Queen of England

5

[On post-apartheid South Africa]: You have become one nation whose spirit of reconciliation is a shining example to the world, and I have come back to see for myself what is little short of a miracle.

Before South African Parliament, Cape Town, South Africa, March 20/ Los Angeles Times, 3-21:(A)10.

Ibrahim Gambari
Nigerian Ambassador to the United Nations

1

[Denying charges that Nigeria's government is repressive]: [It} has not oppressed anyone. [The arrests of activists and politicians have been] because the survival of Nigeria is paramount. We had to maintain stability. These activists wanted to make political points. They were not thinking about what is best for Nigeria.

March/ The Washington Post, 4-3:(A)16.

Victor Gbeho
United Nations Special Envoy to Somalia

2

[On the departure of U.S. and UN peacekeeping forces from civil-war-torn Somalia]: When the history of Somalia comes to be written, it will be seen that we made more gains than losses. Our mistake was the police action taken in the middle of '93, when we mistook the woods for the tree.

Mogadishu, Somalia, Feb. 28/ The New York Times, 3-3:(A)3.

Shaharyar Khan
United Nations Special Representative to Rwanda

3

One has at the back of his mind, always, that civil war can break out again [in Rwanda]. This country is held together by a slender thread . . . And the history of Rwanda tells us that this slender thread breaks from time to time.

Los Angeles Times, 9-14:(A)12.

Nelson Mandela
President of South Africa

4

[On criticism that his government has not delivered on what it promised in last year's election]: There are many political commentators throughout the world who are deaf and dumb. They never see the progress that is made by their rivals.

Speech marking the anniversary of last year's first all-race democratic election in South Africa, April 27/ USA Today, 4-28:(A)10.

5

In the last 18 months, we [in the ruling ANC] have done far more [for the South African people] than the National Party did in 45 years of its rule. But the people have forgotten that. They want houses. They want jobs. They want to see. We go to them and remind them of our achievements. And I've gone to the private sector, to involve them, and they are helping. Now we've finished our planning, and delivery is coming onstream. But it requires a great deal of work on the ground, and that may affect our chances in the coming local elections.

Interview, New York, N.Y./ Newsweek, 11-6:51.

(NELSON MANDELA)

1

The ANC never had a socialistic policy. In 1956, I wrote an article pointing out that implementation of the [ANC's] Freedom Charter would actually lead to the blossoming of capitalism among [South African] blacks for the first time in history. It was based on private enterprise. The only exception was a clause which called for the nationalization of the mines and a ban on monopolies. And we've learned from the experience of the rest of the world that nationalization and state ownership of enterprises has its problems.

Interview,
New York, N.Y./
Newsweek,
11-6:51.

George Moose
Assistant Secretary
for African Affairs,
Department of State
of the United States

2

There is growing evidence that Africa is, in fact, undergoing a major transformation, potentially comparable to what Latin America experienced over the past decade. I think the clearest indicators of this transformation are the growth in the expansion of democratic governments and democratic institutions and the parallel development, the very significant development in terms of economic reform and economic liberalization. I think it's important to note that nearly two-thirds of sub-Saharan Africa's 48 countries are now at some stage in the process of a democratic transition, compared to only four in 1989. Many African nations have taken very difficult, at times courageous, reforms aimed at creating an enabling environment in which the private sector can act as the engine of growth.

At Senate
subcommittee hearing,
Washington, D.C.,
March 28/
The Washington Post,
3-31:(A)30.

Sylvestre Ntibantunganya
President of Burundi

3

[On attempts by other African countries to avert a new conflict in Rwanda between opposing tribes]: If these people want peace, they are going to have peace. If they want war, they are going to have war. It is very simple.

At conference
on peace in Rwanda,
Cairo, Egypt,
Nov. 28/
Los Angeles Times,
11-29:(A)9.

Donald M. Payne
United States Representative,
D-New Jersey

4

[Criticizing the military dictatorship in Nigeria]: Nigeria is not only harming their own people, but military leaders continue to line their pockets with drug payoffs to transport narcotics through Nigeria to our youth on the streets of every city in the United States.

March 16/
The New York Times,
3-17:(A)6.

Randall Robinson
Executive director,
TransAfrica (United States)

1

[On repression in Nigeria]: We will oppose the Nigerian government with as much tenacity as we opposed the military regime in Haiti. It is not easy to publicly criticize black leadership. It is uncomfortable and disquieting. But we are left with no alternative . . . Nigeria should be the bellwether nation of sub-Saharan Africa. It should be a viable democracy with a healthy economy . . . So it is sad to see a country moving in a diametrically opposite direction.

The Washington Post,
3-14:(A)1,13.

Saeed Saadi
Director,
Assembly for Culture
and Democracy (Algeria)

2

[Criticizing Islamic fundamentalists who are trying to take over Algeria]: Algerians have to stop fooling themselves about flirting with fundamentalism. I refuse to give power to a Fascist movement that says, "Okay, we will enter elections to get power, but once we are there we represent the word of God, and that you cannot subject to the will of man."

The New York Times,
6-6:(A)6.

Wilton S. Sankowolo
Chairman,
Council of State of Liberia

3

[On strife-torn Liberia]: I know what it means to dodge bullets and rockets. I know what it means to be incarcerated or killed for belonging to this or that ethnic group, or making the bad mistake of working for the government. I know what it means to live in the bushes, in refugee camps and displaced centers, going without food for days. I know what it means to walk up and down the streets of Monrovia in torn clothes and shoes.

At ceremony installing
the Council of State,
Monrovia, Liberia,
Sept. 1/
The New York Times,
9-2:4.

John W. Sewell
President,
Overseas Development Council
(United States)

4

[Calling on the world to invest in southern Africa]: The outside community has got to put a priority on African countries where they think they can work, where there is competence and a commitment to development. You have an area of great potential [in southern Africa]. There are other countries [in Africa] where in the immediate sense development is not possible, either because they are literally torn apart, like Somalia, or they are in some form of anarchy, like Zaire . . . The four great recipients of United States aid to Africa in the 1980s—under the [Presidents Ronald] Reagan and [George] Bush Administrations, though really starting with [Jimmy] Carter, to be fair—Sudan, Somalia, Liberia and Zaire. The amount of money was horrifying. Something like $800 million for Somalia over the decade, all for Cold War rea-

(JOHN W. SEWELL)

sons. And it was all wasted. Ratholes are bipartisan in the U.S.

Interview,
Copenhagen, Denmark/
The New York Times,
3-9:(A)4.

Tokyo Sexwale
Premier
of Transvaal Province,
South Africa

1

Crime in South Africa has created fear, it has created panic. Crime has frightened foreign investors. Crime has undermined our job-creation strategy. Crime threatens tourism. Crime threatens our total economic activity. Crime threatens our lives.

At rally,
Johannesburg, South Africa/
Los Angeles Times,
11-30:(A)12.

Abdelrahman Sherif
Minister
of the Interior
of Algeria

2

[Criticizing Islamic fundamentalists who are trying to take over Algeria]: We have to do everything we can now to return social and civil peace to Algeria, and we will make every effort toward this goal . . . We are not playing anymore because you cannot talk to people who adopt violence as their creed, people who decapitate, who rape and cut women's breasts, who kill innocents.

The New York Times,
6-6:(A)1,6.

Daniel Simpson
United States
Special Envoy
to Somalia

3

[On the departure of U.S. and UN peacekeeping forces from civil-war-torn Somalia]: People who look at the Somali situation now with even a small amount of optimism operate from the premise that it may be that now that the foreigners are absolutely leaving Somalia, the Somalis themselves may be able to get together, close the door, inside the family, and say, "Okay, now it's time to wrap it up and make a government." It's their turn now. I've told them categorically: You're out of time . . . The world may have bitten off more than it can chew in terms of trying to bring the Somalis to a government . . . None of [the West's approaches] worked very well, or some of them worked partly, but we never quite got there because the Somalis themselves lacked the will to form a government.

Interview/
The New York Times,
3-3:(A)3.

Benjamin Stora
Analyst,
Maghreb-Europe Institute
(France)

4

The French political class thinks about Algeria only in the simplest terms—Algerians are either democrats or non-democrats. After Algeria became independent [in 1962], they were no longer interested in Algeria. The Algerian war was simply forgotten. A collective amnesia set in.

The Christian Science Monitor,
1-4:7.

Liamine Zeroual
President of Algeria

1

[On his victory in the just-held Algerian elections]: [I am] President of all Algerians. [The election is a] victory for democracy [and] a lesson to the internal and external enemies of Algeria.

Algerian broadcast address, Nov. 17/ Los Angeles Times, 11-18:(A)12.

The Americas

Dwayne O. Andreas
Chairman,
Archer Daniels Midland Company
(United States)

1

[On Cuban President Fidel Castro, whom he saw at a recent dinner in New York]: These Communists used to be ideological crusaders. But the Communists of 1995 are managers of businesses. Fidel talked like the general manager of AT&T. Even his language is that of a businessman. He was talking about his working-capital requirements, his depreciation problems, his repair problems.

Time,
11-6:47.

Jean-Bertrand Aristide
President of Haiti

2

Never again will the uniform and a gun be used to suppress the rights of our [Haitian] people. A uniform and a gun will never again lead us to tyranny and brutality. The sons and daughters, and our Constitution, represent our future.

At graduation
of Haitian police cadets,
Port-au-Prince, Haiti,
June 4/
Los Angeles Times,
6-5:(A)20.

3

[On the recent Haitian elections]: [The voting was] a major step toward democracy for my country . . . The Haitian people demonstrated that they wanted to vote, and they did . . . The technical aspect was not what we would wish, [and there were] incidents which we regret . . . [But] we were delighted to be able to cast ballots in a free, calm, non-violent atmosphere [this time]. This year we have ballots, not bullets. This is great.

Interview,
Port-au-Prince, Haiti,
June 27/
The New York Times,
6-28:(A)4.

4

We are building this nation slowly, as in putting pieces of broken glass together.

To foreign journalists,
Port-au-Prince, Haiti,
Nov. 30/
Los Angeles Times,
12-1:(A)14.

Martin Balza
Chief of Staff,
Argentinean Army

5

[Saying that in the 1970s the Argentinean military tortured and killed political prisoners]: Some of the members of the military dishonored the uniforms that they should not have worn. To be fair, all Argentines are guilty of this past conflict, either by action or omission, by absence or excess, by condoning or counseling.

Argentinean
broadcast statement,
April 25/
The New York Times,
4-27:(A)5.

Michael Bliss
Historian,
University of Toronto
(Canada)

1

[On Canadian Prime Minister Jean Chretien's recent suggestion that the countries of the Americas, other than the U.S., get together as a group to counter U.S. economic might in the hemisphere]: This is a historic Canadian strategy. He is telling these countries that anyone that tries dealing with the U.S. one-on-one is bound to be the mouse in bed with the elephant. Not only that, Chretien is trying to get all the mice together.

The Christian Science Monitor,
1-25:1.

Enrique Borgo (Bustamente)
Vice President
of El Salvador

2

[In El Salvador,] peace is not enough. We need social peace. We need to remake whatever was Salvador. We need to walk that last part of the road, and we feel so short of breath.

Interview,
United Nations,
New York,
Jan. 4/
The New York Times,
1-5:(A)7.

Lucien Bouchard
Leader,
Parti Quebecois (Canada)

3

[On the narrow loss for Quebec separatists in the recent referendum on the province's secession from Canada]: Let's keep the faith. Let's keep hoping [for Quebec's independence], because the next time [there is a referendum] will be the right time—and the next time could come more quickly than we believe.

To supporters,
Montreal, Canada, Oct. 30/
Los Angeles Times,
10-31:(A)1.

Jose Cardenas
Director,
Cuban-American
National Foundation
(United States)

4

[Criticizing the positive reception Cuban President Fidel Castro received from business, media and society types during his recent visit to New York]: How dispiriting for Cubans sitting in misery and squalor to see Fidel Castro feted in New York by the powers that be. His acceptance by them could have set back the prospects for freedom and democracy in Cuba by five years.

Time,
11-6:47.

Fernando Henrique Cardoso
President
of Brazil

5

[With] the opening of the Brazilian economy, we are leaving behind xenophobic attitudes. Today, there is no serious specialist who does not forecast for Brazil anything but a long period of growth.

Inaugural address,
Brasilia, Brazil,
Jan. 1/
The New York Times,
1-2:3.

(FERNANDO HENRIQUE CARDOSO)

1

[On criticism that he has had a slow beginning to his Presidency, which started this past January]: You have to set a goal, and then build your road to get there. You lose today. You win tomorrow. You have to have perseverance.

Interview,
Brasilia, Brazil/
The New York Times,
4-15:4.

Fidel Castro
President of Cuba

2

Foreign investment [in Cuba] is working, and we see it as an important source for development; we would not have had another alternative. [But] we don't want to sell the country . . . nor are we prepared to sell the country. We are doing business with factories that are stalled, factories that don't have raw materials, factories that don't have a market.

Interview/
Los Angeles Times,
2-9:(D)4.

3

[On foreign criticism of the limited, one-party local elections held in Cuba]: People want us to have elections where they spend millions of dollars, like in the United States. You have to have a lot of money in the democracy of the rich. Who here does it for money, when they do not even receive a salary for their work? Here is a democracy like no other, where people propose and elect their candidates. We cannot go back to the dirty politics of before [the revolution], where only those with money could run. Here, we spend not one penny. It is democracy for the poor.

News conference,
Havana, Cuba, July 9/
The Washington Post,
7-10:(A)10.

Jean Chretien
Prime Minister
of Canada

4

[Suggesting that the countries of the Americas, other than the U.S., get together as a group to counter U.S. economic might in the hemisphere]: We have to stay united, because the United States will try to divide us to the extent that is possible.

Interview/
The Christian Science Monitor,
1-25:1.

5

[Opposing independence for Quebec, which some Quebecers say would be like a magic wand for a favorable future]: Don't put your trust in magicians. In the real world, there are no magic wands, and people have to pay their bills at the end of the month.

Speech/
Newsweek,
10-30:59.

6

[On the possibility of further Quebec referendums on the separation of that province from Canada, such as the recent one in which separatists had a narrow loss]: We cannot play the game that there will be a referendum every six months or year or two years. This country has the right to political stability. And as

(JEAN CHRETIEN)

the Prime Minister of Canada, I will make sure we have political stability in the land . . . I will do what is needed to keep this country together.

At Liberal Party fund-raiser, Toronto, Canada, Nov. 1/ Los Angeles Times, 11-2:(A)4.

Bill Clinton
President of the United States

1

[Defending his $40-billion assistance plan to help Mexico's faltering economy]: This is not simply a financial problem for Mexico, this is an American challenge. The livelihoods of thousands and thousands of our workers depend upon continued strong export growth to Mexico. That's why we must reach out and not retreat. It is vital to our interests . . . These guarantees [that are part of his plan] . . . are not foreign aid. They are not a bailout. They are not a gift. This is the equivalent of co-signing a note.

At U.S. Treasury Department, Washington, D.C., Jan. 18/ Los Angeles Times, 1-19:(D)1,3.

2

[On criticism that his $40-billion assistance plan for the troubled Mexican economy is really a bailout for Wall Street types who have money invested there]: It isn't a bailout for Wall Street. First of all, helping the economy stay strong down there [in Mexico] is more important than anything else for our [U.S.] working people and our businesses on Main Street that are doing such business in Mexico. If they want to continue to grow and to have that as a market, we can't let the financial markets, in effect, collapse the Mexican political and economic structure. Secondly, there are a lot of pension plans and ordinary Americans that have their investments tied up there [in Mexico].

Washington, D.C., Jan.30/ The New York Times, 1-31:(C)6.

3

[On Mexican President Ernesto Zedillo]: I believe that he's moving in the right direction and Mexico plainly has moved toward more democracy, more openness and more market economics.

News conference, Washington, D.C., March 3/ Los Angeles Times, 3-4:(A)14.

Alfonse M. D'Amato
United States Senator, R-New York

4

[Saying the U.S. Clinton Administration misled the American people into thinking Mexico's economy was strong in 1994 and then had to guarantee billions of dollars to bail out Mexico when its economy faltered]: Key Administration officials . . . were not candid and forthcoming about the true condition of Mexico's economy in 1994 . . . Administration officials repeatedly painted a rosy picture of the Mexican economy. That pic-

(ALFONSE M. D'AMATO)

ture was distorted and not accurate and not true.

At Senate Banking Committee hearing on the nomination of Lawrence Summers for Deputy Treasury Secretary, Washington, D.C., July 21/ The New York Times, 7-22:18.

Lionel Delatour
Haitian political analyst

1

[Saying Haitians should not be impatient for things to improve as a result of last year's U.S. military intervention to restore democracy there]: Haiti is on course for a better life due to events of September 19 [1994]. Haiti has been digging a hole for 200 years, and to think that in five or six months [U.S. President] Clinton will dig us out is not realistic.

The Washington Post, 3-30:(A)20.

Robert J. Dole
United States Senator, R-Kansas; Candidate for the 1996 Republican Presidential nomination

2

[Criticizing the U.S. Clinton Administration's $40- billion assistance plan to help Mexico in its current economic crisis]: Is it politicians from Mexico [who would be helped], or Wall Street? If that's the case, I don't want to cast my vote to expose the American taxpayer to any risk at all. It's not our purpose to bail out people who made bad investments.

Jan. 27/ The New York Times, 1-28:3.

Myles Frechette
United States Ambassador to Colombia

3

[On suggestions that NAFTA has made drug trafficking easier by lifting restrictions on trade]: It was felt by those who supported NAFTA and by the [U.S.] Clinton Administration [which wants to expand NAFTA to more of the Americas] that using the argument that any increase in trade could increase drug trafficking and money laundering was not a sufficient argument to overcome the need of the United States for increasing markets for its exports abroad.

The Christian Science Monitor, 8-2:9.

Alberto K. Fujimori
President of Peru

4

[Saying he should be re-elected to another term as President]: We should not turn Peru into a guinea pig. Let's stop experimenting. I can govern because I know how to get things done.

Peruvian broadcast interview/ USA Today, 4-7:(A)8.

Jim Gaines
Managing editor, "Time" magazine (United States)

5

[On a recent *Time* magazine-sponsored

(JIM GAINES)

tour of U.S. executives, educators, and journalists, which included a stop in Cuba]: Many in our group came away from Havana thinking the U.S. embargo against Cuba is a Cold War anachronism, but that [Cuban President Fidel] Castro's reluctance about reform made him an even bigger one.

Time,
10-23:3.

Cesar Gaviria (Trujillo)
Secretary General,
Organization
of American States

1

[On international dealings with Cuba]: Until now, the policy of all-or-nothing has not gotten us anywhere. The debate on the present and future of Cuba has been monopolized by the most extreme positions.

June/
The New York Times,
7-8:5.

Newt Gingrich
United States Representative,
R-Georgia;
Speaker of the House

2

[Supporting U.S. President Clinton's $40-billion assistance proposal for the troubled Mexican economy]: It's important to do this. It's important to find a way to make sure that we help our next-door neighbor. I am concerned about the real financial impact on Americans and the real financial impact on small business if we go through some kind of significant meltdown [in world markets because of Mexico, which could have] an immediate direct impact on every American as interest rates go up.

Jan. 30/
The New York Times,
1-31:(C)6.

Alexis Guardia
Director, Institute
for National Statistics
(Chile)

3

Chile, between '90 and '93, experienced for the first time in its history—and in an important way—what is called "equitable growth." In other words, the economy grew strongly, at about 6 percent, without deteriorating the distribution of income, in fact improving it slightly. Now the problem is whether this is a one-time thing. I will tell you that is a subject of constant conversation and discussion among government economists.

The Washington Post,
8-21:(A)17.

Jesse Helms
United States Senator,
R-North Carolina

4

Whether [Cuban President Fidel] Castro leaves Cuba in a vertical or horizontal position is up to him and the Cuban people. But he must, and will, leave Cuba.

News conference,
Washington, D.C., Feb. 9/
USA Today, 2-10:(A)4.

5

[On the recent Haitian elections]: Observers have documented countless irregular activities, including some one million lost reg-

(JESSE HELMS)

istration cards, the flagrant use of Xeroxed ballots, tally sheets intentionally altered and ballots substituted with newly market ballots, and widespread disregard for the secrecy of the balloting process.

June 27/
The New York Times,
6-28:(A)4.

Chavannes Jean-Baptiste
Haitian
civil-rights leader

1

[On Haiti since last year's U.S. military intervention aimed at restoring democracy]: The only positive thing we have felt from the occupation is that the President [Jean-Bertrand Aristide] returned. Everything else has been disillusionment. We were hoping the Americans would disarm the paramilitary groups. We get the sense that some of the U.S. military is more tied to the old [Haitian] military than the democratic sectors of society. The U.S. troops are a waste of money, because they are not doing anything. [U.S.] President Clinton wants to portray this as a success, but for the Haitian people it has not been a success.

The Washington Post,
3-30:(A)20.

Bob Kerrey
United States Senator,
D-Nebraska

2

[On possible signs that Haitian President Jean-Bertrand Aristide, who returned to office last year through U.S. military intervention, may decide to stay as President beyond early next year, the time he originally promised he would step down]: We've [the U.S.] put a lot of money and a lot of time and risked a lot of lives down there . . . We've put a lot of energy into supporting democracy; and if he doesn't support democracy, we shouldn't support him.

Broadcast interview/
"This Week With David Brinkley,"
ABC-TV, 11-26.

Jose Lopez (Portillo)
Former President
of Mexico

3

[The function of former Mexican Presidents should be] shutting up and not creating more problems for the next President.

Interview/
The New York Times,
3-6:(A)3.

John McCain
United States Senator,
R-Arizona

4

For years [Cuban President Fidel] Castro has exported subversion and terror, and there has been no noticeable improvement in his abominable human-rights record. If he agreed to and implemented steps toward democratic reform, then I would be willing to consider relaxation of the [U.S.] trade embargo.

USA Today,
7-14:(A)7.

Michael D. McCurry
Press Secretary to President
of the United States Bill Clinton

5

[On U.S. President Clinton's $40-billion

(MICHAEL D. McCURRY)

assistance proposal for the troubled Mexican economy]: I think the President will look for every opportunity he can find to make it clear that this is not a bailout. It is not, you know, welfare for Mexico, that this is in a sense an insurance policy that helps protect our interests as well as the fundamental strength of the Mexican economy.

Washington, D.C., Jan. 30/
The New York Times,
1-31:(C)6.

Maria de Los Angeles Moreno
Member of the Mexican Senate;
President,
Institutional Revolutionary Party
of Mexico (PRI)

1

The [ruling] PRI is not in crisis. The PRI is working. It is acting. Certainly, the impact of [Mexico's] financial problem has repercussions. There is uneasiness in society. It's necessary to provide answers, to look for ways to overcome this crisis as briefly as possible and restore confidence.

At press breakfast,
Mexico City, Mexico,
Jan. 6/
Los Angeles Times,
1-7:(A)6.

Felipe A. Noguera
Argentinean political analyst

2

[The economic crisis in] Mexico has been good for [the re-election prospects of Argentinean President Carlos Saul] Menem because it reintroduced the fear factor into Argentine society. Argentines were suddenly reminded what is was like to live under hyperinflation, and many are afraid to face the future without the man (Menem) who tamed it.

The New York Times,
5-4:(A)4.

Sam Nunn
United States Senator,
D-Georgia

3

[On the $40-billion U.S. assistance proposal to help Mexico during that country's current economic crisis]: Who gets bailed out? Are we bailing out Wall Street bankers [with investments in Mexico]? Or are we bailing out pension funds [with Mexican investments] that affect American workers? Who's getting saved here, and are they taking their part of the loss because they have gone into high-yield, high-risk investments? That's a big question. [A financial rescue of Mexico is] not going to be popular [with the U.S. public], and anyone voting for it [in the U.S. Congress] is going to have to hold their nose because this is not what the public wants out there. But neither does the public want a financial debacle south of our border.

Broadcast interview/
"Meet the Press,"
NBC-TV, 1-29.

William J. Perry
Secretary of Defense
of the United States

4

[On possible signs that Haitian President Jean-Bertrand Aristide, who returned to office last year through U.S. military intervention, may decide to stay on as President beyond early next year, the time he originally

(WILLIAM J. PERRY)

promised he would step down]: We're watching with concern some of the developments in Haiti. I think the situation in Haiti is ambiguous, but I do not consider in any sense that it is unraveling.

Broadcast interview/ "Face the Nation," CBS-TV, 11-26.

Robert E. Rubin
Secretary of the Treasury of the United States

1

[Defending the U.S. Clinton Administration's $40-billion assistance plan to help the faltering Mexican economy last winter]: The objective of promoting United States exports, jobs, security of our borders, in our judgment, is being accomplished. We have also avoided the spillover into other emerging markets [in the Americas] that we think could easily have happened.

Before Senate Banking Committee, Washington, D.C., July 14/ The New York Times, 7-15:17.

Felix Salgado
Mexican Senator

2

[Criticizing a proposed new law in Mexico that would involve the armed forces in fighting crime]: The law is confusing public security and national security. The armed forces would be butting into civilian matters, going against the Constitution. The fear is that it will turn the country into a military state. The government is declaring itself incapable of taking on rising violence and calling in the military, opening itself to increased repression. It could lead to a government controlled by the army. This is Mexico, not Hitler's Germany.

Los Angeles Times, 11-3:(A)5.

Sergio Sarmiento
Mexican political analyst

3

[On the first year of Mexican President Ernesto Zedillo's Administration]: I think he actually is ruling Mexico, but not everyone likes what they're seeing. It takes a lot of courage to maintain an open market system with all the pressures that he—and the Mexican people—have suffered. It takes a lot of courage to accept all the opposition victories the ruling (PRI) Party has suffered. The point is, yes, he's a nerd, but he's a good nerd.

Los Angeles Times, 12-1:(A)10.

Stanley Schrager
Spokesman for the United States Embassy in Haiti

4

[On last year's U.S. military intervention in Haiti aimed at restoring democracy]: We learned a lot from [the previous U.S. intervention in Somalia]. That includes not getting sucked into a morass of things better left to an internal police structure . . . We took a narrow view of creating a "safe and secure environment." We were determined that what went wrong in Somalia would not go wrong here [in Haiti]. What this country has now is a unique window of opportunity to recreate itself in the space of about 18 months. They

(STANLEY SCHRAGER)

have a breathing space and the focus of the international community that will not continue because the world will lose interest. Haiti may never have this chance again.

Port-au-Prince, Haiti/
The Washington Post,
3-30:(A)1,20.

1

[On Haiti's forthcoming elections]: The fact that elections are being held eight months after [President Jean-Bertrand] Aristide returned . . . is a significant credit to this country. I don't deny there were problems along the way, but elections in such a polarized country, with their lack of resources . . . is a major achievement.

The Washington Post,
6-24:(A)14.

2

[On last year's return of Haitian President Jean-Bertrand Aristide, who was restored to power by U.S. military intervention]: One of the things we had hoped for when Aristide came back was that the private sector and foreign investors would jump-start the economy. [But] Aristide has not moved as quickly on economic reform as we had hoped. That did not encourage a positive investment climate.

Los Angeles Times,
11-29:(A)12.

Lawrence Summers
Deputy Secretary of the Treasury
of the United States

3

[On Mexico's early repayment of part of the assistance supplied by the U.S. to help stabilize that country's economy during the recent financial crisis]: What this says is that we kept our promises [to the American people]. [U.S.] President Clinton and Treasury Secretary [Robert] Rubin said that if the United States and Mexico did what they needed to do, this [bailout of Mexico] would work. Now Mexico is moving back into the private capital markets.

Oct. 5/
Los Angeles Times,
10-6:(D)12.

Arturo Uslar (Pietri)
Venezuelan author
and political commentator

4

Oil riches sank us . . . Venezuela is a country unique in Latin America. The country was poor, small and not very developed, with limited possibilities. Then suddenly—without effort, without work—it became immensely wealthy [due to its oil deposits]. That is the short history of Venezuela.

Los Angeles Times,
1-12:(D)4.

Joaquin Villalobos
Former commander,
Farabundo Marti
National Liberation Front
(Salvadoran rebel organization)

5

[On the three years of peace that have reigned in El Salvador since the end of that country's civil war]: This is a new country. After all we have seen [of the conflicts] in Bosnia and Rwanda and Somalia, it is good for the world to know there is at least one

(JOAQUIN VILLALOBOS)

place where a peace process has been successful.

The New York Times,
4-29:1.

Alexander F. Watson
Assistant Secretary
for Inter-American Affairs,
Department of State
of the United States

1

[Arguing against admitting Cuba to the Organization of American States]: It's absurd to think today of admitting a country with a Stalinist government to an organization which increasingly makes efforts to consolidate democracy in the hemisphere.

At meeting of Organization
of American States,
Haiti, June/
The New York Times,
7-8:1.

Togo West
Secretary of the Army
of the United States

2

[On his evaluation of the success of the U.S. military intervention in Haiti six months ago aimed at restoring democracy]: If your vantage point is Secretary of the Army, you evaluate it based on the performance of your soldiers. And that becomes an easy evaluation. [The U.S. Army has not only] been able to restore order and to minimize casualties, but also to breed trust and confidence [among Haitians]. If you look at it from some other vantage point, such as the overall circumstances in the country . . . and compare that with all that still has to be done, measuring success is a little more complex. [But] you still notch it as a success, [because] people who live here are now able to reclaim their role in planning for their country's future.

Haiti/
USA Today,
3-31:(A)9.

Emilio Zebadua
Professor of political science
and economics,
College of Mexico

3

[On Mexican President Ernesto Zedillo]: Zedillo, either willingly or not, has simply removed himself [from the spotlight at various times]. He has realized that his lack of popularity, his lack of charisma, his lack of leadership, his lack of a confidence-inspiring image makes it better for him not to be in the center of things . . . He's distancing himself form the public act of governing. If you want to call this democracy, then you are really stretching the term. It's not a question of intelligence. It's a question of political skill . . . He has no understanding of Mexican politics.

Los Angeles Times,
12-1:(A)11.

Ernesto Zedillo
President of Mexico

4

[Mexico] has been badly damaged by cases of impunity, resulting from the abuse of power, misuse of authority, and corruption. Our duty is to apply the law to everyone without exception. We are fulfilling our promise not to rest until justice has been done in the cases of the brutal assassinations of noteworthy political figures in our country. No one

(ERNESTO ZEDILLO)

and nothing will stop me in my decision to lead the building of the true rule of law Mexicans deserve.

Broadcast address to the nation, Mexico City, Mexico, March 12/ The Washington Post, 3-13:(A)9.

1

[On his austerity plan and the U.S. aid package designed to help Mexico out of its current economic plight]: We have acted with firm decision and swiftness to avoid an even greater financial crisis. The first signs of this strategy are beginning to stand out. Certainly, the adjustment has been very severe. The crisis has had a significant cost in limiting economic activity, income and jobs. However, the extent to which the economy has rapidly adjusted also has made us hopeful for a very quick and fundamental recovery.

To stockbrokers, Mexico City, Mexico, April 4/ Los Angeles Times, 4-5:(A)11.

Asia and the Pacific

Howard L. Berman
United States Representative,
D-California

1

[Criticizing China's involvement in the proliferation of strategic weapons among various countries it trades with]: [China's record is to] proliferate, promise not to, proliferate, promise not to, and proliferate.

At House International Relations Committee hearing, Washington, D.C., June/ The Washington Post, 7-3:(A)17.

Benazir Bhutto
Prime Minister
of Pakistan

2

How tragic it is that the pre-Islamic practice of female infanticide still haunts [an Asia] we regard as modern and civilized. Girl children are often abandoned or aborted. Statistics show that men now increasingly outnumber women in more than 15 Asian nations.

At United Nations World Conference on Women, Beijing, China, Sept. 4/ The New York Times, 9-5:(A)3.

Nicholas Burns
Spokesman for the Department
of State of the United States

3

We [the U.S.] have made abundantly clear from the President [Clinton] on down for the past several months that we have a one-China policy and that we recognize the People's Republic of China as the sole representative of the Chinese people. We've also made it very clear that on the subject of Taiwan, we will retain unofficial relations only. We will not change that policy, and we have assured the Chinese government to that effect.

July 12/ The New York Times, 7-13:(A)8.

Thomas Chen
Director,
China Economic
Research Consulting Company
(Hong Kong)

4

As Taiwan [business] investment on the mainland [of China] has increased, the mainland, Taiwan and Hong Kong have become more closely linked together, and it is already difficult for any man-made factor to split them apart . . . As investment in the mainland increased in amount, its composition changed from short-term, low-risk, labor-intensive processing enterprises in the coastal areas to petrochemicals, machinery, electronics . . . and other capital- and technology-intensive ventures, further and further inland . . . Politics follows economic interests. You will see a gradual shifting in [Taiwanese business executives'] loyalty away from the Taiwanese government because their market is now in China.

Interview/ Los Angeles Times, 11-24:(A)49.

Bill Clinton
President
of the United States

1

[On the forthcoming 50th anniversary of the end of World War II]: The last three leaders of Japan have expressed in the sincerest terms their regret about the war. We have had a remarkable relationship, a partnership and a growing friendship with Japan, and I would hope that we could mark this year by saying this [the war] is something that civilized nations can never permit to occur again.

Press briefing,
Washington, D.C.,
Jan. 11/
Los Angeles Times,
1-12:(A)4.

2

[On a new trade agreement with Japan aimed at opening up that country's market for U.S. auto products]: Today, Japan has agreed that it will begin to truly open its auto and auto-parts markets to American companies. This agreement is specific. It is measurable. It will achieve real, concrete results. [It will produce] thousands of new jobs for American workers. We finally have an agreement that will move cars and parts both ways between the United States and Japan. This breakthrough is a major step toward free trade throughout the world.

Press briefing,
Washington, D.C.,
June 28/
Los Angeles Times,
6-29:(A)1,8.

Hillary Rodham Clinton
Wife
of President
of the United States
Bill Clinton

3

[On her recent trip through India, Pakistan, Bangladesh, Nepal and Sri Lanka]: I don't think the [rights of] girls and women get as much attention on a regular basis as some of the well-publicized other instances of human-rights concerns [in those countries]. I believe we have to emphasize as much as possible that the denial of education, the denial of basic health care, the denial of basic choices for girls [in those countries] is a human-rights issue.

Colombo, Sri Lanka,
April 4/
Los Angeles Times,
4-5:(A)9.

Cui Liru
Director
of North American studies,
Chinese Institute
of Contemporary
International Relations

4

China is a big country. Its first goal is to raise the living standards of its people, develop the economy and defend the sovereignty of its territory. But because it is a big country, when it develops, the reality is that it will be getting stronger [militarily] and more powerful . . . Quite a number of Chinese people at various levels tend to believe that the Americans regard a powerful China as a hindrance to the United States in its bid to maintain world dominance and so are trying hard pur-

(CUI LIRU)

posefully to keep China weak and even divided.

The Washington Post, 7-24:(A)16.

Bob Currieo
Executive director, Veterans of Foreign Wars (United States)

1

[Criticizing former U.S. President George Bush for his planned visit to Vietnam to speak on behalf of American business interests, now that U.S. President Clinton has decided to establish diplomatic relations with Vietnam]: This is a slap in the face of [American] veterans [who fought in the war in Vietnam in the 1960s and '70s]. It's premature for him to be going over there making these business overtures. Here's the person who is adamant about not lifting the embargo against Vietnam [when he was U.S. President], and now he's jumping at the first chance to go. You wonder how sincere he was as President.

Interview, Washington, D.C./ The New York Times, 8-5:1,3.

Robert J. Dole
United States Senator, R-Kansas; Candidate for the 1996 Republican Presidential nomination

2

[On a new U.S. trade agreement with Japan aimed at opening up Japan's market for U.S. auto products]: After 2½ years of negotiations, the final agreement is vague, unenforceable, non-binding—in short, it is virtually empty.

Before the Senate, Washington, D.C./ Time, 7-10:45.

Dianne Feinstein
United States Senator, D-California

3

If we're [the U.S.] really interested in human rights, what as a nation we ought to do is help the Chinese in the evolution of an independent judicial system and one that has due process of law. The Chinese have indicated an interest in pursuing that course.

Los Angeles Times, 11-27:(A)5.

Charles W. Freeman, Jr.
Former Assistant Secretary of Defense of the United States

4

There has been no credible "China [military] threat" . . . The Chinese prefer shots across the bow that produce sensible adjustments in opponents' policies, to shots that strike and sink them. The [current] Chinese choice [for military exercises] of an uninhabited island north of Taiwan as the place to demonstrate their military power is a classic instance of this.

The Washington Post, 7-24:(A)16.

Jeffrey E. Garten
Under Secretary for International Trade, Department of Commerce of the United States

1

[Saying China should open up its economy so that it's large trade surplus with the U.S. can be reduced before there will be American support for China's entry to the World Trade Organization]: China wants entry to the WTO, and we would like to see it enter. But unless they come in on terms that promote a more open economy, we will be unable to support the Chinese entry . . . There's a real big issue here. What is the relationship between what's going on inside China and in the rest of the world? When I asked this question in a room full of Chinese economists, I was met with an enormous silence.

Beijing, China, April 13/ The New York Times, 4-14:(C)3.

2

[On U.S.-Japanese relations]: A relationship between the world's two biggest trading nations that is characterized by one trade confrontation after another seems as anachronistic as the old gunboat diplomacy . . . Virtually all of our time is spent in contentious negotiations.

Speech to foreign correspondents, Tokyo, Japan, July 31/ The New York Times, 8-1:(C)3.

Newt Gingrich
United States Representative, R-Georgia: Speaker of the House

3

[Criticizing China's foreign policy]: They are self-deluding. They are claiming territorial rights a thousand miles away from the Chinese border. They are involved in pressuring the Philippines and other countries in terms of territorial rights in areas that clearly no one is going to recognize in the international arena. And I think it helps the Chinese in the long run for us to be firm and direct in our rejection of their pretensions.

Broadcast interview/ "Face the Nation," CBS-TV, 7-9.

Bonnie Glaser
Authority on Asian affairs

4

The Chinese increasingly suspect that the United States is seeking to thwart China's emergence as a great power and keep China weak and divided. An economically or militarily powerful China, deeply resentful of the United States, could be more stridently nationalistic and determined to resist perceived bullying.

The Washington Post, 2-13:(A)17.

Goh Chok Tong
Prime Minister of Singapore

5

[On censorship in Singapore]: For liberals in the West, these are curbs on personal liberties. But they are necessary safeguards

(GOH CHOK TONG)

which enable Singaporeans as a whole to enjoy more freedom, greater security and a safer environment.

*World Press Review/
June:4.*

Phil Gramm
United States Senator, R-Texas; Candidate for the 1996 Republican Presidential nomination

1

[Saying a new trade agreement with Japan—which U.S. President Clinton says will open up the Japanese market for U.S. auto products—has no teeth]: The White House advertised this as a gunfight at the O.K. Corral. But it turned out that the President was only shooting blanks.

*June 28/
Los Angeles Times,
6-29:(A)6.*

Carla Hills
Former United States Trade Representative

2

[Criticizing U.S. Trade Representative Mickey Kantor for being too tough and demanding too much in trade talks with Japan and for not first going to the World Trade Organization before threatening trade sanctions against Japan]: Our strategy and tactics are unfortunate . . . We are now the outlaws, and there should be individual and collective responsibility for that in the Clinton Administration.

USA Today, 6-27:(B)2.

Jiang Zemin
President of China

3

Only by ensuring the dominant position of the public sector [in China] can we prevent polarization and achieve common prosperity. Any move to shake or give up the dominant position of the public sector will deviate from the direction of socialism.

*Before Chinese
Communist Party
Central Committee plenum,
Sept. 28/
Los Angeles Times,
10-9:(A)6.*

4

Our policy is to reunify peacefully with Taiwan. What we firmly oppose is Taiwan independence. Having two Chinas, or one China and one Taiwan, is unacceptable. All other issues can be discussed. Taiwan can maintain its capitalist system, even its army; no mainland officials will assume leadership positions there. On the contrary, Taiwanese can become officials on the mainland and even be part of the central government—though of course they can't become the President of the People's Republic. But on one thing we are certain: If separatism emerges on Taiwan, whether stemming from international hostile forces or from local separatist forces, then we might use non-peaceful means to achieve reunification. This is the last thing we wish to see happen.

*Interview,
Beijing, China/
U.S. News & World Report,
10-23:72.*

Chalmers Johnson
Professor of economics,
University of California,
San Diego;
President,
Japan Policy
Research Institute
(United States)

1

[Saying the new trade agreement between the U.S. and Japan, aimed at opening up Japan's market for U.S. auto products, will not end trade disputes between the two countries]: The Japanese are going to keep the United States on the string for a few more years. They are essentially buying time to milk the Cold War relationship a little longer until their ascendancy in Asia is irreversible. Japan has profited more from the Cold War than any other nation, and it has an enormous interest in preserving Cold War relations as long as the United States will tolerate it.

June 28/
Los Angeles Times,
6-29:(A)8.

Sam Johnson
United States
Representative,
R-Texas

2

[Criticizing U.S. President Clinton's decision to give full U.S. diplomatic recognition to Vietnam]: It's impossible for me to figure that Vietnam can be honest about anything. [As a POW during the U.S.-Vietnam war of the 1960s and '70s,] I lived with them too long. They never told the truth once.

U.S. News & World Report,
7-24:22.

Mickey Kantor
United States
Trade Representative

3

[On his negotiations with Japanese Minister of International Trade and Industry Ryutaro Hashimoto aimed at opening up Japan's market for U.S. auto products]: When Minister Hashimoto and I first met on Monday evening here in Geneva, I presented him with a kendo *shinai* [sword]. I said at the time that the sport of kendo represents courage, honesty, integrity and patience. After spending a great deal of time with my friend during the last several days, I can assure you that he represents all of these qualities and more.

Geneva, Switzerland,
June 28/
USA Today,
6-29:(B)3.

Paul Keating
Prime Minister
of Australia

4

[Criticizing France's intention to resume testing of its nuclear weapons in the South Pacific]: The sentiment in the countries of the South Pacific is all but universal. If France must test these weapons, let her test them in metropolitan France. Whatever the French government intends by these actions, they are read by a great majority of people in this region as an assault upon the rights of small nations by a large one . . . No one can possibly foresee the longer-term dangers associated with possible [nuclear] leakage from the fragile atoll structures housing the tests.

USA Today,
9-1:(A)8.

Kim Young Sam
President
of South Korea

1

I would like to make it very clear to all of you today—to maintain peace in the Korean peninsula and to maintain stability in the Asia-Pacific region, the U.S. [military] force in the Republic of [South] Korea is necessary . . . For the Asia-Pacific area to fully blossom, the United States must continue to play this role [of providing a defense shield]. Above all, safeguarding peace on the Korean peninsula, situated in the heart of Northeast Asia, has become the key to the stability of the entire region.

Before U.S. Congress,
Washington, D.C.,
July 26/
The Washington Post,
7-27:(A)23.

Yotaro Kobayashi
Chairman,
Fuji Xerox Co.
(Japan)

2

[On a new trade agreement with the U.S. aimed at opening up Japan's market for U.S. auto products]: [The projected figures by the U.S. should] not be viewed as something that the Japanese government has promised. I don't mean to be impolite to the American government, but this is what Japan has been worrying about the most. But the agreement clearly says that the Japanese government is not guaranteeing it.

June 28/
Los Angeles Times,
6-29:(D)3.

Alex Krauer
Chairman and managing director,
Ciba-Geigy Corporation
(Switzerland)

3

We believe China has the potential to make a substantial leap forward. We have quite a few projects in China. We have invested about $300-million to $350 [-million] into different ventures . . . There is much talk now about the impact of changes in political control [in China]. But we feel that this economic reform process has a momentum that will make it impossible to stop.

Interview/
USA Today,
6-9:(B)4.

Anthony Lake
Assistant to President
of the United States
Bill Clinton
for National
Security Affairs

4

[On the effect of China's poor human-rights record on U.S.-China relations]: We will not sacrifice human rights on the altar of economic interest, or [nuclear] non-proliferation on the altar of human rights.

The Washington Post,
2-13:(A)17.

Jacques LeBlanc
French Ambassador
to New Zealand

5

[On criticism in the South Pacific area of France's resumption of nuclear-weapons testing there]: I do not like this word "bomb." It

(JACQUES LEBLANC)

is not a bomb; it is a device which is exploding.

Before National Press Club, Wellington, New Zealand/ Time, 10-23:32.

Martin C.M. Lee
Chairman, Democratic Party of Hong Kong

1

[On his party's victory over pro-China parties in the recent Hong Kong legislative elections]: This election makes clear the will of Hong Kong. This election is a referendum on the aspirations of the people of Hong Kong [bearing in mind China's scheduled takeover of Hong Kong in 1997]. Hong Kong people voted with their hearts and their minds for freedom and genuine democracy. The elections, in short, are a mandate for democratic government in Hong Kong and real constitutional, legal and human-rights reform to ensure basic freedoms in Hong Kong after 1997.

Sept. 18/ The New York Times, 9-19:(A)4.

Lee Teng-hui
President of Taiwan

2

We [Taiwanese] sincerely hope that all nations can treat us fairly and reasonably, and not overlook the significance, value and functions we represent. Some say that it is impossible for us to break out of the diplomatic isolation we face, but we will do our utmost to demand the impossible.

At Cornell University, June 9/ The New York Times, 6-10:4.

3

For many developing nations, the process of moving to a democratic system has been marked by a *coup d'etat*, or by [a] kind of "political decay" . . . In short, it is not unusual for such a process of transformation to be accompanied by violence and chaos. However, the case of the Republic of China on Taiwan is a notable exception. Non-existent is the vicious cycle of expansive political participation, class confrontation, military coup and political suppression which has occurred in many developing countries. The process of reform in Taiwan is remarkably peaceful indeed, and as such is virtually unique. In addition to the "economic miracle," we have wrought a "political miracle," so to speak.

At Cornell University, June 9/ Nation's Business, October:57.

Farooq Leghari
President of Pakistan

4

[Saying the South Asian Association for Regional Cooperation has not made enough progress in bettering relations among its members]: The fact is, our Association has not taken off. The reason is not far to seek. The suspicions and insecurity generated by the

(FAROOQ LEGHARI)

unsettled political issues in our region stand in the way of SAARC moving forward at the pace that it should be.

At meeting of SAARC, Simla, India, May 2/ Los Angeles Times, 5-4:(A)9.

John W. Lewis
Specialist on China, Stanford University (United States)

1

[Criticizing calls by some in the U.S. for closer relations with Taiwan because of China's negative human-rights and nuclear-weapons policies]: United States policy since 1972 has sought to build peace, stability and prosperity between China and Taiwan, and this policy has yielded tremendous results in nurturing economic and political reforms and in creating an environment for Beijing and Taipei to integrate their economies, set aside 45 years of enmity and negotiate their own future under the "one-China" banner. This policy is now dangerously close to being reversed.

The New York Times, 8-19:5.

Winston Lord
Assistant Secretary for East Asian and Pacific Affairs, Department of State of the United States

2

[Despite the end of the Cold War,] China remains just as important geopolitically, if not more important, to us. It's important on regional issues like Korea and Cambodia, or the South China Sea territorial dispute. It's important because it's a nuclear power and also exports advanced technology and nuclear materials to various countries. It's important because it has the world's largest population and will have a tremendous impact on the environment and on energy sources around the world. It's important because if its potentially huge market and its fast, dynamic growth. Finally, it's important because it has a veto in the UN Security Council and therefore is a major actor in terms of being able to move forward with peacekeeping or other actions in the United Nations. So the strategic importance of China, if anything, is growing even though the specific military factor has been removed; it is certainly different than during the Cold War in that sense. It's flirtatious, however. It's a mixed relationship, where we'll have areas of cooperation but also areas of confrontation, which we try to manage.

Interview/ Current History, September:248.

Peter Lynch
Director, and former fund manager, Fidelity Investments

3

[Saying the fall of the U.S. dollar against the Japanese yen is partly due to a low U.S. savings rate and a high Japanese savings rate]: You simply don't have an ability to spend [in Japan]. The money's building up and they can't spend it. We need about 10,000 great

(PETER LYNCH)

American shoppers to go over there and show them how to spend.

To corporate executives, Boston, Mass., April 26/ Los Angeles Times, 4-27:(D)3.

Roderick MacFarquhar
Specialist on China, Harvard University (United States)

1

The political system [current Chinese leader] Deng Xiaoping will leave behind is extremely fragile. It lost its legitimacy as a result of the battering it received from [the late Chinese leader] Mao [Tse-tung] during the Cultural Revolution and in a different way from the reforms of Deng. [But] the reform program cannot be reversed. It has gone too far. The political repercussions of attempting to reverse it would be too enormous.

USA Today, 2-10:(B)2.

Jimmy MacGregor
Representative to the Hong Kong Legislature from the General Chamber of Commerce of Hong Kong

2

[On the Hongkong Bank's decision to move its legal headquarters to London in anticipation of China's taking control of Hong Kong by the end of the decade]: The fact that they have done so [and that many other Hong Kong firms have relocated their legal headquarters] represents a very substantial nervousness about the future . . . Bit by bit, the Bank of China will move into a more dominant position, and the Hongkong Bank will give way gracefully.

The Christian Science Monitor, 7-26:18.

John McCain
United States Senator, R-Arizona

3

[On U.S. industrialist and 1992 Presidential candidate Ross Perot's claim that live American POWs still exist in Vietnam]: He's nuttier than a fruitcake—and that's on the record.

Newsweek, 6-26:35.

4

[Saying he favors full U.S. relations with Vietnam]: [There are] several reasons. One, China is flexing its muscles in a disturbing fashion . . . [Also,] there are opportunities for American businesses [in Vietnam]. The Vietnamese do like us. General Vo Nguyen Giap, the former head of the Vietnamese forces [during the U.S.-Vietnam war of the 1960s and '70s], told me a year and a half ago: "You Americans were an honorable enemy." In 1991, the [U.S.] Bush Administration gave the Vietnamese a road map for normalization: If they got out of Cambodia, closed their re-education camps and showed cooperation on the POW-MIA issue, we in turn would do certain things. It seems to me that we have a commitment. Finally, I have worked for over 20 years to heal the wounds of the war. I believe normal relations between our two countries will help in that effort.

Interview/ U.S. News & World Report, 6-26:21.

(JOHN McCAIN)

1

[Saying he is concerned about China's recent actions]: China has claimed most of the South China Sea where most of the oil reserves are. It has kicked the Filipinos out of the Spratly Islands. And it recently acquired 10 Soviet submarines. China is not only building up its military establishment, but is also in a transition phase as far as its leadership is concerned.

Interview/
U.S. News & World Report,
6-26:21.

Daniel Mitchell
Economist,
Heritage Foundation
(United States)

2

[On a new U.S. trade agreement with Japan aimed at opening up Japan's market for U.S. auto products]: Just to pick the fight [with Japan] in the first place was good politics [for U.S. President Clinton] . . . [But it's] embarrassing [for Clinton to] pathetically go begging a foreign country . . . to have [trade] quotas.

June 28/
USA Today,
6-29:(B)3.

Walter F. Mondale
United States Ambassador
to Japan

3

The one thing I've been increasingly impressed by is the obduracy to real change here [in Japan]. I'm going to recommend that [there be] a metabolism test for the next [U.S.] Ambassador [to Japan]. My advice would be, if you don't have a low metabolism rate, you shouldn't come over.

The New York Times,
1-3:(A)4.

Hitoshi Motoshima
Mayor
of Nagasaki, Japan

4

[Criticizing the U.S. use of nuclear bombs against his city and Hiroshima during World War II]: [They are] one of the two great crimes against humanity in the 20th century, along with the Holocaust . . . Does avoiding the death of [U.S.] servicemen justify the sacrifice of tens of thousands of guiltless non-combatants [in the two cities]? This is tantamount to killing a flea with a sledgehammer. It can hardly be called a justified act, even in wartime.

To foreign correspondents,
Tokyo, Japan,
March 15/
Los Angeles Times,
3-16:(A)1,10.

Hiromu Nonaka
Minister of Home Affairs
of Japan

5

[On recent terrorist attacks in Japan, which have been blamed on the Aum Shinrikyo cult]: The country is facing a crisis. I can't help feeling that these are scenes from a bizarre comic strip. But I think they've been acting as if they were an independent nation, and it's a bit like a war between two countries.

The New York Times,
5-1:(A)1.

Seisuke Okuno
Former Japanese Cabinet Minister; Leader of opposition to a resolution of apology to Asian nations for Japan's role in World War II

1

[Saying Japan should not apologize to those Asian nations it invaded in World War II]: These countries had been colonized and oppressed by whites, so our purpose was to free those nations and stabilize them. [American incendiary bombs fell on Japan like rain and atomic bombs were dropped on Hiroshima and Nagasaki. And the Russian Army committed mind-boggling atrocities against Japanese. So we think there were war crimes more serious than any committed by Japan . . . The Japanese people were brainwashed [by the rewriting of history by the American post-war occupiers]. They started to think that Japan had led a war of invasion and did many bad things. [But now,] people are starting gradually to understand the facts.

The New York Times, 3-6:(A)4.

Chris Patten
Governor of Hong Kong

2

[Advising China not to be too tough on Hong Kong, which is scheduled to come under Chinese rule in 1997]: I'm constantly surprised at how Chinese officials misread the situation and the people here [in Hong Kong]. People aren't aggressive and threatening. The thing that never ceases to amaze me is how moderate political life is in Hong Kong. If Chinese officials recognized that, they'd find themselves overwhelmed by the response.

U.S. News & World Report, 10-2:58.

William J. Perry
Secretary of Defense of the United States

3

[China] does not represent, in my judgment, a significant military threat, either on a global scale or on a regional scale. Nor do I believe the Chinese government has aggressive or offensive intentions.

New Delhi, India, Jan. 13/ The New York Times, 1-14:4.

4

[On the U.S. military presence on Japanese territory as part of the U.S.-Japan security pact]: [If those forces ever have to be used against an enemy,] I will be very glad, and you [Japanese] will be very glad, that they are based where they are. They are located here because this is where they have to be to provide the security umbrella for the Asia-Pacific region. Freedom is never free. Security is never guaranteed. You have to work for it.

News conference, Tokyo, Japan, Nov.1/ Los Angeles Times, 11-1:(A)7.

Nguyen Xuan Phong
Director, Americas Department, Foreign Ministry of Vietnam

5

We are a people who always look to the future. Before, we fought the war for inde-

(NGUYEN XUAN PHONG)

pendence, for freedom, for the reunification of the country. Now our battle is for the development of the country, to modernize the country, to industrialize the county. For that, we know we need relations with the world, to get financial resources, to get technology. In the case of the United States, we have other reasons, too, to leave behind the past. Since the [U.S.-Vietnam] war [of the 1960s and '70s] left behind a lot of consequences for both people, the only way to heal the wounds is to have relations between the two countries. There is no other way.

The Washington Post,
7-17:(A)14.

Jan Prybyla
Specialist on Asia,
Pennsylvania State University
(United States)

1

[On Chinese President Jiang Zemin, who may be in line to take over from Deng Xiaoping when he retires as China's top leader]: [Jiang] doesn't have the character or the power or the personality to put a stamp on anything. He is not very bright . . . And his power base is very shaky . . . I don't think any of us has the slightest inkling of what is going on behind the walls where the guys [China's leaders] live. It's Kremlinology all over again. We're just guessing.

USA Today, 2-10:(B)2.

Qian Qichen
Foreign Minister of China

2

Taiwan is part of China. Taiwan should by no means embark on the road to Taiwan independence. Should such a situation occur, the peace and stability in the region . . . would be damaged.

News conference,
Osaka, Japan,
Nov. 17/
Los Angeles Times,
11-18:(A)6.

P.V. Narasimha Rao
Prime Minister
of India

3

[Saying South Asian countries should form a common-market-type free-trade association]: Collective self-interest has been the fundamental basis of regional cooperation all over the world. Those regional groupings that have succeeded have opened doors to the free flow of goods, services, capital and people. This is also the route we have to adopt.

At meeting
of South Asian Association
for Regional Cooperation,
Simla, India, May 2/
Los Angeles Times,
5-4:(A)9.

Eisuke Sakakibara
President,
Institute of Fiscal
and Monetary Policy
(Japan)

4

[Arguing against too much change in the way Japan operates its economy]: I'm not a nationalist in the narrow sense of the word, but too much deregulation would create great confusion. You could destroy things that are thousands of years old. It's naked market forces against cultures. It would be the end of

(EISUKE SAKAKIBARA)

Japanese-style capitalism if we pushed this kind of change [to more economic openness]. Japan would be split, as America is split.

*Interview/
The New York Times,
1-3:(A)4.*

Sarasin Viraphol
*Senior official,
Foreign Ministry
of Thailand*

1

[On the threat of U.S. sanctions against Japan because of that country's refusal to open its markets more to U.S. products]: Privately, we're saying the U.S. is taking the right approach because the Japanese have to be hit over the head. But publicly we have to say we are concerned about the use of sanctions . . . because we worry that we are liable to face the same treatment.

*Los Angeles Times,
6-5:(A)5.*

John H. Shattuck
*Assistant Secretary
for Human Rights
and Humanitarian Affairs,
Department of State
of the United States*

2

[On the rejection by the UN Human Rights Commission, by a vote of 21-20 with 12 abstentions, of a European-sponsored and U.S.-supported resolution condemning China's human-rights record]: Obviously, we were disappointed not to get that one vote. But the result still is a powerful signal to China and to the world that the Human Rights Commission will not allow any country—no matter how large—to block consideration of its human-rights record . . . The bottom line is that we see in the work of the Commission a growing consensus, a growing majority of countries that are willing to press for international standards of human rights.

*March 8/
Los Angeles Times,
3-9:(A)4.*

Michael Smith
Former United States trade negotiator

3

[On a new U.S. trade agreement with Japan aimed at opening up Japan's market for U.S. auto products]: Both sides blinked, but the U.S. blinked more than Japan. It's perplexing. Seems like we climbed Mount Fuji for no reason at all.

*June 28/
USA Today,
6-29:(B)3.*

John Sommer
*Executive director,
American Legion*

4

[Criticizing ongoing plans to normalize relations between the U.S. and Vietnam]: We certainly oppose any further moves toward normalization until they [the Vietnamese] effect the fullest possible accounting [of U.S. POWs and MIAs from the war of the 1960s and '70s], and they haven't done that by a long shot.

*Jan. 27/
The New York Times,
1-28:1.*

Joan Spero
Under Secretary
of State
of the United States

1

[Trade conflicts with Japan] are like the New York City buses—they seem to travel in packs.

Interview/
The Washington Post,
6-10:(C)6.

Harry Summers
Colonel,
United States Army (Ret.)

2

The Korean War [of the 1950s] was the "forgotten war," and at the same time the paradigm for future wars.

At conference
on the Korean War,
Georgetown University/
The Washington Post,
7-27:(A)21.

Johsen Takahashi
Senior economist,
Mitsubishi Research Institute
(Japan)

3

Unemployment, especially among the young, could be the biggest problem for Japan's economy from now on . . . Companies can no longer afford to hire a bunch of new graduates at the start of every business year and spend huge amounts of money on their in-house training as they have done before. The moves to restrain recruitment of fresh university graduates may signal a turning point in Japan's traditional labor system.

Los Angeles Times, 6-19:(D)5.

Noburo Takeshita
Former Prime Minister
of Japan

4

[On the possibility of Trade Minister Ryutaro Hashimoto becoming a future Japanese Prime Minister]: Except for his tendency to get angry, arrogant and sulky, he is the most qualified.

Newsweek,
7-10:15.

Alan Tonelson
Fellow,
Economic Strategy Institute
(United States)

5

[Saying the U.S. may become reluctant to use its military in the Asia/Pacific area due to economic problems at home and the lack of clear enemies since the end of the Cold War]: East Asians are realizing that just because U.S. forces are stationed in that part of the world does not mean they will be used.

U.S. News & World Report,
5-22:44.

Wang Xingjuan
Founder,
Women's Research Institute
(China)

6

Why are there few women in top leadership (in China)? The answer is that we still have traditional values. It's still very much a man's world in China.

The Washington Post,
8-21:(A)14.

William Westmoreland
General,
United States Army (Ret.);
Former commander
of U.S. forces
in the war with Vietnam
in the 1960s-'70s

1

[Criticizing a new book by Robert McNamara, U.S. Defense Secretary during the U.S. war with Vietnam, in which he expresses regrets about the U.S. involvement there]: He obviously has something to get off his chest, but this is not the McNamara I did business with. None of this [McNamara's now-stated criticisms of U.S. involvement] ever came up, never was indicated to me. Recall that we went into Vietnam promising we would bear any price, any burden to bolster the Vietnamese to self-sufficiency, and we almost did until [the U.S.] Congress cut us off. You can't turn your back on a promise like that. I think McNamara should be reminded of that.

The New York Times,
4-15:8

Kent Wiedemann
Deputy Assistant
Secretary of State
of the United States

2

[On the Dalai Lama, the exiled former ruler of Tibet]: We regard him as an internationally respected religious leader as well as one who deserves special admiration for his advocacy of peaceful resolution of disputes. We do not regard the Dalai Lama as a political figure or political leader. Any discussion the [U.S. Clinton] Administration has with the Dalai Lama does not in any way convey that we recognize the government-in-exile of Tibet.

Sept. 11/
The New York Times,
9-12:(A)3.

James Wold
General,
United States Army;
Chief POW/MIA investigator,
Department of Defense
of the United States

3

[On U.S. efforts since the Vietnam war of the 1960s and '70s to account for American POWs and MIAs in that country]: The United States government has committed more resources, deployed more personnel, used more equipment than ever before in any other conflict to resolve the remaining cases of unaccounted-for Americans in Southeast Asia. Never before in all the history of warfare has so much been done to get this kind of an accounting.

Before House
International Relations Committee,
Washington, D.C.,
July 12/
Los Angeles Times,
7-13:(A)4.

Taizo Yokoyama
Managing director,
Mitsubishi Motors
(Japan)

4

[On the new trade agreement with the U.S. aimed at opening up Japan's market for

(TAIZO YOKOYAMA)

U.S. auto products]: Our announcement today doesn't directly state how many [U.S.] parts are going to be purchased [by Japanese firms]. Therefore, we understand the figures the American side has announced today are calculated upon estimates they made. I don't think they will be taken as ones Japanese manufacturers have agreed to.

June 28/
Los Angeles Times,
6-29:(D)3.

Vladimir V. Zhirinovsky
Member of Russian Parliament

1

[On Russia's relations with India]: We should strengthen India's defense for our own sakes. Look at these fools in Moscow disbanding so many [Russian] tanks, fighters, bombers and battleships and missiles under American pressure. Instead, if they have any sense in their drunken heads, they should send them all to India, free.

Interview/
The New York Times, 3-9:(A)5.

Europe

Susanna Agnelli
Foreign Minister
of Italy

1

[On calls by the political left in Italy for that country to increase its military profile and join in any European intervention in the ethnic conflict in the Balkans]: We have these greens, these radicals who for a long time talked about "don't make war, make love," and now they all want to make war. But this is the spirit of the Italians. One day they are all bellicose, and one day they are all pacifists. They see these things on TV, and they say, Oh my God, how awful; but then when you mention to them about sending troops, then they say, Oh for God's sake, let's not send troops.

Interview/
The New York Times,
8-15:(A)4.

Leon Aron
Russia specialist,
American Enterprise Institute

2

[Russian President Boris] Yeltsin has lost touch with what the country and people want. His back is against the wall. And besides, now there's someone else on the horizon [Prime Minister Viktor Chernomyrdin] . . . Yeltsin's government is showing complete ineptness. His key occupation these days should be to find a leader who could be both electable and guarantee him—and his cronies—freedom from prosection for corruption.

USA Today,
6-29:(A)4.

Edouard Balladur
Prime Minister
of France

3

[On his running for President of France]: France has become a raw and difficult society in which too many people have lost out. I don't promise, "Vote for me and in six months everything will be better." It will take years of hard work. [But] I want France to be better off, and the French to be happier than they are now.

At campaign rally,
Montpellier, France,
March 14/
The New York Times,
3-16:(A)7.

Harley Balzer
Authority on Russia,
Georgetown University
(United States)

4

The reforms [in Russia] are so entrenched, they have a life of their own. People have seen the past and no one wants to go back—with or without [current President Boris] Yeltsin.

USA Today,
1-9:(A)5.

Silvio Berlusconi
Prime Minister
of Italy

5

The moment I entered politics, I made a choice that was ruinous to my own popularity. I had to suffer the envy of moderates. My

(SILVIO BERLUSCONI)

wealth is obvious to many people because I have many houses. So many things. I changed my life for the worse. It's incredible. I have everyone jumping on me. The judges on the one side, the newspapers on the other, the other industrial groups . . . I won the election despite the newspapers and despite television. And I govern despite newspapers and despite television. Berlusconi has always had to struggle against the world of the media. And I continue, practically every day, to wage this battle. And all for the love of my country! And instead of honoring this, the fact that I removed myself from my company, despite all I'm doing for the country— . . . I never would have thought about doing what I'm doing: receiving heads of state, Prime Ministers from foreign countries, addressing Parliament. These things are contrary to my nature! So while a politician likes these things, I can't bear doing them! I suffer doing these things. Suffer physically. Suffer. Suffer. So politics makes me suffer.

Interview/
Vanity Fair,
January:108,109.

1

[On the naming of Lamberto Dini to replace him as Prime Minister]: Only a rapid return to the ballot box will create a coalition government that is capable of insuring full stability and political authority. Arrivederci. I am reasonably sure that mine is a brief goodbye.

News conference,
Jan. 13/
The New York Times,
1-14:3.

Tony Blair
Leader,
Labor Party of Britain

2

[On his Party's recent sweeping victories over the Conservative Party in local British elections]: [The results] are clearly a disaster for the [Conservative-led national] government. More than that, they are a victory for new Labor . . . People are coming straight to us not just because the government is discredited but because they like the alternative we offer.

Los Angeles Times,
5-6:(A)9.

Betty Boothroyd
Speaker of the British House
of Commons

3

Today, when some contemporary writers are busy with their versions of history, I am more than ever certain of one thing: [World War II] was a war worth fighting; it was a fight worth winning. The price was high, but the consequences of defeat would have been unthinkable.

On commemoration
of V-E Day's
50th anniversary, May 5/
Los Angeles Times,
5-6:(A)8.

John Bruton
Prime Minister
of Ireland

4

[On British-Irish proposals for the future of Northern Ireland, which has been racked by strife between Catholics and Protestants for 25 years]: The proposals will challenge

(JOHN BRUTON)

the two traditions on this island, but will do so in an evenhanded way. Neither tradition need fear its contents. It is a framework for discussion and not a blueprint to be imposed over the heads of anyone.

After meeting with British Prime Minister John Major, Belfast, Northern Ireland, Feb. 22/ Los Angeles Times, 2-23:(A)1.

1

[On his forthcoming visit to the U.S. to seek help in settling the ethnic conflict between Protestants and Catholics in Northern Ireland]: [We need to] get a few messages into the political system about the need to get a balanced approach to this problem, to recognize the rights of both communities [in Northern Ireland]. I think I'm realistic to know that people in America don't wake up every morning and ask what's happening in Ireland. They think about Ireland maybe twice or three times a year in a serious way.

Interview, Dublin, Ireland/ The New York Times, 3-17:(A)3.

George Bush
Former President of the United States

2

[Saying the U.S. must remain engaged in Europe]: Throughout our history, trouble in Europe has meant trouble in America. I hope today my own countrymen do not forget this lesson.

At ceremony marking 50th anniversary of Potsdam Conference, Potsdam, Germany, July 24/ Los Angeles Times, 7-25:(A)7.

Charles
Prince of Wales

3

[On the 50th anniversary of V-E day, which is being celebrated this year]: The conscious act of remembering is crucial to our continued survival as civilized human beings.

U.S. News & World Report, 5-22:11.

Sergei Cheshko
Senior researcher, Institute for Social Anthropology (Russia)

4

[Saying Russians suffer from feelings of both superiority and failure]: There is always a rushing back and forth between extremes as the failure to realize this great potential leads to bouts of inferior feelings. This tendency to extremes is obvious in our politics. We embrace a new ideology with vigor, then later denounce it and reject even the elements of worth.

Los Angeles Times, 5-1:(A)6.

Jacques Chirac
Mayor of Paris, France; Candidate for President of France

5

France must firmly oppose clandestine

(JACQUES CHIRAC)

immigration. Too often, the laws of the republic are openly flouted, with the police and the authorities unable to react and make the required expulsions in cases of infractions. Our judicial arsenal and our punitive sanctions should be adapted to circumstances and applied with all necessary firmness. How can we tolerate entire neighborhoods dropping out and opting out of the law? If we continue down the route the Socialists have put us on, we will end up witnessing the confiscation of law and order by ethnic or religious groups that will accelerate the process of ghettoization.

At political rally,
Orleans, France, April 25/
The New York Times,
4-27:(A)7.

1

[Defending France's plans to resume nuclear-weapons testing in the Pacific]: We are prepared to place our force in the service of Europe. A reliable and credible French nuclear deterrent can be an important asset for European defense.

Interview/
The Washington Post,
9-4:(A)18.

Warren Christopher
Secretary of State
of the United States

2

Russia's indiscriminate and excessive use of force in [the secessionist area of] Chechnya has certainly dealt a setback to reform in that country, but it has not altered our fundamental interest in helping Russian reformers build a nation that finally is at peace with itself and its neighbors.

Press briefing,
Washington, D.C., Feb. 6/
The New York Times,
2-7:(A)4.

3

[Criticizing Russia's use of military force in the secessionist Chechnya region]: [It is] tragically wrong . . . really quite foolhardy. The Russians are paying a very high price internationally. They are certainly paying a very high price in terms of American public opinion.

News conference,
Geneva, Switzerland,
March 22/
Los Angeles Times,
3-23:(A)6.

4

[Warning Russia against being isolationist]: What I tell [Russian Foreign Minister] Andrei Kozyrev is this: Do not isolate yourself; do not fail to have the kind of discussion that will ensure that you have a proper relationship with the West.

Interview,
Washington, D.C., April 25/
The Washington Post,
4-26:(A)27.

5

[Saying the U.S. and Europe should create ways to expand their trading relationship]: Although our [U.S. economic] ties have expanded with the Asia-Pacific region and Latin America, it is important to recall that the United States and Europe enjoy the largest combined external trade and investment rela-

(WARREN CHRISTOPHER)

tionship in the entire world . . . We should undertake a trans-Atlantic economic initiative to multiply trade, investment and the creation of new, high-paying jobs. It will make us an even more powerful engine of the global economy . . . Together the Old World and the New World have created a genuinely better world. But we must not take this relationship for granted. It cannot be sustained by nostalgia.

Speech
Madrid, Spain, June 2/
Los Angeles Times,
6-3:(A)8.

Bill Clinton
President
of the United States

1

[Saying the conflict in the secessionist Chechnya region of Russia does not change the U.S. interest in helping Russia become a stable, democratic country]: It would be a terrible mistake [for the U.S.] to react reflexively to the ups and downs that Russia is experiencing and was bound to experience all along, and will continue to experience in the years ahead, indeed, perhaps for decades, as it undergoes an historic transformation.

At trade conference,
Cleveland, Ohio,
Jan. 13/
The New York Times,
1-14:5.

2

[Defending his support for Russian President Boris Yeltsin despite some disagreements and U.S. opposition to some Russian policies]: Boris Yeltsin has been elected the President of a country that has a Constitution and a democratic system. It would be curious indeed if the United States were to say that we have a separate set of rules for these new democracies: When things don't go the way we want or they follow some policy we don't like, well, then we decide that we should invest ourselves in some other person . . . My confidence level in [Yeltsin] is strong. If you ask me, "Do I think he is still the effective President of Russia and is he making those decisions?" Yes, that's what I believe is the case . . . When we differ with Russia, we say so. When they differ with us, they say so. But on the whole, let's not forget that a remarkable amount of progress has been made in that country, and a remarkable amount of progress has been made in our relationship.

News conference,
Washington, D.C.,
March 3/
The New York Times,
3-4:4.

3

[On the sectarian conflict in Northern Ireland]: Paramilitaries on both sides must get rid of their bombs and guns for good, and the specter of violence that haunted Ireland must be banished once and for all. I hope the parties can soon sit down together to discuss the future and their differences. That is the best guarantee of a permanent peace.

At conference
on investment
in Northern Ireland,
Washington, D.C.,
May 25/
Los Angeles Times,
5-26:(A)19.

(BILL CLINTON)

1

[On the current cease-fire in the ethnic conflict in Northern Ireland]: We will stand with those who take risks for peace. If you walk down this path continually, you will not walk alone. We are entering an era of possibility unparalleled in all of human history. If you enter that era determined to build a new age of peace, the United States of America will proudly stand with you. [The struggle today in Northern Ireland is] between those who are in the ship of peace and those who are trying to sink it; old habits die hard. You, the vast majority, Protestants and Catholics alike, must not allow the ship of peace to sink on the rocks of old habits and hard grudges.

Speech, Belfast,
Northern Ireland, Nov. 30/
Los Angeles Times,
12-1:(A)22.

2

[On Ireland]: I know well that the immigration from your country to the shores of mine helped to make America great. But I want more than anything for the young people of Ireland, wherever they live on this island, to be able to grow up and live out their dreams close to their roots—in peace and honor and freedom and equality. Realize that those of you [in the Republic of Ireland] who have more emotional and physical space [than the feuding Catholics and Protestants in Northern Ireland] must reach out and help them to take those next hard steps [toward peace].

Speech,
Dublin, Ireland, Dec. 1/
Los Angeles Times,
12-2:(A)11.

Luciano Di Crescenzo
Italian philosopher

3

[Italy's] state debt actually makes [Italians] feel much richer than they really are because of the huge returns on their money [from government-issued bonds]. There will be a lot of sad people around the day we get responsible political leadership that can bring down the debt.

The Washington Post,
1-16:(A)16.

Anatoly Dobrynin
Former Soviet Ambassador
to the United States

4

Relations between Moscow and Washington have always had a very narrow base, namely disarmament and security issues. This is still true. With China, for instance, America has a broad economic relationship, which influences your behavior on other issues, such as human rights. But we [Russians] still don't have an economic relationship. Our relationship must be broadened at all levels, including economics, cultural ties—everything.

Interview,
Washington, D.C./
U.S. News & World Report,
11-13:70.

Robert J. Dole
United States Senator,
R-Kansas;
Candidate for the
1996 Republican
Presidential nomination

5

Just as it was wrong [for the U.S.] to place too much focus on [then Soviet-President

(ROBERT J. DOLE)

Mikhail] Gorbachev in 1991, it is wrong in 1995 to ignore the fact that [Russian] President [Boris] Yeltsin has made serious errors, has moved toward authoritarian rule and has lost the political support of virtually all reform-minded Russians . . . [Russian foreign policy today] is often in conflict with American interests. [But U.S. President Clinton has a] misguided devotion to a "Russia first" policy, which has turned into a "Yeltsin-first" policy.

At Nixon Center for Peace and Freedom, Washington, D.C., March 1/ The Washington Post, 3-2:(A)13.

Grzegorz Domanski
Professor of law, Warsaw University (Poland)

1

[On the Polish Parliament's ability to overturn rulings made by the Constitutional Tribunal, the country's highest court]: Parliament basically said: Go to hell with the highest court. In the minds of the average Pole, it was like an announcement that everything in this country is political. The idea that I am a citizen, I'm aware of my liberties and I will not allow anyone to violate them and I know where to find justice—this is phantasmagoria in the eyes of the average Pole.

The New York Times, 6-19:(A)5.

Dzhokhar M. Dudayev
President of Chechnya, Russia

2

[On Russia's use of military force to stop Chechnya's move for independence]: You will never solve this problem militarily. Even if you erase every village and raze the Caucasus Mountains to the ground, still the people's ingrained desire for freedom and the right to life cannot be taken away.

News conference, Grozny, Russia, Jan. 11/ Los Angeles Times, 1-12:(A)8.

Jonathan Eyal
Director of studies, Royal United Services Institute (Britain)

3

The reality is that Europe cannot mount a large military operation on its own without American support.

Los Angeles Times, 5-26:(A)5.

Franco Ferrarotti
Sociologist, University of Rome (Italy)

4

We've [Italians] been hearing about how we have fallen into decay and decline ever since the days of the Roman Empire. Italians love to complain, yet deep down inside they know they probably live better than anyone else.

The Washington Post, 1-16:(A)16.

Yegor T. Gaidar
Former Prime Minister of Russia

5

[On the advice Russian President Boris Yeltsin has received on the secessionist re-

(YEGOR T. GAIDAR)

gion of Chechnya, where Yeltsin has committed Russian forces to a controversial war of repression]: When someone in Russia talks in a trembling voice about "strengthening the state," it usually leads to a bloody mess.

U.S. News & World Report, 1-30:22.

Jeffrey E. Garten
Under Secretary for International Trade, Department of Commerce of the United States

1

[On U.S.-Europe economic relations]: We need to invest at least as much time and energy in the development of new economic architecture as we are doing in the restructuring of NATO. This is not now the case, and we have no time to lose.

Los Angeles Times, 5-3:(A)10.

Stanislaw Gomulka
Professor, London School of Economics (Britain)

2

[On Slovakia's tenuous new democracy]: The collapse of the old Communist system, in some [East European] countries, happened in a day. But developing a proper new political system takes time. The distance between the actual situation and the ideal situation varies between countries. Slovakia is probably the most problematic of all.

Los Angeles Times, 11-24:(A)18.

Mikhail S. Gorbachev
Former President of the Soviet Union

3

I cannot praise our current [Russian] government. The political line taken since 1991 has done nothing for reform. When [Russian President Boris] Yeltsin came to power, I gave him my backing . . . But the people have been disappointed and they no longer accept this situation.

At celebration of 10th anniversary of his leadership of the Soviet Union, Italy, March 9/ USA Today, 3-10:(A)4.

4

[Criticizing the use of the Russian military against secessionists in the Chechnya region]: If the authorities are counting on putting an end to the drama of Chechnya by military methods, they are making a serious error.

Los Angeles Times, 6-16:(A)24.

Al Gore
Vice President of the United States

5

[On U.S. backing of Russian President Boris Yeltsin]: We're not siding with him as an individual. We're siding with him as the democratically elected leader of a free people.

Interview, Washington, D.C., Jan. 6/ Los Angeles Times, 1-7:(A)10.

Vaclav Havel
President
of the Czech Republic

1

[Advocating the admission to NATO of former Soviet-bloc countries]: Admission of the new democracies to NATO will make these countries feel safer and more secure and enhance their awareness of their European affiliation.

To NATO
senior military officers,
April 27/
Los Angeles Times,
5-4:(A)15.

Jesse Helms
United States Senator,
R-North Carolina

2

[Saying the U.S. may withhold aid to Russia if that country continues the brutality of its war against the secessionist region of Chechnya]: If [Russian President Boris Yeltsin] can't control his people in terms of killing women and children and other people, then he had better look out as far as foreign aid is concerned or any other aid, in my opinion.

The New York Times,
1-14:5.

Gyula Horn
Prime Minister
of Hungary

3

[On his commitment to privatization of government industries in Hungary]: Being a pragmatic man, I believe in concrete issues. For instance, on June 15, bids will be invited for MVM [the electric utility]. Within the next few weeks, another phase begins with the privatization of the phone company. And in the second half of the year, we'll invite privatization bids for the oil company . . . But on the other hand, we are speaking about strategic corporations. It is vital that government should have a key control function in those companies.

Interview/
The Wall Street Journal,
6-6:(A)12.

4

[On Russia's objection to former Soviet-bloc countries, such as his, joining NATO]: I understand that the Russian people are suffering a major identity crisis. But they must take democracy and the sovereignty of states seriously, or they will never be credible and they'll isolate themselves.

Interview/
The Wall Street Journal,
6-6:(A)12.

Serge July
Editor,
"Liberation" (France)

5

[On revelations of political corruption in France]: These cases of corruption are scandalous. Everyone shut their eyes to the financing of political life in France. And everyone lived with the hypocrisy. What is happening now is a real revolution . . . Politics is in the process of being removed from the pedestal. Long ago, when the Catholic Church was making popes in Italy and saints in Spain, it was making politicians, in the form of cardinals, in France. Politics is at the heart of French culture.

Los Angeles Times, 3-30:(A)7.

Alain Juppe
Foreign Minister
of France

1

[On foreign terrorism in France, such as that by Algerian Islamic militants]: On French territory, the government is determined—we will not let terrorism rot our society.

Jan. 4/
The New York Times,
1-5:(A)7.

Alain Juppe
Prime Minister
of France

2

[On France's controversial decision to resume testing of nuclear weapons in the South Pacific]: France's nuclear deterrence not only guarantees French independence. It is also critical to the peace and security of Europe.

USA Today,
9-1:(A)8.

3

The mastery of nuclear arms has allowed [France] to play a more important role in the world than could have been expected from simple arithmetic. Our influence on the [UN] Security Council, as a permanent member, is an illustration, even if the choice of the five wasn't originally made according to nuclear criteria.

Sept. 7/
The Christian Science Monitor,
10-4:10.

4

[On the budgetary reforms proposed by his government which have resulted in turmoil-causing public-sector strikes]: We can't wait any longer [to institute the reforms]. It's necessary to do this now, and together. France has a rendezvous with history.

Before French Parliament,
Paris, Dec. 5/
Los Angeles Times,
12-6:(A)10.

Oleg Kalugin
Former Director of Foreign
Counterintelligence, KGB (Soviet security police)

5

[Criticizing Russian President Boris Yeltsin's security advisers]: The President has become a willing hostage of the old party apparatchiks, the military-industrial complex. All together, they reflect the old totalitarian, imperial mentality.

U.S. News & World Report,
1-9:36.

Mickey Kantor
United States
Trade Representative

6

[On European criticism of U.S. trade sanctions against Japan for that country's alleged unfair trade practices]: Our European friends are always willing to hold our coats while we get our nose bloodied.

Newsweek,
5-29:46.

Klaus Kinkel
Foreign Minister
of Germany

7

Europe is inconceivable without America, and America inconceivable without Europe.

(KLAUS KINKEL)

The United States and Europe must develop a shared vision for the 21st century.

Chicago, Ill., April/ Los Angeles Times, 5-3:(A)10.

Vladimir A. Kitaev
Professor of history, Volgograd University (Russia)

1

[On his country's part in winning World War II]: Ours can be said to have been a Pyrrhic victory, because what did the people get for this? That the government took advantage of the victory to enhance its own power goes without saying.

Los Angeles Times, 5-1:(A)6.

Helmut Kohl
Chancellor of Germany

2

We need a new culture of self-reliance in Germany. The adventure of doing something new in life is something we have prized too little.

At gardeners' show, Cottbus, Germany/ The New York Times, 9-16:3.

3

From bitter historical experience, we know how quickly inflation destroys confidence in the reliability of political institutions and ends up endangering democracy. It is therefore no German hysteria when, in connection with European economic and monetary union, we stress forcibly that the Maastricht [Treaty] criteria must be met at all costs and under no circumstances are open for discussion.

At Christian Democratic Party meeting, Karlsruhe, Germany, Oct. 16/ The New York Times, 10-17:(A)6.

Alexander Konovalov
Director, Center for Military Policy and System Analysis (Russia)

4

[Saying NATO, by its airstrikes against Serb positions in the current conflict in the Balkans, is showing its aggressiveness and is thus seen as a threat in Russia]: When the West openly demonstrates that Russia has no role to play, it leaves only one way for Russia to react—to find other allies and to contrive a policy that does as much harm to the West as possible.

U.S. News & World Report, 9-25:64.

Sergei A. Kovalev
Former Commissioner of Human Rights of Russia

5

[Criticizing the Russian government's use of military force against the secessionist Chechnya region]: [Russia's use of a hard line in Chechnya] is not only our problem, it is your [the U.S.'] problem and a danger for you . . . Once again, we are hearing great lies from official [Russian] sources. Once again, we are learning to read newspapers between the lines.

(SERGEI A. KOVALEV)

Once again, we are hearing that the interests of the state are above all others.

News conference, Washington, D.C., May 4/ Los Angeles Times, 5-5:(A)4.

Andrei V. Kozyrev
Foreign Minister of Russia

1

[Defending Russia's use of military force to put down a move for independence in Chechnya]: [There is] no other way but to use force to reinstall law and order and to rescue the population [from criminals]. It is just intolerable to have a military gang anywhere—be it in the center of Moscow, be it in Los Angeles or whatever, or Chechnya—and we have to put it down.

Broadcast interview/ "Meet the Press," NBC-TV, 1-1.

2

In order to restore his relations with the reformists [in Russia], the President [Boris Yeltsin] needs only to come up to the mirror, because he himself is the major reformer.

News conference, Geneva, Switzerland, Jan. 18/ Los Angeles Times, 1-19:(A)9.

3

Saying Russia's use of military force against the secessionist Chechnya region should not adversely affect U.S.-Russian relations]: What's important is that nobody makes any artificial linkages or tries to exercise any political pressure on each other. But I don't see any issue which can't be discussed or examined between the two of us, because, after all, that's what partnership is.

Geneva, Switzerland, March 22/ Los Angeles Times, 3-23:(A)6.

Leonid Kuchma
President of Ukraine

4

[On the Commonwealth of Independent States, made up of former, now independent, Soviet republics]: I am clearly and fully aware that a shapeless organization like the C.I.S. has no future. The experience of the C.I.S. up to now confirms that not a single decision made is working.

Interview, Almaty, Kazakhstan, Feb. 10/ The New York Times, 2-11:5.

Eduard Kukan
Former Foreign Minister of Slovakia

5

[On Slovakia's tenuous new democracy]: At this time, the future of Slovakia is being decided: whether we will be a truly democratic country or some sort of "Slovak way" will develop which is reminiscent of the old Communist times. We risk being left out, of becoming an isolated island in Europe, like Albania used to be.

Los Angeles Times, 11-24:(A)19.

Anatoly Kulikov
Minister
of Internal Affairs
of Russia

1

[On a just-signed cease-fire agreement between the Russian government and Chechnya, which has been fighting for independence]: [The agreement] will not be met enthusiastically either in [the Chechen capital of] Grozny or in the mountains or even in Moscow. There are forces interested in the fire of war continuing or burning or at least smoldering.

News conference,
July 30/
The Washington Post,
7-31:(A)14.

Aleksander Kwasniewski
Candidate for President
of Poland

2

[On the Social Democracy of the Republic of Poland, the Communist Party's successor, which he leads]: The [former Communist] hardliners are older and older, and they are not active, thank God, in politics. There has been a change in generation in my party. The leaders are now in their 30s and 40s, and for us it is very important to organize Poland as a democratic state.

Interview/
Los Angeles Times,
11-4:(A)17.

3

Any serious politician in Poland should protect all of the successes, all of the elements of Polish reforms since 1989. Communism is the past. It is not possible to come back, and there is no sense for Communism to come back anywhere.

Warsaw, Poland, Nov. 5/
Los Angeles Times,
11-6:(A)4.

Aleksander Kwasniewski
President-elect
of Poland

4

[Saying that, although he is a former Communist, his election will not mean Poland will go back to its old Communist ways]: I would like to assure all of you, those who voted for me and those who today have a lot of doubts, that Poland is not going to get off the road to reform. The choice we made in 1989 [to end Communist rule] is the right choice, supported by a majority of Poles . . . Those who voted for [current President] Lech Walesa and those who voted for Aleksander Kwasniewski, you are neighbors. We work together; we meet on different occasions. Really, if you look into each other's eyes, you will see that a lot of things unite us, and very little divides us.

Broadcast address
to the nation,
Warsaw, Poland, Nov. 20/
Los Angeles Times,
11-21:(A)12.

Mart Laar
Former Prime Minister
of Estonia

5

[On the politically unpopular, but which he says were necessary, economic reforms instituted during his time as Prime Minister following Estonia's independence from the broken-up Soviet Union]: Yeah, it was a dirty job.

(MART LAAR)

But somebody had to do it, and I did it. And Estonia is totally transformed as a result.

Interview,
Tallinn, Estonia/
Los Angeles Times,
3-4:(A)2.

Patrick J. Leahy
United States Senator,
D-Vermont

1

[Criticizing Russia's plan to build nuclear reactors in Iran]: The political reality is that [U.S.] aid [to Russia] may well be cut off because of inexplicably stupid moves on the part of Russia. The Russians could try the patience of a saint.

Interview/
The New York Times,
2-23:(A)6.

Alexander Lebed
Lieutenant General,
Russian Army (Ret.)

2

[On the now-broken-up Soviet Union]: There is a big difference between being a citizen of a great power and being a citizen of a third-rate developing country—which is what has become of all the former [now independent] Soviet republics. Western Europe is gradually uniting, but each [of the former Soviet republics] sits behind its own fences, sucking on its own stale bread. This is unnatural. There will be a new union, whether the West likes it or not.

Interview, Moscow, Russia/
U.S. News & World Report,
10-9:60.

John Major
Prime Minister
of the United Kingdom

3

[On the current cease-fire in the ethnic conflict in Northern Ireland and the new British-Irish framework document for negotiations to end the strife there permanently]: Consent and free negotiation are fundamental to me, and they are the foundation of this Joint Document. I know that many people will be worried, perhaps some pessimistic, about the future. [But] the dialogue of the deaf has ended. The British government is engaged in talks with paramilitaries on both sides. We have had nearly six months of peace. Prosperity and a normal life are returning to Northern Ireland.

Belfast, Northern Ireland,
Feb. 22/
The New York Times,
2-23:(A)3.

Luigi Manconi
Italian sociologist

4

[On the increasing number of immigrants coming to Italy]: In the course of a century, we've gone from being a land of emigrants to one that takes in immigrants. We're just not equipped.

The New York Times,
1-5:(A)4.

Mitch McConnell
United States Senator,
R-Kentucky

5

If Russia's political leadership does not embrace free-market democracy, our [U.S.] aid [to Russia] is at best an irrelevant waste,

(MITCH McCONNELL)

and, at worst, serves corruption, authoritarianism and imperialism.

At Senate appropriations subcommittee hearing, Washington, D.C., Feb. 9/ USA Today, 2-10:(A)4.

1

[Criticizing Russia's plan to build nuclear reactors in Iran]: I would like the message to be very clear: This deal threatens Russian aid [from the U.S.], period . . . This is not the kind of behavior we expect of a country that purports to be an ally [of the U.S.] and aid recipient. This thing could really be a [U.S.-Russia] deal-breaker.

Interview/ The New York Times, 2-23:(A)6.

Michael A. McFaul
Russian-based senior associate, Carnegie Endowment for the Humanities (United States)

2

[In Russia today,] there is a return to old-style Soviet politics, with [President Boris] Yeltsin in the middle and four or five powerful groups around him. We get hints of how it works, but we are not privy to the inner workings the way we were two or three years ago.

The New York Times, 5-23:(A)4.

Roy A. Medvedev
Russian historian

3

[On the terror government of Josef Stalin in the post-World War II Soviet Union]: Five million [Soviet soldiers] who returned [from the war] immediately vanished to die in the [Soviet prison] camps. The losses were staggering. Among the generation born in the 1920s and 1930s, there are almost no men left. Think of all the talented scientists and artists and writers who never lived to fulfill their potential. [Despite the coming 50th anniversary of V-E Day,] I don't feel victorious, because as a historian I see the criminal errors that were committed after this war.

Los Angeles Times, 5-1:(A)6.

Francois Mitterrand
President of France

4

[Calling for progress on European unity]: The first common victory should and will be the victory of Europe over itself.

U.S. News & World Report, 5-22:11.

Teodor R. Pekarski
Director, Motherland Memorial Park, Volgograd, Russia

5

[On the former Soviet leader Josef Stalin]: If it hadn't been for Stalin, there would have been no victory [over Nazi Germany in World War II]. After the war, he oversaw the reconstruction [of the Soviet Union], he built up a nuclear state, he created a country that put the first man in space. He made mistakes, but people today are too quick to forget what good he did for this country.

Los Angeles Times, 5-1:(A)6.

Pascal Perrineau
Director,
Center for the Study
of French Political Life
(France)

1

[On the current turmoil in France involving strikes by public-sector workers opposed to the government's austerity proposals]: [Non-public-sector] people aren't opposed to reform, but they [support the strikers because] they feel deceived by [President Jacques] Chirac. They feel they've been "rolled in flour" [set up] by a man who promised them one thing and now is doing another . . . This hostility is more directed at the government than at reform. The French know that reform is justified. We all realize we can't go on with this deficit. But it's being done in an authoritarian style that makes the French feel it's a *fait accompli*. . . France only changes through crisis. We don't have the habit of changing in a consensual way. And this crisis underlines how much the politicians are cut off from the population. They think they know everything and that the people just have to change.

Los Angeles Times,
12-6:(A)10.

Romano Prodi
Italian economist;
Candidate for Prime Minister
of Italy

2

[On the difficulties of Italian coalition governments made up of disparate groups]: We are obliged to unite under one symbol, or else we will repeat [former Prime Minister Silvio] Berlusconi's mistake. We don't want to put together different people, and then have a government that is forever fighting [with itself]. We are building a previous common program, before the [election] campaign. If we don't do this, then the crisis in Italian politics will never be solved.

Interview, March 3/
The New York Times,
3-6:(A)3.

3

I have a saying which is that you can't be wealthy and stupid for more than one generation. I think that Italy at the moment has a contradiction between its [high] standard of living and its [lower] level of skills.

Interview, March 3/
The New York Times,
3-6:(A)3.

Peter Reddaway
Political scientist,
George Washington University
(United States)

4

The more U.S. policy supports [Russian President Boris] Yeltsin, the more it provokes anti-Americanism among the Russian population. By backing someone who's unpopular, you're helping opponents to overthrow him. It happened with [former Soviet President Mikhail] Gorbachev, and it happened with the Shah of Iran.

Los Angeles Times,
1-7:(A)10.

Sergio Romano
Italian political commentator
and former diplomat

5

[On Italian Prime Minister-designate Lamberto Dini, who promises to form a government that will restore discipline to the

(SERGIO ROMANO)

economy]: For so long, we've had governments [in Italy] that tried to please everybody. Now maybe it's good that we will have a government that tries to please nobody, which is basically what Dini says he intends to do.

The Washington Post,
1-16:(A)16.

Andrzej Rychard
Sociologist,
Polish Academy
of Science

1

The perception of politics is changing in Poland. In the beginning of [President Lech Walesa's term], voters believed in the people who were involved in politics, [but] the institutions themselves were less trusted. Now people are starting to put their trust in the institutions of democracy. [Walesa] was quite efficient in destroying the old Communist institutions. But his ability to build new ones is limited, and I think people perceive that.

The Washington Post,
9-11:(A)12.

Dmitri K. Simes
President,
Nixon Center on Peace
and Freedom
(United States)

2

[On the U.S. Clinton Administration's support for Russian President Boris Yeltsin]: The Administration has put Yeltsin above Russian democracy . . . The Administration still believes that Yeltsin is the best Russian leader that America can bargain for. It's very difficult for me to understand why the Administration feels that way . . . I remember when [U.S. officials] felt there was no alternative to [former Soviet President Mikhail] Gorbachev—and there were quite a few alternatives at the time.

Los Angeles Times,
1-7:(A)10,11.

Yuri Skokov
Leader,
Congress of Russian Communities
(Russian political party)

3

[Saying NATO, by its airstrikes against Serb positions in the current conflict in the Balkans, is showing its aggressiveness and is thus a threat to Russia]: In [Russian] society, the opinion is forming that the West is simply trying to destroy us. We made friends and said, "Let's live together in peace." And suddenly it seems our new friend has deceived us. You couldn't take us by force, so you took us by deception.

U.S. News & World Report,
9-25:64.

Masayoshi Takemura
Minister of Finance
of Japan

4

[Criticizing France for its plans to resume nuclear-weapons testing in the Pacific]: It is not too late for [French] President [Jacques] Chirac to turn back from nuclear testing. Nuclear weapons are a relic from a previous era.

Papeete, Tahiti/
The Washington Post,
9-4:(A)18.

Margaret Thatcher
Former Prime Minister of the United Kingdom

1

[Criticizing U.S. President Clinton's giving a red-carpet welcome to Northern Ireland's Sinn Fein leader Gerry Adams, who many accuse of being a terrorist]: It would be the equivalent of having the Prime Minister of England invite the Oklahoma City [U.S. Federal building] bombers to 10 Downing Street, to congratulate them on a job well done.

Newsweek, 5-15:19.

Valentin I. Varrenikov
General (Ret.) and former commander of ground forces, Soviet Army

2

[Criticizing the reforms going on in Russia today]. In the 1950s, under [then-Soviet leader Josef] Stalin, we were not buying wheat from the West, we were selling it on the international market. We didn't go around the world asking for humanitarian aid and loans, we were granting them. Here lies the paradox.

Los Angeles Times, 5-1:(A)6.

Philippe Vasseur
Minister of Agriculture of France

3

[On the declining sales in France of "baguettes," the type of bread that has been a part of the French scene for a long period of time]: Bread is part of our national identity . . . If there isn't any left, we won't know who we really are.

Newsweek, 10-2:29.

Katalin Vasvary
Secretary general, Hungarian League Against Cancer

4

[On Hungary's high cancer rate]: We have to undo all those years of Communism, when people were told not to care about the wellness of their whole being. People were viewed as bodies, not as human beings with souls.

Los Angeles Times, 5-30:(A)6.

Dmitri A. Volkogonov
Russian historian; Colonel General (Ret.), Soviet Army

5

[In Russia,] democrats are wonderful in opposition. Unfortunately, when they come to power they use it badly and make many mistakes.

Interview, Moscow, Russia/ The New York Times, 8-1:(A)3.

6

Communism with a human face is impossible, and [former Soviet President Mikhail] Gorbachev never understood. He thought he was saving Communism [by reforming it], but objectively he destroyed it; or more exactly,

(DMITRI A. VOLKOGONOV)

he didn't interfere in the process of its self-destruction.

Interview,
Moscow, Russia/
The New York Times,
8-1:(A)3.

Vladimir Volkov
Adviser
on the Balkans
to Russian President
Boris N. Yeltsin

1

[Expressing concern about NATO airstrikes against Serb positions in the ethnic conflict in the Balkans]: NATO has put the UN beneath it. A new mechanism for interfering in other countries is being developed. [It] could be used toward Russia.

U.S. News & World Report,
9-18:63.

Lech Walesa
President
of Poland

2

[On the tough battle he is having with his opponent in the forthcoming Presidential election, Aleksander Kwasniewski, a young and good-looking candidate]: Do you want me to look nicer? I will try, but it is impossible. I am not reformable. But I am absolutely sure those of us responsible for Poland have proved what we can do in dangerous moments. I think all of the people who feel responsible for Poland know who should lead Poland.

Los Angeles Times,
11-4:(A)17.

Boris N. Yeltsin
President of Russia

3

The efficiency of the state authorities is to a great extent determined by their handling of crime. We have made little progress in this area. [And] as the major crime networks . . . have grown more and more impudent, the law-enforcement agencies have virtually assumed a policy of non-interference.

Before Russian Parliament/
The Washington Post,
2-27:(A)13.

4

[On his government's efforts to create a new government in the Russian region of Chechnya, which has been at war with Moscow in a bid for independence]: We are talking with the elders, district representatives, city representatives and leaders [in Chechnya]. We have already set up the [new] government of Chechnya, and are looking forward to organizing elections to the Chechen Parliament. [But] we realize that until such democratic elections are held, we will be unable to convince the world that the situation in Chechnya is really positive, really democratic and there are no human-rights violations.

Interview,
Moscow, Russia,
March 16/
The New York Times,
3-17:(A)5.

5

[On his concern about NATO expanding closer to Russia by the membership of former Soviet-bloc countries]: What's happening is that we have just recently abandoned the bloc

(BORIS N. YELTSIN)

divisions. Now assume that some East European and Central European countries would join NATO and the border would move immediately closer to Russia, so the situation would appear to suggest that we would again have a bloc situation with NATO. Is it really consistent with all-European security? No, it is not. The situation will not be calm.

Interview,
Moscow, Russia, March 16/
The New York Times,
3-17:(A)1.

1

[Saying he is concerned about the growing military aspect of NATO]: The political leaders who are championing the rapid bloating of NATO should be very careful and accurate in their thoughts. NATO is already showing [in its current bombing campaign against Serb positions in the ethnic conflict in the Balkans] what it is capable of. Only of bombing, and then counting the trophies, of how many are killed among the civilian population . . . When [through the expansion of membership] NATO approaches the borders of the Russian Federation, you can say that there will be two military blocs, and this will be a restoration of what we have already had.

News conference,
Moscow, Russia,
Sept. 8/
The New York Times,
9-9:3.

2

[On the increasing crime and corruption in Russia]: All this is connected with free-market economy, which creates the corruption, the mafia and so on. It has become easy to trade, cheat and behave like hooligans.

Interview,
Moscow, Russia,
Oct. 19/
The New York Times,
10-20:(A) 3.

3

[The expansion of NATO] will mean a conflagration of war throughout all of Europe, for sure, for sure.

September/
Newsweek,
11-6:50.

Naina I. Yeltsin
Wife of Russian President
Boris N. Yeltsin

4

[On the economic problems in Russia]: We shouldn't paint all this in dark colors. The shops are full. Russia is building up. If you travel by plane, you can see construction under way. If people are building houses, it is a sign the country is surviving. It is too early to bury Russia.

Russian
broadcast interview,
Oct. 31/
Los Angeles Times,
11-1:(A)15.

THE ETHNIC CONFLICT IN THE BALKANS

All of the quotations in this sub-section relate to the ethnic civil war which broke out following the self-declared independence in 1992 of the Yugoslav republics of Bosnia-Herzegovina and Croatia. In this conflict, Bosnian Serbs, with support from Yugoslav Serbs, aim to conquer Muslim territory in Bosnia to form a larger Serbian-ruled area. The fighting has also involved Croatia.

Yasushi Akashi
Ranking United Nations representative in Bosnia-Herzegovina

1

[On the just-signed four-month cease-fire in Bosnia]: There have been many cease-fires, but this is the first time we have a cessation-of-hostilities agreement. I hope that we are turning a very important corner in this most tragic conflict in Europe since the Second World War.

Jan. 1/ The New York Times, 1-2:3.

Richard K. Armey
United States Representative, R-Texas

2

[On the reluctance of the U.S. Congress to formally vote on whether to support President Clinton's decision to commit American ground troops to help enforce the recently agreed Bosnia peace treaty]: Getting a vote on this matter would be like pulling teeth through the back of your head.

To reporters, Nov. 28/ Los Angeles Times, 11-29:(A)14.

James A. Baker III
Former Secretary of State of the United States

3

[Arguing against U.S. President Clinton's suggestion that the U.S. might send ground forces to help the UN forces]: This is a slippery slope, in capital letters. This is exactly the kind of mission creep that led to disaster in Somalia. This is incrementalism at its worst—and a sure recipe for disaster.

The New York Times, 6-2:(A)4.

4

If this thing spreads [from Bosnia] to Macedonia, you could well have Bulgaria, Serbia, Albania, Greece, even Turkey involved. And America, whether we like it or not, would be back over there, because history shows us America cannot stand general instability in Europe. We've fought three wars

(JAMES A. BAKER III)

over there in this century—two hot ones and a cold one. And we would have to be right back again.

Broadcast interview/ "This Week With David Brinkley," ABC-TV, 6-4.

Paul Beaver
Editor, "Jane's Balkans Sentinel" (Britain)

1

[Saying a lifting of the UN arms embargo against the Bosnian Muslims to help them fight the Serbs would not be a quick and easy operation for the Muslims]: Like fighting a war, equipping an army requires a major logistics chain. There is a hiatus while equipment is marshaled, located and fed into it. And then you can't just supply an army with howitzers and tanks and say, "Here you are, guys, off you go." They have to learn how to operate them.

Los Angeles Times, 8-10:(A)12.

Howard L. Berman
United States Representative, D-California

2

[On U.S. policy in the conflict]: Every option is fraught with tremendous political risks. [The U.S.] Congress will carp and criticize and hold hearings and second-guess and in the end do everything it can to avoid taking a firm clear-cut position because it doesn't want to bear the responsibility of the consequences.

June 2/Los Angeles Times, 6-3:(A)4.

Joseph R. Biden, Jr.
United States Senator, D-Delaware

3

[Criticizing U.S. President Clinton's handling of the conflict]: We know enough to know when a policy stinks.

U.S. News & World Report, 8-7:20.

Boutros Boutros-Ghali
Secretary General of the United Nations

4

[On UN peacekeeping efforts in Bosnia]: If there is not the political will among the protagonists, we cannot achieve peace. Must we stay for an indefinite period, like Cyprus, for 30 years? The fact is that we maintain a huge operation in Bosnia at the expense of other operations.

At conference on peacekeeping sponsored by International Peace Academy and the Austrian government, Vienna, Austria, March 2/ The New York Times, 3-3:(A)3.

5

[On the problems the UN has had in intervening in the conflict]: In Bosnia, the mandates were clear at first. When attempts were made to change them, problems arose. In [the former] Yugoslavia, we were told to keep the peace, not to make war. But we also were not given the means to apply that mandate. Member states could not agree on what was to be done in [the former] Yugoslavia, or they were

(BOUTROS BOUTROS-GHALI)

not willing to put everything they had into resolving that crisis.

Interview/ World Press Review, June:14.

Patrick J. Buchanan
American political commentator; Candidate for the 1996 Republican Presidential nomination

1

[Arguing against sending U.S. ground troops to help enforce the recently agreed Bosnia peace treaty]: Bosnia is Beirut [Lebanon] all over again. A bloody, religious, ethnic and civil war, in which all sides have perpetrated horrors and all sides have been victims of horrors.

Los Angeles Times, 12-11:(A)18.

Nicholas Burns
Spokesman for the Department of State of the United States

2

[On the current wave of NATO air attacks on Serbian positions]: The Bosnian Serbs, especially after the events of the last 12 hours, ought to have concluded that there is no military victory in sight for them, the tide of the war has turned against them, their dream of a Greater Serbia is no more, [and] it's time to face the responsibility of peace.

Aug. 30/ Los Angeles Times, 8-31:(A)6.

3

There won't be peace until the Serbs sit down with the Bosnian government and the Croatian government and negotiate a peace arrangement. Like it or not, you deal with people who have made war to make peace. We don't like negotiating with some of these people on the Bosnian Serb side, but it's going to be absolutely necessary for them to be there to make the peace.

Los Angeles Times, 10-30:(A)8.

George Bush
Former President of the United States

4

[Saying U.S. President Clinton, by committing himself to sending American ground troops to help enforce the recently agreed Bosnia peace treaty, has placed U.S. credibility on the line and thus must be supported by the American Congress]: If the President shifts direction now—or if it is seen that the President does not have the support of the Congress [even though many in that body oppose sending troops]—our standing as leader of the free world and the standing of [NATO] would be dramatically diminished. That must not happen.

Dec. 5/ Los Angeles Times, 12-6:(A)14.

Ted Galen Carpenter
Director of foreign-policy studies, Cato Institute (United States)

5

[On the increasing spread of the conflict into Croatia]: All parties to this conflict are

(TED GALEN CARPENTER)

maneuvering for position and advantage. And the increasing blend of fighting in Croatia and Bosnia simply highlights the fact that this is one large civil war, with several fronts.

USA Today,
5-3:(A)9.

Ismet Ceric
Chairman,
department of psychology,
Kosevo Hospital,
Sarajevo, Bosnia

1

[On the conflict]: We thought there were rules in the modern world. But as time has passed, we have seen that only with a stone in your hand can you defend yourself.

The New York Times,
6-28:(A)6.

Jacques Chirac
President of France

2

[On France's military involvement in the conflict]: [France] will not accept the return of ethnic hatred and barbarism to the continent. [Neither will it accept its soldiers] being humiliated, wounded or killed with impunity.

At funeral
for French soldier
killed in Bosnia,
Vannes, France, June 1/
The New York Times,
6-2:(A)5.

3

[Criticizing the continuing advance of Serb forces in Bosnia]: I call on all the great democracies to think again and to impose respect for human rights and international law. [The UN] must at the very least be ready to protect the remaining [safe-haven Muslim] enclaves [in Bosnia] and notably Sarajevo.

News conference,
Paris, France,
July 14/
Time, 7-24:44.

Warren Christopher
Secretary of State
of the United States

4

[Saying the U.S. Congress should be careful if it is considering ending U.S. participation in the UN arms embargo against Bosnian Muslims so they can fight against the Serbs more effectively]: What I ask all of you to do when you talk to [Bosnian Prime Minister Haris Silajdzic], when he comes here [next week] is to be frank with him, to be honest with him as to what the Congress is likely to do. The easy step, perhaps, for him to advocate is a unilateral lifting of the arms embargo; but you must tell him what you feel you will next do. If the arms embargo is unilaterally lifted, and the Muslims get in trouble, will you send United States troops to help him?

To members
of U.S. Congress,
Washington, D.C./
The New York Times,
1-31:(A)3.

5

The Bosnian Serb leaders are now on notice that an attack against [the UN "safe haven" of] Gorazde will be met by substantial and decisive [NATO] air power. Any air campaign in Gorazde will include significant

(WARREN CHRISTOPHER)

attacks on significant targets. There will be no more pinprick strikes.

London, England, July 21/
The New York Times,
7-22:1.

1

[On the possibility that the U.S. Congress will deny President Clinton's desire to send U.S. peacekeeping troops to Bosnia in the event of a peace agreement there]: If we get a peace settlement and the United States does not participate in the enforcement, I believe it would be the end of NATO. If we do not join our NATO allies in that important endeavor, it would undermine NATO, which has been the most effective military alliance in the history of the world.

Interview,
Washington, D.C., Oct. 3/
Los Angeles Times,
10-4:(A)16.

2

[On the beginning of peace talks among the parties to the conflict being held in Dayton, Ohio]: We're embarking today on a process that well may be the last, best chance for peace. I hope that someday Dayton, Ohio, will be remembered as the site of the place where the killing finally was brought to a halt, and we started building a better future for all the people of former Yugoslavia—especially the people of war-torn Bosnia-Herzegovina.

Welcoming the participants,
Dayton, Ohio, Nov. 1/
Los Angeles Times,
11-2:(A)1.

3

[Saying not sending U.S. ground troops to help enforce the recently agreed Bosnia peace treaty would adversely affect American leadership throughout the world]: Whether we take action now in Bosnia is an acid test of American leadership. I can tell you from my personal experience as Secretary of State that if our country doesn't follow through on this initiative, no nation around the world will follow us—not in Europe, not in the Middle East, not in Asia, not anywhere.

Before House International
Relations Committee,
Washington, D.C., Nov. 30/
Los Angeles Times,
12-1:(A)27.

4

[Supporting the use of U.S. ground troops to help enforce the recently agreed Bosnia peace treaty]: In Bosnia, we have a fundamental choice. If the United States does not participate, there will be no NATO force. And if there is no NATO force, there will be no peace in Bosnia, and the war will reignite.

Before Senate Foreign
Relations Committee,
Washington, D.C., Dec. 1/
Los Angeles Times,
12-2:(A)10.

5

[On the planned U.S./NATO deployment of ground troops to enforce the recently agreed Bosnia peace treaty]: For NATO, this is, without exaggeration, a moment worthy of being called historic . . . [This] will be a noble mission, unique in the history of Eu-

(WARREN CHRISTOPHER)

rope. It will be a defining challenge for this [NATO] alliance. It will have profound consequences for our interests today and for our hopes for the future.

Brussels, Belgium, Dec. 5/ Los Angeles Times, 12-6:(A)1,14.

Bill Clinton
President of the United States

1

[On the possibility of the U.S. becoming more involved militarily in the conflict]: If the UN forces want to stay in Bosnia but have to relocate so they can concentrate themselves in more secure areas, if they needed help from us, we would be willing to give it. As long as the mission was strictly limited for a very narrow purpose and it was something that we could do for them that they couldn't do for themselves—upon proper consultation with [the U.S.] Congress, I would be inclined to do that. But [U.S. forces] would not be going there to get involved in the war or to be part of the United Nations mission.

Interview/ The New York Times, 6-2:(A)4.

2

The difference between the Croatians and the Serbs is that the Croatians . . . if they can think to the future, what they want is an economic, a political, a security relationship with the West—which is the point of leverage we never had with the Serbs, because they were always looking eastward.

To newspaper columnists, Washington, D.C., Sept. 27/ Los Angeles Times, 9-28:(A)6.

3

[On the possibility of the U.S. sending ground troops to Bosnia]: If we were to send a substantial number of troops in there, it would have to be for a limited amount of time, just to deal with all the phaseout that has to be done when people begin to lay down their arms . . . I think the American people have been exposed to such horrible violence in Bosnia . . . that they may assume that if the United States were to go there to be part of implementing the peace process, that our troops would automatically be in a conflict. I think that would be a false assumption . . . Of course, whenever you send people into a situation where there has been hatred and violence, there's always the prospect that something could happen. But I think the likelihood is far greater that they will be there to enforce a peace agreement and that they will not be subjected to combat-like circumstances.

To newspaper columnists, Washington, D.C., Sept. 27/ Los Angeles Times, 9-28:(A)6.

4

[Saying up to 25,000 U.S. troops would be needed to act as peacekeepers if a peace agreement is reached]: We have a long way to go, and there's no guarantee of success. The United States will not be sending our forces into combat in Bosnia. We will not send them into a peace that cannot be maintained. But

(BILL CLINTON)

we must use our power to secure that peace. In Bosnia, as elsewhere, if the United States does not lead, the job will not be done.

Before Freedom House,
Washington, D.C., Oct. 6/
The New York Times,
10-7:5.

1

[On polls that show the American people do not approve of sending U.S. ground forces to Bosnia, which Clinton wants to do if a peace agreement is reached]: I know that. But public opinion is very volatile on an issue like this. It will change if the President acts. I've got to decide this not on the basis of what public opinion is today, but on what people are going to say 20 years from now.

At White House meeting
with members
of Congress,
November/
Los Angeles Times,
11-22:(A)17.

2

[On the just agreed Bosnia peace treaty]: After nearly four years of [war with] 250,000 people killed, 2 million refugees, atrocities that have appalled people all over the world, the people of Bosnia finally have a chance to turn from the horror of war to the promise of peace . . . [But] without [the U.S. as part of a peacekeeping force on the ground in Bosnia], the hard-won peace would be lost, the war would resume, the slaughter of innocents would begin again, and the conflict that already has claimed so many people could spread like poison throughout the entire region.

Press briefing,
Washington, D.C., Nov. 21/
Los Angeles Times,
11-22:(A)1,16.

3

[On his decision to send U.S. ground troops to help enforce the recently agreed Bosnia peace treaty]: America cannot and must not be the world's policeman. We cannot stop all wars for all time, but we can stop some wars. We cannot save all women and children, but we can save many of them. We cannot do everything, but we must do what we can . . . If we're not there in [in Bosnia], NATO will not be there. The peace will collapse. The war will reignite. The slaughter of innocents will begin again . . . For nearly four years, a terrible war has torn Bosnia apart. Horrors that we prayed had been banished from Europe forever have been seared into our minds again—skeletal prisoners caged behind barbed-wire fences, women and girls raped as a tool of war, defenseless men and boys shot down into mass graves—evoking visions of World War II concentration camps and endless lines of refugees marching toward a future of despair . . . In Bosnia, we can succeed because the mission is clear and limited. Our troops are strong and very well-prepared. But no deployment of American troops is risk-free, and this one may well involve casualties . . . Our mission will be limited, focused and under the command of an American General. In fulfilling this mission, we will have a chance to help stop the killing of innocent civilians, and especially children, and at the

(BILL CLINTON)

same time bring stability to Central Europe, a region of the world that is vital to our national interests.

Broadcast address to the nation, Washington, D.C., Nov. 27/ Los Angeles Times, 11-28:(A)1,8.

1

We must help peace to take hold in Bosnia, because so long as that fire rages at the heart of the European continent—so long as the emerging democracies and our allies are threatened by fighting in Bosnia—there will be no stable, undivided, free Europe.

Before British Parliament, London, England, Nov. 29/ Los Angeles Times, 11-30:(A)6.

2

Our nation . . . has a vital stake in a Europe that is stable, strong and free. But we know such a Europe can never be built as long as conflict tears at the heart of the continent in Bosnia.

Before Irish Parliament, Dublin, Ireland, Dec. 1/ Los Angeles Times, 12-2:(A)11.

3

[On the recently agreed Bosnia peace treaty]: [Yugoslav] President [Slobodan] Milosevic made strong commitments which he will have to fulfill to secure the support of the Bosnian-Serb leaders for this agreement. We fully expect [he] will take the appropriate steps to ensure that this treaty will be honored as it is written and that we will not have undue interference with implementing it.

News conference, Madrid, Spain, Dec. 3/ Los Angeles Times, 12-4:(A)8.

4

[Saying U.S. troops, sent to help enforce the recently agreed Bosnia peace treaty, will leave after a year even if the war there resumes]: For a force of this size to stay any longer than that would run the risk of [turning] into an occupation force. We don't believe that's right. Neither do they [the Bosnians] . . . If we leave after a year, and they decide they don't like the benefits of peace and they're going to start fighting again, that does not mean NATO failed. It means we gave [the Bosnians] a chance to make their peace and they blew it.

Broadcast interview/ "60 Minutes," CBS-TV, 12-10.

Robert J. Dole

United States Senator, R-Kansas; Candidate for the 1996 Republican Presidential nomination

5

[On the just-held U.S. Senate vote to lift the arms embargo against the Bosnian Muslims]: [This vote] is not about politics [U.S. President Clinton is against lifting the em-

(ROBERT J. DOLE)

bargo]. It is about whether some small country that has been ravaged on all sides, pillaged, women raped, children killed, do they have any rights in this world?

July 26/
Los Angeles Times,
7-27:(A)1.

1

[On U.S. President Clinton's decision to send American ground troops to help enforce the recently agreed Bosnia peace treaty]: We now have an unfortunate situation. Either [the U.S.] Congress agrees to a military deployment that looks suspiciously like [the disastrous U.S. deployment to Lebanon in 1983, or, on the other hand, we unravel a Presidential commitment . . . which would be at great cost to the solidarity and credibility of NATO and America itself.

Before National
Jewish Coalition,
Washington, D.C.,
Nov. 28/
Los Angeles Times,
11-29:(A)26.

Lawrence S. Eagleburger
Former Secretary of State
of the United States

2

None of the parties [in the conflict] are particularly nice people. Any of them would be doing to the other side what Bosnian Serbs are doing [now], if they could get away with it.

USA Today,
9-1:(A)6.

Fred Eckhard
Spokesman for
Yasushi Akashi,
ranking United Nations
representative in
Bosnia-Herzegovina

3

[On the inability of UN peacekeeping forces to prevent breaks in cease-fires during the conflict]: We'd like to believe we are not legitimizing aggression in any case, but just moving, falling back each time the parties break another agreement between themselves or with us, and try to stabilize or push them back in the direction of a negotiated settlement . . . We've been quite flexible in that sense, and we've been pushed around in the process.

Los Angeles Times,
5-5:(A)12.

Dianne Feinstein
United States Senator,
D-California

4

[On U.S. President Clinton's decision to send American ground troops to help enforce the recently agreed Bosnia peace treaty]: [I have] come to the conclusion that the risk of not doing [anything] is greater than the risk of doing [something] long-term. I think the cause is noble, and there's nothing wrong with the strongest democracy in the world being part of a noble cause.

At Senate
Foreign Relations
Committee hearing,
Washington, D.C., Dec. 1/
Los Angeles Times,
12-2:(A)10.

Ejup Ganic
Vice President of Bosnia-Herzegovina

1

[Saying the Bosnian government will not renew the current cease-fire when it expires this month]: If you extend the cease-fire, they [peace negotiators] will wait until the end to try hard for a settlement. They are like a student who waits until two weeks before the exam to study.

Interview, April 2/ USA Today, 4-3:(A)9.

Newt Gingrich
United States Representative, R-Georgia; Speaker of the House

2

[On the possibility of the U.S. sending ground troops to Bosnia]: We should wait to see what's happening. [It is unlikely that] we would say to our [European] allies of a half-century [that] the U.S. won't do anything. But at the same time, we don't want to go and get involved. It's very important for us to be very cautious.

To reporters, Georgia, June 1/ The New York Times, 6-2:(A)1.

3

[Criticizing the ineffectiveness of UN peacekeeping and protection efforts in Bosnia]: The UN acts totally impotently and undermines the morale of every law-abiding democracy.

July 13/ USA Today, 7-14:(A)4.

Patrick Glynn
Resident scholar, American Enterprise Institute

4

[On the downing of a U.S. fighter plane by Bosnian Serbs]: I hope the [U.S. Clinton] Administration doesn't overreact to the downing of the plane. This is not about honor; it's about damage control. Whatever face we could have lost, we've already lost. Going in deeper would just be worse . . . If the British and French are willing to go to bat [in the conflict] without our forces being there, we can probably keep standing on the sidelines—and that's where [U.S. President] Clinton would clearly prefer to be.

June 2/ Los Angeles Times, 6-3:(A)6.

Philip Gordon
Analyst, International Institute for Strategic Studies (Britain)

5

[Saying a lifting of the UN arms embargo against the Bosnian Muslims to help them fight the Serbs would not be a quick and easy operation for the Muslims]: Even with the mere announcing of a lifting of the embargo, one can assume the Bosnian Serbs will take full advantage before it's too late. How quickly you can get the Bosnian [Muslim] forces up to speed [with the new military equipment] to prevent [a massive Serb offensive] is an open question. Some people say there would be no Bosnians left by the time you get [the army] armed and trained.

Los Angeles Times, 8-10:(A)13.

Al Gore
Vice President
of the United States

1

[Supporting U.S. President Clinton's decision to send American ground troops to help enforce the recently agreed Bosnia peace treaty]: The risks of not undertaking this mission are overwhelming: the destruction of NATO; the loss of a significant measure of U.S. influence in the world; the restarting of the war with the ethnic slaughter; and the risk that the war would spread, bringing Greece and Turkey into a much broader Balkan war . . . This cup has passed to us. And we are going to lead and keep this peace.

Broadcast interview/
"Meet the Press,"
NBC-TV, 12-10.

Dan Goure
Deputy director
of political and military studies,
Center for Strategic
and International Studies
(United States)

2

[Expressing concern that the U.S. may be poised for a gradual increase in its involvement in the Balkans conflict, which could lead to a situation similar to its "gradual escalation" policy in the 1960s-'70s war in Vietnam, which then-U.S. Secretary of Defense Robert McNamara has condemned in a new book]: If you liked Dien Bien Phu, you'll love Sarajevo—this policy is nuts. We're at the stage where [Defense Secretary] Bill Perry is going to write his McNamara *mea culpa* 30 years from now.

Los Angeles Times,
6-3:(A)4.

Phil Gramm
United States Senator, R-Texas;
Candidate for the 1996 Republican
Presidential nomination

3

[Arguing against U.S. President Clinton's plan to send American ground forces to Bosnia to enforce the recently agreed peace treaty]: I have always tried to give the President the benefit of the doubt on foreign-policy issues. But even allowing for the fullest possible benefit of the doubt, I cannot support sending troops to Bosnia. I intend to do everything in my power to give the troops going to Bosnia every ounce of support needed to make their deployment short, safe and successful. But I believe they are being sent to enforce an unenforceable treaty; and I fear that when they are ultimately withdrawn, we will have lost some heroes and there will be no peace for Bosnia.

Nov. 27/
Los Angeles Times,
11-28:(A)8.

4

[Criticizing U.S. President Clinton's decision to send American ground troops to help enforce the recently agreed Bosnia peace treaty]: I am opposed to sending American troops to Bosnia. I intend to fight the President's resolution that will ask Congress for their endorsement of that policy. The President has failed to make his case; [the failure was] for the simplest and most basic of all reasons: That case cannot be made.

Before National
Jewish Coalition,
Washington, D.C., Nov. 28/
Los Angeles Times,
11-29:(A)1.

Lee H. Hamilton
United States Representative,
D-Indiana

1

[Arguing against a unilateral U.S. lifting of the UN arms embargo against Bosnian Muslims]: The impact of lifting the embargo is 25,000 Americans going to Bosnia. That's the result—and it's not in doubt.

June 8/
USA Today,
6-9:(A)6.

Francois Heisbourg
Former director,
International Institute
for Strategic Studies
(Britain)

2

[On Europe's handling of the conflict without U.S. help]: All of a sudden, Europeans found themselves without Big Brother's guidance. They were lost.

Los Angeles Times,
5-3:(A)10.

Richard C. Holbrooke
Assistant Secretary
for European
and Canadian Affairs,
Department of State
of the United States

3

Wars must end and enemies must live and work together. It's happened in Western Europe. It's happened in Asia. It must happen in the former Yugoslavia.

To reporters,
Geneva, Switzerland, Sept. 8/
The New York Times,
9-9:4.

4

[On the problems that must be overcome in peace negotiations during the pending 60-day cease-fire]: You name it, and it's an obstacle: The map. Sarajevo. The Posavina [Serbian supply route] corridor . . . Political structures. Constitutional arrangements. Election procedures. There isn't an issue we [haven't] talked about. Any of you who think these issues are irrational or minor must remember that the whole war, from the point of view of most of us, is irrational. We are going to have to plow through these issues one at a time.

Zagreb, Croatia, Oct. 5/
Los Angeles Times,
10-6:(A)6.

5

Given the lessons of history, Bosnia is not likely ever to have a strong central government. A loose federation, a weak Presidency, seems to me inevitable.

Time, 11-6:50.

Kay Bailey Hutchison
United States Senator,
R-Texas

6

There will be a very big eruption [among the American people] if [U.S. President] Clinton agrees to U.S. troops on the ground in Bosnia . . . I think we are risking dissipating our security resources on border and ethnic conflicts that don't warrant that kind of financial effort. This is not a U.S. security interest.

Sept. 14/
USA Today,
9-15:(A)2.

Henry J. Hyde
United States Representative

1

[Arguing against the U.S. getting more involved militarily in the conflict]: I don't see that the U.S. has to be at the eye of every storm over the globe. This is a European matter, and there ought to be enough resources in Europe 50 years after World War II to deal with it.

Illinois, June 1/ The New York Times, 6-2:(A)4.

Alija Izetbegovic
President of Bosnia-Herzegovina

2

The war must not last a day longer than it has to, but peace at any price cannot and will not be accepted. We will negotiate [with the Serbs] where we can and make war where we have to.

Radio address, Jan. 1/ The New York Times, 1-2:3.

3

[Criticizing the Bosnian Serbs' recent shooting down of a U.S. fighter aircraft and their taking hostage of hundreds of UN peace-keepers]: Only a firm response can resolve this new form of mass terrorism. [Negotiation can lead only to the] humiliation of defeat [for the Bosnian government and the West] . . . I have to express my personal discontent at the astonishingly mild attitude of Western governments.

June 5/ The New York Times, 6-6:(A)7.

4

[Supporting the current wave of NATO air attacks against Serbian positions]: The world has finally done what it should have done a long, long time ago . . . We are seeing not the beginning of a war, but the start of a peace.

Aug. 30/ Los Angeles Times, 8-31:(A)6.

5

[On the just-agreed Bosnia peace treaty]: This may not be [a] just peace, but it is better than continuation of war. In the world as it is, a better peace could not have been obtained.

Dayton, Ohio, Nov. 21/ Los Angeles Times, 11-22:(A)16.

Ahmad Jannati
Spokesman on Bosnian Affairs for Iranian Islamic mullahs

6

Bosnia is a bleeding limb of the body of Islam and the body of Islamic society. An Islamic town [the Bosnian city of Srebrenica], which was supposed to be a safe area, has fallen [to the Bosnian Serbs]. Other towns are under threat and the whole world is aware of this . . . Why is the world silent on the plight of the Bosnian Muslims?

Sermon, July 21/ The Washington Post, 7-24:(A)18.

John Paul II
Pope

7

Very near to us, in the winter cold, the peoples of Bosnia-Herzegovina continue to

(JOHN PAUL II)

suffer in their own flesh the consequences of a pitiless war. Faced with this tragedy, which in a way seems like the shipwreck of the whole of Europe, neither ordinary citizens nor political leaders can remain indifferent or neutral. There are aggressors and there are victims. International law and humanitarian law are being violated. All of this demands a firm and united reaction on the part of the community of nations.

To foreign ambassadors, Vatican City, Jan. 9/ Los Angeles Times, 1-10:(A)4.

Vladislav Jovanovic
Foreign Minister of Yugoslavia

1

What does [foreign diplomatic] recognition mean in Bosnia? How could you define it? There is a messy situation: You have the former Yugoslav republic of Bosnia, a Muslim-Croat federation and a Serbian entity. Whom are you to recognize? Early recognition of Bosnia by the European Union and the United States only led to an ongoing civil war.

Interview, Belgrade, Yugoslavia, Feb. 22/ The New York Times, 2-23:(A)6.

Radovan Karadzic
Leader, Bosnian Serbs

2

[Criticizing NATO airstrikes against Bosnian Serb positions]: We are under terrible attack by NATO. They are bombarding us so terribly that it hasn't been seen since the Second World War in Europe, and it can't be justified by any reasons.

Broadcast interview, Pale, Bosnia/ CNN-TV, 9-6.

3

[On the recently agreed Bosnia peace treaty]: We [Bosnian Serbs] have lost some things [in the treaty] and we have gotten some things. We have half of Bosnia, more than 40 cities, good land . . . We are one step forward toward [international] recognition.

Nov. 24/ Los Angeles Times, 11-25:(A)18.

4

[Criticizing the recently agreed Bosnia peace treaty]: What is wrong with the . . . agreement [is that it] has created a new Beirut in Europe [by giving control of Sarajevo to the Bosnian government]. It is going to bleed for decades.

British broadcast interview/ Los Angeles Times, 11-27:(A)1.

Momcilo Krajisnik
Speaker of the unofficial Bosnian Serb parliament

5

[Criticizing the just-agreed Bosnia peace treaty]: What's been done is an especially big mistake . . . What I am saying is that our [Bosnian Serb] delegation did not accept this

(MOMCILO KRAJISNIK)

plan, nor did it sign, nor will it sign either these maps or the plan itself.

Bosnian Serb broadcast interview, Nov. 21/ Los Angeles Times, 11-22:(A)17.

Jim Leach
United States Representative, R-Iowa

1

[On U.S. President Clinton's decision to send American ground troops to help enforce the recently agreed Bosnia peace treaty]: I believe [the U.S.] Congress has the responsibility to recognize that the President has the Constitutional right to act and we have the obligation to support our troops. Indeed, at this point, it strikes me that, except for second-guessing, the arguments are largely over, and what the Congress now has to cope with is the question [of] how we can help make this mission successful.

At House International Relations Committee hearing, Washington, D.C., Nov. 30/ Los Angeles Times, 12-1:(A)27.

Jerry Lewis
United States Representative, R-California

2

[Opposing the U.S. sending ground troops to help enforce the recently agreed Bosnia peace treaty]: I think our role in NATO is very significant, and we should continue to exercise that role. I am not one of those who feel that America should be putting the wall back up. [But] the Europeans have a responsibility to provide the leadership [on Bosnia]. It is their region. If they'd have taken the responsibility early, we would not be in this position today.

Los Angeles Times, 12-2:(A)10.

Edward Luck
President-emeritus, United Nations Association of the United States

3

[On the UN peacekeeping role in the current conflict in Bosnia]: I think it's been not only a mission impossible, but it has been a very murky mission . . . An example of the absurdity is that you have had over 100 resolutions and statements from the Security Council on the crisis. In Desert Storm [the Persian Gulf war of 1991], when they were serious, they had only a dozen resolutions. [Security Council members] keep postponing the decisive decision. They don't want to say there are no moral values to defend in Bosnia and get out. They also don't want to accept the logic of staying, which is to choose sides . . . The whole idea of peacekeeping has been given a black eye unnecessarily.

Los Angeles Times, 6-10:(A)6.

Richard G. Lugar
United States Senator, R-Indiana; Candidate for the 1996 Republican Presidential nomination

4

[Saying the U.S. Congress will not deny President Clinton's decision to send Ameri-

(RICHARD G. LUGAR)

can ground troops to help enforce the recently agreed Bosnia peace treaty]: If you are asking if there are ways that Congress can deny troops going to Bosnia, the answer is no. They are going to go . . . Charitably [those in Congress who oppose sending troops] are folks who have not grappled with very much in terms of foreign affairs or defense policy . . . I would say: "You'd better grow up. Better begin to think through again what the stakes for this nation are."

To reporters, Nov. 28/
Los Angeles Times,
11-29:(A)26.

Charles William Maynes
Editor,
"Foreign Policy" magazine
(United States)

1

Once [U.S. Assistant Secretary of State Richard] Holbrooke took the forward position that he did [on peace talks], we totally changed the political calculus of failure. Before Holbrooke got involved, if the talks collapsed it was Europe's failure. Now if the talks collapse, it is America's failure. By bringing the negotiations here [to the U.S.], the failure will be not Holbrooke's but [U.S. President Clinton's].

Los Angeles Times,
10-30:(A)8.

2

What brought the Serbs to the negotiating table in the first place [which resulted in the recently agreed Bosnia peace treaty] was not the [NATO] bombing; it was the fact that we recognized the Serbs' separate republic [within Bosnia] . . . We started with a totally unrealistic policy: the imposition of a multi-ethnic ideal in Bosnia. Only when the United States stopped its moralizing . . . did we make any progress.

Los Angeles Times,
11-24:(A)26.

John McCain
United States Senator,
R-Arizona

3

[On the use of U.S./NATO airstrikes against Serb positions]: If escalation of the airstrikes fails, then what do you do? If they fail, then you have stiffened Serb resolve. Not to mention the fact that [we] have de facto entered the war on the side of the Muslims.

U.S. News & World Report,
9-18:62.

4

[Reluctantly supporting President Clinton's decision to send U.S. ground troops to help enforce the recently agreed Bosnia peace treaty]: When the President's word is no longer credible abroad, all Americans are less safe.

Nov. 30/
Los Angeles Times,
12-1:(A)1.

Mitch McConnell
United States Senator,
R-Kentucky

5

[On whether the U.S. should get more involved militarily in the conflict]: Nobody's gotten it right yet, not [former U.S. President George] Bush, not [U.S. President] Clinton. It's easy to jump on the President. I've done

(MITCH McCONNELL)

that on a variety of issues. But frankly, I don't have any clearer idea of how to proceed from here than I believe he does.

June 1/
The New York Times,
6-2:(A)4.

Michael D. McCurry
Spokesman
for the Department of State
of the United States

1

[Criticizing proposals, such as one by Senator Robert Dole, for the U.S. to unilaterally lift the UN arms embargo against the Bosnian government to allow them to more effectively fight the Serbs]: If you take on the unilateral responsibility of lifting the arms embargo, the United States would also unilaterally take on the consequences of that action; and that would include, in our view as a moral responsibility, the arming, training and equipping of the Bosnian Muslims who would have to defend themselves . . . How that could be achieved without massive use of U.S. force unilaterally, and very, very likely the introduction of U.S. ground troops, is a question that someone I hope will pose to Senator Dole.

To reporters, Jan. 4/
The New York Times,
1-5:(A)3.

2

[Saying the U.S. will not unilaterally lift the UN-imposed arms embargo against Bosnia's government in its fight against the Serbs]: We are sympathetic to the views of the Bosnian government. We understand their frustration. But we respectfully disagree [about lifting the embargo] because, at the end, we would like to see the killing and the dying ameliorated, and we don't believe the answer to the conflict in Bosnia is to escalate the war.

Washington, D.C., June 9/
The Washington Post,
6-10:(A)12.

3

[On U.S. President Clinton's desire to send U.S. ground forces to Bosnia to enforce the recently agreed peace treaty, despite the reluctance of the American public to become so involved]: It is a given that the President will be going before the American people to make a case about the urgency of U.S. participation in helping to implement this peace. The American people have questions about this. They know very little about the Balkans, but they know about the horror and the bloodshed that they've seen for the last 3½ years, and they know that the United States is in a position to do something about that.

Nov. 21/
Los Angeles Times,
11-22:(A)17.

Milan Milutinovik
Foreign Minister of Yugoslavia

4

[Saying Yugoslavia may have to enter the conflict if Bosnian peace talks fail]: [If that happened,] it would no longer be a war of bows and arrows. All means would be used, and this war would not end quickly. Yugoslavia is at least 10 times, even 20 times stronger from a military point of view than all the states around it.

Paris, France, Sept. 22/
The New York Times, 9-23:1.

Sue Myrick
United States Representative,
R-North Carolina

1

[Opposing U.S. President Clinton's plans to send American ground troops to help enforce the recently agreed Bosnia peace treaty]: For the past two or three weeks, we have been receiving phone calls and letters [from constituents about whether or not to send the troops]. Today, we got our first phone call in support. Before that, there were none. People are saying: "Don't do it . . . " The moms of this country don't want their kids to be sacrificial lambs.

Nov. 30/
Los Angeles Times,
12-2:(A)10.

William J. Perry
Secretary of Defense
of the United States

2

[On the UN peacekeeping forces in Bosnia]: They have demonstrated that, in the present configuration, the present rules of engagement, they are not capable of performing their mission. They're there to protect the civilian population. They have failed to do that. Therefore, the status quo is not acceptable. We have to fix the UNPROFOR. If we don't fix it, it's going to be pulled out . . . I think the combination of those 12,000 [new European combat] forces, plus a really vigorous use of NATO air, can do it. But it takes the will to use the NATO air.

Broadcast interview,
Washington, D.C./
"This Week With David Brinkley,"
ABC-TV, 7-16.

3

[On the decision to send U.S. ground troops to help enforce the recently agreed Bosnia peace treaty]: Our military planners, who have looked at this quite carefully, believe that one year [of U.S. military commitment in Bosnia] will be sufficient to break the cycle of violence and to create a secure environment.

Broadcast interview/
"Face the Nation,"
CBS-TV,
11-26.

4

[On negotiations between the U.S. and Russia aimed at having Russia involved as a consultant in NATO's enforcement of the recently agreed Bosnia peace treaty]: It's important to get this right, because this will affect the security relations in Europe between NATO and Russia, between the U.S. and Russia, for years to come. As important as it is to get this right for Bosnia, it also casts a larger shadow.

Brussels, Belgium,
Nov. 28/
Los Angeles Times,
11-29:(A)14.

5

[Saying the disarmament of Bosnian-Serb forces will be a key element in making the recently agreed peace treaty work]: I believe the imbalance of arms, particularly between the Bosnian government and the Bosnian Serbs, was a significant factor four years ago in starting the war. We [U.S. and NATO peacekeepers] don't want to leave Bosnia a year from now with the same imbalance . . . I have a high level of confidence [that] the build-

(WILLIAM J. PERRY)

down [in Bosnian-Serb arms] will work, but we've made it known we're willing to take any action necessary to redress the imbalance.

Brussels, Belgium, Nov. 29/ Los Angeles Times, 11-30:(A)6.

Vinko Cardinal Puljic
Roman Catholic Archbishop of Sarajevo, Bosnia-Herzegovina

1

I, like so many in Bosnia-Herzegovina, am astonished and bewildered . . . at the international community's indifferent, half-hearted, inconsistent and ineffectual response to aggression and "ethnic cleansing" [in Bosnia]. Not only has [it] not acted decisively, it has even contributed to the ethnic division of Bosnia and has legitimized aggression by failing to uphold basic moral and legal norms. If the principles of peace and international justice are buried in the soil of the Balkans, Western civilization will be threatened . . . I am convinced that there are moral means to thwart immoral aggression. The international community must have the will to use the means available to it to protect threatened populations, to encourage demilitarization and to establish other conditions necessary for progress toward peace. The solution cannot be simply to give up and withdraw.

Washington, D.C., March 30/ The Washington Post, 4-5:(A)18.

Peter Rodman
Scholar, Richard M. Nixon Center for Peace and Freedom (United States)

2

[Saying the West, in its reluctance to use anything more than limited force, has not done all it could to bring the conflict to an end]: The great powers frittered away their advantage in Bosnia by exerting their power in pathctically ineffectual ways . . . It was a mismatch between our objectives and our will to act, a misunderstanding of what you have to do to coerce people . . . The lesson is clear: When you really do use power in a fairly ferocious way [as NATO finally did recently], it does make a difference. The tragedy is that we could have imposed our will this way two or three years ago.

Los Angeles Times, 11-24:(A)26.

Michael Rose
Lieutenant General, British Army; Commander of United Nations forces in Bosnia

3

[On an agreement between Bosnian Muslims and Serbs to expand the features of their current, temporary cease-fire]: I believe this is a very major step forward. I believe this agreement is a demonstration of the firm intent on all sides to make real progress down the path to peace, to achieve during this four-month [cease-fire] period the final, lasting solution to the problems of this country so the people can return to normal, civilized living.

Jan. 11/ Los Angeles Times, 1-12:(A)4.

Volke Ruhe
Minister of Defense
of Germany

1

[On Germany's decision to send military forces to bolster UN peacekeepers in Bosnia]: [Our mission is] to avoid a collapse of the United Nations mission so that there are better chances of providing humanitarian aid to the population and above all so that the window for negotiations remains open . . . The Americans are clearly standing on the sidelines of developments. The decisive initiative is coming from the French and the English. If our most important European partners judge the situation in [the former] Yugoslavia this way, then Germany must show its solidarity.

June 26/
The New York Times,
6-27:(A)3.

Christian Schwarz-Schilling
German mediator
to the Bosnian-Croat
federation

2

If we [in the West] don't do anything [to help the Bosnian Muslims fight the Serbs], we will slither into a wider war. Brush fires are coming up everywhere because people see that brute power [as displayed by the Serbs] is the way to victory. If this goes on, the U.S. is going to end up being a world policeman quicker than ever before. It is very simple. If you don't risk anything, you will never achieve anything.

The Washington Post,
6-12:(A)14.

John M. Shalikashvili
General,
United States Army;
Chairman, Joint Chiefs of Staff

3

[On suggestions that the U.S. should have insisted on using more Western military force against the Serbs in Bosnia since the conflict started]: There are probably people in hindsight who will say that we [in the armed forces] all should have jumped up and down and insisted on the way we wanted to do it earlier. That's probably a valid criticism, because obviously we didn't get our way. It's not something we woke up to. While it was going on, I thought I was doing the counseling, the arguing and the persuasion, but clearly not successfully.

Interview/
The New York Times,
7-29:4.

Haris Silajdzic
Prime Minister
of Bosnia-Herzegovina

4

[Expressing disappointment that the U.S. has decided not to unilaterally lift the UN arms embargo against his government]: We leave the White House knowing that the position has not changed and that we shall have more suffering. [The embargo is] an instrument of genocide and a failure. If it takes going to a big war [against the Serbs, the Bosnian government is ready], but do not tie our hands because it is very difficult to explain to the Bosnians back home that the big world is not letting them defend themselves.

To reporters,
Washington, D.C., June 9/
The New York Times, 6-10:5.

(HARIS SILAJDZIC)

1

Bosnia is like an organism that has gone through a terrible disease. All of its parts, for example the legs, went numb all of a sudden, so you have to wait for the blood—in this case for democracy and human rights and common sense—to stream through in order to come back to life.

U.S. News & World Report,
9-25:64.

Paul Simon
United States Senator,
D-Illinois

2

[Supporting U.S. President Clinton's decision to send American ground troops to help enforce the recently agreed Bosnia peace treaty]: The President is showing the leadership that the world expects from the United States. He deserves bipartisan support for this task. If we don't make this effort to restore stability, the war in Bosnia will spread and will represent a long-term security threat to our national interests.

Nov. 27/
Los Angeles Times,
11-28:(A)8.

Helmut Sonnenfeldt
Scholar,
Brookings Institution
(United States)

3

If the fighting continues, there are other areas that could become inflamed. The refugee flows to places like Germany will pick up. Between the corrosive effect on our principal alliance and this unsettled and highly unstable situation in southeastern Europe adjacent to areas where we have alliance commitments, there is a pretty serious national-security justification for American action.

Los Angeles Times,
10-30:(A)8.

Hans Stark
Authority on Bosnia,
French Institute
of International Relations

4

The Bosnian Serbs are not satisfied with the military situation on the ground because they don't control all the territory they occupy, and they will try to push to the south. But the Western world, though sympathetic to the [Bosnian] Muslims, wants to maintain its impartiality. and that is the contradiction of our policy.

Los Angeles Times,
6-5:(A)8.

Peter Tarnoff
Under Secretary
for Political Affairs,
Department of State
of the United States

5

[Arguing against a unilateral U.S. lifting of the UN arms embargo against the Bosnian Muslims]: It would lead to a wider and bloodier conflict with a very uncertain outcome for which the U.S. would have ultimate responsibility.

Before Senate
Foreign Relations Committee,
June 8/
The New York Times,
6-9:(A)5.

Marc Thiessen
Spokesman for
the Foreign Relations Committee
of the United States Senate

1

[Speaking for those on the U.S. Senate Foreign Relations Committee who are pushing for a unilateral U.S. lifting of the UN-imposed arms embargo against the Bosnian Muslims]: You're already seeing hundreds of thousands of Bosnians dying. At least [with a lifting of the arms embargo] they'd be dying fighting, and not with their hands tied behind their backs.

June 9/
The Washington Post,
6-10:(A)12.

Anton Tus
Chief military adviser
to Croatian President
Franjo Tudjman

2

[On Croatian territory being held by Croatian Serb rebels since 1991]: We would very much prefer to recover the occupied territory peacefully, but we are coming to the conclusion that the international community is not going to bring us a solution. We have to do it ourselves. If we do nothing, we are essentially giving away part of our country and permitting the establishment of a Serb-run state on our territory.

Interview/
The New York Times,
7-15:5.

Marko Vesovic
Bosnian writer;
Former associate
of Bosnian Serb leader
Radovan Karadzic

3

[Bosnian Serb leader Radovan] Karadzic was a failed poet and psychiatrist, but now at last he thinks he has succeeded. He says history will judge him. Maybe he is finally right. In 100 years no one will ask how many Croats and [Bosnian] Muslims were killed while Karadzic carried out his mission. He'll simply be the man that made Serbia bigger.

U.S. News & World Report,
7-24:26.

The Middle East

Yasir Abed-Rabbo
Minister of Information
of the Palestinian Authority
(the governing entity
of the now self-ruled areas
of Gaza and Jericho)

1

[Criticizing Israel's Jewish-settlement expansion in areas now ruled by the Palestinians, saying such expansion violates the spirit of the 1993 self-rule agreement]: What we see is not a pull-back of [Israeli occupation], but an expansion of settlement and reinforcement of settlement activity. The basic supports of the Palestinian-Israeli agreement have collapsed. The Israeli bulldozers have bulldozed the agreement itself.

The New York Times,
1-10:(A)3.

Abdul Mohsen Akkas
Saudi Arabian
political scientist;
Managing director,
Saudi Research and Marketing

2

[On recent economic and social problems in Saudi Arabia]: The country is still in good shape. Between 1974 and 1982, some kind of cultural change set in. People's expectations became high, and they were justified, because every opportunity was available. But human beings have this strange capacity to adapt. Put them in luxury, and they will change their clothes three times a day. Put them in misery, and they will sweat.

Los Angeles Times,
1-3:(A)15.

Shulamit Aloni
Minister of Culture
of Israel

3

[Criticizing the expansion of Jewish settlements in the West Bank as being counterproductive to peace negotiations with the Palestinians]: The [Jewish] settlers and their friends are the world's last imperialists, who by the force of the occupation rob the locals of their land and uproot their plants. The whole world sees the pictures and hears the voices. We should stop this arrogance, robbery and falsehood.

Los Angeles Times,
1-12:(A)6.

Yasir Arafat
Chairman,
Palestine Liberation
Organization

4

[On the current difficult negotiations between Palestinians and Israelis over Israeli occupation]: There is no magic wand that will help us solve all the problems in one sweep, but I hope we can reach concrete results. I know the European Union will be able to help us, the Palestinians, as well as the Israelis, to head forward toward this "peace of the brave" while equally taking into account each side's security needs.

Paris, France,
Feb. 20/
The New York Times,
2-21:(A)4.

(YASIR ARAFAT)

1

[On Palestinian terrorist attacks on Israelis in the now Palestinian self-ruled Gaza]: I have no magic stick [to stop the terrorists], but we are doing our best . . . Don't forget, these kinds of groups have been established by the help of the Israeli government before my arrival. You know that. And you can ask the Israeli officials.

News conference, Gaza, March 10/ The New York Times, 3-11:5.

2

[On the recent assassination, by an Israeli extremist, of Israeli Prime Minister Yitzhak Rabin]: I'm very shocked about this awful and terrible crime against one of the brave leaders of Israel and the peace-makers.

Time, 11-13:61.

Hanan Ashrawi
Palestinian negotiator and spokesperson

3

The majority of the Palestinian people tend to be [politically] independent, frankly speaking, as I am. Whether they are nationalist independents, secular independents, Islamic independents, et cetera, most people want to see the evolution of a system that would respond to their immediate needs and doesn't have to be reduced to the either/or [pro-PLO or anti-PLO] situation we have now. Most people want to see a genuinely democratic and representative system emerge, in which people are elected. So if we have elections, or once we have elections that are genuinely free and fair, I think you will see the emergence of people who will bring a new type of discourse and platforms—democratic platforms based on issues and on ability.

Interview/ "Interview" magazine, July:89.

James A. Baker III
Former Secretary of State of the United States

4

[On the recent assassination of Israeli Prime Minister Yitzhak Rabin]: Peace [with the Arabs] is going to be Yitzhak Rabin's legacy . . . The process will continue now with even more effort and emphasis . . . [But] the real question, I think, is Syria, and whether or not this means that the Syrian-Israeli track will be even more deadlocked and gridlocked. And, unfortunately, I think that perhaps [that] will be the case, because it is possible that there will be an earlier election in Israel.

Broadcast interview/ "This Week With David Brinkley," ABC-TV, 11-5.

Yossi Beilin
Deputy Foreign Minister of Israel

5

[Criticizing possible U.S. cuts in aid to Middle Eastern countries]: There is a sort of lack of understanding [in the U.S.] regarding the terrible price—also in money but not only in money—that the United States could pay if, God forbid, there is another war in the re-

(YOSSI BEILIN)

gion or in other regions [because the U.S. cuts its financial support for the Middle East peace process].

Interview, March 3/
The New York Times,
3-4:4.

1

[With Israeli-Syrian peace talks,] the problem is not so much with the solution as with the [framework of the] negotiations . . . With [Israeli peace talks with] the Palestinians, it is the other way round: The problem is with the solution rather than the negotiations.

The Christian Science Monitor,
3-8:7.

Warren Christopher
Secretary of State
of the United States

2

[Arguing against easing UN sanctions against Iraq imposed after the Persian Gulf war of 1991]: We do not believe that Iraq is even close to fulfilling [UN] requirements. Iraq's record of compliance [with UN mandates] is genuinely a travesty.

News conference,
Jiddah, Saudi Arabia,
March 13/
The Washington Post,
3-13:(A)12.

3

[Criticizing Russia's plans to sell nuclear reactors to Iran]: [Russia will] rue the day [it sells nuclear reactors to the] terrorist state [of Iran]. It is too dangerous to be permitted.

At Indiana University,
March 29/
The Washington Post,
3-30:(A)24.

Shahram Chubin
Authority on Iran,
Graduate Institute
for International Studies
(Switzerland)

4

[On the possibility of Iran having nuclear weapons in five years]: How will a few weapons, that can't be developed very far, get them anywhere? Here is a country that can't make its own missiles; it has had a missile program for 10 years and still imports missiles; it has had a missile program for 10 years and still imports missiles with 1950s technology from North Korea. Any [nuclear] bomb they would make would probably be a greater threat to themselves than anyone else. No one suggests they have any major functioning installations today in the country, although no one questions their intent.

Interview,
Geneva, Switzerland/
The New York Times,
1-5:(A)5.

Tansu Ciller
Prime Minister of Turkey

5

[On her country's recent military intervention against Turkish Kurds in northern Iraq who were using that area for bases from which to stage separatist actions against Turkey]: Now that we have achieved our primary objectives, we have begun to bring our troops

(TANSU CILLER)

home. We will continue this carefully staged withdrawal in the coming weeks as we bring maximum stability and security to this difficult territory . . . Any Western government bordered by a no-man's land that is used as a terrorist base to invade its own country and kill its citizens would not stand idly by. I must tell you that the Turkish people are deeply disappointed by the harsh criticism [of Turkey's intervention] from some of Turkey's allies, just as we are grateful for the support of [U.S.] President Clinton and the United States government.

Speech sponsored by Council on Foreign Relations and American Turkish Society, New York, N.Y., April 17/ The New York Times, 4-18:(A)3.

David Clayman
Jerusalem director,
American Jewish Congress

1

[On the recent assassination of Israeli Prime Minister Yitzhak Rabin by an Israeli extremist]: [Before the assassination,] the [political] right liked to portray the left in this country as decadent. The right was seen as somehow morally pure, the true Zionists. But since the assassination, we have seen on our television screens night after night young people from the left speaking sensitively and with great understanding and great patriotism about their concern for the nation. It is the right that is looking morally bankrupt now.

Los Angeles Times, 11-8:(A)6.

Bill Clinton
President
of the United States

2

[On recent Palestinian suicide bombings near Jewish settlements in the Gaza Strip]: Once more, the enemies of peace have sought to abuse the opportunity peace presents—to kill it, to kill hope, to kill all possibility of a normal life for the people of Israel, for the Palestinians who are struggling to do the right thing there. Let us stiffen our resolve to say to those who seek to abuse human life so that they can continue to kill and to keep peace from people who want it: You will not succeed.

Before Jewish Federation, Los Angeles, Calif., April 9/ The Washington Post, 4-10:(A)13.

3

[Announcing a U.S. trade embargo against Iran]: I do not take this step lightly. But I am convinced that instituting a trade embargo with Iran is the most effective way our nation can help curb Iran's drive to acquire devastating weapons and support for terrorist activities . . . Some have argued that the best route to changing Iranian behavior is by engaging with it; but the evidence of the last two years proves otherwise. Iran's appetite for acquiring and developing nuclear weapons and the missiles to deliver them has only grown larger. Even as prospects for peace in the Middle East have grown, Iran has broadened its role as inspiration and paymaster to terrorists.

Before World Jewish Congress, New York, N.Y., April 30/ The New York Times, 5-1:(A)1,6.

(BILL CLINTON)

1

[On the recent assassination of Israeli Prime Minister Yitzhak Rabin, who was killed by an Israeli religious extremist opposed to Rabin's peace initiatives with the Arabs]: [Rabin] cleared the path [to peace], and his spirit continues to light the way. His spirit lives on in the growing peace between Israel and her neighbors. It lives in the eyes of the children, the Jewish and the Arab children who are leaving behind a past of fear for a future of hope. It lives on in the promise of true security. So let me say to the people of Israel: . . . Your Prime Minister was a martyr for peace, but he was a victim of hate. Surely we must learn from his martyrdom that if people cannot let go of the hatred of their enemies, they risk sowing the seeds of hatred among themselves.

At funeral for Rabin, Jerusalem, Israel, Nov. 6/ Los Angeles Times, 11-7:(A)7.

Mohammad Dahlan
Director, Palestinian Preventive Security Service in Gaza

2

[Saying the Palestinian Authority, which now rules Gaza and Jericho, is reluctant to extradite to Israel Palestinians suspected of violence against Israel]: We have reached a decision, and it has been taken in our highest echelons, of course agreed to by [PLO] chairman [Yasir] Arafat. We shall not extradite to Israel our people, even if they are [the militant] Hamas people who are wanted [by Israel]. We do not want that our history books will say that we extradited Palestinians to Israel.

Interview/ Los Angeles Times, 9-14:(A)4.

Ali Hillal Dessouki
Dean of political science, Cairo University (Egypt)

3

Egypt, in the mainstream, prides itself on having taken the leadership role in making peace [with Israel]; and now it looks at Jordan and the others [who are seeking better relations with Israel] with a sort of "see-I-told-you-so" attitude. Yes, there's opposition to normalizing relations with Israel from the Nasserites and Islamists. But you don't hear that from intellectuals or others. No political party in Egypt, for instance, has as part of its official platform scrapping the Camp David accords [the 1978 peace agreement between Egypt and Israel]. With the exception of the crazies, the debate now isn't whether to normalize relations [between Arab states and Israel], but the terms of normalization. It's a new ballgame.

Los Angeles Times, 9-28:(A)8.

Uri Dromi
Israeli government spokesman

4

Syria is speaking for all those voices of the past that are becoming more and more obsolete. People in the Middle East are finally starting to turn away from those things that brought so much devastation, and they are

(URI DROMI)

turning toward those options that will bring prosperity. Except the Syrians. So they look obsolete.

Los Angeles Times,
10-31:(A)8.

Haim Drukman
Israeli rabbi

1

[On the call by a group of Israeli rabbis, including himself, that the Israeli Army should refuse to abandon bases in West Bank areas slated to revert to Palestinian control in the future]: We ruled that the Torah forbids evacuating army camps and transferring them to gentiles, because it nullifies a commandment and endangers lives and the existence of the state. A permanent army camp is for all intents and purposes a Jewish settlement. Uprooting it and leaving it to gentiles is tantamount to uprooting a settlement from the Land of Israel. So it is clearly and simply forbidden for any Jew to assist in the evacuation of a settlement, a camp or facility. The army has never put its soldiers in a situation in which they were forced to act against their religious, moral or national conscience. We call on the government and the army leadership not to force soldiers to choose between their values and army orders.

July 12/
The New York Times,
7-13:(A)3.

Nabil Fahmy
Senior official,
Foreign Ministry of Egypt

2

Returning to the traditional Arab-Israel conflict is virtually impossible. So many mistakes would have to be made on both sides for that to happen that the question is really hypothetical.

Los Angeles Times,
9-28:(A)1.

Newt Gingrich
United States Representative,
R-Georgia;
Speaker of the House

3

[Criticizing the U.S. policy of having its Embassy in Israel situated in Tel Aviv instead of Jerusalem, Israel's capital]: I strongly favor moving the American Embassy. I think it is absurd for us to single out Israel as a country where we define what we think the capital should be.

To Israeli television,
January/
The New York Times,
2-4:3.

Hassan II
King of Morocco

4

[Islamic] fundamentalists [in Arab countries] preach their ideology because they consider Islam the elevator to take power. The day I see a fundamentalist who preaches religion for the love of God, then I'll say, "Fine, let's listen." But so far, I haven't heard that.

Los Angeles Times,
10-8:(A)6.

Anat Hoffman
Member of the City Council
of Jerusalem, Israel

5

[Saying women in the Israeli armed forces

(ANAT HOFFMAN)

do not get combat training equal to that of men]: A woman has a better chance of hitting a terrorist with her handbag than with a bullet.

U.S. News & World Report, 5-22:47.

Hussein ibn Talal
King of Jordan

1

[On the recent defection to Jordan of Iraqi Lieutenant General Hussein Kamel Majid]: He got fed up with the way his country was run [by Iraqi President Saddam Hussein]. This man [Majid] was very troubled by mistakes made by his country's leadership: internally, toward the citizens of Iraq; regionally; and also in the context of Iraq's relations with other countries in the world . . . The things I heard from [Majid] contradicted what I heard from other senior Iraqis who visited [Jordan]. They tried to create the impression things were going well . . . When I understood what was really happening in Iraq . . . it was a terrible shock for me.

Interview/ Los Angeles Times, 8-17:(A)7.

2

[On Egypt's criticism that Jordan is moving too fast toward peace with Israel and not coordinating its move with other Arab nations]: If moving toward peace is rushing, then Egypt rushed in 17 years before us [when it made peace with Israel]. And if restoring our own rights and what we have missed over the years is rushing, we will not only rush but run swiftly toward achieving an honorable life for our people.

At economic summit of business and political leaders, Amman, Jordan, Oct. 29/ Los Angeles Times, 10-30:(A)12.

3

[On the late Israeli Prime Minister Yitzhak Rabin, who was recently assassinated]: You lived as a soldier. You died as a soldier for [Arab-Israeli] peace. And I believe it is time for all of us to come out openly and to speak of peace . . . Never in all my thoughts would it have occurred to me that my first visit to Jerusalem in response to your invitation . . . would be on such an occasion [Rabin's funeral]. Let us not keep silent. Let our voices rise higher to speak of our commitment to peace. Tell those who live in the dark, who are the enemies of peace . . . this is where we stand. This is our camp . . . We are not ashamed. We are not afraid. Nor are we anything but determined to fulfill the legacy for which my friend fell . . . As long as I live, I will be proud to have known [Rabin], to have worked with him as a brother, as a friend and as a man.

At funeral for Rabin, Jerusalem, Israel, Nov. 6/ Los Angeles Times, 11-7:(A)9,6.

Martin Indyk
United States Ambassador to Israel

4

[On the recent assassination of Israeli Prime Minister Yitzhak Rabin]: We [the U.S.]

(MARTIN INDYK)

will be determined in every way to press forward to ensure that the great achievements that this great man was able to make in the last few years, in terms of ending the conflict [with the Arabs] and ending the bloodshed, that legacy will be preserved and maintained and taken to a higher level.

Broadcast interview/
"Face the Nation,"
CBS-TV, 11-5.

Erdal Inonu
Foreign Minister
of Turkey

1

[On foreign criticism of his country's recent military intervention against Turkish Kurds in northern Iraq who were using that area for bases from which to stage separatist actions against Turkey]: The [foreign] press is reporting things as if we were going to stay months or years [in Iraq and] that Turkey was going to occupy this area. No, this is not true. Our goal is and was from the beginning to take out [the separatists'] arms depots and to create a security situation in which the [separatists] cannot attack our country . . . When we accomplish this objective, our soldiers will immediately return to Turkey.

News conference,
Bonn, Germany, April 3/
The Washington Post,
4-4:(A)18.

Marwan Kanafani
Spokesman for the
Palestine Liberation Organization

2

[Criticizing the closure of the border between Palestinian self-ruled Gaza and Israel, which Israel instituted many months ago because of violent attacks on Israelis by militant Palestinians]: Closures are the biggest problem we have. Two hundred of the 450 days we've had [self-rule] freedom in Gaza have been closure days. This is a catastrophe. For 200 days, workers stay at home, they don't buy food, grocery stores stop working, the whole economic cycle stops. This encourages extremists who say that peace has brought nothing. The entire homeland of Gaza is held hostage. We did not sign this [peace] agreement [with Israel] to be kept like animals behind bars.

The New York Times,
8-25:(A)5.

Lofti al-Khouli
Egyptian columnist

3

Israelis think they have fulfilled all their obligations on peace by talking about peace with Arabs. But we are finding that the ordinary Arab person only sees continuing Israeli occupation of Arab lands, continued mistreatment of Palestinians. They see this on their television every evening and on the front pages of newspapers and in searing cartoons, every morning. I think it is high time to move in the struggle to another stage that is neither military nor absolute; but I wonder if the popular current allows that.

Interview/
The New York Times,
3-7:(A)3.

Andrei V. Kozyrev
Foreign Minister of Russia

4

[On U.S. criticism of Russia's planned

(ANDREI V. KOZYREV)

sale of a nuclear reactor to Iran]: I don't see why [the sale] should be stopped. It is only beneficial, if Iran buys Russian light-water reactors—safe from the point of view of [nuclear-weapons] proliferation—rather than [that] we abrogate the deal and they try to buy, somewhere, probably much more dangerous equipment . . . We will not give Iran or any other country any nuclear-weapons capability or technology.

At Johns Hopkins University, April 28/ Los Angeles Times, 4-29:(A)13.

David Libai
Minister of Justice of Israel

1

[Criticizing the reluctance of the Palestinian Authority, which now rules Gaza and Jericho, to extradite to Israel those Palestinians suspected of violence against Israel]: I view with concern the fact that the Palestinian Authority is exploiting the [Israel-Palestinian peace] agreement [in order to] give refuge to all of the murderers and to thereby create an image that it supports the murder of Jews . . . We cannot accept a situation where the Palestinians set their own parameters for the war against terrorism and force us to accept them.

Sept. 13/ Los Angeles Times, 9-14:(A)4.

David Mack
Former Deputy Assistant Secretary for Near Eastern and South Asian Affairs, Department of State of the United States

2

[On recent significant defections from Iraq]: [Iraqi President] Saddam [Hussein] has always survived through a combination of what he can do *for* people and what he can do *to* people. [With the recent defections,] the question is how much can Saddam do for people these days? As [foreign] sanctions continue, not much. And it is also clear he can do less and less *to* them, because more and more are getting out of his reach.

Los Angeles Times, 8-17:(A)7.

Moshe Maoz
Specialist on Syria, Hebrew University (Israel)

3

The only thing that will move [an Israel-Syria peace agreement] forward is if [Israeli Prime Minister Yitzhak] Rabin utters the magic words that [Syrian President Hafez] Assad is waiting to hear. Rabin has got to whisper in [U.S. President] Clinton's ear that Israel is willing to withdraw on the Golan Heights to the international border . . . The Americans hold the key. They can bring a blueprint for peace; they can offer to take the Syrians off the [U.S.] State Department's terrorism list; they can help the Syrians secure aid from the Europeans and Japan.

Los Angeles Times, 5-5:(A)10.

Amr Moussa
Foreign Minister of Egypt

1

[On Egypt's dispute with Israel over the latter's nuclear policy and economic dominance]: [U.S.] Secretary [of State Warren Christopher] said it is a policy priority to work for an indefinite extension of the [nuclear non-proliferation treaty, which Egypt is reluctant to go along with if Israel doesn't make concessions on its nuclear-weapons program], that it is in [the U.S.'] best interests and the best interests of the international community. Fine, but we can't accept that with Israel's nuclear program anonymous, vague and in doubt . . . If people say relations between us [and Israel] are at their most tense, fine, we have to live with that. Egypt will not say yes to everything Israel says . . . [And] it cannot [be that Israel's economy will dominate the Middle East]. It just cannot happen, because Egypt is half of the Arab world. If the Israelis want to leave us out, let them try. If half of the Arab world is left on the side, the region will move on one leg.

Interview, Cairo, Egypt, March 8/ The New York Times, 3-9:(A)3.

2

[Criticizing Israel's alleged development and possession of nuclear weapons]: If things go on like this, there will be a nuclear race in the region. In the past we have wasted numerous opportunities to build up a power that can stand up to the Israeli nuclear-armaments program. We cannot afford to do this any longer.

Interview/ The Washington Post, 5-19:(A)30.

Hosni Mubarak
President of Egypt

3

[Criticizing Israel for not signing the Nuclear Non-Proliferation Treaty, which Israel says it will not do until it has peace agreements from some countries which are not even on its borders]: [Israel appears to want to] enlarge the Middle East until it reaches North Korea. We [Egypt] signed a peace treaty for 17 years. The Jordanians have already signed a peace treaty. The Palestinians signed a declaration of principles. And the Syrians are on their way negotiating peace [with Israel] now . . . [So] we are asking the Israelis to join the NPT or to tell us when they will join it.

Interview, Washington, D.C./ Los Angeles Times, 4-5:(A)7.

4

[On criticism that the large amount of U.S. aid to Egypt over the years has not produced positive results in his country]: First of all, the aid which we take from the United States is for mutual interest. It's not given for the sake of the eyes of Egypt. The money is spent in the United States by American authorities. We are not taking money and spending, like other countries, as we like. We buy equipment or arms from the United States . . . It's being supervised by the United States or the aid organization. They interfere or participate in the purchasing of anything from the United States.

(HOSNI MUBARAK)

So to say the aid is not used very well, I can tell you I'm sorry, the aid is well looked after by the American authorities. The second point is that it didn't [help] employment when you start with a very high rate of increase in population, which created a hell of a problem for us. The rate of increase in population was 3. Now we made a very good program, and it's 2.2 and is decreasing.

Interview,
Washington, D.C./
Los Angeles Times,
4-9:(M)3.

1

[On criticism by some in the U.S. that Egypt's crackdown on Islamic terrorists goes too far]: I keep telling our friends in America that these terrorist groups are an international phenomenon. They are not a problem for Egypt alone. Terrorism is spreading everywhere. Look at what happened at the World Trade Center [in New York], or [the Federal building] in Oklahoma, or in Japan . . . We understand this area very well. [U.S.] media said that the Americans were "advising Egypt with their dialogue." Never. And whoever says to me, "Dialogue," I tell him, "No. Go have a dialogue in your own country. We know our people, and how to deal with them."

Interview, Cairo, Egypt/
Newsweek, 6-19:45.

2

[On the late Israeli Prime Minister Yitzhak Rabin, who was recently assassinated]: [He was] a true hero of peace. His earnest efforts to achieve peace in the Middle East area are a testament to his vision, which we share, to end the suffering of all the peoples of Arab regions. He defied the prejudices of the past to tackle the most complicated of problems, namely the Palestinian problem, in a forthright manner.

At funeral for Rabin,
Jerusalem, Israel, Nov. 6/
Los Angeles Times,
11-7:(A)6.

Benjamin Netanyahu
Leader, Likud Party of Israel;
Former Deputy
Foreign Minister of Israel

3

[Criticizing Israeli Prime Minister Yitzhak Rabin for his policy of extending self-rule to Palestinians in Gaza and the West Bank]: The question before the [Israeli] public is who can best guarantee their short-term and long-term security. The question is where Israel's borders are. Who will determine that we do not return to the borders of 1967 and that Jerusalem is not divided? . . . As [the Israel-Palestinian peace agreement] progresses, the public will become more aware of what is involved and suffer the consequences of terrorist enclaves near Jewish cities . . . The government has created a security nightmare with a patchwork quilt of perimeters that can hardly be defended.

Interview/
Los Angeles Times,
10-5:(A)14.

4

[Criticizing Israeli Prime Minister Yitzhak Rabin's policy of granting autonomy to Palestinians in more and more of the Israeli-occupied territories]: [The Rabin government is] the most alienated, most distant

(BENJAMIN NETANYAHU)

from the Jewish heritage of the people of Israel than has ever been in our history.

Before Israeli Knesset (Parliament), Jerusalem, Israel, Oct. 5/ Los Angeles Times, 10-6:(A)14.

1

[On the recent assassination, by an Israeli extremist, of Israeli Prime Minister Yitzhak Rabin]: We must vomit from among us those who do not abide by one of the most basic rules of society: Thou shalt not kill.

Time, 11-13:62.

2

[Criticizing those who blame his Likud Party, which disagreed with Israeli Prime Minister Yitzhak Rabin's accommodations with the Palestinians, for creating a hostile atmosphere that culminated in the recent assassination of Rabin by an Israeli extremist]: Any attempt to use this tragedy to achieve political gain and to incite against half the nation [who agree with Likud] is totally unacceptable. We must be careful not to put collective blame on a whole public that is loyal to the state and respects its laws, and I'm referring to the religious public and the settlers of Judea and Samaria [who are against Rabin's policies], a public that is being harshly attacked these days.

Before Israeli Knesset (Parliament), Jerusalem, Israel, Nov. 13/ Los Angeles Times, 11-14:(A)12.

Ehud Olmert
Mayor of Jerusalem, Israel

3

[Criticizing the Israeli government's decision not to seize 134 acres of land in mostly Palestinian areas of Jerusalem, as it had previously planned to do]: This is a government of surrenderers, a government lacking self-respect and principles, a bunch of cowards.

May 22/ The New York Times, 5-23:(A)6.

Amos Oz
Israeli author and political commentator

4

[On the recent assassination, by an Israeli extremist, of Israeli Prime Minister Yitzhak Rabin]: This will not kill the [Arab-Israeli] peace process [that was being pursued by Rabin], because under [new Prime Minister Shimon] Peres the new government will continue the same policy and perhaps act with even more determination and with more anger. I believe the right-wing opposition in Israel [which was against Rabin's land-for-peace policy with the Palestinians] as a whole will become rhetorically more responsible. In the short run, we are going to have a kind of restraint and perhaps a relative unity [among Israel's political factions], which we haven't had in a long time.

Time, 11-13:65.

Shimon Peres
Foreign Minister of Israel

5

[On the importance of an Israel-Syria peace agreement now that Israel has made

(SHIMON PERES)

peace with most of its Arab neighbors]: The difference between a peace treaty with Syria, if we achieve it, and all the previous peace agreements is that, in the past, any agreement was between us and one country. If we reach an agreement this time, it will in fact put an end to the state of war in the Middle East.

To reporters/
Los Angeles Times,
5-5:(A)10.

1

[Saying Israel will have to give the Golan Heights back to Syria if it wants a peace agreement with that country]: We must not allow the chance for comprehensive peace in the Middle East to slip through our fingers. No one will forgive us if children learn one day that it was possible to end the wars . . . and we ran away from a decision.

At Israeli
Labor Party meeting,
May 25/
Los Angeles Times,
5-27:(A)5.

2

[On Israel's 1993 peace agreement with the PLO]: The risk is that the aspect of security, which for us is so essential, will only be realized after a very long period of time. Judging objectively, I feel very strongly that we are gaining historically but losing politically. Which means that for the fruits of our decisions, which we'll be seeing in five or 10 years, we have to pay the [political] cost now. And because of that, I fear we may lose the opportunity to complete the peace process. So there are many risks involved, especially in the short term, but I think it is better to win peace than to win elections.

Interview/
"Interview" magazine,
July:88.

3

[On the recent assassination of Israeli Prime Minister Yitzhak Rabin, who was killed by an Israeli extremist]: I asked myself, if this happened to me, what would I want to have happen later? I have one answer: to continue the path of peace [with the Arabs].

Nov. 4/
Los Angeles Times,
11-6:(A)1.

4

[On the late Yitzhak Rabin, the Israeli Prime Minister who was recently assassinated soon after attending a peace rally in Tel Aviv]: I have never seen him as happy, soft, content, at peace with himself, as in those two hours [at the peace rally] when he was surrounded with the masses of the Israeli people—young, adult, old people, bereaved families. He felt the wind and spirit of love, of appreciation coming from these people—feelings he did not know often over the last few years.

Nov. 5/
Los Angeles Times,
11-6:(A)11.

5

[On the late Israeli Prime Minister Yitzhak Rabin, who was recently assassinated]: This is the crowning glory of your efforts, all of us here together. The man who murdered you will not be able to murder the idea that you carried . . . I see our Arab neigh-

(SHIMON PERES)

bors and I want to tell them that peace is attainable both here and with you.

At funeral for Rabin,
Jerusalem, Israel, Nov. 6/
Los Angeles Times,
11-7:(A)9.

1

[On the recent assassination of Israeli Prime Minister Yitzhak Rabin by an Israeli extremist]: Yitzhak, you were murdered because you were right [about trading land for peace with the Palestinians]. The bullets which tore through your chest did not kill the fruits of your labor . . . The dawn of peace has broken and it shall never be eclipsed by anyone.

Eulogy for Rabin,
Jerusalem, Israel,
Dec. 5/
Los Angeles Times,
12-6:(A)4.

William J. Perry
Secretary of Defense
of the United States

2

[On what a possible U.S. involvement would be in the Golan Heights if Israel and Syria reached an agreement for Israel's withdrawal from that area]: We have provided some monitoring in the Sinai Peninsula to help monitor the accord after the Camp David agreement [between Israel and Egypt]. It is conceivable that we will be asked to do something like that in the Golan. That would not be providing security; these would not be security forces. It would be strictly monitors to monitor the peace process. If the parties asked us to do that, we would certainly consider the request.

News conference,
Tel Aviv, Israel, Jan. 9/
Los Angeles Times,
1-10:(A)4.

Leah Rabin
Widow of the late
Israeli Prime Minister
Yitzhak Rabin

3

[Blaming the opposition Israeli Likud Party for creating an atmosphere that led to the recent assassination of her husband by an Israeli extremist]: Surely, I blame them. If you ever hear their speeches, you would understand what I mean. They were very, very violent in their expressions [of opposition to Rabin's peace overtures to the Palestinians]: "[Rabin is] selling the country down the drain." "There will be no Israel after this peace agreement." I mean, this was wild. You understand it on the merit of the political game, but still. This was really enough to create the climate that thinks like this.

Interview, Nov. 7/
Los Angeles Times,
11-8:(A)6.

Yitzhak Rabin
Prime Minister
of Israel

4

[Denying that his country has violated agreements with the U.S. not to sell to China Israel's U.S.-supplied military technology]: Israel is not stupid [enough] to risk what we get from the United States by even the slightest temptation to sell something. We have to bear in mind that we have to keep all our com-

(YITZHAK RABIN)

mitments in accordance with the United States laws.

News conference,
Tel Aviv, Israel,
Jan. 9/
Los Angeles Times,
1-10:(A)4.

1

[Criticizing new Jewish settlements in the West Bank as obstacles to peace with the Palestinians]: Settlements add nothing, absolutely nothing, to Israel's security. They are a liability rather than an asset. [The settlers] are making the [Israeli] soldiers' task much more difficult. The soldiers would do far better in combating terror if they didn't have to protect convoys of [Israeli settlers'] school buses every day.

To Israeli
Labor Party members,
Jan. 26/
The New York Times,
1-28:3.

2

[Blaming terrorist attacks for slowing Israel's move toward granting more autonomy to Palestinians in the West Bank and Gaza]: There is no political obstacle to implement everything we are committed to with the Palestinians. The obstacle is terror.

Satellite broadcast
to Paris conference
on Mediterranean peace,
Feb. 20/
The New York Times,
2-21:(A)4.

3

[Criticizing a number of Israeli rabbis for saying the Israeli Army should refuse to abandon bases in West Bank areas slated to revert to Palestinian control in the future]: There has never been anything like this in Israel. It is inconceivable that we will turn the State of Israel into a banana republic. It's unbelievable that in Israel, as a democracy, a very small number of rabbis will take upon themselves the right to act against the law. To call on a soldier to refuse legitimate orders means anarchy. We will not accept it. We will not allow it.

July 12/
The New York Times,
7-13:(A)3.

4

United Jerusalem is the heart of the Jewish people and the capital of the state of Israel. United Jerusalem is ours! Jerusalem forever!

At ceremony
marking the 3,000th anniversary
of Jerusalem,
Jerusalem, Israel, Sept. 4/
The New York Times,
9-5:(A)6.

5

For me what is most important is to have a Jewish state in which at least 80 percent of its population is Jewish. [But] the non-Jewish citizens—the Palestinians, Muslims, Christians—should entertain all a person's civilian political rights, because I believe that racism and Judaism by essence are in contradiction. The Palestinians in their schools, government-paid schools, are entitled—be they Muslims or Christians—to have their religion,

(YITZHAK RABIN)

to have their culture, their language, their heritage. I believe that they can be loyal Israeli citizens while maintaining their special identity.

Interview,
New York, N.Y.,
October/
Time, 11-13:64.

1

In 1977 very few of us believed that in our life we'd see a real possibility of [Arab-Israeli] peace. It started with [the late] President [Anwar] Sadat of Egypt. Allow me to say that I don't believe President Sadat—or any Arab leader with whom we have been engaged in peace—woke up one morning and discovered the justice of the right of the Zionist movement to establish a Jewish state. He came to the conclusion after trying wars, violence, boycott. I believe President Sadat realized that he could never get back the Sinai by force. There was no altruistic or philosophic change of their minds.

Interview,
New York, N.Y.,
October/
Time, 11-13:64.

2

[Calling for Israel to grant Palestinians control over more of the West Bank]: The Jewish people, who have suffered so much after 2,000 years of exile, returned to our homeland, only we found it occupied with the Palestinians. Thousands of people from both sides were killed in the struggle for this piece of land. Today, after wars and numerous acts of bloodshed, we rule over more than 2 million Palestinians and run their lives . . . This is not a solution for peace. We can continue to kill and be killed, but we can also try to stop this bloody cycle. We can give peace a chance.

Before Israeli Knesset
(Parliament),
Jerusalem, Israel, Oct. 5/
Los Angeles Times,
10-6:(A)14.

Hashemi Rafsanjani
President of Iran

3

[Criticizing U.S. plans for tough economic sanctions against Iran]: The Iranian revolution cannot be isolated. America will only deprive itself of opportunities in an important center where everyone wants to have a presence.

At service at mausoleum
of former Iranian leader
Ruhollah Khomeini,
Teheran, Iran,
April 28/
The New York Times,
4-29:5

Gunter Rexrodt
Minister of Economics
of Germany

4

[Saying Germany does not support the recently announced U.S. trade embargo against Iran to protest that country's involvement in international terrorism]: We do not believe that a trade embargo is the appropriate instrument for influencing opinion in Iran and bringing about changes there that are in our interests. The right thing to do is to conduct a political dialogue with Iran. Only po-

(GUNTER REXRODT)

litical dialogue can bring Iran to behave responsibly.

German radio interview, May 2/ The New York Times, 5-3:(A)6.

Barry Rubin
Political scientist, Begin-Sadat Center for Strategic Studies, Bar Ilan University (Israel)

1

[On the possible reason for the recent assassination, by an Israeli, of that country's Prime Minister Yitzhak Rabin, whom many Israelis criticized for making peace with the Palestinians by giving back Israeli-occupied lands where Israelis now live]: [Jews] have lived for 50 years with the fear of annihilation of Israel, of a unified Arab assault on their borders. These people believe that Jewish history has taught that the worst can happen. That they can be destroyed. It is irrational, but there is a strong material basis for it . . . They fear losing everything they worked for.

Los Angeles Times, 11-6:(A)12.

Saud Nasser al-Saud al-Sabah
Minister of information of Kuwait; Former Kuwaiti Ambassador to the United States

2

There's going to be a continued U.S. [military] presence [in the Persian Gulf area] for the foreseeable future. As long as the region is going through the turbulence it's going through, the United States, as well as the British and French, will have to be here.

Los Angeles Times, 6-3:(A)9.

Jasem Sadoun
Kuwaiti economist

3

[Expressing doubts about the U.S. policy of isolating Iran, as well as Iraq, using economic sanctions]: Squeezing Iran, as well as Iraq, with their huge populations . . . will just mean . . . more poverty, and that means more political instability. The price that might have to be paid will be paid directly by us [in the Persian Gulf countries].

Los Angeles Times, 6-3:(A)9.

Nasser Saidi
Vice Governor, Bank of Lebanon

4

In the past, Lebanon played a regional and international role as a commercial-banking center. But I don't think we can go back to playing the commercial-banking role we did in the past. Rather than being a conduit for funds flowing out of the region, we are now poised to play the reverse role of attracting funds form the rest of the world—Arab funds and expatriate Lebanese funds—to be invested in Lebanon for reconstruction and in other parts of the region. This will be a radical departure from the role we played in the past.

Interview, Beirut, Lebanon/ The Christian Science Monitor, 8-16:9.

Ahmed Sayed
Egyptian Ambassador to the United States

1

[On the recent bombing in the U.S. of an Oklahoma City Federal building]: [Arabs] are deeply hurt by the fact that immediately after this horrendous crime, fingers were raised without any basis to accuse Arabs, Muslims and Middle Easterners of being responsible for this crime. [But Arab countries, too] have suffered from such acts of terrorism . . . and we deeply understand . . . all the feelings of the American people. I am talking to all the American friends who are here with us today. We can work together to better the image of the Arab and the Muslim in [the U.S.], to show that Arabs and Muslims are not all terrorists.

Before National Arab American Association/ Los Angeles Times, 4-17:(A)5.

Zeev Schiff
Senior military-affairs analyst, "Haaretz" (Israeli newspaper)

2

[On the recent assassination of Israeli Prime Minister Yitzhak Rabin and the naming of Foreign Minister Shimon Peres as his successor]: I worry about the lack of balance now. Rabin and Peres served as a check and balance to each other, and they made the process [of making peace with the Arabs] work. Now the balance will be gone, I fear.

Los Angeles Times, 11-6:(A)11.

Christine Shelly
Spokeswoman for the Department of State of the United States

3

[On Iraq's negative attitude toward a UN resolution that would ease some of the sanctions against that country imposed following 1991's Persian Gulf war]: We hoped that the Iraqi government would recognize that accepting the resolution and all of its provisions would be in the interests of the Iraqi people. But I think that to the degree to which they don't respond in that way once again provides more indication that they are not responsive and concerned about the suffering of their own people and, in fact, they continue to use the suffering as a kind of propaganda tool, particularly through the media and other public forms of expression, to try to seek the lifting of sanctions.

April 17/ The New York Times, 4-18:(A)3.

Fathi Shukaki
Leader, Islamic Jihad

4

[Criticizing U.S. President Clinton's referring to radical Palestinian groups such as his as terrorists]: We reiterate that we are not terrorists; we are freedom fighters like [first U.S. President] George Washington and [South African President] Nelson Mandela; and we are not committing aggression against anybody. We are seeking to live in dignity.

Jan. 25/ Los Angeles Times, 1-26:(A)4.

Ephraim Sneh
Minister of Health
of Israel

1

[On the Israel-Palestinian peace negotiations that produced the Oslo accord in 1993 and built on that afterward]: A process that began in secrecy, with a handful of negotiators, now involves hundreds of people—experts, soldiers, lawyers and others. They are discussing everything from elections to the environment. It is a very good thing, a process of dialogue that will lead us, finally, to find common ground.

Los Angeles Times,
10-26:(A)11.

Tim Sullivan
Chairman,
department of political science,
American University (Egypt)

2

[On the U.S. attempt to isolate Iran through international economic sanctions]: Where is the consensus on Iran? There isn't one. Other countries don't agree with us, and they aren't all going to cooperate.

Los Angeles Times,
6-3:(A)9.

Ahmed Tibi
Adviser to Palestine
Liberation Organization chairman
Yasir Arafat

3

[Criticizing the recent vote by the U.S. Congress to move the American Embassy in Israel from Tel Aviv to Jerusalem]: This step is aimed against Islamic feelings and the Arab world position. Nobody can say to Palestinians that Jerusalem is the capital of Israelis alone. East Jerusalem is occupied—even according to longstanding American policy. It will be the capital of Palestine.

Oct. 25/
Los Angeles Times,
10-26:(A)10.

Philip C. Wilcox
Coordinator
for Counterterrorism,
Department of State
of the United States

4

Iran continues to assassinate dissidents abroad. It maintains direct support for Hezbollah, one of the most dangerous and lethal terrorist organizations. It continues to support the *fatwa* [death sentence] against [British author] Salman Rushdie. And it is using its resources, money, material to support those groups which are using terrorism against the peace process.

Press briefing,
Washington, D.C., April 28/
Los Angeles Times,
4-29:(A)13.

Mahmoud al-Zahar
Senior official,
Islamic Resistance Movement
(Hamas)

5

[On PLO leader Yasir Arafat and the Palestinian Authority, which now rules Gaza]: There has to be a management system that enables the right person to be in the right position. This is not what has happened. In every field, the person most loyal [to Arafat] is appointed. Now the Palestinian Authority is protecting the [Jewish] settlers with joint patrols. The Authority collects arms held by

(MAHMOUD AL-ZAHAR)

Hamas members. People can't stand what is happening. I am convinced that the Authority is not interested in creating civilian conditions. It is interested in military force. Israel failed with its military force in trying to rule here. Why does the Authority want to mimic a force that failed? The fighters of the *intifada* [Palestinian attacks on Israelis] can start it again, and in a tougher form.

Interview, June/
World Press Review,
September:12.

Abdul-Rahman Zamil
Deputy Minister
of Commerce of Saudi Arabia

1

During the oil boom, people said the decision to modernize and bring in so many foreigners would threaten our values. And what happened? We are more religious today than we were 20 years ago. I go to my mosque, and 80 percent of the men there are younger than 30 years old. All the best doctors, all the best engineers and businessmen are there.

Los Angeles Times,
10-8:(A)6.

PART THREE

General

The Arts

Jane Alexander
Chairman,
National Endowment
for the Arts
of the United States

1

Since 1979, the NEA has lost almost 50 percent of its purchasing power and is now threatened with elimination [by the new Republican-controlled Congress] . . . I'm intent on making Congress understand how the non-profit arts stimulate the economy and how the commercial sector needs the non-profits as a feeder. I would say anyone in show business after 1965 has had their lives touched by the NEA . . . If we are zeroed out, the U.S. would be the only major nation to have no governmental voice about the arts. We must acknowledge that the non-profits are the percolators, the farm teams, for the commercial sector. Congress needs to understand this.

Speech at entertainment-industry gathering, Beverly Hills, Calif., Feb. 23/ Daily Variety, 2-27:7.

Robert Altman
Director

2

In the end, I don't know what my benefactors get from me, but I always come away [from a project] enriched. Whether it's an opera or a crass commercial or a public-service message that I do, it ends up on the usable palette, the place where everything gets added. All theatrical experiences are akin.

Opera News, 2-18:24.

Maya Angelou
Poet

3

[On political conservatives who want to eliminate Federal funding for the arts]: The conservative right has decided that artists are apart from the people. That's ridiculous! I mean, at our best the writer, painter, architect, actor, dancer, folksinger—we *are* the people. We come *out* of the people, and remain *in* the people. What we ought to be doing is singing in the parks, talking to children, going to gatherings of parents, doing whatever it is we do—dancing, reading poetry, performing—all the time, so that people know, "These artists are my people—you can't kill them, you can't stop them." We then re-establish our footing with the people. All artists must do that, or we will be defanged . . . My own work is not threatened, financially. But the *spirit* from which my work comes is forced into a corner. When younger writers and poets, musicians and painters are weakened by a stemming of funds, they come to me saddened, not as full of dreams and excitement and ideas. *I* am then weakened and diminished, and made less rich.

Interview/ Mother Jones, May-June:23.

Francois Barre
Director,
Georges Pompidou Center,
Paris, France

4

[On why France spends so much of its government budget on the arts]: First, there

(FRANCOIS BARRE)

is a tradition. We have always believed . . . that anything that enhances education, knowledge and creation is a public service—in the same category as health services or the fire department. So people consider this something owed to all citizens. We may have economic inequalities, but there is a minimum which must be our common heritage and must be accessible to all citizens. Public financing guarantees that knowledge, education and access to culture and creation is equally accessible, in a way that the laws of the marketplace don't permit.

Interview, Paris, France/ Los Angeles Times, 2-12:(M)3.

Eli Broad
Chairman,
SunAmerica, Inc.

1

[Economically], the '80s are over for art institutions, just as for business and government. Cultural institutions have to do more with less. But when they demonstrate they can do that, we donors will open our purse strings even further than before.

Los Angeles Times, 3-15:(D)7.

Cary Carson
Historian;
Vice president for research,
Colonial Williamsburg Foundation

2

Museums are complex institutions, complex teachers. They do different things at different times. Sometimes the intent of an interpretation or presentation is primarily to pass along information, realizing, of course, that the selection of information is itself a form of interpretation. Other times, a museum's purpose is openly celebratory, to present history in ways that make people both understand and feel good about something—an important part of creating the myths, the accepted truths, that we call our national history. It is also very important, it seems to me, for museums to enter into this discourse that a democracy has to have with itself about those issues that remain unresolved and which can be informed in part by taking a historical perspective. And while museum historians should certainly show respect for those who hold other opinions, they make their most valid contribution if they take a point of view and try to present that point of view as persuasively as they can.

Interview/ Humanities, Jan.-Feb.:50.

Gordon Davidson
Artistic director-producer,
Center Theater Group/
Mark Taper Forum,
Los Angeles, Calif.

3

[Criticizing cutbacks in Federal funding for the NEA]: [Losing] a third of the arts budget is out of whack with increases at the Pentagon, you know? A part of me doesn't want to believe it's going to happen, but it's going to happen. It's a myth to think that, just because we are a big organization, we can take care of ourselves. If I lose $200,000 [in NEA grants], that's a serious number. And I worry in the same breath about the organizations that depend heavily on the Endowment. The mix of disciplines, the mix of big and small and that most dreaded [category], the individual

(GORDON DAVIDSON)

artists, have added up to an extremely important profile of culture in America, in its diversity and complexity and troublesomeness.

Los Angeles Times,
8-17:(F)1.

Philippe de Montebello
Director,
Metropolitan Museum of Art,
New York, N.Y.

1

Last week I was asked by a journalist whether this museum [the Metropolitan] would survive as long as there was a city of New York. And I must confess that I replied then that the real question should have been whether the city of New York could survive if there were no Metropolitan Museum.

At celebration
of 125th anniversary
of the Metropolitan Museum of Art,
New York, N.Y., April 13/
The New York Times,
4-14:(B)9.

David Frum
Political columnist;
Commentator,
"Morning Edition,"
National Public Radio

2

[On the Republican Party's possible alienation of wealthy supporters by its desire to cut Federal spending on the arts]: It's just political reality. The sort of people who love the opera and support their local arts organizations are also the sort of people who make $100,000 donations to the Republican Party. We're [Republicans] not going to be fighting with uneducated people; we're going to be fighting with the most powerful people in American society.

Panel discussion,
Washington, D.C./
Harper's, March:51.

Rudolph W. Giuliani
Mayor
of New York, N.Y.

3

Culture is to New York what steel was to Pittsburgh 30 years ago. It brings us jobs, money and stimulation.

At celebration
of 125th anniversary
of the Metropolitan Museum of Art,
New York, N.Y., April 13/
The New York Times,
4-14:(B)9.

Kay Bailey Hutchison
United States Senator,
R-Texas

4

[Supporting Federal funding of the NEA, but warning against the money being used for grants to controversial projects]: Taxpayers have been required to fund offensive art. But is the answer to do away with the American commitment to our culture? Absolutely not.

Before the Senate,
Washington, D.C., Aug. 9/
Los Angeles Times,
8-10:(A)30.

Chuck Jones
Cartoon animator,
Warner Bros. Pictures

5

All art is working under the deprivation

(CHUCK JONES)

of freedom. Running in all directions is not art. Art is choice, not chance. The more restriction there is, the more possibility there exists for creativity and ingenuity. Character is the most severe restriction. Every great comedian obeys rules consistent with his comic persona.

Interview,
Corona del Mar, Calif./
The Wall Street Journal,
7-11:(A)12.

Jonathan Katz
Chief executive,
National Assembly
of State Arts Agencies

1

[Criticizing proposed cuts in Federal funding for the NEA]: This is not an issue of government agencies. It's an issue that affects people who live in cities and suburbs and rural areas. It's about the frequency and quality of the art available to them to participate in. The war isn't lost. The thing that arts organizations do have is the power to get elected officials to an arts event and turn them into arts advocates.

The New York Times,
7-15:13.

Alonzo King
Choreographer and founder,
Lines Contemporary Ballet,
San Francisco, Calif.

2

Contrary to popular belief, art is not a matter of whimsy and emotion. Art is the knowledge of how things are done. Dancers are as serious as a committed surgeon who knows that an operation can save someone's life. They are like those who give themselves fully, whether it be in government or child-rearing; they have to make definitive choices, with the highest part of their brains. This takes intuition, born of insight. A truth cannot be created, only perceived.

Interview/
Dance Magazine,
June:43.

Rainer Klemke
Press Officer,
Cultural Affairs Administration
of Germany

3

[Comparing the German government's heavy support for the arts with the lesser enthusiasm toward arts subsidies in the U.S.]: [In the U.S.,] either you survive in the arts, or you don't and you're gone. [In Germany,] we think more in historical dimensions. We are protecting a cultural legacy that we've inherited from our grandparents—and we have to pass it on.

The Wall Street Journal,
2-10:(A)7.

Uwe Lehmann-Brauns
Cultural officer
for Berlin Christian
Democratic Union (Germany)

4

[Comparing Europe's history of heavy government financial support for the arts with the lesser and less-enthusiastic government support in the U.S.]: Our ideology says that it's the duty of the state to distribute public funds to support the arts, while at the same time allowing the artists total autonomy . . . It's the Magna Carta of European culture . . .

(UWE LEHMANN-BRAUNS)

If I may put it somewhat brutally, we do not want American-style conditions here.

The Wall Street Journal,
2-10:(A)7.

Julius Lester
Author;
Professor of Judaic studies,
University of Massachusetts,
Amherst

1

People's feelings get bruised very quickly, so it would seem to me that artists have to take extra care in exercising their license to say whatever they want to say. I don't have a problem being sure I'm not stepping on somebody's toes. It doesn't impinge on my freedom as an artist. It makes me a better artist.

U.S. News & World Report,
6-26:20.

Nathan Leventhal
President,
Lincoln Center,
New York, N.Y.

2

[Criticizing proposed cuts in Federal funding for the NEA]: [It is] not only short-sighted, but it ignores the fact that the arts, unlike almost everything else that's funded by the government, are an economic engine. The sad fact is that after all these years we still have to justify support for the arts. It's discouraging to have to make the same arguments over and over.

The New York Times,
7-15:13.

James Levine
Artistic director,
Metropolitan Opera,
New York, N.Y.

3

If you ask a writer to tell you what his best book is, perhaps he can do that—but it won't tell you the answer to any of a number of more interesting questions, since nothing happens in a vacuum and even those he thinks are *not* his most important books are part of the process. I would be surprised, if you looked at a retrospective by a great painter, if it didn't give you a little more of the feeling of what I'm saying. You walk from room to room and you look at the whole history of that artist's work and something may mean more—be more important, *matter* more—to you than something else on a purely subjective basis. But clearly something is gained from being able to see all of his work in proximity and continuity—and that's rather what a performing artist feels, I think. Incidentally, I'd have the same problem if you asked me to name my favorite piece [of music] or favorite composer.

Interview/
Opera News,
September:14.

Christopher Reeve
Actor

4

[Supporting Federal funding for the NEA]: Under the distinguished leadership of [NEA Chairman] Jane Alexander, the agency is doing its job properly. Merit is the guiding principle [for the issuing of NEA grants] more than ever before. Reforms have been instituted that make sure the money goes to worthy projects. [The funding of] obscenity is no

(CHRISTOPHER REEVE)

longer a legitimate issue. The NEA is not in the business of funding obscenity or pornography, as some critics charge. Art can be disturbing; art can be challenging. Most art sponsored by the NEA has no political content at all. People who think the NEA is causing the moral decline of America are in the minority. The serious problems society has—violence, racism, welfare, education—are not caused by artists, and the American public knows it. There is no leading nation in the world that does not support the arts, usually two, three, 10 times as much as we do . . . We must convince our representatives that they will have helped the U.S. take its place among other nations that do not fear the arts but employ their governments to put them in service to the future.

At Advocacy Day for Arts & Culture Congressional Breakfast, Washington, D.C., March 14/ Daily Variety, 3-14:4.

David Ross
Director, Whitney Museum of American Art, New York, N.Y.

1

[On the trend toward the use of electronics and computers in the operation of, and communication among, art museums]: We are at the edge of something that has the potential of changing everything. It will make people more comfortable with engaging art, whether in cyberspace or concrete space . . . There are museum directors who believe these changes are a threat to the integrity of museums. I say, these changes are going to take place and we'd better make sure we are in control of them.

The Wall Street Journal, 10-26:(A)20.

Roche Schufler
Executive director, Goodman Theater, Chicago, Ill.; Chairman, American Arts Alliance

2

[Criticizing the anticipated cut in Federal funding for the NEA]: [The blame is on] people in Congress who are determined to misrepresent the picture of what the agency has accomplished over the past 30 years. [But] this didn't start yesterday and it isn't going to end tomorrow. We are going to keep working and we are going to prevail in the end. We aren't going away. The arts are not going to cease to exist. And people in the arts are not going to stop speaking out.

The New York Times, 7-15:13.

Linda Shapiro
Co-founder, New Dance Ensemble, Minneapolis, Minn.

3

[Saying arts funding has become politicized]: As someone put it to me, "You're not only an artist, you're a social worker." I feel that there's a great deal of pressure by funders and by presenters that if you don't have a hook to hang it on—some kind of issue hook—then forget it. In some ways it's a dangerous thing, because it leads to a kind of very subtle censorship.

Dance Magazine, January:86.

Jac Venza
Director of cultural programming, WNET-TV (PBS), New York, N.Y.

1

[Lamenting the cutback in private funding for the arts and calls for cuts in government funding for the NEA and PBS]: I remember when I started in this [in the 1960s], it was a time when American culture dominated the world's imagination. If you were an artist, you wanted to get to New York. It was almost a challenge among cities to get your own version of Lincoln Center thrown up, and a resident company there. When I think of that period of optimism about the arts in the 1960s, I can't believe all this [the cutbacks] is happening such a short time later.

Interview/ The New York Times, 6-13:(B)4.

Martha Wilson
Director, Franklin Furnace Archive, New York, N.Y.

2

[On proposed cuts in Federal funding for the NEA]: The small [arts] institutions have seen the writing on the wall for years. Since 1990 we've been aware that the avante-garde is not popular. The big [institutions] are now seeing that the waves of conservatism are lapping at their steps, too. The climate that was once warm is now cold, and we will have to find other ways to survive.

The New York Times, 7-15:13.

Franco Zeffirelli
Motion-picture director

3

[On the state of the arts today]: We [will] leave behind a desert. In generations, people will ask what happened between 1980 and 2000. Nothing happened.

World Press Review, May:32.

Journalism

Hal Bruno
Political director,
ABC News

1

Most of the criticism [of the press] is because we're telling people what they don't want to hear. On political coverage, we report the campaign that's there. We don't invent the campaign. And every year it gets worse.

U.S. News & World Report,
1-9:46.

Everette Dennis
Executive director,
Freedom Forum
Media Studies Center,
Columbia University

2

[In the press,] there is a sense of superiority. I think a lot of journalists think they could do a better job of running the country than anyone in office.

U.S. News & World Report,
1-9:46.

Don Edwards
Chairman, department of
broadcast journalism,
Syracuse University

3

When it comes to immediacy, CNN has just taken away from the [traditional broadcast] networks the sense of urgency that television news delivers. When you're competing with CNN, which has 24 hours a day and treats every 22 minutes as a new deadline, there has to be some hard thinking done over what news function is going to be best served by the traditional networks with half an hour a night.

The Christian Science Monitor,
8-2:13.

Steve Florio
President,
Conde Nast Publications

4

All these folks who talk about how interactive television and the [Internet] and all the rest of that will render magazines a dinosaur, not only do not believe it, but I think that there have been so many cases, even in this century, that have proven that type of thinking wrong. For instance, when television came out, everybody said, "Radio will be dead." Well, radio is bigger today than it ever was. When TV came out, they also said, "It's over for movies. Why would you go to a movie? You can see it right in your house." But there's something that happens when you go into a theater and you see a movie with an audience, and that's why we keep going to the movies. I went up to Radcliffe [College] to do the publishing course, lecturing these very smart kids. I said to them, "We've got a wonderful interactive system that is also extraordinarily efficient. For about 33 cents, we can deliver something that has complete portability, that you can take anywhere with you. It has great shelf life; it will, in fact, last at least 50 to 75 years. And the level in quality of product is unsurpassed." There was this buzz of "what is it?" I said, "It's a magazine." Everyone went, "Oh!" I said, "Well, think about it. You get in bed on a winter night, you've got nothing to

(STEVE FLORIO)

do, and you open up this magazine—and you're there, man! It's something that is really moving you! Or it catches your interest or informs you. Somehow I just can't see myself in bed with a PowerBook on my lap. It's not there." If anything, I think all this new information technology is only going to cause more interest in magazines. It's amazing that the more media available, the more people consume.

Interview/ "Interview" magazine, November:70.

Barney Frank
United States Representative, D-Massachusetts

1

The general media has a left-wing bias?—that is patently untrue. The mainstream media has a bias, but it's not left-wing. It's negative. The mainstream media has become increasingly hooked on negativism and nastiness and bad news.

Interview, Washington, D.C./ Mother Jones, May-June:72.

Bob Furnad
Executive vice president and senior executive producer, Cable News Network

2

[On TV's coverage of the murder trial of former football star O.J. Simpson]: We're getting high [audience] ratings for our trial coverage, and all of our other shows, even on the weekend, are benefiting. But while this is a good news story and obviously one of high [public] interest, it's not one of those stories that as a journalist you necessarily feel deserves the audience thirst it's getting. I'd like to see us get high numbers for covering the revolt in Moscow or the war in Bosnia, stories that affect many people's lives. But this [Simpson] is clearly a story that people are thirsty for.

Los Angeles Times, 2-11:(A)16.

Newt Gingrich
United States Representative, R-Georgia; Speaker of the House

3

[Criticizing newspapers that have a socialist editorial bent, and saying businesses should reconsider advertising in such papers that oppose free-market views]: I think it's perfectly legitimate in a free society for people to decide where they'll put their money and their impact . . . I'd be glad to get you a collection of editorials that only make sense if people believe that government's good and the free market is bad. Surely you can't really argue that there aren't a substantial number of news editorial pages that start from an extraordinary pro-government, anti-free-market bias.

Broadcast interview, March 8/ The New York Times, 3-9:(A)9.

Donald E. Graham
Publisher, "The Washington Post"

4

[On the decision by *The Washington Post* and *The New York Times* to publish a "mani-

(DONALD E. GRAHAM)

festo" by a person known as the "Unabomber," who promised to stop his terrorist acts if it was published]: Both *The Post* and *The Times* felt there was no journalistic reason to publish it, but clearly there was a public-safety issue raised, and we both felt [that] before we could make a decision we should talk to the people who are responsible public officials and ask their opinion.

The Christian Science Monitor,
9-20:3.

Christopher Harper
Professor of journalism,
New York University

1

[Criticizing *The Washington Post*'s and *The New York Times*' decision to publish a "manifesto" by a person known as the "Unabomber," who promised to stop his terrorist acts if it was published]: [Even though the newspapers say they consulted with law-enforcement officials before deciding to publish the manifesto,] consulting with the FBI and the Justice Department also led to the [controversial] Waco and Ruby Ridge incidents [in which many people lost their lives] . . . The Unabomber is a terrorist, and *The New York Times* and *The Washington Post* have acceded to terrorist demands. It sets a dangerous precedent for any future case.

The Christian Science Monitor,
9-20:3.

Robert Harris
Author, Journalist

2

[On being an author and a journalist]: I think you really have to ask yourself: "Am I a journalist or am I a novelist?" . . . The skills you need for journalism are different. A journalist's virtues are clarity, simplicity, truth—versus the novelist's skills at being allusive.

Interview/
Publishers Weekly,
10-30:42.

Carl Hiaasen
Author;
Newspaper columnist

3

Newspaper training is invaluable [to an author]. You learn to write on deadline every week, in an environment where there's no such thing as writer's block. You get writer's block in a newsroom and you'll soon have employment block . . . The reason a lot of successful writers come out of a journalism background is that they've been forced to write in a structured environment. The hardest thing in the world is to get up in the morning and face all the other distractions of life and shut them out so you can write.

Interview/
Writer's Digest,
January:40.

Peter Jennings
Anchor, ABC News

4

It is because we [in the news media] are powerful and important that we must think about our role as citizens . . . I know this is a very complicated subject, and it isn't much of a contribution for me to simply say that we've gone overboard about O.J. [the current murder trial of former football star O.J. Simpson], which we have, or that those of us in the so-called establishment or mainstream

(PETER JENNINGS)

press have been unduly influenced by those who publish or produce the tabloids, which in some cases we have . . . More important is the general tendency in the press to treat all public figures as suspect. By doing so, I think we contribute unquestionably to cynicism in the electorate at large.

Upon receiving Paul White Award from Radio & Television News Directors Association, New Orleans, La./ The Washington Post, 9-11:(B)6.

Marvin Kalb
Director, Barone Center on the Press, Politics and Public Policy, Harvard University

1

[There is] a mean-spiritedness to American journalism, a desire to tear down rather than build up. You cannot be positive today. You cannot even give a public official the benefit of the doubt. [And] the first White House correspondent who says something nice about the President is going to be withdrawn from the beat.

U.S. News & World Report, 1-9:46.

2

[On CBS News' removing Connie Chung from her co-anchor slot on its "Evening News" program]: Connie Chung, a good reporter, is not to be guillotined, nor CBS to be savaged as sexist and stupid. Both are, sadly, reminders that all network pursuit of ratings and profits is deplorable.

USA Today, 5-26:(A)15.

Olga Karabandova
Official, Glasnost Defense Fund (Russia)

3

[Saying the Russian government is trying to control press reports about its war in Chechnya]: There is a big government campaign to prevent journalists from receiving full information, and a tendency to deliver the kind of information that is good for the government. Russian journalists have the possibility to deliver independent information, but it is difficult and dangerous.

The Christian Science Monitor, 1-4:4.

Andrew Kohut
Director, Times Mirror Center for the People and the Press

4

The [public] accusations that the press is a watchdog gone out of control are increasingly evident in our surveys. [People think] it's excessive even in the things they value the most, which is keeping the politicians honest. They appreciate the watchdog role [of the press], but they hate the way it practices its craft.

U.S. News & World Report, 1-9:45.

Robert MacNeil
Co-host,
"MacNeil/Lehrer NewsHour,"
PBS-TV

1

I'm worried about [TV network news shows]. In 1966, when the first national survey showed a majority of Americans got their news from television, the network news departments commanded about 90 percent of the television audience at suppertime. These were serious journalists, responsible news organizations. [Thirty] years later, if those same news programs—two of them anyway [CBS and NBC]—night after night say the O.J. Simpson [murder] trial is the most important thing of the day in the world, that bothers me. And you know perfectly well the journalists in those shops, if asked, would say O.J. is *not* the most important thing in the world but, come on, we've got to do it.

Interview/
Newsweek,
10-30:88.

Mary Jo Meisner
Editor,
"The Milwaukee Journal Sentinel"

2

[Saying editors today need to be business-oriented regarding their own newspapers]: I don't think you can be an editor anymore and sit in an ivory tower and know all about foreign policy or state politics but not necessarily know that much about what makes your company tick every day. It's a lot more complicated now.

Interview,
Milwaukee, Wis./
The New York Times,
6-19:(C)1.

John S. Reidy
Managing director,
Smith Barney, Inc.,
investments

3

[On family-owned newspapers]: Once a newspaper's owners take it public [by issuing stock], they are obliged to deliver reasonably competitive [financial] returns. Family members who want to do the hard work should stay onboard. The aspiring surfers should head to Malibu.

USA Today,
7-21:(A)13.

Bernard Shaw
Anchor,
Cable News Network

4

[On the success of Ted Turner's CNN]: People laughed in his face and ours, saying we'd go broke because there wasn't enough news to fill the airwaves 24 hours a day. But his character and his sense of history wouldn't let him give up. After the boys and girls at the other networks stopped sneering, they started looking over their shoulders.

Los Angeles Times,
8-31:(D)5.

Paul Simon
United States Senator,
D-Illinois

5

When I was a young reporter, the great weakness of journalists was whiskey. Today, the great weakness of journalists is cynicism.

U.S. News & World Report,
1-9:45.

Arthur Sulzberger, Jr.
Publisher,
"The New York Times"

1

[On his newspaper's decision to publish a "manifesto" by a person known as the "Unabomber," who promised to stop his terrorist acts if it was published]: Whether you like it or not, we're turning our pages over to a man who has murdered people. But I'm convinced we're making the right choice between bad options . . . It's difficult to put complete faith in the word of someone with the record of violence that the Unabomber has. But the best advice available, from the FBI and others, is that the Unabomber may well not bomb again if his material is published.

Interview, Sept. 18/
The New York Times,
9-19:(A)1.

Literature

Martin Amis
Author

1

Novels are very long [to write], and long novels are very, very long. It's just a hell of a lot of man-hours. I tend to just go in there, and if it comes, it comes. A morning when I write not a single word doesn't worry me too much. If I come up against a brick wall, I'll just go and play snooker or something or sleep on it, and my subconscious will fix it for me. Usually, it's a journey without maps but a journey with a destination, so I know how it's going to begin and I know how it's going to end, but I don't know how I'm going to get from one to the other. That, really, is the struggle of the novel.

Interview,
London, England/
"Interview" magazine,
May:125.

2

I think every writer has felt burning hatred for other writers. There is this kind of late-night glinting of completely uncontrolled ambition and egotism that is always there. And that is necessary; it's a job qualification.

Interview/
Vanity Fair,
May:135.

Elizabeth Arthur
Author

3

[On writing fiction and non-fiction]: I love both forms. They're freeing in different ways. Fiction gives you the freedom to make up anything that comes to mind and to serve your own purposes within the text. Non-fiction already has a frame,so it's a completely different kind of discipline. It's like yoga: You're working in a very limited area, but within it you can do amazing postures. Fiction just allows you to start running toward the horizon.

Interview/
Publishers Weekly,
1-2:55.

4

I learned from building [my] house that I was capable of organizing a project, following through with it, understanding its different parts, and keeping going when it got really tough. The process of making a book is very similar: You start with nothing, you have a pile of raw materials you have to figure out how to put together, and those qualities of organization, architecture and discipline all come into play.

The Writer,
May:3.

Rick Bass
Author

5

[As a writer,] when you're really in love with something you're working on, 90 percent of the time you think: Man, this is it; this is the only thing in the world. It takes on its own light and magic. The other 10 percent, you have this huge despair—you saw the way you wanted it, but you just missed it. You're

(RICK BASS)

the only one who sees it; it's invisible, it's vaporous.

Interview, Montana/
Publishers Weekly,
6-26:84.

Mario Benedetti
Uruguayan author

1

The short story is a very demanding genre. Argentine writer Jorge Luis Borges used to say that if novels were written with the same rigor as short stores, writing novels would be an impossible task. One word can make a story.

Interview/
World Press Review,
June:45.

James Billington
Librarian of Congress
of the United States

2

[With the increasing use of computers,] this is a time of very rapid change [in libraries], and libraries as an institution are somewhat change-resistant. I'm excited to the extent to which libraries are improvising or rising to the challenge. But there's a long way to go.

The Washington Post,
8-28:(A)9.

Kate Braverman
Poet

3

I love writing the "new" poetry. And the newer, the better. "Form" is dead. I think this [current] interest in formalism is just an aberrational moment. It only appeared fashionable because nobody is really reading poetry anymore. I don't think we can pretend that Freud didn't happen. I don't think we can pretend Einstein didn't happen. [Formalism] is a kind of intellectual game, but it doesn't serve the purpose of women. It doesn't serve the purposes of, oh, shall we call them issues of freedom that have defined this century. [Writing in form] is the same tyranny as that of the patriarchy. And I despise it. And I despise the people who practice it. To go back and straitjacket poetry into forms that never worked to begin with and pretend that they work now is an absurdity to me.

Interview/
Los Angeles Times,
1-19:(E)7.

Sandra Brown
Author

4

I've got this love-hate relationship with writing. Yes, it has been commercially rewarding, but that's not what drives me. It's this compulsion to tell a story that people want to read. And I never get over my amazement that people have an interest in what I have to write. Maybe I keep at it to prove myself wrong.

Interview/
Publishers Weekly,
7-10:40.

Cary Carson
Historian;
Vice president for research,
Colonial Williamsburg Foundation

5

Historians, I've always insisted, are ultimately fiction writers no less than novelists.

(CARY CARSON)

They simply play by a stricter set of rules. In the end, it all is art. That is, historians can often agree on certain basic facts, but when we begin assembling those facts into something larger and more meaningful, our choice of the facts we do and don't select and how we put them together, that's the art of what we do. And in doing that, we are constrained in ways that, say, [novelist] William Styron isn't when he writes about Nat Turner. That isn't to say that he doesn't feel a tremendous sense of obligation to the same set of facts that historians writing about this subject would. On the other hand, we permit him, a novelist, some license that we don't permit ourselves. That is the difference between his work and our work. In a larger sense, we're all making selections from this body of agreed-upon truths we call facts and putting them together in ways that we think address the larger truths that are certainly far more interesting and important than the facts by themselves.

Interview/
Humanities,
Jan.-Feb.:9.

Michael Chabon
Author

1

I like to read books that are in the first person. I like the intimate confessional tone, as though the person has pulled up a chair and is telling you about his life.

Interview,
Los Angeles, Calif./
Publishers Weekly,
4-10:45.

Deepak Chopra
Author

2

Non-fiction, in fact, doesn't tell the truth, because non-fiction is arranging facts in a certain way to try and convince other people of your hypothesis. It's your best representation of what you think the truth is. But fiction tells the truth, because it reveals your innermost feelings and fantasies about situations, circumstances, people and events. If you write fiction and you do it with intensity and passion, you reveal yourself—and you write the truth.

Interview, La Jolla, Calif./
Publishers Weekly,
7-24:44.

Jim Crace
Author

3

As an ex-journalist I don't believe in "writer's block," so I've never had any problem about getting on with it. I also have this sense of what I have to achieve by the end of the week—5000 words. If I have written only 1600, I can't enjoy my weekend in good conscience. It doesn't mean I am not passionate about my writing, but I am very measured about it.

Interview/
Publishers Weekly,
10-2:49.

Robert Darnton
Author;
Professor of European history,
Princeton University

4

[In the 18th century], there was a monopoly in the official book trade that con-

(ROBERT DARNTON)

trolled the quality and the material being printed. People recognized literature as something that *mattered*, something that should be controlled and something that should be manipulated in the service of the ruling monarchy. Every book that appeared legally had to be censored. The censors were not just snuffing out heresy; they were worried about quality, reinforcing a higher, nobler kind of literature. And this mental set on the part of the authorities just excluded a very large part of the literature people wanted to read.

Interview, Princeton, N.J./ Publishers Weekly, 3-13:50.

Stephen Dixon
Author

1

[On the many jobs he had before he became a successful writer]: I would not have wanted the recognition to have come earlier. All those jobs made me tougher; they forced me to become a stronger person. When you work like that for 20 years, you meet the real people you can write about. I'm glad it worked out this way. If it had come earlier, I might not have written that hard—nor as much.

Interview, Baltimore, Md./ Publishers Weekly, 6-19:41.

Shannon Drake
Author

2

I'm happier as a writer of popular fiction who pays her bills than I would be as a struggling genius.

The Writer, August:3.

Rikki Ducornet
Author, Poet

3

Poetry is a curious process. It seems to me to get down to the darkest spaces very quickly, down to the bones of things. It's a baptism of fire in a way for a beginning writer—it was very much that experience for me.

Interview, May/ Publishers Weekly, 10-9:66.

Greg Gatenby
Executive director, International Festival of Authors (Canada)

4

If you were to ask critics around the world to name the 50 most important writers of fiction in the English language, probably six to 10 of them would be Canadian. Well, that's way out of proportion to the population.

Interview, Toronto, Canada/ Los Angeles Times, 10-27:(A)5.

Nadine Gordimer
Author; Winner, 1991 Nobel Prize in Literature

5

I've always thought, and I think you see it in my writing, that it is the significance of detail wherein the truth lies. These are invisible connections, invisible stitches, that really connect the narrative in a way that chronology and any other method doesn't do.

The Writer, September:3.

Winston Groom
Author

1

There's a reason why [we] Southerners make good storytellers. We're surrounded by big families and old friends, and we spend a lot of time talking. Those stories we live by may get embellished over the years, but they make it into our interior and become part of what we are.

Interview,
Los Angeles, Calif./
Publishers Weekly,
4-17:35.

Donald Hall
Poet

2

When a poem, any work, is private to me, its spirit and possibilities are limitless. Once I show it to anyone . . . somebody else's spirit, psyche, tone of voice, has entered the poem. There is something mysterious in the way in which I know when it is right for another mind to come into this poem. This holding back is essential to me, perhaps more for me than others, but too many people rush to show work to their best friends or spouses.

The Writer,
September:3.

Robert Harris
Author,
Journalist

3

Today, when a writer says, "I am a storyteller," it is practically shorthand for saying "it's crap." Of course, it is perfectly legitimate to write novels which are essentially prose poems. But in the end, I think, a novel is like a car; and if you buy a car and grow flowers in it, you're forgetting that the car is designed to take you somewhere else.

Interview/
Publishers Weekly,
10-30:43.

Carl Hiaasen
Author;
Newspaper columnist

4

Some of [my characters] start like a spark from a conversation, or maybe a newspaper story. I start my novels with a list of characters, and I spend a lot of time with them before I even work on the plot. Characters are what hold my readers' attention, so their development is crucial. They can't be forgettable. You won't find my character in Central Casting—they're all a little off-center. In real life, people are really like that. Nobody is all good or all evil. Even the most despicable criminals live by some code . . . A writer needs to tap into that moral code, find out what these bad guys will stand up for or believe in. Then you have an interesting character. Pure evil is easy to write about. Common evil is more complicated, and often more of a riddle.

Interview/
Writer's Digest,
January:39.

Thomas Keneally
Author; Professor of English,
University of California, Irvine

5

[For a writer,] when an editor leaves [a publishing house], it's sort of like having your wife shot on your honeymoon, and you have to get married again.

Interview, Irvine, Calif./
Publishers Weekly, 4-3:41.

Andrew Klavan
Author

1

I started out thinking that the thriller form had to be about violence, about evil—and to be perfectly honest, even now I am not opposed to cheap thrills. I think a book like *Silence of the Lambs*, which genuinely made me sick, was a wonderful thriller. What loses me is stylized violence, especially when someone says "I am showing you how the humanity has gone out of these men"—because it never does that, really.

Interview,
London, England/
Publishers Weekly,
6-12:41.

Paul LeClerc
President,
New York Public Library System

2

[On the increasing availability of computers in libraries]: [Access to information is] a national good. The more people can access accurate information, the more productive they'll be as citizens. Libraries provide the one logical, existing place that the nation can invest in to bring people up to speed on satisfying their information needs.

The Washington Post,
8-28:(A)9.

John T. Lescroart
Author

3

I start out writing various stories—they're all on my word processor, and I sort of move back and forth between them. I don't get writer's block, but sometimes it's difficult for me to decide which story to commit to. When that happens I just sit back in a sort of zen state and wait to see which gate will open. When *that* happens, I do a very detailed plot outline. I hate doing that, because it's hard work, but it's worth it. The twists and turns of the plot are tricky, and I need a good map. Then I turn off the plot-writing part of me and let the writing take over. The characters are what really drive my plots. They begin in the dark and they go through hell and come out of it with some kind of knowledge of redemption.

Interview, Davis, Calif./
Publishers Weekly,
8-14:61.

Julius Lester
Author;
Professor of Judaic studies,
University of Massachusetts,
Amherst

4

Writing for children is a curious thing because you're writing for people who don't buy books. So what I have consistently done is write for both audiences, children and adults. I put things in my books for the enjoyment of the teacher, parent or librarian who is reading to the child. And I also try to spark the child to ask, "Oh, gee, what does this mean?" What I strive for is an interaction between the adult and child as they read the book.

Interview/
Booklist, 2-15:1090.

Mark Leyner
Author

5

There's a stunning contrast between my discipline and organization and the

(MARK LEYNER)

unpredictability of my writing. But I think one is necessary for the other. This is where, each day, I go to war with my imagination.

Interview/
Publishers Weekly,
3-6:44.

Myra Cohn Livingston
Poet

1

Poetry is more than an appeal to the head; it's an appeal to the body; it's physiological. A good poem will grab your sense of rhythm. I remember going to a school and hearing a teacher tell her students, "I want you to sit perfectly still when Mrs. Livingston reads." That's the *wrong* thing to tell children. If they really enjoy the poetry, they're going to move. Their bodies are going to respond to it. That's what [poet] Emily Dickinson meant, I think, when she said she knows she's hearing a poem if she gets a chill up her spine.

Interview/
Booklist, 6-1:1745.

David McCullough
Pulitzer Prize-winning author

2

[Calling for more support for U.S. libraries]: If we want libraries open again, if we want a generous, exciting education for our children, and a culture that counts for something, it's up to us.

Before American
Library Association,
Philadelphia, Pa./
Publishers Weekly,
2-13:11.

W.S. Merwin
Poet

3

The thing that makes poetry different from all of the other arts [is that] you're using language, which is what you use for everything else—telling lies and selling socks, advertising and conducting law. Whereas we don't write little concerti to each other, or paint pictures.

The Writer,
April:2.

Michael Mewshaw
Author

4

I'm extremely responsible to place. It's important to me as a person and it's important in my fiction. Sometimes editors have said, "There's an awful lot here about place; maybe we should cut some of it out"; and then reviewers would say, "What a terrific sense of place he has." Ultimately, I realized that for me, place is a character.

The Writer,
January:3.

Don Napoli
Director,
St. Joseph County
Public Library,
South Bend, Ind.

5

The [computer] Internet is going to become the medium for transmitting or providing information in almost every field you can think of. But you'll still need a public entity that acts for the community in providing access. That's the [public] library.

The Washington Post,
8-28:(A)9.

Mary Oliver
Poet

1

I never had any other notion than that the *eye/I* of the poem should be not the writer of the poem but the reader of the poem . . . It's not that I care whether I'm a male voice speaking or a female voice speaking, or anything on a this-world basis; it's that I believe very much and always have that readers want poems that will bring them news of their lives, not news of the poet's life.

The Writer, January:3.

Cynthia Ozick
Author

2

The sentence is my primary element, my tool, goal, bliss. Each new sentence is a heart-in-the-mouth experiment.

The Writer, June:3.

3

I am a literary obsessive. I believe a writer can weave in and out of genres—do it all. It is a gluttonous point of view, to be sure. Then again, when it comes to writing, that is what I truly am and nothing less: a glutton.

The Writer, November:3.

Robert B. Parker
Author

4

The key to writing believable fiction is a powerful, yet controlled, imagination. Before you begin to write about any fictional happening—be it a gun battle, the meeting of two lovers, or something as innocuous as a stroll through a park—you, the author, must be certain that you have imagined it fully. If you can't manage to part the curtain that veils what is essentially your daydream, if you can't see the event unfolding in its entirety with your mind's eye, [then] when you translate that vision into words, it will surely be shrouded in a thick, oily gray mist. Then, to make the action more vivid, you'll be tempted to litter the landscape with mangled corpses and buckets of gore.

Interview/ Writer's Digest, September:28.

Robert Pinsky
Poet

5

[On his translation into English of Dante's *Inferno*, which originally was written in Italian with a triple-rhyming scheme]: To write triple rhymes in English is not easy. English has an immense vocabulary, larger than Italian. And one of the classic mistakes you can make is to draw on that huge wealth of synonyms to supply rhymes. If you do that, you have an extremely unnatural, unidiomatic language; you end up with phrases that no one would ever say.

Interview/ The New York Times, 1-31:(B)1.

Nancy Taylor Rosenberg
Author

6

I wrote all my life. I was a very troubled child, and I was also a gifted child. The combination made me very dark, and the only real

(NANCY TAYLOR ROSENBERG)

happiness I felt was when I picked up a pen and reinvented my world *beyond* my world.

Interview,
New York, N.Y./
Publishers Weekly,
1-16:434.

Salman Rushdie
Author

1

Fiction has been dangerous for its authors *always* [he himself has to hide from a death sentence by Iran because of one of his novels]. It's also dangerous for the world in the way that's a necessary danger. Without it, you can't change anything; you can't shake things up in people's heads. It's always been dangerous, and it will be a sad day when it stops being dangerous.

Interview/
Publishers Weekly,
1-30:81.

2

One of the things that's interesting about the nature of reading is that you *assume* that your response is universal. If you like something, you don't think: I *like* this. You think: This is *good.* In a way, all readers are absolutists. Which is all right in the context of a variegated response. If everybody was saying the same things about the same stories, then they must be right.

Interview/
Publishers Weekly,
1-30:81.

3

One of the things a writer is for is to say the unsayable, to speak the unspeakable, to ask difficult questions.

At literary debate,
London, England/
Los Angeles Times,
9-14:(E)1.

Vern Rutsala
Poet

4

I think there is a naturally subversive role that writers play in any society, simply because they are trying to use language *precisely*, whereas nearly everyone else in society is trying to use language to pull the wool over our eyes or sell us something or make us vote for a particular candidate.

The Writer,
August:3.

Luis Sepulveda
Chilean author

5

I write four hours a day. To put together a good novel, you need 95 percent discipline and 5 percent of what some people call talent and what, to me, is keeping a clear idea of where you are going. The 95 percent demands that you work every day, in any situation you may find yourself in, and that you make it clear to those around you that those four hours of the day are your own.

Interview/
World Press Review,
August:46.

Timothy Steele
Poet

1

Being labeled as a "formalist" [poet] troubles me. It's sad that we've reached a point where a poet who uses meter, rhyme and stanza is regarded as an oddity and is praised or damned on that basis. It would be risible to call Shakespeare, Keats or Dickinson a formalist. When I sit down to write, I don't say, "Iambic pentameter, here I come!" The traditional instruments of poetry are merely means to an end—that end being to say something moving or interesting in a memorable and compact manner.

Interview/
Los Angeles Times,
1-19:(E)7.

2

I'm often asked what I think will be the future of poetry, and I have to say I honestly don't know. People who, in the 19th century, would have read Longfellow, Dickens and George Eliot today are spending more time around the television, watching videos or going to films. And this is something poetry can't compete with. Moreover, much of modern poetry is so difficult to read, it's hard to imagine that anyone except a specialist in poetry would find it engaging.

Interview/
Los Angeles Times,
1-19:(E)7.

Gloria Steinem
Author;
Women's-rights advocate

3

I've always used personal anecdotes [in my writing], because I think the reader has a right to know the life experience a particular conclusion came out of—unlike the traditional style [of writing] that makes everything seem as if it came from Mount Olympus.

Interview/
"Interview" magazine,
June:99.

Gore Vidal
Author

4

Reading, with the power of television, has really been a lost art. There are far more good writers in America than we have good readers. I want to give the Nobel Prize for the best reader in the world . . . They'll hand out a golden lamp, a reading lamp.

Interview,
Beverly Hills, Calif./
Los Angeles Times,
10-30:(E)1.

Mary Willis Walker
Author

5

[As a writer,] I think I've become a junkie for how it feels to be totally involved in a fictional world that you're creating. There's nothing like it—being called back to it every morning, to want to expand on it. It's total involvement.

Interview, Austin, Texas/
Publishers Weekly,
8-28:90.

Richard Wilbur
Former Poet Laureate
of the United States

6

There is no such thing as an inherently hackneyed rhyme; there is only rhyme used

(RICHARD WILBUR)

well or badly. The best statement ever made about rhyme was made by [the poet] Robert Frost; he said that good poets don't rhyme *words*, they rhyme *phrases*.

At National Arts Club Literary Award Dinner/ The Writer, June:3.

1

[In poetry,] rhyme and meter present difficulties which, if overcome, turn into added force. And any poet who can't use them on occasion, and at the same time pursue his thought, is in the wrong racket.

At National Arts Club Literary Award Dinner/ The Writer, August:3.

Jeanette Winterson
Author

2

[As a writer,] I think you must get more and more and more ambitious. Writers do run out [of writing]; with hindsight, we know that "writing lives" are concentrated in a relatively short span, and it doesn't matter to me whether mine ends next year or in 20 years. [And when I recognize that moment,] I will bc glad, because then I'll have done my work in the world. Then perhaps I'll retire and breed bulls.

Interview, London, England/ Publishers Weekly, 3-20:39.

Tim Winton
Australian author

3

I had always been a very hard-nosed sender-outer of manuscripts. I had a system, a grid which listed all the publications, and I used to send things out in huge multiples. I didn't feel anything when I got a rejection. Sometimes I would send them back to the same editor a second time and get accepted. You can never underestimate enough the intelligence of people who work for magazines.

Interview/ Publishers Weekly, 5-29:63.

Medicine and Health

Ron Anderson
Administrator,
Dallas (Texas)
County Hospital District

1

[On public hospitals]: People see that the product we provide is a quality product not just for indigents but for the entire community. Public hospitals that work have to have a governing structure like a not-for-profit hospital. They have to be accountable to the community but not be whipsawed back and forth by political intrusion.

Los Angeles Times,
11-2:(A)13.

Bill Archer
United States Representative,
R-Texas

2

[Part B of Medicare] has not been paid for [by recipients] during the work life of the individual. I think there's a majority [in Congress] that favors means-testing the Part B premiums, and I think that's justifiable. . . . [Part A of Medicare] is already means-tested by virtue of the fact that, no matter what you make in salary, you pay [1.45 percent]. This is the most heavily means-tested program at the Federal level.

Interview/
AARP Bulletin,
January:6.

3

We [Republicans] said we would save Medicare from bankruptcy, and we have offered a plan that does indeed save it. Our plan is bold, it is innovative, and most importantly, it protects Medicare for today's retirees, and it preserves it for the next generation of seniors.

At House Ways and Means
Committee hearing,
Washington, D.C.,
Sept. 22/
The New York Times,
9-23:8.

Richard K. Armey
United States Representative,
R-Texas

4

The Democrats have a craven approach to Medicare, which is to let it go bankrupt in the long-run [by not wanting to cut Medicare spending growth] for what they perceive to be short-term political gain. What they fail to realize is that public tolerance for demagoguery is at an all-time low.

Sept. 15/
The New York Times,
9-16:1.

Marianna Bauder
President,
St. Joseph Hospital,
Denver, Colo.

5

Medicine is not just black and white. It's a matter of judgments . . . We have 1,250 doctors on staff. They are all human.

Los Angeles Times,
8-24:(A)14.

Judith Bell
Co-chairman,
San Francisco office,
Consumers Union

1

[Criticizing HMOs for trying to reduce medical costs at the expense of patient medical treatment]: You don't want these kinds of decisions made by a company staring at its bottom line. To the extent that we're making them as a society, they should be made by public-policy-makers, not by insurance executives . . . [Health care is] different from going out to buy any other service because there is a big imbalance in knowledge. The patient really has to rely on doctors [because] consumers are not used to having to advocate for themselves, as they have to in [HMO] managed care.

Los Angeles Times,
8-31:(A)14.

Ruth Berkelman
Deputy Director,
Center for
Infectious Diseases
of the United States

2

[Criticizing the lack of sufficient Federal funding for her organization]: Mortality from infectious disease has gone up 50 percent in a decade, and a lot of policy-makers still think we don't have a problem . . . We're losing our expertise. When a guy who's our expert on botulism retires, that's it; we no longer have anybody who knows about botulism. During the hanta outbreak, our people were working day and night to figure out what was doing the killing. We had people in the field, trapping rodents, sending samples and animals back to the lab. Our people in the lab were working day and night to identify the pathogen. And during all this, we get the word that we have to cut our staff by 100. People were coming to me saying, "What am I doing this for? We work like dogs and this is the thanks we get?"

U.S. News & World Report,
3-27:55,56.

Brian Bilbray
United States Representative,
R-California

3

[Criticizing suggestions that Congressional cuts in Medicaid funding growth would be catastrophic]: Easing back on the throttle does not mean the train is going to stop. It simply means we are trying to slow a train that is speeding out of control. Until a formula is finalized, it is irresponsible to make allegations of an impending crisis. This is merely a scare tactic, one with no basis in fact.

Los Angeles Times,
7-27:(A)3.

Michael Bilirakis
United States Representative,
R-Florida

4

[On Democrats who are criticizing the Republican Medicare-reform proposals]: Shame on those politicians who over the years, not just now, use scare tactics and misinformation to frighten our senior citizens all in the interest of getting votes through fear. These actions are unconscionable. Only the most affluent retirees are having their [Medicare] Part B premium raised substantially [under the Republican plan]. We are not raising

(MICHAEL BILIRAKIS)

Medicare deductibles or co-payments. We would not be reducing services or benefits. Our legislation insures that the core services and the current Medicare program will be retained and must be offered to all beneficiaries. I also want to make it clear that no one will be forced into HMOs. If Medicare beneficiaries wish to keep the current fee-for-service benefit where they have complete choice of their doctor, they will be permitted to do so. If beneficiaries want to enroll in an HMO, which might include additional health benefits or some other Medicare-plus plan, they can do so.

Before the House,
Washington, D.C.,
Oct. 19/
The New York Times,
10-20:(A)10.

David Branding-Bennett
Deputy Director,
Pan-American
Health Organization

1

[Saying increased life expectancy due to advances in medicine are creating new problems]: The millions of lives that have been saved and the better chance of survival have led to an increase in the number of older persons throughout the world, many of whom develop heart disease, diabetes, cancer and other chronic diseases. Unfortunately, developing countries are poorly equipped to deal with these new diseases.

Interview/
The New York Times,
5-2:(B)9.

Richard M. Burr
United States Representative,
R-North Carolina

2

[Criticizing proposals by the FDA to begin regulating tobacco products because of its decision that nicotine is a drug]: As long as tobacco is a legal product in the United States and Congress decides not to change that status, then the Agriculture Department and any other Federal agency should treat it as a legal commodity.

July 12/
The New York Times,
7-13:(A)9.

Bill Clinton
President
of the United States

3

[On criticism of his nomination of Dr. Henry Foster for U.S. Surgeon General, criticism which centers on the number of abortions Dr. Foster has performed]: Henry Foster's record can be seen in the lives of thousands of babies that he has helped come into this world in a healthy way, in the people he has tried to educate, and the people he has tried to help. He deserves to be more than a political football in the emerging politics of this season.

At White House luncheon
for the group Emily's List,
Washington, D.C., May 1/
The New York Times,
5-2:(A)13.

4

Gay people who have AIDS are still our sons, our brothers, our cousins, our citizens. They're Americans, too. They're obeying the

(BILL CLINTON)

law and working hard. They are entitled to be treated like everybody else.

At Georgetown University,
July 6/
The New York Times,
7-8:7.

1

There's a lot of wonderful people in this country who make a living as tobacco farmers. [But] we cannot pretend that we're ignoring the evidence, that one of the greatest threats to the health of our children is teenage smoking, and it's rising. If you wanted to do something to reduce the cost of health care, help over the long run to balance the [Federal] budget and increase the health care of America, having no teenagers smoke would be the cheapest, easiest, quickest thing you could ever do.

At Baptist convention,
Charlotte, N.C.,
Aug. 9/
Los Angeles Times,
8-10:(A)19.

2

[Criticizing the Republican proposals for Medicare]: Their plan would increase premiums and other costs for senior citizens. It would reduce doctor choice. It would force many doctors to stop serving seniors altogether. It threatens to put rural hospitals and urban hospitals out of business. Brick by brick, it would dismantle Medicare as we know it . . . You can have a healthy Medicare trust fund, you can have reductions in cost inflation in Medicare and Medicaid, without these Draconian consequences.

To senior citizens,
Washington, D.C.,
Sept. 15/
The New York Times,
9-16:7.

3

[Criticizing the Republican proposals for Medicare]: Their proposal to double the premiums, double the deductibles, stop giving Medicare to anybody under 67 years old, to raise three times as much as it takes to bail out the trust fund, has nothing to do with saving Medicare. It has everything to do with their budget priorities.

Before Congressional
Hispanic Caucus,
Washington, D.C.,
Sept. 27/
Los Angeles Times,
9-28:(A)14.

Howard Coble
United States Representative,
R-North Carolina

4

[Criticizing proposals by the FDA to begin regulating tobacco products because of its decision that nicotine is a drug]: I think tobacco has become the convenient whipping boy on Capitol Hill. It is lawfully grown, lawfully packaged and lawfully marketed, and I am getting annoyed by these efforts to make it seem like there is something illegal about tobacco.

July 12/
The New York Times,
7-13:(A)9.

Richard Corlin
Physician;
Former president,
California
Medical Association

1

[Saying that non-profit HMOs run by doctors would provide better and cheaper health care for Medicare patients]: The fear the insurance companies have is that the doctors will do it successfully and then the companies would have real competition and no more big stock options [for their executives]. If we didn't think we could do a better job for what patients need, we wouldn't be trying to do it. The issue is not, is managed care good or bad, but are the for-profit HMOs committing abuses for which we need a correction in our policies?

Los Angeles Times,
11-25:(A)29.

Martin Corry
Director
of Federal affairs,
American Association
of Retired Persons

2

[On discussions about the future of Medicare]: It's a good, strong program that serves millions of beneficiaries and it ought to be able to sustain a debate and scrutiny very well. On the other hand, it's certainly going to be a more difficult dialogue if, at the same time, we're trying to fend off billions of dollars in spending cuts that we hear coming down the pike whenever members of either [political] party talk about entitlement cuts.

The New York Times,
1-31:(A)8.

David R. Dantzker
President,
Long Island (N.Y)
Jewish Medical Center

3

[Saying too many doctors want to enter medical specialties rather than general practice]: In some specialties we could probably turn off the spigot for 10 years and still have plenty. The pity is there are a number of people involved in years of specialty training who are not going to use it, who aren't going to practice their subspecialty [because of an over-supply of specialists] . . . I tell students that unless they have an underlying love for a subspecialty, they should go into general medicine. Because if they go into something like cardiology, they are going to find themselves in a very compromised position.

The New York Times,
4-15:6.

Richard Daynard
Professor of law,
Northeastern University;
Chairman,
Tobacco Production
Liability Project

4

[Saying tobacco companies target much of their marketing to teenagers]: People now understand that this is an industry that needs to get its people under-age, when it's illegal to sell the product to them, or they are not going to get new customers.

Los Angeles Times,
7-25:(D)16.

Horace B. Deets
Executive director,
American Association
of Retired Persons

1

[Criticizing proposed cuts in the growth of Medicare spending]: Even now, Medicare pays doctors and hospitals considerably less per person than does the private sector. Over time, you'll find a greater reluctance on the part of doctors to accept Medicare patients. The bottom line is that these cutbacks could adversely affect access to care and quality of care—how much time doctors spend with Medicare patients. Or hospitals could cut their staffing . . . The proposed [Medicare] cuts are too much, too fast.

Interview/
AARP Bulletin,
Fall:14.

Robert J. Dole
United States Senator,
R-Kansas;
Candidate for the 1996 Republican
Presidential nomination

2

[On the controversy over U.S. Surgeon General nominee Dr. Henry Foster's performing abortions during his career]: This is not about abortion; this is about credibility. This is about telling the truth. This is about the White House leveling with the American people [about the number of abortions Dr. Foster performed] and not letting it drip and drip and drip out so the American people don't find out the truth.

At Republican
Party gathering, May 1/
The New York Times,
5-2:(A)13.

Henry W. Foster, Jr.
Surgeon General-designate
of the
United States

3

[On criticism of his having performed abortions and of his having recently understated the number of abortions he has performed]: I am a doctor who delivers babies. My life's work has been devoted to bringing healthy lives into this world, and trying to assure that every child born is a wanted child and who has parents that can meet its needs. I have dedicated my career to taking all appropriate medical steps to meet the health needs of my patients, and that includes performing legal abortions. In America, a woman has a right to choose, and I support [President Clinton's] position—and most Americans—that abortions in this country should be safe, legal and rare. But again, my life's work [has been devoted] to making sure that young people don't have to face that difficult choice . . . [When I was recently asked how many abortions I have performed,] I answered based on my memory without reviewing the record. That was a mistake; I should not have guessed. But it was an honest mistake. I am a doctor. I had never experienced anything like the media scrutiny that I attracted following my nomination [for Surgeon General]. In my desire to provide instant answers to a barrage of questions coming at me, I spoke without having all of the facts at my disposal, and since that time I have made every human effort possible to review my records so I could be as accurate as possible . . . I do regret the initial confusion that this caused, but there was never any intent to deceive. I had no reason to do so. I have worked very, very hard and have established an impeccable record of credibil-

(HENRY W. FOSTER, JR.)

ity and ethical conduct. It is open to anyone who chooses to scrutinize it.

At Senate Labor and Human Resources Committee hearing on his nomination, Washington, D.C., May 2/ The New York Times, 5-3:(A)14.

Robert Friedland
Executive director, National Academy on Aging

1

[On suggestions that non-profit HMOs run by doctors would provide better and cheaper health care for Medicare patients]: Just because an HMO is run by doctors does not mean it will be different from [for-profit] HMOs. They will still need to be solvent, still need to make a living and have a management structure, still need an MBA, accountants and lawyers to make it work.

Los Angeles Times, 11-25:(A)29.

Bill Frist
United States Senator, R-Tennessee

2

[Saying he will vote for confirmation of Dr. Henry Foster as Surgeon General, despite the reservations of other Republican Senators]: I know Hank Foster. I know him as a fellow Tennessean. I know him as a fellow physician and colleague who worked four miles from my office. And I know him as a fellow Nashvillian, who has done what few physicians do—step out of the operating room, out of the clinic, into their community to address the really tough problems in our society.

At Senate Labor and Human Resources Committee hearing on Foster's nomination, Washington, D.C., May 26/ Los Angeles Times, 5-27:(A)1.

Richard A. Gephardt
United States Representative, D-Missouri

3

We cannot change Medicare without changing the entire health system. If we hack away at Medicare year after year, all we're going to do is wreck Medicare.

Before National Legislative Council of American Association of Retired Persons, Washington, D.C./ AARP Bulletin, March:8.

Newt Gingrich
United States Representative, R-Georgia; Speaker of the House

4

We need a new set of strategies for health in America, we need new projects for health in America, and we need different tactics for health in America. It has to start with a vision of health care within a balanced Federal bud-

(NEWT GINGRICH)

get, but with every citizen having far more responsibility than they have today.

Before National Hospital Association, Washington, D.C., Jan. 30/ The New York Times, 1-31:(A)8.

1

We will improve Medicare by offering a series of new Medicare options that will increase senior citizens' control over their own health care and guarantee them access to the best and most modern systems of health research and health innovation . . . [And] no one will touch your Social Security, period . . . Our goals are simple. We don't want our children to drown in debt. We want baby-boomers to be able to retire with the same security as their parents. We want our senior Americans to be able to rely on Medicare without fear.

Broadcast address to the nation, Washington, D.C., April 7/ The New York Times, 4-8:8.

2

Our goal will be by September to bring in a bill that will save the Medicare system for a generation . . . What you currently have is a system designed to be a centralized bureaucracy, with all of the inefficiency and all of the obsolete technology and all the obsolete approaches and all the waste and fraud you would associate with a large centralized bureaucracy. Everything we've ever told [Russian President] Boris Yeltsin about centralized bureaucracies is also true of the [U.S.] Health Care Financing Administration.

Before Seniors Coalition, April 28/ The New York Times, 5-1:(A)14.

3

We [Republicans] have decided that we're taking Medicare into a separate box [isolating it from the rest of government-spending cuts]. Every penny saved in Medicare should go to Medicare. It should not be entangled in the budget debate.

April 30/ The New York Times, 5-1:(A)14.

4

[Criticizing the Clinton Administration for what he says are untrue negative forecasts about Republican plans to reform Medicare]: In an Administration whose capacity for truth is highly limited, their recent effort to scare senior citizens, I think, is among the most despicable I have seen, and it is patently false. [But] I don't detect any panic by senior citizens when a dishonest Administration issues another dishonest number.

At conference sponsored by Congressional Institute, Atlanta, Ga., Aug. 7/ The New York Times, 8-8:(A)8.

5

[Saying he believes the Republican Medicare-reform plan will result in more seniors leaving fee-for-service treatment to go into

(NEWT GINGRICH)

HMOs]: We don't get rid of [fee-for-service] in Round 1 because we don't think that's politically smart and we don't think that's the right way to go through a transition. But we believe it's going to wither on the vine because we think people are voluntarily going to leave it voluntarily—voluntarily.

Before Blue Cross/ Blue Shield Association, Washington, D.C., Oct. 24/ Los Angeles Times, 10-26:(A)16.

1

[Conceding that President Clinton has apparently had success in his campaign to sway public opinion against the Republican proposals for Medicare reform]: The President, frankly, was deliberately misinforming the American people . . . So he got an early advantage. But it's a year to the election. And in a free society, I think the truth beats the big lie.

Broadcast interview, Nov. 15/ Los Angeles Times, 11-16:(A)23.

Rudolph W. Giuliani
Mayor of New York, N.Y.

2

[On his plan to sell at least three of New York City's municipal hospitals]: The care in public hospitals is below what it should be, and it's below the care that people are entitled to. And the tragic part of it is that New York City spends more money on that care than any city in America, by a large margin . . . A lot of people are resisting [the plan to sell the hospitals]. There's a tremendous amount of internal union pressure. There's a tremendous amount of political pressure to keep it the way it is. [But] as each of these reports [about poor health care in these hospitals] comes out, it will underscore the need for reform that we've been championing for some time now.

To reporters, Staten Island, N.Y., March 5/ The New York Times, 3-6:(A)13.

Charlene A. Harrington
Professor, School of Nursing, University of California, San Francisco

3

[Criticizing Republican proposals to ease Federal quality standards for nursing homes]: Republicans say states will maintain standards for the quality of care. But states don't have the money. The money is being cut back, and states will not pay for either regulation or the nursing-home services needed to comply with those regulations. States will lower their nursing-home reimbursement rates, which are already outrageously low. Quality of care will deteriorate.

The New York Times, 10-7:8.

Earvin "Magic" Johnson
Former basketball player, Los Angeles "Lakers"

4

[On his being HIV-positive]: I don't know how long I'll live—who does? In the meantime, I'm proving to people who have the vi-

(EARVIN "MAGIC" JOHNSON)

rus that you don't have to hide in a corner and feel sorry for yourself. You can still accomplish a lot. And I'm showing people who aren't infected that you don't have to treat people with the virus any different than you did before. You can still be friends with them. There's a lot of discrimination toward people with the [HIV] virus—rejection by their family and friends, getting thrown out of their apartments, losing their jobs. But if you embrace them, if you love them, they'll trust you and love you back.

Paris, France/ Esquire, January:74.

Michael Kendrick
Physician;
President,
Central Oregon Independent
Physicians Association

1

[Criticizing the idea of having Medicare patients belong to HMOs]: To turn all of medicine into the hands of a bunch of primary-care people, pay them not to take care of people and give them incentives not to get things done to people is a terrible mistake.

Los Angeles Times, 11-24:(A)33.

David A. Kessler
Commissioner,
Food and Drug
Administration
of the United States

2

[On tobacco addiction among young people]: If we could affect the smoking habits of just one generation, we . . . could see nicotine go the way of smallpox and polio . . . A person who hasn't started smoking by age 19 is unlikely to ever become a smoker. Young people are the tobacco industry's primary source of new customers . . . replacing adults who have either quit or died . . . It is easy to think of smoking as an adult problem. It is adults who die from tobacco-related diseases. We see adults light up in a restaurant or bar. We see a colleague step outside for a cigarette break. But this is a dangerously shortsighted view. Nicotine addiction begins when most tobacco users are teenagers, so let's call this what it really is: a pediatric disease . . . It's a ritual that often, tragically, lasts a lifetime. And it is a ritual that can cut short that lifetime . . . We owe it to our children to help them enter adulthood free from addiction.

At Columbia University Law School, March 8/ Los Angeles Times, 3-9:(A)15.

John Kitzhaber
Governor
of Oregon (D)

3

[On his state's experience with Medicare HMOs]: Managed care is not as frightening a prospect to patients and providers here as it is in the rest of the country. I would defy anybody to show that our elderly population suffers any less quality of care than anywhere else in the country.

Los Angeles Times, 11-24:(A)33.

Calvin M. Kunin
Professor, Ohio State University School of Medicine; Former president, Infectious Diseases Society of America

1

[Saying antibiotics are being over-prescribed, which leads to resistant bacteria]: The old people in the nursing homes are going to die [because of the over-use and misuse of antibiotics], and the young kids with ear infections are going to progress to mastoiditis, sinusitis, meningitis. I think there ought to be a new organization called MAMA, Mothers Against the Misuse of Antibiotics. Because it's the mothers' children who are going to die.

The Washington Post, 6-26:(A)13.

Richard Kusserow
Former Inspector General, Department of Health and Human Services of the United States

2

[On fraud against the Medicare and Medicaid systems by doctors, hospitals, etc.]: There were always a limited amount of resources [for government investigations of such fraud]. When you think about the gigantic programs and the very limited number of investigators available, it's shocking. On the Federal side, there are only 125 [full-time] investigators. Now it's going to be cut again. You'll have 100 investigators left for some 250 programs, among them Medicare and Medicaid.

Mother Jones, March-April:71.

John Lewis
United States Representative, D-Georgia

3

[Criticizing the Republican Medicare-reform proposals]: A scam, a sham and a shame. I know it, you know it, now the American people know it. On this day, the 19th of October, let the word go forth from this place to every state, every city, every town, every village, every hamlet, that it was the Republicans who voted to cut Medicare . . . This vote, this debate is something more than one vote. It is bigger than one bill. It is about two contracts. The Republican contract with the rich, and the Democratic contract with the American people, Medicare.

Before the House, Washington, D.C., Oct. 19/ The New York Times, 10-20:(A)10.

Susan Love
Director, Revlon/UCLA Breast Center

4

We like to think that medicine is somehow pure and true and not influenced by market forces. But drug companies market so strongly to doctors—especially gynecologists—that some physicians lose their objectivity.

Interview/ U.S. News & World Report, 7-24:17.

William J. Mahon
Executive director,
National Health Care
Anti-Fraud Association

1

[On criticism of HMOs for delaying or denying care to patients]: [In managed-care,] there is a reversal of the profit motive. In managed care, a provider agrees to treat patient Jones for a fixed payment; and if he is unscrupulous about it, he will try to do as little as possible for patient Jones, to maximize profit. Where you have the provider assuming greater financial risk, you have a good starting point for susceptibility to fraud.

Los Angeles Times,
3-18:(D)1.

Michael D. McCurry
Press Secretary
to President
of the United States
Bill Clinton

2

[Criticizing the Republicans' proposals to reform Medicare, saying Republicans want Medicare to die]: You know, that's probably what they'd like to see happen to seniors, too, if you think about it.

Press briefing,
Washington, D.C., Oct. 26/
Los Angeles Times,
10-27:(A)12.

Walker Merryman
Vice president,
Tobacco Institute

3

[Criticizing FDA Commissioner David Kessler for blaming the tobacco industry for campaigning to hook young people on smoking]: There's no way in the world he can logically lay that on the doorstep of the tobacco industry. We don't have anything to do with creating or maintaining "childish curiosity" [about tobacco] or "a youthful need to rebel" [by taking up smoking].

March 8/
Los Angeles Times,
3-9:(A)15.

Dan Miller
United States Representative,
R-Florida

4

We [Republicans] agree with so many things that our [Democratic] colleagues on the other side of the aisle are talking about. We agree Medicare is going bankrupt and we need to save it. Where we disagree is: We don't want to just have a Band-Aid to fix it for a year or so. We want to fix it before the baby-boomers retire in the year 2010. We want to give choices. And it's amazing why the people on the other side [the Democrats] are opposed to choices . . . What's wrong with giving people the right to choose? We're going to give people the right to stay in the plan they have now . . . [But] those that want to choose a medical savings account—great! Let them choose it. Those that want to go [into] managed care—great! Let them choose it . . . [The Democrats] talk about $270-billion in cuts [to Medicare under Republican proposals]. [But] let's look at how much we're *increasing* it—whether the glass is half full or half empty. We [Republicans] are increasing spending on Medicare by $354-billion over seven years compared to the last seven years. That goes

(DAN MILLER)

from $4,800 to $6,700 [per person]. That is an increase.

Before the House, Washington, D.C., Oct. 19/ The New York Times, 10-20:(A)10.

Wendy Moyle
Nursing program coordinator, Griffith University (Australia)

1

Nursing education and health are generally so focused on the technical side of things. [But] being a good nurse is not just being able to push a button.

U.S. News & World Report, 11-6:17.

Susan Pisano
Spokeswoman, Group Health Association of America

2

HMOs are the one system where we have every incentive—medical, philosophical, financial—to make sure people get the appropriate treatment promptly.

Los Angeles Times, 3-18:(D)2.

Dan Quayle
Former Vice President of the United States

3

[On the controversy over the nomination by President Clinton of Dr. Henry Foster to be Surgeon General]: When you nominate someone for Surgeon General, you ought to have a person that can unify the country as much as possible. And when you have someone [like Foster] that has performed a number of abortions, there will be a large segment of the population . . . that will be opposed to that. The White House did not do its homework. This was handled poorly and shows incompetence.

Broadcast interview/ "Meet the Press," NBC-TV, 2-12.

Charles B. Rangel
United States Representative, D-New York

4

I know that Republicans have fought Medicare from the inception. Every time it comes up, you've [Republicans] always been there. Always been there to vote it down. And here you come again, where hospitals that service the poorest of the poor, in the rural areas, in the inner cities, when they have no support system, there you are reducing the benefits. [Republicans] get up here time and time again saying that's just not so. Well, why don't you go to the hospital people and ask them why they believe that you're destroying them. Why don't you go to those that are in nursing homes and ask why they are so frightened [by Republican Medicare-reform proposals].

Before the House, Washington, D.C., Oct. 19/ The New York Times, 10-20:(A)10.

Kenneth E. Raske
President, Greater New York Hospital Association

5

[Criticizing Republican proposals to cut

(KENNETH E. RASKE)

the growth in Medicare spending]: What people need to understand is that these cuts reach beyond the Medicare population. There is no such thing in a hospital as a Medicare nurse or a Medicaid nurse or a Blue Cross-Blue Shield nurse. Hospitals combine different streams of revenue to pay for everything they do, and so cuts in Medicare payments affect everyone who comes through their doors.

The New York Times,
10-21:1.

Robert B. Reich
Secretary of Labor
of the United States

1

[On the hearing, which he is attending, being held by some House Democrats on the White House lawn, in the rain, to protest that Republicans are shutting them out of the Medicare-reform process]: In some ways, it's absurd that we're out here. In some ways it's funny. In some ways it's pathetic. But it is symbolic, on a day like this, of what is now transpiring.

At the Democrats'
outside hearing,
Washington, D.C.,
Sept. 22/
The New York Times,
9-23:1.

Uwe E. Reinhardt
Professor
of political economy,
Princeton University

2

[On the growing competition among hospitals for patients]: What you have on now is a hunt for bodies.

The New York Times,
4-29:16.

Robert D. Reischauer
Senior fellow,
Brookings Institution;
Former Director,
Congressional
Budget Office

3

[On suggestions that "managed care" programs for the elderly would save Medicare money]: There is some hope that managed care might save money, but not in the next few years. Managed care involves structural changes that take time to implement, and it requires a marketing campaign to convince beneficiaries that it is in their interest. That will take a long time.

The New York Times,
5-2:(A)13.

Fortney H. "Pete" Stark
United States Representative,
D-California

4

Any Medicare beneficiary can go to any physician in the United States, if they can afford the fare to get there. They can go to any hospital in the United States. They can join a wide variety of approved HMOs. There is no insurance plan in the country that offers a broader choice than Medicare.

Jan. 30/
The New York Times,
1-31:(A)8.

Gerald Stern
Special Counsel
for Health Care Fraud,
Department of Justice
of the United States

1

[On the growing incidence of fraud in the health-care industry]: It's small providers, it's large companies. It is even those who are not in the health-care industry but prey upon the system, not providing health care but creating scams.

To reporters,
Washington, D.C.,
March 2/
Los Angeles Times,
3-3:(D)2.

Alan A. Stone
Professor
of law and medicine,
Harvard University

2

[On managed-care health-care systems]: You get paid a certain amount of money at the beginning of the year to treat a certain number of people. The more you have left at the end of the year, the richer you are. A patient comes in with a stomachache, and you say, "Here's an antacid. Don't bother me." When you introduced the profit motive into health care, the whole industry became permeated with greed . . . Ordinary market principles cannot apply to the health-care industry. The basic problem is the problem of information. The patient knows he's sick, but he relies on the physician to identify the illness. Take the doctor in Rhode Island who implanted a pacemaker into every elderly patient who came in. He was putting pacemakers into every patient with mild congestive failure, just to make money. But how were the patients to know that?

Mother Jones,
March-April:74.

Thomas A. Travers
Vice president
for health-care delivery,
Oxford Health Plan

3

[On major hospitals which previously shunned managed-care organizations such as his, but now need patients and want to become allied with such companies]: In 1987, I would have loved to have had [New York's] Mount Sinai or some of these other places on our panel. They would listen cordially [to us]; [but] then they would remind us who they were and that they didn't need us. Now that we have over 353,000 covered lives [patient-members], I get at least three calls a day from people and facilities in the greater New York area making a pitch to us.

The New York Times,
4-29:16.

Reed Tuckson
President,
Charles Drew University
of Medicine and Science

4

[Criticizing proposed Congressional cuts in Medicaid spending growth]: There can be no question the impact would be extraordinary. People are going to die by the thousands, and their deaths will not make it on the [political] radar screen.

Los Angeles Times,
7-27:(A)22.

Sten Vermund
Chairman,
department of epidemiology,
University of Alabama,
Birmingham

1

[To fight AIDS,] we have to have the political will to make investments in drug treatment and drug control [among illegal-drug users, especially in inner cities]. If we are hostile to drug [-abuse] treatment and job creation, then the epidemic will rage . . . I'm talking about removing the waiting lists for drug treatment. Now a motivated addict who wants treatment in a city like New York is put on a waiting list for six months. That is a national disgrace . . . It's a tough nut to crack. [But] we pay the price, and not merely in diseases like HIV and sexually transmitted diseases and hepatitis, but also in our crime losses and correctional institutions. [As a society,] we reap what we sow.

The New York Times, 2-28:(B)6.

Ron Wyden
United States Representative,
D-Oregon

2

[Criticizing the way Medicare's regional insurance-company administrators handle the approval process of Medicare claims]: The government's loose reins on these private insurance contractors has produced a program in which Medicare doesn't pay claims that should be paid, Medicare pays claims that ought to be denied, and doesn't have a systematic approach to knowing the difference. This free-lance approach to Medicare management has produced an astonishing degree of inequity for elderly citizens.

AARP Bulletin, March:2.

The Performing Arts

BROADCASTING

Richard K. Armey
United States Representative,
R-Texas

1

[Criticizing a proposal requiring all TV sets to be equipped with a "V-chip" to allow parents to block out programs they don't want their children to watch]: [Such an idea is] so typical of liberal Democrats: First, let's make sure we advocate something that is not currently available—it's probably 10 years—that's going to be very costly, and then make it mandatory . . . [Parents must] exercise, in their own viewing habits, good judgment and good taste [to limit objectionable programming]. If we quit, for example, watching smutty shows, people will quit producing smutty shows.

At National Press Club,
Washington, D.C., July 19/
Daily Variety,
7-20:8.

William J. Bennett
Former Secretary of Education
of the United States

2

The worst of television is the daytime talk shows . . . In these shows, indecent exposure is celebrated as a virtue. It is hard to remember now, but there once was a time when personal or marital failure were accompanied by guilt or embarrassment. But today, these conditions are a ticket to appear as a guest on the Sally Jessy Raphael show, the Ricki Lake show, the Jerry Springer show, or one of the dozen or so like him . . . The shows we target are not close calls. They're the bottom of the barrel . . . This is a test on whether there is a sense of shame in the broadcast industry.

News conference,
Washington, D.C., Oct. 26/
Los Angeles Times,
10-27:(A)19;
Daily Variety,
10-27:13.

Matthew Blank
President,
Showtime Networks

3

[On the proposed "V-chip," which would allow parents to lock out objectionable TV programs they do not want their children to watch]: We have some serious societal issues here. The V-chip seems like an overly simple solution to a very complicated problem.

Time,
7-24:64.

Leo Bogart
Sociologist;
Specialist in communications

4

[Criticizing TV for a lack of quality, responsible programming]: I see an erosion of the conscience that may have troubled TV executives in the past . . . [TV] is increasingly controlled by a handful of people who wield enormous power, but whose interests and energies are spread too thin to permit them to take pride in any non-commercial aspect of their endeavors.

Interview/
Daily Variety,
6-14:38.

David E. Bonior
United States Representative, D-Michigan

1

[Supporting proposed legislation that would require TV sets to be equipped with a "V-chip" to allow parents to lock out violent and other types of programs they don't want their children to watch]: Parents should be the ones who choose what kind of shows come into their homes, not some programmers in New York. We believe parents should be able to choose to let [PBS'] Big Bird in, and keep *The Texas Chainsaw Massacre* out.

Daily Variety, 7-14:20.

Allan Burns
Producer

2

Television is cyclical. In three years they'll be back to family shows. A new *Cosby* show will come around and everybody will be looking for those. All the networks want to do original things, but they don't want to be the first ones to do it. Everything will be aimed toward the 25-35-year-old audience, at the exclusion of everything else, until a different type of show slips in there and works.

Daily Variety, 6-12:56.

James Burrows
Director

3

I think somebody told me there are now 59 half-hours [of comedy shows on TV]. And there are probably really good writers for about 20 percent of those. It's a little bit like the National Football League: There are so many teams now that the quality of players, the average quality, has diminished. I think that's true of television . . . Good writing—that's the paramount thing. You need good writing.

Interview, Universal City, Calif./ American Way, 12-1:92.

Stephen J. Cannell
Producer, Writer

4

[Criticizing those in the U.S. Congress who want to crack down on violence in TV programming]: I just think we [in TV] are being scapegoated by a bunch of unpopular Congressmen and an Attorney General [Janet Reno], and I think it is really depressing. It is so transparent. One of the things I have found is that there are no advocates for TV. Even in our own business, if you ask executives what their favorite shows are, they say they don't really watch TV. They work here but don't really watch it. There is this whole attitude that TV is trash and if you smack us around it's okay. These people can attack us without any fear. We are the perfect target. The fact of the matter is that if you were to give an MPAA rating to what you saw on TV, most of it would be a PG, including my action [shows]. Canada gets all the same TV we [in the U.S.] get and has nowhere near the violence. So what's the difference? Hey, maybe it is environmental.

Interview/ Daily Variety, 8-17:48.

Bill Carroll
Vice president and director of programming, Katz Television

1

[On criticism that many TV talk shows are sleazy]: There's a definite feeling that a lot of these talk shows are going too far, that they've become too outrageous and exploitative. Producers say the audience is demanding that guests lay bare their innermost feelings and secrets. But that's not a justification. These shows are tapping into volatile situations and the rage of some of these guests is genuine and real.

Daily Variety, 3-13:30.

Peggy Charren
Founder, Action for Children's Television

2

[Saying TV lacks enough quality programming for teenagers]: It's teenagers that we keep talking about when we talk about trouble in America. We talk about teenagers on the street corners, teenagers on drugs. All the problems we focus on teenagers and yet we don't want to take care of them. We don't want to build recreational facilities, we don't want to make sure their high schools work, and we don't want to do anything about their television programming . . . If [individual] stations wanted to, they could make the networks do better [teen programming], but stations don't care. They want the largest number of eyeballs on those commercials.

Interview/ Daily Variety, 6-14:33,34.

Bill Clinton
President of the United States

3

[Criticizing some radio talk shows]: [The nation's airwaves are frequently used] to keep some people as paranoid as possible and the rest of us all torn up and upset with each other. They spread hate; they leave the impression that, by their very words, that violence is acceptable . . . It is time we all stood up and spoke against that kind of reckless speech and behavior. When they talk of violence, we must stand against them. When they say things that are irresponsible, that may have egregious consequences, we must call them on it.

To community-college educators, Minneapolis, Minn., April 24/ The Washington Post, 4-25:(A)1.

4

[Arguing against proposals to lift the ceiling on TV-station ownership limits]: I do think it would be an error to set up a situation in the United States where one person could own half the television stations in the country, or half of the media outlets; and we don't have a Fairness Doctrine anymore, and we don't have . . . any kind of maintenance of competition or any kind of maintenance of a competitive environment. [The U.S. has] the most successful telecommunications operations in the world, partly because we have had the proper balance between a highly competitive environment and an openness to new forces and new technologies and new entries in it from all around the world.

News briefing, Washington, D.C., Aug. 1/ Daily Variety, 8-2:3.

Richard Dominick
Executive producer,
"The Jerry Springer Show"

1

[Defending daytime TV talk shows, such as his, that critics say are harming society because of the perversion they present]: I don't think daytime talk shows are putting drug dealers or gang members on the street. There is not a pregnant teen who blames [talk-show host] Ricki Lake for getting pregnant, and [convicted killer] Susan Smith didn't kill her children because she watched Jerry Springer. We take real people with real lives and real issues and put them on TV. These shows are one of the only forums left for an average person to go and speak their mind. That's what makes this country so great.

Oct. 26/
Los Angeles Times,
10-27:(A)19.

Burt Dubrow
Television
talk-show producer

2

[Responding to criticism that daytime TV talk shows are too sleazy]: How has talk [TV] had a negative effect on the country? If these shows are influencing the country, then that is fascinating. Should [the critics] be telling us what [soap operas] to watch? Maybe we shouldn't watch [the nighttime hit hospital series] *ER* because it has too much blood . . . Most people or a lot of people watch these [daytime talk] shows for the entertainment value, and the audience is hip enough to know that when some nut starts yelling, it is not serious.

Daily Variety,
10-27:13.

Ervin S. Duggan
President,
Public Broadcasting Service

3

[On proposals to cut Federal funding for PBS]: The fundamental nature and mission of the system changes [if public funding is cut]. And inevitably, just another commercial channel would be the result . . . Public television cannot serve the gods of education, culture and citizenship and also serve the god of commerce at the same time. It cannot be done.

USA Today,
1-9:(D)2.

4

Take away public broadcasting's [government-supplied] seed funding and you force it headlong into the alien world of ad agencies and costs-per-thousand and merchandising, rather than the world of teachers and historians and community volunteers.

Interview/
Christianity Today,
3-6:43.

5

[Criticizing suggestions that PBS be privatized and its stations become commercial channels]: As newly minted commercial licensees—faced with the necessity to generate millions in new revenue—consider what will happen to their programming decisions. Inevitably, those decisions will be driven more and more by the need to attract mass viewership. And so these "non-profit commercial" licensees will become competitive bidders not only for advertising dollars, but also for viewers and programs that once were the preserve of commercial broadcasters . . . We have lots of commercial television, but only

(ERVIN S. DUGGAN)

one PBS—only one television service whose mission is clearly cultural, educational and non-commercial; only one quality alternative which reaches every home and doesn't send out a monthly bill of $30 to $50.

Before International Radio & Television Society, New York, N.Y., April 11/ Daily Variety, 4-12:4.

1

[Criticizing those who want to cut Federal funding of PBS]: Certainly if one wants to have real impact on the Federal budget, public television is not the place to begin. So I can only conclude that the effect on public television is primarily done for symbolic value. And one could say generally about symbolism that in the old Judaic ritual of the sacrifice of the lamb, the symbolism may have been very powerful and useful for everybody except the lamb.

Interview, Alexandria, Va./ The New York Times, 6-26:(B)4.

Fred Franzwa
Vice president, Kodak Motion Picture and Television Imaging

2

[On criticism of the lack of quality, responsible TV programming]: The success and longevity of the medium is a big factor to us at Kodak since so much of our business is film. We are aware—and always have been—that television has a tremendous responsibility. We are anxious to bring to the table a range of issues that need to be discussed . . . We don't want to wake up 10 years from now and ask, "Was someone asleep at the switch?"

Interview/ Daily Variety, 6-14:36.

Larry Gelbart
Playwright, Screenwriter

3

Truth to tell, there's probably more [respect for writers] in television than in film. Writers are so necessary to the lifeblood of television production that they have a different, more powerful, position than they do in films.

Interview, Palm Springs, Calif./ Writer's Digest, April:39.

Newt Gingrich
United States Representative, R-Georgia; Speaker of the House-designate

4

[Calling for cutting Federal funding of PBS]: [The late President] Lyndon Johnson created this little sandbox for the rich, and they love it, and they give out the money to the particular producer they favor. I'm glad they love [PBS commentator] Bill Moyers. [But] Bill Moyers can get programs funded [elsewhere]; he doesn't need to take it from the taxpayer . . . [PBS children's character] Big Bird makes money; Barney makes money. These are profit-making centers; they would survive just fine [without Federal funding] . . . I understand why the elite wants the money, but I think they ought to be honest.

(NEWT GINGRICH)

These are a bunch of rich, upper-class people who want their toy [PBS] to play with.

Broadcast interview/ C-SPAN, 1-2.

1

[Saying government funding for PBS should not be eliminated]: The Federal government should keep national assets.

U.S. New & World Report, 7-24:14.

2

If you were to look at the five most popular [daytime] talk shows in America in terms of television, and look at the level of ignorance and misinformation which substitutes for learning, you would understand better why we are an increasingly ignorant culture.

Speech, Atlanta, Ga., Oct. 30/ Daily Variety, 10-31:5.

Al Gore
Vice President of the United States

3

[Criticizing Republicans who want to cut Federal funding for PBS]: If you're like most Americans, you will see what a great value [PBS] is . . . Ask the 40 percent of Americans who don't have cable. Ask the parents and teachers . . . if [the] *Mr. Rogers* [program] is "elitist" [as critics say of PBS] or if *Sesame Street* is elitist. Their kids will tell you right quick they don't want any epithets applied to Mr. Rogers. What sounds elitist is the small group of ideologues in Washington, D.C., telling the American people that public broadcasting isn't good for them. When the overwhelming majority of the American people say [they] support it, leave it alone.

At American University, March 2/ Daily Variety, 3-3:5.

Phil Gramm
United States Senator, R-Texas; Candidate for the 1996 Republican Presidential nomination

4

My mother about five years ago called me up and said, "Phil, you got to do something about the sex on the [TV] soap operas. I've gotten to where I can hardly watch them. They're either gettin' into bed or gettin' out of bed." So I go to visit her at Thanksgiving and one o'clock comes. She turns on the television, and she says, "Don't bother me, I can hardly keep up with my soap opera." And so I say, "Mother, if you don't like it, turn it off. If you don't want to watch it, don't buy the products of the people who advertise." My view is that every institution in America should be more responsible, and so should the entertainment industry. But we [the audience] have to be more responsible too.

Interview, Savannah, Ga./ Vogue, September:608.

Jeff Greenfield
Correspondent, ABC News

5

[Criticizing TV talk and "tabloid" shows]: To put it as bluntly as I can, why shouldn't people believe in television's capacity to con-

(JEFF GREENFIELD)

tribute to societal breakdown, or to crime, or to violence, when we prove every morning, every afternoon and every evening that we can be supremely indifferent to the way we treat vulnerable and helpless human beings [on those shows] . . . It does not help TV's cause one bit that lots of people love to watch these shows. We all know that we do not always reach for the highest shelf in the library of good taste . . . Just sit back one afternoon, and turn on the set and realize that what you are seeing is a result of the deliberate, conscious decisions of some of the most powerful, respected people in this business—that this is what we choose to put over the public airwaves . . . and it would not be there if we did not want it to be.

Before National Association of Broadcasters, Las Vegas, Nev./ Daily Variety, 4-11:16.

Charles Grodin
Actor;
TV talk-show host

1

[On being a talk-show host]: Very few people have an interest in other people, and very often the people who are hosting talk shows are the last people that have an interest in other people . . . I don't think people really understand what makes a good host. If I was producing a [talk] show, I would ask [a prospective host], "Are you interested in people? Are you comfortable in front of a camera? Would you be comfortable talking in front of an audience? Do you have a wide variety of interests?" But [when I was hired] nobody asked me even one of those questions. They just said they wanted me because I was funny as a guest on *[David] Letterman* or something.

Interview, Fort Lee, N.J./ Vogue, May:168.

Billy Grundfest
Producer

2

[Saying the TV audience wants more authentic characters and stories]: We are an affluent society where people can afford to live by themselves. People are isolated from each other and, as a result, their primary relationship is with that box [the TV set]. What they want is not escape but a connection to something that feels like human reality.

Daily Variety, 6-12:42.

Reed E. Hundt
Chairman,
Federal Communications Commission

3

[Saying the FCC has a role to play in ensuring that there is adequate children's programming on TV]: I'm not suggesting that government should control content. I'm suggesting that because broadcasters have the spectrum for free . . . we should make sure that they have the opportunity to create some suitable programming if they want a guarantee that their license will be renewed. We want to avoid creating a big, vicious, meddlesome

(REED E. HUNDT)

bureaucracy, but we also want the communications revolution to include all Americans.

Interview/
The Christian Science Monitor,
5-3:4.

Larry Irving
Administrator,
National Telecommunications and Information Administration of the United States

1

[Arguing against lifting rules that bar foreign ownership of more than 25 percent of U.S. radio and TV properties]: We should not be too hasty in lifting restrictions on the amount of foreign influence over, or control of, broadcast licenses due to the editorial discretion of broadcasters over the content of transmissions . . . It doesn't make sense to open [U.S. radio and TV stations] to foreign concerns.

Before Senate
Commerce Committee,
Washington, D.C.,
March 2/Daily Variety, 3-3:1.

Tommy Lee Jones
Actor

2

[On the "information superhighway"]: It's a monstrous industry with enormous tentacles, and I don't know if we can control it to the betterment of mankind or not. It goes all through life, and it affects government, politics, culture, the spiritual quality of our lives. Think of the difference between how people spent their evenings before the advent of television, when you were a boy, and how people spend their evenings now. What has that done to the decent art of conversation?

Interview,
San Saba, Texas/
"Interview" magazine,
June:110.

Larry King
Television and radio talk-show host

3

[On being a talk-show host]: I ask very short questions [of his guests]. I leave myself out of it—I don't use the word *I*. But since childhood I always knew I had a way of making people respond to me, and I was sincerely interested in what they had to say. People fascinate me, and I think I transmit that. And I'm not there to embarrass them . . . What matters to me is the four things I want in an interview: passion, a sense of humor, a little anger and an ability to explain what you do very well.

Interview/
Ladies' Home Journal,
August:54.

Norman Lear
Writer, Producer

4

The [TV] networks are in the business of short-term, bottom-line thinking. In television that translates into, "Give me a hit on Tuesday night at 8:30, and [forget] everything else" . . . Any idea that inherently requires some time for the audience to get acclimated to . . . has no opportunity to develop.

The Christian Science Monitor,
8-16:12.

David Levy
Secretary,
The Caucus for Producers,
Writers & Directors

1

[TV and cable are examples of] instruments of mass communication that have become, in a substantial way, contributors to the cultural pollution engulfing us. [Broadcasting has become] something of a murky swamp—as dangerous to our well-being as environmental pollution. [The best TV] does not need the crutch of profanity, of excessive violence, or titillating sex to capture audience numbers. [TV and cable producers should] acknowledge their moral responsibilities to programming in the interest of the general welfare of the nation.

Interview/
Daily Variety,
6-14:36.

Ann Lewis
Vice President,
Planned Parenthood;
Democratic Party
activist

2

[On the proliferation of politically oriented radio talk shows]: The old media acted as gatekeepers, deciding what people should know. The new media involves the "democratization" of political knowledge. Ordinary people are taking over some of that power, and often in a more honest way. Talk-show hosts don't masquerade as "objective journalists."

The Wall Street Journal,
4-4:(A)14.

Joseph I. Lieberman
United States Senator,
D-Connecticut

3

[Criticizing daytime TV talk shows]: These shows have enormous potential to act as the worst kind of sex educators. [It is] clear that talk is indeed cheap—and too often on those shows demeaning, exploitative, perverted, divisive, or, at best, amoral . . . The proliferation of perversion on daytime television [talk shows] is affecting our entire society by the example it sets, pushing the envelope of civility and morality in a way that drags the rest of the culture down with it. It is a vicious circle, fueled by the competition among talk-show hosts to be the most sensational, and one with no apparent end in sight.

News conference,
Washington, D.C.,
Oct. 26/
Daily Variety,
10-27:13;
Los Angeles Times,
10-27:(A)19.

Edward J. Markey
United States Representative,
D-Massachusetts

4

[On suggestions that U.S. law be changed to permit foreigners to own more than 25 percent of American broadcast properties]: I have real problems with foreign interests controlling ABC, CBS and NBC for the same reason that [Americans] won't be able to purchase networks in Paris, Tokyo or Berlin. This is central to the control of culture.

Daily Variety,
5-4:22.

Newton N. Minow
Former Chairman,
Federal Communications Commission

1

[Saying TV lacks enough quality programming for young people]: I don't know of any TV executive who gets up in the morning and says, "How many children can I harm today?" What one meets are people who simply don't think about it; who don't think that quality is any of their business. What I often hear is, "It's just an entertainment medium." And those who say that are belittling their own importance, when you consider that kids spend more time today with television than with their teachers. We have a mind-set today that dictates that selling eyeballs [audience size] is the nature of the business. I know some in the industry who say with pride, "I don't let my children watch what I produce" . . . In 1961, I worried that my children would not benefit much from television. Today, I worry that my grandchildren will actually be harmed by it.

Interview/
Daily Variety,
6-14:38.

Don Ohlmeyer
President
of West Coast operations,
NBC-TV

2

[Saying TV networks should not be expected to limit their primetime programming to shows that are appropriate for children]: It is not the role of network television to program for the children of America . . . Television's obligation is not [to be] the nation's babysitter.

Before Television
Critics Association,
Pasadena, Calif./
Daily Variety, 7-18:3.

James Quello
Commissioner,
Federal Communications Commission

3

[Criticizing FCC Chairman Reed Hundt's call for quotas to ensure sufficient TV children's programming]: Any activist claim of a "marketplace failure" in children's programming is a farcical notion in today's multicultural, multifaceted era, and represents only the viewer's failure to locate the desired programs . . . It is simply not right to treat the First Amendment as an inconvenient impediment to regulatory empire-building.

Before Media Institute,
Washington, D.C., Nov. 14/
Daily Variety,
11-15:21.

Geraldo Rivera
Television talk-show host

4

[On those who criticize TV talk shows for presenting sleaze]: They're on to something. The frayed edges [of these shows] should be cut off. These shows have great relevance to tens of millions, but sometimes the moral message is obscured by a burlesque theater. What comes next? Fornication on the air?

Newsweek,
11-6:46.

Ira Rosen
Senior producer
for investigations,
"PrimeTime Live,"
ABC-TV

1

[On TV "magazine" shows]: The journalism makes the piece. Good characters are important, but the key is to tell me something I didn't know. Surprise me. That takes reporting, working the story, time. Today, it's patient kills doctor, let's go get it. You would have 12 bookers from 12 magazine shows, none knowing what the story really was, offering the killer 30 minutes on the air.

Esquire,
January:80.

Scott Sassa
President,
Turner Entertainment Group

2

In the near future, when we have expanded distribution and total interactivity, the consumer won't need to subscribe to a 24-hour [TV] channel. He or she will just get it on demand. The future won't be 500 channels—it will be one channel, *your* channel. So instead of subscribing to some a la carte, 24-hour channel, you'll just get the show you want on demand, whenever you want it. It'll be W-cubed: whatever, wherever and whenever you want it.

Interview/
The Wall Street Journal,
2-16:(A)16.

Diane Sawyer
Anchor, ABC News

3

[On "magazine" or "reality" TV programs]: This is not the way of the future. This *is* the future. Reality is riveting. It has so depleted the material of fiction that entertainment cannot keep up.

Interview,
New York, N.Y./
Esquire,
January:78.

Andrew Schwartzman
Executive director,
Media Access Project

4

[Criticizing a just-passed Senate bill with sweeping changes in TV and communications regulations]: There is a strong prospect of a veto of this bill in light of the concentration and anti-competitive problems created by this legislation. Right now the only thing that will certainly happen as a result of this bill is that cable [TV] rates will go up. Everything else in the legislation is premised on the development of competition that does not yet exist, and may never come to pass.

June 15/
Los Angeles Times,
6-16:(A)30.

Ruth Seymour
General manager, KCRW
(Los Angeles Public Radio station)

5

[Criticizing attempts to cut Federal spending for public TV and radio]: We feel this is a public trust. Those of us who are in the business feel we are extraordinarily talented. After all, we get people to pay for something they can listen to for free. It's a real challenge. We are also idealists. When we make a vow, we don't make it on behalf of my own job—

(RUTH SEYMOUR)

I can get a job elsewhere. We make it on behalf of a cause, something we believe in. We would be derelict in our responsibility if we didn't fight to preserve it. The public will support stations which are passionate about their mission, their responsibility to serve the public.

Interview,
Santa Monica, Calif./
Los Angeles Times,
1-22:(M)3.

Donna E. Shalala
Secretary of Health
and Human Services
of the United States

1

[Criticizing daytime TV talk shows]: You could fill hour after hour with shows that are bizarre, carnival-esque or even degrading. But we surely don't gain anything, and indeed we lose, when we spotlight absurd antisocial or even violent behavior and portray it as the norm . . . After you [talk-show producers] deliver the heat, I challenge you to add some light. You know what separates an "issue" show from a "tissue" show. Instead of having 95 percent of the show be conflict and 5 percent resolution, I believe we can strike a better balance. [It is understandable that programs] need to be ever mindful of the [financial] bottom line. But there is another role and another bottom line that I'm challenging you to pay more attention to: It's your role as professionals, as citizens, and as guardians of the public trust.

Before Talk Summit,
New York, N.Y., Oct. 27/
Daily Variety, 10-30:3.

Paul Simon
United States Senator,
D-Illinois

2

[On proposed legislation that would require TV sets to be equipped with a "V-chip" to allow parents to lock out violent and other types of programs they don't want their children to watch]: We have to be careful about where we go in terms of government involvement. I don't want the V-chip to become a proxy that will allow the [TV] industry to shift responsibility [for violent programs] to parents.

The New York Times,
7-13:(C)4.

Tom Snyder
Television
talk-show host

3

[Years ago,] I discovered radio, and to this day I love it. I love it more than I will ever love television because, to me, it is the most intimate and the most powerful medium in all broadcasting. The 5½ years that I worked for ABC Radio were the best years of my life.

Interview,
Los Angeles, Calif./
Los Angeles Times,
1-1:(Calendar)3.

John Spratt, Jr.
United States Representative,
D-South Carolina

4

[Supporting proposed legislation that would require TV sets to be equipped with a "V-chip" to allow parents to lock out violent and other types of programs they don't want their children to watch]: We're trying to chill

(JOHN SPRATT, JR.)

the violence, the vulgarity, the bloodshed that's coming into TV sets.

Daily Variety,
7-14:20.

Rod Steiger
Actor

1

The ability to replay scenes over and over in film and television today can make mediocre talent into stars. So can good film editors. But in live television, you had to be good. You had to be able to improvise your way out of mistakes in front of millions of people. So those actors in the early years of television came from the stage where they had been well trained. Even so, I've always contended that if actors could visualize that many people watching, they would drop dead right there.

Interview,
Malibu, Calif./
The American Patriot,
Summer:6.

Peter Strauss
Actor

2

Television is in a particular "women's period." They are the central focus. It makes playing interesting men more difficult to find. The characters in movies are more dark and sophisticated, and there's less chance for that in television. In the last few roles I've played in TV, it's really been limited to men who were either brutalizing, or being brutalized by, women.

Interview, New York, N.Y./
Daily Variety,
4-25:41.

Howard Stringer
Chairman, Tele-TV;
Former president,
CBS/
Broadcast Group

3

[On the quality of TV programming]: During the late part of the 20th century, Americans, in the guise of being democratic, have become so aggressively egalitarian and anti-elitist, many feel that only the lowest denominator will sell. Actually, there are plenty of notable exceptions to that. I think there is some great writing on television today. [But] ours is a quantitative society, not a qualitative one. We judge politicians by polls, business by quarterly reports, movies by the box office and television by ratings. None of this relates to quality. This is where democracies, in the end, get themselves in trouble.

Interview/
Daily Variety,
6-14:38.

4

[Comparing broadcast TV with cable TV]: Broadcasting is restricted by economics. Which is to say, you have to have 23 episodes of every program, and you have to appeal to as many people as you can get to satisfy the advertisers. Cable television initially started to imagine itself as a "niche" [specialty] programmer, but then got trapped into wanting higher ratings just like everybody else.

Interview,
Beverly Hills, Calif./
Esquire,
August:75.

(HOWARD STRINGER)

1

In the '70s and '80s, the [U.S. TV] networks were, by their nature, much like the BBC in England. Their job was to preserve traditions, and preserve standards, and maintain this and maintain that. All very appealing and understandable. But it nonetheless became very dated by events. Once the marketplace crossed international borders, the rules changed dramatically.

USA Today,
8-4:(B)4.

Tom Tauke
Executive vice president
for government affairs,
Nynex Corporation

2

[Supporting a just-passed Senate bill with sweeping changes in TV and communications regulation]: The consumer groups [that are against the bill] are locked into the mind-set that the only way consumers can be protected is by heavy government regulation. But the monopoly model no longer fits the technology or the marketplace.

June 15/
Los Angeles Times,
6-16:(A)30.

Jack Valenti
President,
Motion Picture Association
of America

3

[Criticizing legislative proposals to deal with the problem of violent, sexual and other types of TV programming many deem objectionable]: I most respectfully suggest to the Congress that a quick surge to legislative judgment without knowing where that law takes you is neither prudent nor sensible. Passing laws without first exposing the hazards of invading that place where governments should not go doesn't fit our governing system . . . [We must return to the] essential civic duty of individual responsibility. We have the right not to watch television programs we do not find suitable to our families . . . But if we don't exercise these rights, do we blame someone else for our derelictions? . . . [The TV industry] must and will rise to the challenge of responsibility and do that which is right to be done. We are obligated to do no less.

Before Los Angeles
World Affairs Council,
July 20/
Daily Variety,
7-21:7.

Oprah Winfrey
Television
talk-show host

4

[On whether, as a pioneer of the TV talk show, she feels any responsibility for today's glut of what many people believe are sleazy and exploitive talk shows]: No, I absolutely do not. What I feel is that, just as *Donahue* created the path for me, I have created the path for a lot of other people. The reason why there are so many talk shows today is because people were specifically coming after the Oprah deal and looking for the bucks. But how each host has chosen to use their voice is not my responsibility . . . From the beginning, my philosophy has been that people deserve to come to and to leave [my show] with their dignity. I never did what you see on the air today—nowhere close to it—because I never wanted people to be humiliated and embarrassed. And that is why I will not accept any kind of responsibility for the crap that we see on TV every day.

Interview/
Ebony,
July:23.

MOTION PICTURES

Gillian Armstrong
Australian director

1

Hollywood *is* hard on women. It's still that terrible cliche that when men stand up for what they believe in, it's considered artistic expression; a woman is being a troublemaker and a bitch.

Interview, New York, N.Y/
The New York Times,
3-8:(B)2.

Robert Benton
Director

2

That ability [of a director] to use an actor to anchor a film just by their presence is really something. I mean, what [Ingmar] Bergman does with just a closeup of Ingrid Thulin or Bibi Andersson is extraordinary. And it has nothing to do with stardom; it has to do with knowing the power of certain faces.

Interview/
Film Comment,
Jan.-Feb.:45.

Jeff Berg
Chairman,
International Creative
Management (talent agency)

3

Reformatting content has been a critical part of entertainment economics for years. It has been most pronounced in the music business in the last 20 years, where we have seen LPs, cartridges and cassettes, CDs, and now mini-CDs. New delivery systems have constantly driven the music catalogue, and each title can be sold all over again. The same thing is now happening in film. Just 15 years ago, there was no such thing as home video. There's a high likelihood that the movie cassette will be replaced by some form of laser disk, and eventually we'll see on-line [home computer] delivery. Technology will always provide artists with new outlets for their work.

Interview,
Beverly Hills, Calif./
The Red Herring,
February:77.

John Boorman
Director

4

When we're making films, we're struggling to speak a language we can't quite grasp. It's a curious thing. Film-making is such a groping process from script to shooting to editing, it's constantly taking two steps forwards and two steps back. It's as though you're half blind, as though it's a foreign language that we don't really yet quite understand. I feel that's because we're groping toward connecting film to the unconscious, and in good films this is only achieved in odd moments, those marvelous cinematic moments that we all recognize where suddenly everything comes together and there's this extraordinary jolt of recognition—something extraordinary's been achieved or understood, we've penetrated the impenetrable surface of the world and reached something that lies underneath.

Interview/
Film Comment,
July-Aug.:49.

(JOHN BOORMAN)

1

The process of film-making is taking material things—wood and metal, sets and costumes, technology and equipment and money—and transforming them into light. That's why it's always difficult to get money to make films, because you take all this money and these resources and all you have at the end of the day is a light flickering on the screen. It's true that chemistry is involved, emulsions and celluloid; but finally everything is left behind and that's all you have, this light. And it only exists one frame at a time; it only exists in the present. The rest of it is past or future. And so it is an extraordinary kind of metaphysical object, much more so even than the printed word. A poem is printed, it's signs, it has a physical substance. Film doesn't. It's the only art form that is utterly transcendent. That's why I think we have such an appetite and expectation for film. Every time we go see a movie and the lights go down, we get that thrill that This May Be It. And how only occasionally we have that elation of the spirit that comes through truly cinematic moments: But we always hope for more. Film is connected to that just as it is connected and so similar to the process of dreaming—the way that it can shift location, point of view, and the fact that it is so vivid the way dreams are. Film can simulate life without being it. The thing I always say to my collaborators when we're making a film is, "Film is not life." If you behave as though it *is* when you're making a film, hopeless failure is going to dog you, if you're trying to make it lifelike. It has to be something different from life.

Interview/
Film Comment, July-Aug.:54.

Bill Bradley
United States Senator,
D-New Jersey

2

[On what the public can do about excessive sex and violence in entertainment-industry product]: If you see something that offends you, take control of your own circumstances. You can create a rivulet of pressure that falls into a big stream. Find out who the sponsor is; write the board of directors; talk at their churches or synagogues. Send a letter and ask, "Why are you making money out of trash?" Shame them into accepting moral responsibility for what they do.

Interview/
U.S. News & World Report,
6-19:19.

James L. Brooks
Director,
Screenwriter

3

It's driven everybody crazy when we've tried to do a screwball comedy [today] or our version of a landmark Preston Sturges or Billy Wilder film that we all hold dear. We have to accept that they're just masterworks that we admire, and it's hard to be a master.

Los Angeles Times,
2-12:(Calendar)9.

David Brown
Producer

4

At the end of the game, it's the director who will attract the actors and it's the script that will attract the director. It all starts with the screenplay.

Cosmopolitan,
June:197.

Don Burgess
Cinematographer

1

Good films are made by directors who have a vision of what the story is about. You have to put that ahead of everything else. Bad things happen when everybody [involved in a production] is making their own movie.

Daily Variety, 4-11:7.

Mark Canton
Chairman, Columbia-TriStar Motion Picture Group

2

[On Senator Robert Dole's criticism of films he says promote violence and debase the culture]: We're all concerned about the quality and content of movies. The family market has, in fact, grown in recent years. But this is a clear case of political finger-pointing. It's very dangerous for anyone to single out Hollywood, as if we all thought one way; just like it would be dangerous for anyone to single out Congress, as if everyone in Congress had the same values and accomplishments. The issue here is creative rights. We have to retain the right to make creative choices with diversity and freedom.

June 1/ The New York Times, 6-2:(A)10.

Bill Clinton
President of the United States

3

Today, going out to the movies is one of the most popular things we do together as people. The movies have a way of binding us together and reminding us of what we share. Going to the movies is one of the things that the President still gets to do, and I go every chance I get.

Taped message to NATO-Showest convention, Las Vegas, Nev., March 9/ Daily Variety, 3-13:32.

4

[On Senator Robert Dole's recent criticism of the entertainment industry for debasing the culture with excessive violence and sexual content in its product]: I don't believe in censorship, and I don't believe in singling Hollywood out. I agree with a lot of what Senator Dole said . . . But I think that we need to do this in a spirit, not of dividing each other, but of asking everybody to come forward and be accountable.

Broadcast interview, "Larry King Live"/ Los Angeles Times, 6-19:(A)10.

Allen Daviau
Cinematographer

5

The more you work in film, the less tied to reality you are.

Daily Variety, 2-17:28.

Bill Dill
Cinematographer

6

Cinematography is ultimately about passion. But the truth is that passion without technique is like a car without an engine. Technique gives you the freedom to express what

(BILL DILL)

you feel about a character or a song at that moment. I'm not talking about being a soloist and forcing a visual style on a picture. That's not my style. I never think of it as *my* movie. It's always *our* movie. Ultimately, it's the director's movie. I don't have a problem with that. What I mean is that anyone can dream up ideas about how something should look. [But] unless you can do the physical part of getting the story on film within the limitations of the budget and time, your talent is meaningless.

Daily Variety,
5-23:13.

Robert J. Dole
United States Senator,
R-Kansas;
Candidate for the
1996 Republican
Presidential nomination

1

Every parent knows the greatest challenge to family values is the way our popular culture ridicules them. Our music, movies and advertising regularly push the limits of decency, bombarding our children with destructive messages of casual violence and even more casual sex . . . Shame is a powerful tool. We should use it . . . Let's put the heat on the entertainment industry.

Speech, April 11/
Daily Variety,
4-12:40.

2

Too much of today's entertainment continues to operate in a moral vacuum, without a redeeming hope and without any suggestion that virtues are important, that morality is, in fact, preferable to immorality.

Before the Senate,
Washington, D.C., May 18/
The Washington Post,
5-19:(A)6.

3

[On a story in a Boston newspaper about two accused murderers who reportedly linked their crime to seeing the violent film *Natural Born Killers*]: [This story] should send shivers down the spines of all Americans, especially those who have criticized my call to the entertainment industry to exercise good citizenship when it comes to producing films that celebrate mindless violence. Of course, no movie caused this brutal killing. We are all responsible for our own actions, period. But at the same time, those in the entertainment industry who deny that cultural messages can bore deep into the hearts and minds of young people are deceiving themselves. If the *Boston Herald* story is true, and if these are the kinds of role models that Hollywood is content to promote, then perhaps some serious soul-searching is in order in the corporate suites of the entertainment industry.

Before the Senate,
Washington, D.C., June 27/
Daily Variety,
6-28:15.

Faye Dunaway
Actress

4

[Addressing theater owners]: We [filmmakers] may be the people who make movies, but the ones who bring them to the people are you. You complete the magic because a movie isn't really finished until it has touched

(FAYE DUNAWAY)

someone in your darkened theaters and moves them to laughter or to tears.

At NATO-Showest convention, Las Vegas, Nev./ Daily Variety, 3-13:32.

Clint Eastwood
Actor, Director, Producer

1

Producers get the least amount of attention and gratification on a film. They're not as hands-on as the director and the actors. But by and large they finance and envision the project. The producer is the person who puts together the elements and then lets the director run with the ball . . . A producer has to be a salesman for the project. He has to raise enthusiasm to finance it. You have to sell it to actors if you want a name cast. You have to sell the different elements to a director . . . Producing is also something that you don't go to school for. You can go to cinema schools and learn cinematography and editing. [But] you can't teach someone how to be a good producer.

Interview/ Daily Variety, 3-27:38.

Farrah Fawcett
Actress

2

I'm too passionate about my work. In my profession, you may do a job intensely for three months, and that is your only life. And I have a son now whom I take on location. But am I able to give to him what I give to him when I'm not working? No. Because acting takes not only concentration, it takes creativity; it takes . . . your soul.

Interview, New York, N.Y./ "Interview" magazine, February:92.

Sally Field
Actress

3

Acting has been my lover and best friend. My confidant and my tormentor. It has given me support and broken my heart and mended it.

Before New York Women in Film & Television/ Ladies' Home Journal, March:109.

Freddie Fields
Former talent agent

4

Actors are getting $10-million to $15-million to $20-million a movie; directors are getting $5-million; writers are getting $3-million. Those are gigantic multiples. Supply-and-demand is what drives the prices up. How can an agent drive a price up unless someone says, "I'll pay it"? . . . There was a time when if you couldn't get Paul Newman, you might take Rock Hudson. Everything was done on the basis of "We can't afford it" . . . That's not happening today.

Interview, West Hollywood, Calif./ Los Angeles Times, 6-16:(D)4.

Jodie Foster
Actress, Director

5

[As an actress,] it's such a luxury to be

(JODIE FOSTER)

able to work [things] out in a therapeutic way in certain roles. Otherwise, standing on a movie set in someone else's clothes with a bunch of people putting compresses on your face is not that interesting to me. I have to have this huge monologue or dialogue about what I'm doing in a movie or I just don't know why I'm doing it. I've no idea why it's becoming harder and harder for me to find movies that fit into that category now.

Interview/
"Interview" magazine,
November:114.

Bill Fraker
Cinematographer

1

Every time you do a picture, you extend yourself. And try to do something new or original. Or else you would end up doing the same kind of picture every year.

Daily Variety,
2-17:29.

Michael Fuchs
Chairman,
Home Box Office;
Chairman,
Warner Music Group

2

The truth is, there is a problem with American entertainment. More and more of what is produced has a tendency to "program down," to appeal to the lowest common denominators of sensationalism and tabloidization: sex, violence and sleaze . . . We have a glut of enormously expensive movies with non-stop action and super high-tech special effects all in search of an intelligible script . . . [But] the dirty little secret of the entertainment industry is that *quality* sells.

At Edinburgh
International Television Festival,
Edinburgh, Scotland, Aug. 26/
Daily Variety,
8-28:5.

Carlo Fuscagni
President, RAI
(Italian broadcasting network)

3

Nothing unites Europe in fiction the way the American cultural model of optimism, uplift and the ability to make something of oneself is reflected in the [U.S.] movies. There's simply no European vision of life that unites our people in the same way and which can be translated onto the screen.

At conference
at Mip TV market,
Cannes, France, April 8/
Daily Variety,
4-10:12.

Larry Gelbart
Playwright, Screenwriter

4

A film is rarely a writer's vision. It might start out to be a writer's vision, but it quickly goes into the machinery, and the machinery is designed to eat writers. That's a very tough thing to face, but you have to. It's essential that you have the enthusiasm and the need to write a film, but it's equally important to prepare yourself for the inevitable process by which your work gets passed around. Opinions are formed not according to the quality or the execution of the idea, but on market and research, on ego and power . . . There's very little respect for the writer in film; we

(LARRY GELBART)

are traditionally low man or woman on the totem pole. Prices [for screenwriting] are extraordinarily high, but they're just paying more money to insult you.

Interview, Palm Springs, Calif./ Writer's Digest, April:39.

Mark Gill
President of marketing, Miramax Films

1

[On the advertising and promotion of films]: We spend a lot of time making movies look more provocative than they really are. Our cheap cliche is: "Sex, betrayal, murder." People want to see things that are provocative. You'll see a lot of women with no clothes on their backs in our ads. We'll put a gun in [the ad] if we can. It works. You can scorn me for this. But it works.

At Toronto International Film Festival symposium, Toronto, Canada, Sept. 12/ Daily Variety, 9-13:22.

Newt Gingrich
United States Representative, R-Georgia; Speaker of the House

2

[On the recent Academy Awards]: I can't tell you how glad I am that *Forrest Gump* won [for best picture] and that *Pulp Fiction* lost. I've refused to go see *Pulp Fiction* on the grounds that there's a certain level of degeneration that shouldn't be honored with your cash.

Los Angeles Times, 3-30:(A)5.

Jerry Goldsmith
Composer of music for motion pictures

3

[As a composer,] I want the interplay between the [film's] director and me to be open. It's a real trap for the director to say, "Go ahead, do whatever your instincts tell you," because you don't get enough landmarks. And besides, I have to say that sometimes my instincts aren't always the right ones. That's one of the things I love about writing music for films: It's a collaborative process, and it usually turns out best if that's the way it's done.

Interview/ Daily Variety, 9-8:53.

Brad Hall
Producer, Screenwriter

4

[On the difficulty today in making romantic comedies such as those produced decades ago]: The world has changed, especially in the way the romance is played out. The roles have changed. These movies [in the old days] were breaking social boundaries that no longer exist. A lot of these movies have powerful women as a source of comedy. That's no longer comedy [today]; that's life. Women competing with men is just not funny in the same way; women have come such a long way.

Los Angeles Times, 2-12:(Calendar)20.

Conrad Hall
Cinematographer

1

[As a cinematographer], what I like to do is abuse film. But usefully. Artistically. That is what creates the artistry and the mood of the story.

Daily Variety,
2-17:28.

Christopher Hampton
Screenwriter,
Director

2

Life is hard, and it should be written about truthfully. What is common in all my work is the view that life's a struggle and people are victimized and ill-treated. The subjects I choose are guaranteed to terrify producers. [But] you can't write a screenplay without being an optimist every time. This is one job that truly is a triumph of hope over experience. I just keep having to tell myself I've written 30 screenplays and had 10 accepted, which is a pretty good average.

Interview/
"W" magazine,
November:54.

Tom Hanks
Actor

3

The foreign market [for U.S. motion pictures] is incredibly important. I've gotten a better grasp of publicity over the years and I've learned that one of the most exhausting things for me is selling pictures in foreign lands. My travel is not horizon-broadening; it's hard work. And there's no substitution for it. You have to do it to be competitive in the marketplace. Publicity is the difference between your film being seen and not being seen.

Interview,
Los Angeles, Calif./
Daily Variety, 3-9:35.

Amy Heckerling
Director

4

I don't believe that love goes on forever and that there's one person for anybody . . . I don't believe in any of that. I don't believe in marriage; I don't believe in eternal love; I don't believe in any of the stuff that will probably be the ending of all my movies.

Los Angeles Times,
2-12:(Calendar)8.

Holly Hunter
Actress

5

[On preparing for a role]: I'm like a little reporter in the field. Anything I can grab. I may get nothing, but it may send me down an unanticipated little road. It's kind of the same philosophy I have about my life, too. If I follow anything that people offer, it may be a dead end, but sometimes it isn't. I like that total immersion in a world that you don't know anything about. When you leave [after making] the movie, you may never touch that world again. But you will, because that information—you have it now.

Interview/
"W" magazine,
November:133.

Anjelica Huston
Actress

6

It's our obligation as working actors to use what we have—to use life to show life, to

(ANJELICA HUSTON)

live life. Every actor has responsibility to the original truth. If it means you have to relive some suffering, then that's part of the alchemy of what actors do. It makes you a little richer.

Interview,
Los Angeles, Calif./
"W" magazine,
October:164.

Tommy Lee Jones
Actor

1

[On acting]: It's certainly not instinctive. I mean, birds fly south by instinct; I don't think people make movies or act or write by instinct. I don't have a fixed method, because here in this country we have so many different cultural influences, and people come to cinema from so many different places and sources, with so many different intentions and so many different destinations they aspire to. You have to be rather eclectic in your appreciation of style and your use of style. Even your concept of style has to be rather versatile to work in the movies these days. You have to invent a method for every movie. Different directors have different requirements, and actors are really there to serve the company.

Interview,
San Saba, Texas/
"Interview" magazine,
June:84.

Jessica Lange
Actress

2

[On acting]: There was a time when I really tried to have a technique. But I find the best way for me to work is really like a child, in the sense that I can make myself believe so completely in the situation that it doesn't become acting choices. It becomes like *living*.

Interview,
New York, N.Y./
Vanity Fair,
March:188.

3

[On acting]: It's amazing what this work can do to you physically. When you're acting, your nervous system doesn't understand that it's just pretend, and lying in bed last night I could feel everything trembling. [I have] realized it was imperative that I learn how to *not* be devoured by the characters I play, and I'm working much differently now. Instead of setting specific tasks for myself or thinking about what the expectations of the scene are, I try to get myself into a neutral state and then I just start. I've found that if you get yourself into the right state, the emotions will come and they'll come very purely and powerfully.

Interview/
Los Angeles Times,
3-19:(Calendar)3.

Sherry Lansing
Chairman,
motion-picture group,
Paramount Pictures

4

[Movies are] all I ever cared about. It's like an adrenaline rush when I walk onto a soundstage or a set. It's alive. Creative. Everybody is friendly. Everybody eats together. You make friends with people who in ordinary walks of life you wouldn't know. Everybody's dressed the same. Everybody lives the same. You block out the rest of the

(SHERRY LANSING)

world. You can see why people fall in love on movie sets. It's a magical place, and nothing else exists.

Interview,
Los Angeles, Calif./
Working Woman,
April:87.

Art Murphy
Film scholar,
School of Cinema,
University
of Southern California

1

[The film business is] a cash business. Every morning, a studio receives real cash, [and] puts it in a safe only long enough to decide what new project to risk it on. The money is always moving around.

Los Angeles Times,
4-9:(D)7.

Molly Ornati
Senior producer,
"The Hollywood Style,"
PBS-TV

2

We live in a visual culture, constantly being bombarded by the media. The cinema is such a prominent part of our lives, yet we seem inarticulate in discussing it. We want the audience to see that every film image is the result of historical, economic and cultural forces. To fully understand it is to see it as having these dimensions.

Interview/
Humanities,
Jan.-Feb.:26.

Jack Palance
Actor

3

I think it's time to sit back and not be involved with being an actor anymore . . . What does it mean to say the words someone else wrote? Nothing.

Interview,
Tehachapi, Calif./
Los Angeles Times,
4-30:(Calendar)83.

Sean Penn
Actor

4

[On why he wants to direct]: When I say direct, I mean write, direct and edit, because for me, it's all one thing. I would say that a non-writer-director has as much to do with a writer-director as a grocer does to a barber: It's got nothing to do with it. When you act in a film, you're inevitably surrounded with people whom you didn't choose, right down to the set painter. I like being able to pick the family I'm waking up to in the morning that's going to make this group effort to tell a story that applies to what's interesting to me at that stage in my life. When I sit down to write and direct, it comes out of something I'm looking into, something I don't have an answer to. If I'm acting, I'm going back and looking at something I already know. I know this guy I'm playing either emotionally, metaphorically or literally from my past—I've already got that done. And if I know how a movie ends before I start it, or what it means, I don't want to make it.

Interview,
New York, N.Y./
"Interview" magazine,
October:141.

Nicholas Pileggi
Screenwriter

1

There's a big difference between writing a play and a screenplay. In a play, the words are delicate. You can't improvise onstage; it doesn't really work. [But] in a movie, you might do one scene 12 times. I feel that as a [movie] writer, I'm laying out a terrain, and if the actor is good at it, he can improvise in that terrain.

Interview,
New York, N.Y./
"W" magazine,
October:187.

Roman Polanski
Director

2

I love the technical side of film-making—the creating a reality, an atmosphere, an emotion in the audience . . . That's the reason I still do it. For me, it's about emotion. If art doesn't move me, it has no interest. Mondrian was never my kind of artist. I'd rather pick up a Chagall.

Interview,
Paris, France/
The Wall Street Journal,
1-6:(A)8.

3

Everything must come down to expressing what is essential. The most hateful thing to me is a production where you can see the director scratching his head to come up with a concept, desperate to be original.

Opera News,
2-18:25.

Sydney Pollack
Director

4

One of the things that made filmgoing such a wonderful experience is it was kind of a dazzling journey that you took to a place and a life that bore little resemblance to your own. And you measured the success of it sometimes by the distance between you and that world.

Interview,
"American Cinema,"
PBS-TV/
Humanities,
Jan.-Feb.:25.

David Puttnam
British producer

5

[Saying European and other foreign film industries can learn something from Hollywood about marketing movies]: [Although Hollywood studios] have from time to time lacked any identifiable artistic or cultural ambition, *our* fault is that we have so often lacked something just as essential—the commercial ambition to earn the revenue to make the next picture . . . Are we going to allow the Hollywood industry to go on consolidating its grip on entertainment [worldwide], while we [outside the American industry] survive with varying degrees of success on the margins? Or are we going to develop an alternative scenario?

Speech at
Screen Producers
Association of
Australia convention,
Melbourne, Australia, Nov. 8/
Daily Variety,
11-9:18.

Allen Sabinson
Executive vice president of original programming, Turner Network Television

1

[On the effect on creative people of the recent giant media mergers]: Is this a good time for writers, producers and artists seeking to give voice . . . to individual visions of diversity and creativity? With the huge accumulated debt associated with these mergers and the enormous stakes associated with the success and release of every major theatrical [film], it's hard not to be worried that diversity, innovation and risk-taking are going to take a back seat to profit-and-loss analysis.

At Toronto International Film Festival symposium, Toronto, Canada, Sept. 12/ Daily Variety, 9-13:22.

Van Gordon Sauter
Former president, CBS News

2

[On the current criticism of the entertainment media for excessive sex and violence]: Boycotts [against the media] don't work and government threats of censorship no longer work. But one of the great tools of advocates of any stripe is shame.

U.S. News & World Report, 6-19:57.

John Schlesinger
Director

3

[Saying many people have never heard of him, despite his long career]: Oh well, when [his 1969 film] *Midnight Cowboy* was revived last year, people came out of the woodwork. They didn't think I was functioning. It's par for the course for most directors . . . Most directors have been through the mill one way or another. Even the great directors. I remember once meeting William Wyler in Malibu. I went up to him and said, "Oh, Mr. Wyler, you're such a great director." And he was so surprised and very touched that anyone remembered him. Can you believe it? He said, "I thought nobody knew who I was" . . . [As for me,] people probably say, "Who is this guy?" I appear for a year and then disappear for three years, either making European films or not getting films off the ground or working on television. And then I come back.

Interview, Los Angeles, Calif./ The New York Times, 6-28:(B)1.

Barbet Schroeder
Director

4

There is one thing I hate more than anything. I have a total, profound aversion to power, anything that expresses power. Casting [a film] especially is excruciating for me because you're supposed to be selecting people right in front of their eyes. Walking among a group of extras, selecting ones for the scene—you feel like you're in a concentration camp. Yet in the film-making process, if you don't have the power to impose what you think is right, the movie is going to suffer. I just try to live with it, but do everything I can to make it less apparent and less painful—for me, and for the others.

Interview/ Film Comment, March-April:71.

Martin Scorcese
Director

1

I've always been fascinated by the ability of people—whether directors or producers or, in the old style of Hollywood films, even writers and actors—to create a body of work that ultimately had a certain personality to it, especially certain directors. The films not only were phrased eloquently, with visual images and sound, but they had something to say . . . [Today there is too much] surface film-making. Just for the thrills.And no content, no depth . . . Cinema—whether it is going to be shown on disc or projected inside the mind's eye with some sort of electrode in your brain—is a story.

Interview/
Daily Variety,
10-17:31.

Steven Spielberg
Director

2

It starts with the writer—it's a familiar dictum, but somehow it keeps getting forgotten along the way. No film-maker, irrespective of his electronic bag of tricks, can ever afford to forget his commitment to the written word.

Interview,
Universal City, Calif./
Daily Variety,
10-30:15.

Rod Steiger
Actor

3

[As an actor,] you never know where the instinct that ignites a performance will come from. Although I didn't know it at the time, my years in the [military] service were the best education I could have gotten for acting. I was living on ships with hundreds of men of different backgrounds and ways of speaking. We visited many countries. I saw men fighting with other men, men fighting over women, people happy and people sad. The world was revealed very quickly. And to this day, when a young person says "I want to be an actor," I ask: "Would you *like* to be an actor, or do you *need* to be an actor?" If the answer is the latter, my advice is to get out of the cocoon of your own society. Join the Merchant Marines for a year. Go around the world. Then go to New York to study for the stage.

Interview,
Malibu, Calif./
The American Patriot,
Summer:7.

Vittorio Storaro
Cinematographer

4

Cinema is a language spoken with images formed by the conflict between light, shadows and color. We are trying to write a story with light.

Daily Variety,
2-17:29.

Quentin Tarantino
Director

5

[On Senator Robert Dole's criticism of films he says promote violence and debase the culture]: This is the oldest argument there is. Whenever there's a problem in society, blame the playwrights: "It's their fault; it's the theater that's doing it all" . . . My biggest problem with [Dole's] statement is that it's so disingenuous—he hasn't even seen the

(QUENTIN TARANTINO)

movies [that he is criticizing]. How can you take seriously someone talking about art he admittedly hasn't seen? But then, that's politics. I'll return Bob Dole the favor and only listen to the soundbites of what he has to say.

June 1/
The New York Times,
6-3:(A)1.

Bertrand Tavernier
Director

1

[On suggestions that today's movies promote violence in society]: [I] would never say that an image could transform a person into a killer. But when people become a slave to the image, when they have no curiosity, motivation or thoughts of their own, then it can be a dangerous thing . . . But one of the problems is that many people have no barriers or standards. When the old ways and ideologies fell, they were not replaced by democratic values but by Mafia-like values, creating socially and morally bankrupt societies. And the fact that things are so available and accessible makes people less curious. For a lot of us, films were a way to learn things, to learn about other people and places and times. When you lose a sense of history, you lose a sense of the present as well . . . Maybe it's like the audiences of the Depression. They want big stars, and now, if there's a problem, [action star Arnold] Schwarzenegger will come along and blast it away. People want to be reassured. But the danger all over the world is to have films without roots, without passion.

Los Angeles, Calif./
Daily Variety,
8-4:27.

Daniel Toscan du Plantier
President, Unifrance
(French motion-picture association)

2

[Saying the importance of motion pictures in France is reflected in the solicitous attitude toward the film industry by the current French Presidential candidates]: Cinema is a topic of consensus in the French election campaign. The candidates have run after us.

The New York Times,
5-4:(B)1.

Kathleen Turner
Actress

3

[The film industry today] begins and ends with money. It's absurd in this day and age—when we need so much money for education, for health, for people—that a hundred million dollars can be spent on a film. It's obscene to me that an actor would take a fee of $15-million for a film . . . Those values are seriously askew to me.

Interview, New York, N.Y./
"Interview" magazine,
August:69.

Liv Ullmann
Actress, Director

4

[On directing]: I choose actors who I believe have their own fantasy, their own creativity, their own experience; so I am there to be the best audience . . . On the day when they are going to do it, I am looking for their offer. If there is something that I think will really add to their offer, I give them a little cue, a little word or whatever. But I want them to build on the best that they are, and if they do it too big or too small—if they are too the-

(LIV ULLMANN)

atrical or too anonymous—I can say so. But it is their offer. They are the creators, and I am there to allow their creation to look as good as possible . . . The creation, the fantasy, belongs to the actors and always should. But you have to make it bloom. A bad director makes a wonderful creative person die because he gives it too much or too little water. He doesn't allow it. You just have to give actors love, and you'll get love back.

Interview/
The Christian Science Monitor,
1-25:16.

Jack Valenti
President,
Motion Picture
Association
of America

1

[Disagreeing with those who criticize motion pictures for promoting violence and other social problems]: There is a certain view [of] some public officials that if we cut the wires of every TV set in the nation, and darken every movie theater, the surly streets would become tranquil. True? Not very likely . . . [While some movies have] too much violence, too much sexuality [and] too much vulgarity, [the vast majority of film today] are rising toward the highest point to which the creative spirit can soar, without eroding the central values of society.

At Faith &
Media Conference,
Miami, Fla., Nov. 30/
Daily Variety,
12-1:33.

Peter Weir
Australian director

2

Americans hate ambiguity [in films]; they like neat endings; they like everything explained. [Hollywood] is nauseating in its shallowness: I dare not call it creative. There are tokenistic nods to race issues, feminism and gay issues . . . American mainstream [cinema] is in a terrible state; they always had a terrible problem. By not living there I manage to keep ideas somewhat alive.

At Australian
Screen Directors
Conference/
Daily Variety,
8-30:11.

Haskell Wexler
Cinematographer

3

We, as film-makers, are privileged. We can make people cry or laugh. We can make them think and feel. It is a great privilege and a great responsibility.

Daily Variety,
2-17:28.

Bruce Willis
Actor

4

Actors don't have control of films. We're only a little part of them. There are a hundred and fifty people, easy, who go into making a film from start to finish—and sometimes you get lucky, and sometimes it's a dog.

Interview/
Cosmopolitan,
June:159.

Dick Wolf
Producer

1

[On those in government who are criticizing the entertainment media for excessive sex and violence]: We are on the verge of some kind of censorship in this country if the people shouting the loudest get heard. There is no such thing as a little censorship.

U.S. News & World Report,
6-19:57.

James Woods
Actor

2

[Criticizing those in government who are speaking out against excessive violence and sex in movies and music]: We are unequivocally discussing censorship. I think you cannot be cavalier about your trashing of the First Amendment . . . Some of these movies, some of these lyrics, they disgust me. They disturb me. But they are the price I must pay to live in a free society.

Broadcast interview/
"Face the Nation,"
CBS-TV, 6-4.

Robert Zemeckis
Director

3

There's nothing better than an actor or a group of actors clicking—that works like gangbusters. If you look at the Marx Brothers, Charlie Chaplin and all these guys, there's no editing. Buster Keaton—none of his stuff is edited. These guys have perfect timing. But I believe it to be for anything, even drama. The actors' own rhythms and their own feelings, not being cut up, is the most powerful, magical thing.

Interview/
Daily Variety,
3-7:34.

Vilmos Zsigmond
Cinematographer

4

For me, movies should be visual. If you want dialogue, you should read a book.

Daily Variety,
2-17:28.

Christopher Alden
Opera director

1

The financial austerity [of some opera companies] is quite attractive to me. It forces one to use imagination, which is what I try to do . . . I've never been a director who's had a need to spend a ton of money to create an interesting opera production. I feel the more operas are about ideas and strong feelings, the more interesting they are. They're not about creating a lavish succession of visual pictures, but about stripping that down so that the focus is on the singing actors.

Los Angeles Times,
4-30:(Calendar)57.

Julianne Baird
Classical-music singer;
Associate professor,
Rutgers University

2

Musicologists don't want to make the music their own; they want to make it the composer's. That's the dilemma. You get a noncommittal performance. It's a cold-blooded approach. But in the 18th century, the music was a blueprint—at best—for what happened onstage. I have a more humanist approach. Let's do away with "authentic" practices if they alienate the audience. Let's do away with the fear of taking chances.

Interview/
Opera News,
October:33.

William J. Bennett
Former Secretary
of Education
of the United States

3

[Criticizing excessive violence and sex in the lyrics of music released by major recording companies]: This stuff is not fit for human consumption. And it certainly is not fit for promotion and sales to children by what is the largest entertainment company in the world [Time Warner] . . . I'm seeking some drawing of the line by the companies themselves, some degree of self-regulation, some sense of shame, if you will.

Broadcast interview/
"Face the Nation,"
CBS-TV, 6-4.

Joanna Berman
Ballerina,
San Francisco Ballet

4

[On being "musical"]: I think that's something you either have or you don't. It's not something you learn. I think there are people who feel the highs and lows of music well, but can get lost during the rest. And there are those who are more mathematical and can be with the music, but they don't *feel* it; they're just doing the correct thing. And then there are those who are musical, who hear the music and feel it.

Interview/
Dance Magazine,
March:60.

Gary Burton
Dean of curriculum,
Berklee College of Music

1

[Criticizing the notion that you can't teach jazz]: People get confused with what is talent and what is musical information. A typical classical musician studies how music works, how harmony works, what the grammar of this music is in order to play better. You study your instrument with a master player. You study these same things as a jazz musician, but instead of using as an example a piece by Beethoven, you use a piece by [Thelonious] Monk or [Duke] Ellington. You're still learning musical information, which helps you be a more knowledgeable, proficient player.

Interview/
Down Beat, May:23.

James Carter
Jazz musician

2

[On the social status of jazz]: If this music had come up in a rifle club instead of a brothel, it would get the same respect as Beethoven or Bartok.

Interview/
Vogue, April:203.

James Conlon
Chief conductor,
Cologne Opera (Germany])
Principal conductor-designate,
Paris National Opera (France)

3

[On being an American conductor who has found success working in Europe]: I remember once being told [that] Americans prefer foreigners [to head their orchestras] and foreigners prefer foreigners [to head *their* orchestras]. It's not a gift to be an American conductor. It was my conviction 20 years ago that, given the same capabilities, American institutions will always pick non-Americans. And I have seen nothing in 20 years to make me change my mind.

Paris, France, March 6/
The New York Times,
3-7:(B)13.

Victoria De Los Angeles
Opera and recital singer

4

The public has diminished [for opera]. I thought the world would become more interested in classical music, but it has become more indifferent. There are groups of young people, but records show that crowds have shrunk by 25 percent. It goes with the society, with the way of life. People like a lot of sound. There is a minority of people interested in the intimacy of music, of poetry. It is a pity that this is finishing, this kind of communication between the stage and the people. For other kinds of music, there is still a big reception, and it is nourished by the media. The example is set by Coca-Cola. So you have thousands of people and big communication, but it has nothing to do with the great quality of cultivated human souls.

Interview/
Opera News, 1-7:14.

Robert J. Dole
United States Senator,
R-Kansas;
Candidate for the
1996 Republican
Presidential nomination

5

[Criticizing entertainment companies,

(ROBERT J. DOLE)

such as Time Warner, for releasing films and music that promote violence and other anti-social behavior]: [Time Warner is involved in the] marketing of evil through commerce . . . I cannot bring myself to repeat the lyrics of some of the music Time Warner promotes. But our children do . . . I would like to ask the executives of Time Warner a question: Is this what you intended to accomplish with your careers? You have sold your souls, but must you debase our nation and threaten our children as well? . . . The American entertainment industry is at the cutting edge of creative excellence, but also too often the leading edge of a culture becoming dangerously coarse.

At fund-raising dinner, Los Angeles, Calif., May 31/ Daily Variety, 6-1:3.

Marta Eggerth
Former operetta singer

1

[Saying American operetta productions lack the advantages of the true German and Austrian tradition]: The words are there to be *interpreted.* You can't just sing them. You must understand the emotions and the *sentiment*—which is different from sentimentality. And most American singers don't have the opportunity to see these works! Their mothers can't tell them about Vienna if they're living in Virginia. There is no company here [in the U.S.] where they play one day *Countess Maritza,* one day *La Belle Helene,* one day *La Vie Parisienne.* I feel sorry for these young [American] singers. It's not their fault that they don't know what the real goulash tastes like.

Interview/ Opera News, August:33.

Peter Hemmings
General director, Los Angeles (Calif.) Music Center Opera

2

My own experience when running [an opera] company in London that specialized in doing contemporary operas is that there is a finite audience for such pieces, and it's almost impossible to increase it beyond those few hundreds.

Los Angeles Times, 4-30:(Calendar)57.

Raymond Hughes
Chorus master, Metropolitan Opera, New York, N.Y.

3

[On what he looks for in a chorus singer]: I look for voice, of course—a blendable voice. I look for musicality. It's also a matter of personality—a chorister has to have patience, discipline, a strong sense of self-worth. Working in a collective situation requires a certain kind of balanced temperament, a sense of being happy with oneself, and I've had great luck in finding so many people who are like that. But what I want to see more—and this is one of my 90 theses to nail to the door—is people with more *language experience.* That's where we are really, really far behind. I get so tired of people citing chapter and verse from this or that diction book. That has nothing to do with the language. Diction books are a won-

(RAYMOND HUGHES)

derful aid, but oh, please! No one should presume to think they can sing opera if they can't be lost in the back alleys of Rome and find their way out in the language of Rome.

Interview/
Opera News,
4-15:31.

Elton John
Rock musician

1

For some of [my] records, I haven't been 100 percent there, in part because of advances in the technology of making records. You become very comfortable with having great producers around you, with being able to program a computer for a drum track and let the technology sort of take over. I'm not knocking that, because it's a way of doing stuff. But while all that was being done, I would tune out. I would sit on the couch, or go shopping, or play table tennis, because it takes five or six hours to record one song that way. You get removed from the music . . . To my mind, there hasn't been a record since 1976 which has had all of me on it.

Interview/
"Interview" magazine,
April:74.

Quincy Jones
Musician,
Composer

2

[In composing and arranging music,] you start with a blank page . . . you start out with nothing there. When you start out with an album, there's absolutely nothing there in the beginning. All you have to do is visualize it and if you believe it's there, it's there. I think that's what keeps you young, always being in deep water, and not becoming complacent . . . The process is the most beautiful part. You know, there are two kinds of composers: one who sees the goal across the park and just runs straight to it; and the other who goes to the park, stops, takes a leaf and feels it, takes his shoes off, and puts his feet in the water for a while. You're going across the park anyway, so you might as well take the trip, you know.

Interview/
"Interview" magazine,
November:30.

James Levine
Artistic director,
Metropolitan Opera,
New York, N.Y.

3

There are times—and always have been and always will be—when a constellation of artists working on [an opera] is all one could wish for; and then there are certain times—and, surprise, always have been and always will be—when it isn't. And I guess one regrets the times when it isn't; but there isn't any way to avoid that. If you could always tell in advance, you would avoid it, obviously. But anyone who does opera planning will tell you that even if you are able to get everyone you think is the best possible person to get, even that may exist in ideal form only on paper, in your imagination of how it will be. In reality, people arrive at the rehearsal period and interact with one another based on chemistry, on where they are in their own technical and interpretive developments, and at various stages in their growth in life. So I suppose I could say I regret "anything I found

(JAMES LEVINE)

disappointing." But I don't see how you can have one thing without the other.

Interview/
Opera News,
September:14.

Lyle Lovett
Singer, Songwriter

1

To me, [sincerity in music is] the goal. Art is sincere. Somehow you can tell the difference when a song is written just to get on the radio and when what someone does is their whole life. That comes through in [Bob] Dylan, Paul Simon, Willie Nelson. There is no separating their life from their music. The craft of it becomes their life, too. Most of my songs I write as a way to communicate with a particular person and they are full of personal references.

Interview, Syracuse, N.Y./
Los Angeles Times,
1-1:(Calendar)78.

Wynton Marsalis
Jazz musician

2

Jazz is like a good conversation: You have to listen to what others [in the group] have to say [musically] if you're going to make an intelligent contribution.

Interview, New York, N.Y./
Down Beat,
May:20.

3

[Comparing jazz with democracy]: You have to be willing to hear another person's point of view and respond to it. Also, jazz requires that you have a lot of on-your-feet information, just like a democracy does. There are a lot of things you simply have to know. In jazz you have the opportunity to establish your equality—based on your ability. That's the chance you have in a democracy. It doesn't mean you're going to be even, but you do have an opportunity. And often things won't go your way; they'll go the way the majority takes them. So you'll have to go with them, and make the best out of a situation you might not like. The principle of American democracy is that you have freedom; the question is, How will you use it? Which is also the central question in jazz. And in democracy and in jazz, you have freedom with restraint. It's not absolute freedom; it's freedom within a structure. The connection between jazz and the American experience is profound. Believe me, that's the heart and soul of what jazz is. That's why jazz is so important. And that's why the fact that it has not been addressed has resulted in our losing a large portion of our identity as Americans. Because the art form that really gives us a mythic representation of our society has not been taught to the public.

Interview/
American Heritage,
October:80.

Reba McEntire
Country-music singer

4

I'm gonna sound like a greedy, driven, possessed woman, but that's pretty much what you have to be to get ahead. It is still hard for a female to break into this business. We have to work five times harder. You have to think up better things, and you have to put on a show that costs your butt for the first half of the

(REBA McENTIRE)

year until you get it paid for. Women still face a lot of obstacles, and I have done everything in the world to break through.

Interview, Memphis, Tenn./ Working Woman, August:36.

Donald McIntyre
Opera singer

1

[For an opera singer, the key is to find] an understanding of a role, something you can identify with, whether or not it's the type of person you would identify with in real life. We certainly don't have all the experiences the characters in opera have. If you get killed onstage, you don't actually go through the process of dying. But you can imagine from a small thing what it's like, and magnify it.

Interview/ Opera News, 4-15:16.

Michael Milenski
General director, Long Beach (Calif.) Opera

2

Minimalism here is a philosophy. It is not dictated by budget. If we had a budget three times as large for the same work that we do now, if we were sensible we would save most of it because we simply don't need that, and, in fact, it might even be detrimental to what we do. If you tell somebody not to worry about a budget, then all of a sudden you don't have to think nearly as hard, do you, as a creator? . . . If you do more productions, pretty soon they're not hand-made anymore, pretty soon you're cranking out a season. For our philosophy, a three-opera season is about what can be handled. By the time you get bigger than that, you're going to have to have a bigger staff, you're going to be much more organized in the sense of being sure that the sets are designed months in advance so that they can get to the shop. You see what I mean? What it does is that it takes away a lot of the hands-on thing.

Interview/ Los Angeles Times, 4-30:(Calendar)57.

Kent Nagano
Orchestra conductor

3

At the Berkeley Symphony, democracy is not just a word. If a passage is slow in coming together, ranting and raving won't help. I need to work with the orchestra toward a constructive solution. We have to remember that our job is not to serve ourselves, it's to serve music and the community.

Interview/ Harper's Bazaar, June:71.

Willie Nelson
Country-music singer

4

I never pretended to have a great voice. It works and I can carry a tune. If you have a good song, that's about all that's required.

Interview/ The New York Times, 2-23:(B)4.

Stanford Olsen
Opera singer

5

The young audience for opera and vocal

(STANFORD OLSEN)

recitals is almost non-existent. I think it's a shame we can't find a way to turn people on to *Mozart*—not the spectacle of a [Franco] Zeffirelli finale with a thousand supers and three stage orchestras. What I fear is that an already "elitist" art form is going to become so super-elite that it will have no validity. And that will be a shame, because then that wonderful place in *Le Nozze di Figaro* that always moves me to tears, and where Figaro says, "I may look like I'm lying, but I'm not," and the ground bass comes in—boom!—will be *gone*, and nobody will feel that ever again.

Interview/
Opera News, 3-4:38.

Oscar Peterson
Jazz musician

1

I have exact peeves with certain jazz writers, no names. I believe they pose as self-appointed discoverers who want more than anything to say they saw the next new wave coming before anyone else. So they patrol the fringes. They don't regard any music as having value unless it's removed and utterly esoteric. Then they write and people get curious. But audiences aren't dumb. No amount of publicity can force audiences to accept music they don't like.

Interview/
The Wall Street Journal,
1-11:(A)12.

Marshall Pynkoski
Co-director, Opera Atelier,
Toronto, Canada

2

The baroque period [in opera] was a literal time. The characters were archetypes; things were black or white, and this simplicity gave the theater its power to stir the emotions. There was also an acceptance that the audience exists, and that what is onstage is staged. Today we never deal with the obvious.

Interview/
Dance Magazine,
February:47.

Sonny Rollins
Jazz musician

3

This summer when I was playing festivals, I found out that now anything goes under the title "Jazz Festival." Maybe it's a good thing, but I just lament the fact. The reason why, quite frankly, was because I have to maybe follow some guy that's really playing crowd-pleasing, accessible music . . . I still am playing straightforward jazz. And that's still not as accessible as a guy singing, "Come back, baby! Everybody clap your hands!" It's still not the same thing as that. Blues is great. Pop-jazz is great. I'm not putting down any of that. [But] I'm saying that if we [jazz purists] have to follow that, or compete with that, it makes it hard for [us]. If the jazz musician doesn't compare favorably, isn't that putting a nail in jazz's coffin?

Interview, New York, N.Y./
Down Beat, January:21.

Bruce Springsteen
Rock singer

4

[On his recently winning four Grammy awards]: You stick around long enough and they give these things to you.

Newsweek, 3-13:19.

Joan Sutherland
Opera singer

1

[When judging opera competitions,] I look for technique and a certain personality [in an aspiring singer]—the fact that they deliver the aria, that they *know* what they are singing . . . Today I find there is a lack of technical background. So many of the young singers are singing music they can cope with musically, but they have not worked on their technique sufficiently to be *in command* of what their voices are doing. And they sing sloppy coloratura and get away with it! I don't understand. And they sing off-pitch and get away with it! I actually said at one competition, "Are you all deaf? This person has been singing sharp through the whole competition, and you've put her in the finals!" And, I mean, there were 12 other adjudicators . . . Some of the young singers seem to have in their mind what the music is, but they don't actually sing it. And they *think* they're singing it! I don't know how they can do that, nor do I know how their teachers let them get away with the inaccuracy of pitch and the lack of correctness.

Interview,
Australia/
Opera News,
October:13.

Al Teller
Chairman, MCA
Music Entertainment Group

2

From a long-term perspective, your ability to find talent and nurture them from their very early days is what determines whether or not you're a great record company. If you can't do that, you're going to fail.

Hong Kong/
Los Angeles Times,
5-5:(D)4.

THE STAGE

Edward Albee
Playwright

1

The writer has a responsibility to look as clearly and honestly as he can at the society around him—how people behave toward themselves and others, their participation in their own lives—and to put that down as accurately and as honestly as he possibly can.

The Writer,
February:3.

Martin Amis
Author

2

I think [drama] has been largely superseded by the written culture, and now by the audiovisual culture. If you compare English drama to English poetry—when you get wave upon wave of mighty geniuses—and if you take Shakespeare's godlike singularity out of it, there's practically nothing there. There are few distinguished dramatists now.

Interview,
London, England/
"Interview" magazine,
May:124.

Trisha Brown
Choreographer

3

[On her choreographing to the music of Bach]: I've been dancing to my own drummer for years, and not in a small way. The rhythmic structures of my choreography are derived from the movement itself. The timing of a phrase is so inextricably bound to the action of the phrase that you don't have to count it. Suddenly, with Bach, it's like there is a sea of notes all over the floor, and I've got no place to put my foot! I found that Bach's music makes my hand-chiseled movement geometries and my willful excursions into space look like old-fashioned modern dance! I've tried many, many incursions on this problem, all the way from just dancing to the music—Isadora Brown!—to very deliberate attempts to find a vocabulary that holds the music at a distance. The question is, how do I set up a separate identity concurrent with this music? How do I make up dance to this music? What is my relationship to any music?

Interview/
Dance Magazine,
April:48.

Gary Dunning
Executive director,
American Ballet Theater

4

[On the trend toward presenting classic, full-lengthy ballets rather than mixed bills]: The audience for repertory evenings is not declining. It's just that the full-lengths bring in a broader audience . . . The classics are the touchstone of who we are. Ballet technique was defined and formed in the 19th-century classics.

Dance Magazine,
July:36.

Horton Foote
Playwright

5

Some writers are very detailed and make

(HORTON FOOTE)

specific outlines and don't vary very much from their outlines. I'm of the school that I like to take the journey into the unknown. I have a rough kind of road map, but I'm always amazed at what just comes to me and what's unplanned that's usable. Whether it's inspiration or whatever it is . . . I keep myself ready for these unfoldments. I don't know a better word. It's kind of an unfolding that takes place, and sometimes I'm in awe of it.

Interview,
New York, N.Y./
The Christian Science Monitor,
3-22:14.

1

I've seen New York theater go through many, many stages, and the enemy always has been, to me, commercialism. The so-called golden day of the theater, which I was here and part of, I found very stifling, because I found that only the most conventional plays got done. I think there's more experimenting going on now. I have great hopes for the theater. You just have to get away from the fact that the only stamp of approval is to have a play done in the so-called Broadway district.

Interview,
New York, N.Y./
The Christian Science Monitor,
3-22:14.

Larry Gelbart
Playwright, Screenwriter

2

I don't have any set idea about [writing a specific number of] pages [a day]. A good day can mean no pages. A good day can mean a breakthrough in understanding a character, or a progression required in the story. Very often that happens without ever once setting pen to paper, or finger to keyboard. We tend to forget just how much *thinking* goes into writing. A lot of time can go by before you ever see a word. It's very easy to be discouraged, thinking "I haven't written anything; I haven't got any pages to show for it." In fact, there *are* pages—they're waiting to make their appearance.

Interview,
Palm Springs, Calif./
Writer's Digest,
April:38.

3

There's no question in my mind that the theater is the best of it all [for a writer]. Your work is not taken away from you. You don't sit with a committee. You aren't "instructed" to rewrite. Best of all, nobody says, "You're off the show—we're having seven or eight other people come in and do this." Your work remains your own.

Interview,
Palm Springs, Calif./
Writer's Digest,
April:39.

John Hart
Artistic director,
Ballet West

4

We [in ballet] have to be more conscious of box office than ever in this country, because the grants are running out and there's very little private patronage anymore. I've always been very practical in the sense that you are dependent on audiences. It's no good

(JOHN HART)

being the most creative if you're playing to an empty house.

Dance Magazine,
July:36.

Alonzo King
Choreographer
and founder,
Lines Contemporary Ballet,
San Francisco, Calif.

1

An opinion that's often expressed is that classical ballet is obsolete, that it's classist, useless, and Eurocentric, and dramatically opposed to all other cultures. This deduction came about because of its patronage by European royalty, its secularization, the trivialization of the art form by the media, bad teachers, and the methodic secrecy that dancers often maintain about their art. But, in fact, classical ballet is a science, which through symbolic movements reveals universal truths.

Interview/
Dance Magazine,
June:46.

Tony Kushner
Playwright

2

When I teach writing, I always tell my students you should assume that the audience you're writing for is smarter than you. You can't write if you don't think they're on your side, because then you start to yell at them or preach down to them.

Interview/
Mother Jones,
July-Aug.:64.

Kevin McKenzie
Artistic director,
American
Ballet Theater

3

[On the trend toward audiences preferring classic, full-length ballets rather than mixed bills]: Full-lengths are the ultimate challenge for choreographers as well as dancers. It's one thing to do a 20-minute piece; it's quite another to hold an audience's attention and carry them through an entire evening . . . I'd prefer it to be half-and-half. More repertory allows you to give more people opportunities. But it's not only my decision. Presenters who are paying the bills want the full-lengths, and they know their audiences. In the end, it's as much about fiscal responsibility as it is about creativity. I can't just say, "This is a good idea, so we'll do it and figure out how to pay for it." Those days are gone.

Dance Magazine,
July:36,38.

Terrence McNally
Playwright

4

[On his advice to young people seeking a stage career]: The theater is something to give your life to. It gives your life value and joy . . . Just stick it out like I did. It doesn't happen overnight, and when it does, the network of friends and extended family and the feeling of having an impact on other people's lives is so amazing. I don't think we in the theater can change the world, but I think we can leave it a better and a different place than it was if we hadn't written our plays and acted in them. It's exciting, too—that you have to be there. It's like a good party. You can't hear *about* a

(TERRENCE McNALLY)

party; you want to be *at* the party. And the theater's the party I want to be at.

Interview/ Vogue, May:154.

Marc Scorca
Chief executive officer, OPERA America

1

As long as people seek the mysteries of life, they will want to come together in a theater.

Interview/ Opera News, 2-4:49.

Neil Simon
Playwright

2

[On his plays that get bad reviews from critics]: Yes, it hurts, but not for very long, because sometimes you see the truth in it. I know when I haven't done really well. That doesn't bother me. It's when I do really well and there are a couple [of] critics who will just cut you down because your kind of theater is not what they want to see.

Interview, Los Angeles, Calif./ Los Angeles Times, 4-30:(Calendar)86.

Ben Stevenson
Artistic director, Houston Ballet

3

[On the trend toward audiences preferring classic, full-length ballets rather than mixed bills]: I would love to be able to do three world premieres by three choreographers on three rep programs each season and see them sell out because people love dance so much. That's the goal, that's the dream. But that doesn't happen. If you are directing a ballet company, you have to program thinking, What can I do that will pay people's salaries, that will keep the company going? That's as much part of the job as "Dream, baby, dream."

Dance Magazine, July:41.

Tom Stoppard
Playwright

4

I can start by writing almost anything, and I just have a sense that I am going to find a way to get there, and then *there* . . . You pull things in from the thoughts of other weeks and other months, other years, other books; you cross your fingers and write your way down and hope things come out . . . You have to bow down before the true god of theater, who is merciless and is saying, "This is not a text, this is an event happening in this room at this time in front of people who are under no obligation to remain."

Interview, London/ Harper's Bazaar, March:127.

Paul Taylor
Choreographer

5

Touring no longer pays for itself. That used to be our [his dance company's] real dependable source of income. As long as we got the dates, we knew there would be money coming in. Now that is no longer the case.

(PAUL TAYLOR)

These days it costs us money to tour. One problem is that the local presenters used to get support from the NEA, and now they [don't]. As a result, they are less able to afford a lot of things, and they are tending more and more toward booking things they think will be popular. They're more interested in what they consider [will have] commercial success, and the media is largely responsible.

Interview,
New York, N.Y./
Los Angeles Times,
3-19:(Calendar)81.

Kathleen Turner
Actress

1

I love Broadway—the flowers backstage, the standing ovations. There is nothing in the world like dying onstage. It's wonderful . . . In a film, you can make people breathe together, laugh together, cry together—and it's a communal experience for *them*, but not for *you* [as an actor]. But there are nights in the theater when you feel your arms go like this [spread wide] and they sneak right down the walls of the theater and they go right around the people in standing-room and you hold everyone.

Interview,
New York, N.Y./
Harper's Bazaar,
April:96.

Vladimir Vasilyev
Artistic director-designate,
Bolshoi Ballet
(Russia)

2

When people say, "Oh, the poor Bolshoi! So many people are leaving; they are irreplaceable; it will never be the same," it reminds me of [the late Soviet leader Josef] Stalin's funeral—people said the same things then.

Interview/
The New York Times,
3-28:(B)4.

Alcine Wiltz
Professor of dance,
University of Maryland,
College Park

3

Dancers are team players and individuals at the same time. And it's probably one of the professions in which students think about the excitement it can give them, rather than how much money they're going to make. Salary is Number 1 elsewhere. Dance people don't ever ask that. They should, in a sense, but they want to dance and it doesn't matter. It's always secondary how they're going to live. That in itself is what is beautiful about the human spirit.

Interview/
Dance Magazine,
January:64.

Isabel Allende
Author

1

There must be only a handful of very privileged people who can believe that life is a party, all celebration. But they are wrong. I am not a pessimistic or sad person, but accepting this has made me able to enjoy the good moments all the more.

Interview,
California/
World Press Review,
April:47.

Martin Amis
Author

2

[On turning 40 years of age]: You're sort of glad you made it, even to that modest age. You get a dawning awareness of certain things, but it doesn't come on your 40th birthday. It comes around 38 or 39; some people get it much earlier. There's a youthful illusion that age and death are just a rumor and that, funnily enough, you've been picked to defy this law. Intellectually, you're satisfied that you're going to get old and die, but you don't feel it in your gut. That feeling of exclusion from time as a universal process might even be the definition of youth. But around 40 the jig is up, really, and it's a full-time job looking the other way. You can't get out of the road. It even puts shadows in the orbits of your eyes, that realization, and it changes your balance, your sense of your place in time. Also, you begin to make quite logical but obvious comparisons between what's gone and what's to come, and it isn't good news, on the whole.

Interview,
London, England/
"Interview" magazine,
May:125.

Maya Angelou
Poet

3

The most delicious piece of knowledge for me is that I am a child of God. That is so mind-boggling, that this "it" created everything, and I am a child of "it." It means I am connected to every thing and every body. That's all delicious and wonderful—until I'm forced to realize that the bigot, the brute, the batterer is also a child of "it." Now, he may not know it, but I'm obliged to know that he is. I *have* to. That is my contract.

Interview/
Mother Jones,
May-June:24.

Henry Beard
Co-founder,
"National Lampoon" magazine

4

[On sarcastic, off-the-wall humor]: I don't know how you would outrage anyone today . . . [And] if nobody cares how far you go, a little bit of the drama is gone. Part of the power of the kind of parody and satire we were doing [when *National Lampoon* began] was that there was still a sense of outrage.

Interview, Universal City, Calif./
Los Angeles Times,
1-5:(E)7.

William J. Bennett
Former Secretary
of Education
of the United States

1

I'm convinced that efforts aimed at improving people's lives that don't have a moral and spiritual dimension are a waste of time. I think religion is the anchor for most people's morality. I would rather be judged by people from the Christian Coalition than by my former colleagues in university philosophy departments, thank you.

Interview/
Modern Maturity,
March-April:28.

Patrick J. Buchanan
Political commentator;
Candidate for the
1996 Republican
Presidential nomination

2

Whether the choice of weapons is words or guns, men fight to preserve the most beautiful of the pictures in their minds.

Los Angeles Times,
3-21:(A)17.

Marcy Carsey
Television producer

3

[On the worst job advice she has ever been given]: "That which you do, do with your might. That done half is never done right." There must be mental institutions chock-full of people who thought they had to do everything perfectly. There are lots of things that ought to be only half done, and only a very few things that need to be done with all your might. The most important thing you can ever do is to figure out the difference.

Working Woman,
July:38.

Bill Clinton
President
of the United States

4

It's important not to take criticism personally. That is, a lot of times people try to hurt you personally, and you can't let that happen. So if someone criticizes you, ask yourself, "Is it true what they're saying?" And if it's true, then say, "Well, I'm going to try to improve. I'm going to try to do better."

To students at
Clinton Elementary
Magnet School,
Sherwood, Ark.,
Jan. 4/
The New York Times,
1-5:(A)13.

5

[What] will [people] say about World War II 100 or 200 or 300 years from today? I believe the lesson will be that people, when given a choice, will not choose to live under empire; that citizens, when given a choice, will not choose to live under dictators; that people, when given the opportunity to let the better angels of their natures rise to the top, will not embrace theories of political or racial or ethnic or religious superiority.

At World War II
commemoration ceremony,
Honolulu, Hawaii,
Sept. 3/
The Washington Post,
9-4:(A)4.

(BILL CLINTON)

1

There will be problems in this old world as long as people like you and me inhabit the planet, because we're not perfect. But the issue is, are we gaining on it, are we getting closer every day to living by the values we believe in, to lifting up the potential of every person, to giving everybody the chance to be the kind of person that they ought to be?

At fund-raising luncheon,
Dallas, Texas,
Oct. 16/
The New York Times,
10-21:9.

Hillary Rodham Clinton
Wife of President
of the United States
Bill Clinton

2

[On teenagers and sex]: My theory is, don't do it before you're 21—and then don't tell me about it.

Newsweek,
6-26:15.

Farrah Fawcett
Actress

3

[On aging]: To me, the gift we have in life is the knowledge that [as we get older] the exterior becomes less important. [What's important is] whatever I didn't get in my early years: the wisdom and the confidence, the power. You don't usually have those things when you're young, unless you're really an exceptional person. That's why I prefer where I am now in my life than where I was then, not knowing what I had or what to do with it.

Interview,
New York, N.Y./
"Interview" magazine,
February:92.

Horton Foote
Playwright

4

The qualities of people that appeal to me are this sense of courage and desire to, sometimes in spite of terrific odds, keep going and try to work things out . . . It's amazing what people can go through and endure and can come out on top somehow . . . And I don't think they all do. I think some people fail, and that's part of the human equation. That's one of the great questions: Why, under given circumstances, some people survive and some people don't? And that's a question that interests me very much.

Interview,
New York, N.Y./
The Christian Science Monitor,
3-22:14.

Phil Gramm
United States Senator,
R-Texas;
Candidate for the
1996 Republican
Presidential nomination

5

The easiest way for me to get melancholy is to walk over to the Library of Congress and look down those endless stacks of books, and realize there's information in there I need to know and am going to die not knowing.

The Atlantic Monthly,
March:86.

Hanna Holborn Gray
Historian,
University of Chicago

1

History is above all the study of complexity. The capacity to live and come to terms with complexity may be the hardest and most important thing we have to learn, and we have to learn it over and over.

World Press Review,
May:31.

Elton John
Rock musician

2

I think most actors, most singers, most creative people are self-destructive people. I don't know whether they've used their profession as a form of escape from who they are. But I know for me the work was partly an escape route. I was an overweight, shy kid who had very little self-esteem, who was always timid, who was always on the fringe of being in the gang; and so I created my own world and I blotted out everything else. And I think that's what a lot of creative people do. It's a blotting out of reality.

Interview/
"Interview" magazine,
April:74.

John Paul II
Pope

3

I am convinced that although war and violence are, alas, contagious, peace is equally so. Let us give it every chance!

To foreign ambassadors,
Vatican City, Jan. 9/
Los Angeles Times,
1-10:(A)4.

4

Hope and trust: These may seem matters beyond the purview of the United Nations. But they are not. The politics of nations . . . can never ignore the transcendent, spiritual dimension of the human experience, and could never ignore it without harming the cause of man and the cause of freedom.

At United Nations,
New York, Oct. 5/
Los Angeles Times,
10-6:(A)27.

Krzysztof Kieslowski
Polish
motion-picture director

5

I don't meet "bad" people. Yes, people behave selfishly, with cowardice and stupidity, but they do so because they find themselves in situations where they have no other option. They create traps for themselves, and there's no escape. People don't want to be dishonest—life forces them into it.

Interview,
Los Angeles, Calif./
Los Angeles Times,
2-12:(Calendar)18.

Carole King
Singer, Songwriter

6

I think friends are important at all times. But I think it's really important to remember that *you* are your very best friend. And if *you* are your very best friend, you will have lots of friends.

Interview,
New York, N.Y./
"Interview" magazine,
February:59.

Vladimir A. Kitaev
Professor of history,
Volgograd University
(Russia)

1

History is not always just to those who make it.

Los Angeles Times,
5-1:(A)6.

Sherry Lansing
Chairman,
motion-picture group,
Paramount Pictures

2

You can be strong without being tough. What I have found in life is that most people just want you to tell them the truth. They can take a "no" if you say it to their face. What's painful is when you don't give people the truth. And when you don't do it yourself.

Interview,
Los Angeles, Calif./
Working Woman,
April:87.

Julius Lester
Author;
Professor
of Judaic studies,
University of Massachusetts,
Amherst

3

[Some people believe they] only live in one world, and that simply is not true of any of us. We all live in and move back and forth between many worlds. One of my worlds is the world of black culture. Another of my worlds is the world of Western culture. Another is the world of Jewish culture, and the culture of the university, and then there's the culture of New England. We all live in multiple cultures, and move back and forth between them and put on and take off identities and parts of identities as we go; and we do it pretty effortlessly.

Interview/
Booklist,
2-15:1091.

Jerry Lewis
Entertainer

4

[On the timid, juvenile character that has become his trademark over the years]: Your world out there is that character. Think about it. Everybody you see today is that character. They've covered it a little bit with makeup, but the bottom line is, everybody's nine [years old]. And the very thing that spirits an individual to passion and energy and inspiration is coming from the child within. The adult isn't smart enough to know there's something to be inspired about. The child of nine still feels excitement and awe and all the things that make humanity. It doesn't come from the poet-laureates; it comes from nine-year-olds . . . A lot of people suffocate the child within because they have waited a long time to light a cigarette and to get on the jet-set party list. All of those things are the things that get in the way of having a wonderful time without any bravado and without any covers or shadings. I'm having the best time of my life and I'm 69 years old this year. But really I'm nine.

Interview,
New York, N.Y./
"Interview" magazine,
April:93.

Antanas Mockus
Mayor of Bogota, Colombia

1

Political mediation is a necessary illness that is crucial in a democracy.

Interview, Bogota, Colombia/ The New York Times, 4-29:4.

Toni Morrison
Author

2

[On loneliness]: Don't call it loneliness. Call it something else. Call it solitude. I don't mean to be glib, but if you're not good company for yourself, you have to work to become the kind of person whose company you enjoy. If you enjoy your own company, there is no loneliness.

Interview/ Essence, May:274.

Gerard Mortier
Artistic director, Salzburg Festival (Austria)

3

Tradition is not a document of the past but an inexhaustible treasure for future generations.

Opera News, June:43.

Bill Moyers
Broadcast journalist

4

[On his having open-heart surgery last year]: I think it was that quick, unexpected brush with a premature exit that called me for the first time to see that the hourglass had fewer grains of sand in the upper half of it than it had in the bottom. I mean, I still think of myself as a young man with a future. I think a lot of us do. And coming out of bypass surgery and turning 60 made me realize that the only future one really has . . . is the one grain of sand that falls through that hourglass a piece at a time. And I want to see it in all of its mystery and beauty and glory as it falls.

Interview/ Ladies' Home Journal, March:74.

Charles Murigande
Cabinet Minister of Rwanda

5

It doesn't take a lot of people to do harm. It is the nature of human beings that people who want to do bad have more commitment and energy and determination than those who want to do good.

Los Angeles Times, 9-14:(A)1,12.

Gaylord Nelson
Former United States Senator, D-Wisconsin

6

The distinguished British jurist Lord Moulton neatly summed it all up in one sentence. As he put it: "The measure of a civilization is the degree of its compliance with the unenforceable." In other words, what you do when nobody is looking is what counts. That is what ethics is all about.

Speech/ The Washington Post, 4-12:(A)24.

Shimon Peres
Foreign Minister
of Israel

1

I don't think anybody who carries a rifle carries the future. Because I don't believe that you can really change the world by killing and shooting. You have to change it by creating and competing. And the people who don't understand this will disappear, not by the kinds of enemies we have seen in the past, but by the judgment of history.

Interview/
"Interview" magazine,
July:102.

Henry Petroski
Chairman,
department of civil
and environmental engineering,
Duke University

2

I see the process of creativity in synthesizing ideas or objects or things as being very similar. We tend to segregate things—engineering, architecture, legislation—but there are a lot of common features. We're all human beings, just focusing on different aspects of what effectively is a single big problem.

Interview,
Durham, N.C./
Publishers Weekly,
9-4:44.

Colin L. Powell
General,
United States Army (Ret.);
Former Chairman,
Joint Chiefs of Staff

3

We've got to restore a sense of shame to our society. Nothing seems to shame us or outrage us anymore. We look at our television sets and see all kinds of trash, and we allow it to come into our homes. We're not ashamed of it anymore.

Speech/
Time,
7-10:26.

Ann Richards
Governor
of Texas (D)

4

The people who are truly powerful are the ones who give it away, not the ones who hang on to it and are conscious of it. I know people who have power where the power itself is important to them, and they're some of the unhappiest people I know—truly miserable. Because all their time is spent hanging on.

Interview,
Austin, Texas/
Working Woman,
March:85.

Bruce Springsteen
Rock singer

5

I've found that giving 100 percent to your job isn't the same as giving 100 percent of your *life* to your job. Very often when I thought I was giving 100 percent of my life to my job, I was simply obsessing over something. I think that changes as you get older because you want more out of life. You've got your kids and your wife, and your overall family becomes more important. You see your parents differently. Hopefully, one of the things you learn as part of your craft is how

(BRUCE SPRINGSTEEN)

to focus your abilities and your energy into a shorter span of time.

Interview,
Los Angeles, Calif./
Los Angeles Times,
3-6:(F)4.

Sylvester Stallone
Actor

1

All friends are like flawed jewels, and when you understand that none of them are going to be outstandingly perfect, but that through all the crap they will still shine because they have integrity and they can be brutally honest with you and have the pride to tell you to go to hell if you step on them—those are real friends. Those are people that you can count on when your back is to the wall. When you're on top and you lead the parade, everyone's there throwing lilies and lilac water on your head. But when those parades have gone by and there's a storm in your heart, there are very few people that are going to sit there and listen to you bemoan life.

Interview/
"Interview" magazine,
July:78.

Rod Steiger
Actor

2

I was on my own as a boy. I became my own father and mother, my own protector and provider. But I learned that you need another person in your life, whether you like it or not. I wrote a poem at the age of 17 about the differences between men and women. That difference contains desire, and that desire pursued with respect makes us both more completely ourselves. I have yet to meet a man or woman who can live their lives alone and be fully happy.

Interview,
Malibu, Calif./
The American Patriot,
Summer:7.

Jim Stowers, Jr.
Chairman,
Twentieth Century
Mutual Funds

3

[On being a millionaire]: I naturally could be extravagant, but I think I'm probably tighter now than I was [before becoming a millionaire]. You want to be able to get the most you can for the least amount of money—it's the same thing as when I was younger. The biggest disease a millionaire has is being afraid of running out of his money. He's got the same identical problem as the person who has just a little bit of money, because a millionaire's expenses are a lot greater than the other person's.

Interview,
Kansas City, Mo./
The Christian Science Monitor,
1-9:8.

David Weeks
Neuropsychologist,
Royal Edinburgh Hospital
(Scotland)

4

Many people in society today are unhappy and don't know exactly why. Most people want to be unique and popular and happy. My definition of eccentric people is almost an

(DAVID WEEKS)

oxymoron. They are able to attain all these things, whereas most people think in terms of a tradeoff: If you're too unique, you run the risk of being unpopular. If you're too popular, you tend to be conformist. Eccentrics get away with more than most people can, and they do it through the sheer thrust of their personality. It's not magic. It's the way they behave and relate to other people. They are often seen as taking a certain number of steps too far.

The Wall Street Journal,
11-2:(A)12.

Andrew Young
Former United States Ambassador/
Permanent Representative
to the United Nations;
Former Mayor of Atlanta, Ga.

1

We all know that our lives are going to end, but we don't live that way. Great men are the ones who do. [The late President] Franklin Roosevelt, [the late civil-rights leader] Martin Luther King and [former President] Jimmy Carter all knew they were going to die and lived that way.

Life,
November:114.

Religion

Zine el-Abidine Sebti
Moroccan Ambassador to Italy

1

[On the opening of a new Islamic mosque in Rome, the largest in Europe]: [This is a major step] toward demolishing the campaigns of information which paint Islam as a violent and extremist religion, while Islam has proclaimed equality and peaceful coexistence.

Rome, Italy, June 21/ Los Angeles Times, 6-22:(A)14.

Catherine L. Albanese
Professor of religious studies, University of California, Santa Barbara

2

If you look at the record of American religious history, it's quite clear that there is a kind of gradation of tolerance. Groups that are most like the public Protestantism that informed the founders of the nation are the most tolerated, and as groups get further and further away from looking and acting and behaving like Protestants, they become less and less tolerable.

The Washington Post, 7-25:(A)6.

Aleksii II
Patriarch of the Russian Orthodox Church

3

I am sincerely grateful to all of those American Christians who have unselfishly aided [the church in] Russia at a time when our country especially needed it [in the last several years after the fall of Communism]. The tensions arise only in those instances when people come to us who are too self-assured and unfamiliar with our real needs. They often bring with them primitive, semi-literate books and Bible-course translations intended for low reading levels. Along this line, they take part in proselytism and try to inveigle Orthodox people or the unchurched members of Orthodox families into those communities that they have created. At a recent meeting between the Constantinople Patriarchate and the heads of 14 Orthodox churches, we drew a fine line between proselytism, on the one hand, and evangelization by Christian missionaries, on the other. It was emphasized that approaches made to an already Christian people through various forms of seduction poison the ties between Christian denominations and damage the path toward unity.

Interview/ Christianity Today, 6-19:15.

Nancy T. Ammerman
Sociologist of religion, Hartford Seminary

4

It is within the teachings of the Christian church that one should be willing to lay down one's life for one's beliefs. Throughout Christian history, you find people going on crusades, willing to be killed in defense of holy ground, in defense of the holy cross. That is

(NANCY T. AMMERMAN)

very much a part of what we as the human race have found religion to be about.

Interview/
The Washington Post,
7-25:(A)6.

Jack Bemporad
Rabbi;
Director,
Center for Christian-Jewish Understanding,
Sacred Heart University

1

Most Jews and Catholics are not aware of the [positive] changes in Christian-Jewish relations in the last 30 years. We are ready for a new kind of dialogue: How can I be true to my faith without being false to yours?

At conference on
Catholic-Jewish relations,
New York, N.Y./
The New York Times,
2-25:10.

William J. Bennett
Former Secretary
of Education
of the United States

2

The [Christian] Coalition has earned itself a central place at the conservative table now. And yeah, there are [religious] excesses; there are dupes; there are some TV hucksters out there who just want people's money. But religious people for the most part are really fine people to whom you would entrust your children. They are God-fearing and responsible and I like them. I'd take that audience over a Grateful Dead [rock group] audience anytime.

Interview/
Modern Maturity,
March-April:28.

David Berger
Professor of history,
Brooklyn College;
Board member,
Association
for Jewish Studies

3

For women, the advanced study of Jewish texts outside formal academic settings does not exist in Israel and has a limited extent in the United States. For women, the academic route becomes the avenue for the most advanced achievement for Jewish learning.

The New York Times,
2-4:9.

Lisa Berkman
Epidemiologist,
Yale Medical School

4

Having a strong [religious] faith and being embedded in a web of relationships like churchgoing have definite health benefits . . . For years, the research was unclear on whether it was the social participation in temple or church that was beneficial, or the underlying religious faith. It turns out from the accumulated data to be both.

Before American
Heart Association,
Santa Barbara, Calif.,
Jan. 18/
The New York Times,
2-4:9.

Darrell Bock
Professor
of the New Testament,
Dallas Theological Seminary

1

I wouldn't say the evangelical mind is emerging as much as it is *re*-emerging. The church was bleeding at the beginning of this century in the face of modernism, and it had to withdraw, retreat and rebuild itself, almost from scratch. As a result, the church had little energy to do reflective, calm, deep thinking. When a body is in trauma, its first priority is to save itself. If I can change metaphors, the evangelical movement is like a teenager coming of age in which she is now facing major decisions about adulthood. So the question is this: Now that we have the potential for recovery, how do we move on from here?

Panel discussion/
Christianity Today,
8-14:22.

Thomas Cahill
Director
of religious publishing,
Doubleday & Co.,
publishers

2

[On the increase in sales of religious-oriented books]: If you walked through the American Booksellers Association [summer convention], you would have heard everywhere that religion is hot, as if it sort of broke like a wave from nowhere on top of big mainstream publishers. [In fact,] I'm not sure religion is a new trend. It's a deep, pervasive, abiding need of many people, and publishers have simply rediscovered it.

The Washington Post,
8-21:(A)6.

Conrad Cherry
Professor of religion,
and director of the Center
for the Study of Religion
and American Culture,
Indiana University-Purdue University,
Indianapolis

3

[On the U.S. fondness for organized, public expressions of religious faith]: It's an outcropping of the sense that God is clearly associated with the future and the destiny of this nation, a longstanding belief in this country.

The New York Times,
5-4:(A)8.

Bill Clinton
President
of the United States

4

[On criticism of him by Christian conservatives]: If they could look into my soul, they would see someone whose belief in God and of faith is as sincere and deep and genuine as theirs is. And they would probably see someone who is, perhaps rightly or wrongly, much more humble in his Christian faith than many of them are . . . I don't see any conflict between a person having deep religious convictions and being an active citizen. But I do think that it calls for a little more humility than we sometimes see in condemning the motives and character of people with whom you disagree.

Broadcast interview/
"This Morning,"
CBS-TV, 2-20.

5

[The First Amendment of the U.S. Constitution] does not convert our schools into religion-free zones . . . I am deeply troubled

(BILL CLINTON)

that so many Americans feel that their faith is threatened by the mechanisms that are designed to protect their faith. When the First Amendment is invoked as an obstacle to private expression of religion, it is being misused. Religion has a proper place in private and a proper place in public, because the public square belongs to all Americans.

At James Madison High School, Vienna, Va., July 12/ The New York Times, 7-13:(A)1.

Paul Davies
Professor of natural philosophy, University of Adelaide (Australia); Winner, 1995 Templeton Prize for Progress in Religion

1

Most people think that as science advances, religion retreats. But the more we discover about the world, the more we find there's a purpose or design behind it all.

Telephone interview, March 8/ The New York Times, 3-9:(A)11.

Yechiel Eckstein
Rabbi; President, International Fellowship of Christians and Jews

2

Private prayer, which is something many of us engage in, is critical. But I do believe there is a place for [public] symbolism. When the [U.S.] Senate is opened with a prayer, it's making a statement about that body. It's bringing transcendence to our national polity.

The New York Times, 5-4:(A)8.

Dean Hoge
Director, American Congregational Giving Study

3

Boomers [the baby-boom generation born after World War II] feel less desire to be involved in church at all; they feel that it's optional. And they have less denominational loyalty as well. Now it seems like the kind of loyalty you have when you're buying a car—not much.

Christianity Today, 4-24:49.

Ernest Jim Istook, Jr.
United States Representative, R-Oklahoma

4

[Calling for a Constitutional amendment that would allow prayer in public schools]: The decision of whether to have a prayer at some kind of school activity should properly be made by the people that are involved in that activity, not by a Federal judge, not by an ACLU attorney. This [should be] a community decision, not a Federal decision . . . Nobody is proposing that we return to a practice of compulsory prayer, or mandatory recital, or reading from Scripture. We are talk-

(ERNEST JIM ISTOOK, JR.)

ing about *permitting* religious expression, not about compelling it.

Before House Constitution Subcommittee, Washington, D.C., June 8/ The New York Times, 6-9:(A)1.

John Paul II
Pope

1

In recent years, the number of canonizations and beatifications has increased. These show the vitality of the local churches, which are much more numerous today than in the first centuries and in the first millennium.

Los Angeles Times, 1-5:(A)1.

2

They say the Pope is getting old and that he can't walk without a cane. But, one way or another, I'm still around. I've got my hair, and things aren't so bad with my head either.

To Polish pilgrims, Vatican City, Jan. 6/ Los Angeles Times, 1-12:(A)6.

3

My task is not to speak in purely human terms about merely human values, but in spiritual terms about spiritual values, which are ultimately what makes us fully human.

At St. Joseph's Seminary, Yonkers, N.Y., Oct. 6/ Los Angeles Times, 10-7:(A)16.

Mark Juergensmeyer
Sociologist, University of California, Santa Barbara

4

Religion provides an ideology of stability and moral certainty in a world rapidly changing or in a world that seems unstable or corrupt.

Los Angeles Times, 11-6:(A)12.

Richard D. Land
Executive director, Christian Life Commission, Southern Baptist Convention

5

[Saying the "separation of church and state" idea some say is inherent in the U.S. Constitution has been carried too far in schools]: We believe that seeking to make the public schools an artificially sanitized religious-free zone is religious segregation.

Los Angeles Times, 4-5:(A)13.

Barry Lynn
Executive director, Americans United for the Separation of Church and State

6

The problem [with government-sponsored or government-involved religious expression] is [that] civil religion is never a substitute for authentic religious experience. [The involvement of politicians] tends to cheapen the whole process.

The New York Times, 5-4:(A)8.

Richard Mouw
President,
Fuller Theological Seminary,
Pasadena, Calif.

1

A lot of us Protestants wish we had a stronger sense of the teaching and shepherding authority of the church, whereas Catholics are loosening up on that. There's a kind of passing each other in opposing directions. Many of us on the Protestant side of things worry a little about the breakdown of authority in the Catholic Church. We simply don't want to see them make all the mistakes we've made.

Time,
10-9:68.

Bill Moyers
Broadcast journalist

2

Religion is a source of values and ideas. It drives us, in the same way that hunger, the need for nutrition, drives us. It is a force . . . that motivates human behavior . . . This whole surge [in religious belief] is taking place in people's hearts. I mean, forget for the moment the religious right that you see in politics. Forget the civil-rights movement, [which was driven] by religiously motivated men and women. The search to find meaning today, short of the political process, is the kind of experience that people don't talk about very easily. Religion is subjective. It's deeply personal. And this is not something people talk about easily or discuss openly on television.

Interview/
Ladies' Home Journal,
March:74.

Laura Murphy
Director,
Washington office,
American Civil Liberties Union

3

[On President Clinton's recent statement that prayer should be permitted in schools]: There's good news here in that the President made a strong case against any changes in the First Amendment. But there is also an attempt to push the envelope on what is permitted . . . I've already been getting calls from worried Jewish parents asking: "Does this mean my child is going to have to listen to Christian prayers?" This [Clinton's statement] is an olive branch to the conservative Christian groups. This is a way of portraying the President as a centrist. We have no illusion about that.

Los Angeles Times,
7-13:(A)11.

John Navone
Biblical theologian,
Gregorian University
(Vatican City)

4

Saints are the friends of God. They mirror the church's concept of Christian perfection and are meant to be imitated. Saints help us to envision what the good Christian life really is.

Los Angeles Times,
1-5:(A)6.

Mark Noll
Professor of Christian thought,
Wheaton College

5

American evangelicalism is wonderful in that it has no boundaries. The terrific fellow-

(MARK NOLL)

ship, helpfulness and lack of concern for authority and place have all positively affected Christianity in this country. But American evangelicals often function like an engine run amuck when it comes to intellectual questions. And this explains why, generally speaking, there are fewer active believers in Britain than in America but much better Christian thinking. We have the virtues of our vices and the vices of our virtues.

Panel discussion/ Christianity Today, 8-14:25.

Lloyd John Ogilvie
Chaplain-designate of the United States Senate

1

[On suggestions that a taxpayer-supported Chaplain of the Senate is un-Constitutional]: I believe there is a real difference between separation of church and state and the separation of God and state. I will constantly affirm the oneness of God, [not the oneness of church and state].

Christianity Today, 3-6:46.

Thomas Oxman
Psychiatrist, Dartmouth Medical School

2

[Saying religious faith may help people with serious illnesses]: It seems that being able to give meaning to a precarious, life-threatening situation—having faith there is some greater meaning or force at work—is medically helpful. If you can't make sense of what's going on, it's much harder to bear . . . It may be that having faith translates into your being more soothed physiologically. If your mind is calmer, that might make arrhythmias less likely.

The New York Times, 2-4:9.

Richard W. Riley
Secretary of Education of the United States

3

Public schools should not be hostile to religion. On the contrary, there are significant religious freedoms for individuals that they carry with them into the school house and the school room

Interview, Aug. 25/ The New York Times, 8-26:8.

4

[On the controversy over whether or not to allow prayer in schools]: Nothing can be more sensitive to people than their religion. Add that with their children, and then add the public space of a school where you have different views and teaching is taking place. We need to stop and think about it, and it is not something to take a dogmatic approach on.

Washington, D.C./ Los Angeles Times, 8-31:(A)28.

Pat Robertson
Evangelist

5

[On why he founded the American Center for Law and Justice organization]: Back in the early '80s, I took a long look at what the [American] Civil Liberties Union was do-

(PAT ROBERTSON)

ing to take religion from the public square of America. It was like an all-out vendetta against religious values. There didn't seem like there was any champion to stand up against them.

Interview/
The New York Times,
7-8:8.

Cecil Roebuck
Professor of church history and ecumenics, Fuller Theological Seminary, Pasadena, Calif.

1

I think about the way Protestant churches are continually looking back to [the Catholic Pope in] Rome. We're always looking with our heads turned over our shoulders, if not straight on, to find an authority figure who can speak on behalf of the church. The World Council of Churches doesn't speak for the church. My suspicion is there is still this kind of twinge inside of us [Protestants] that says there is something more to this papacy than meets the eye.

Los Angeles Times,
6-3:(B)4.

Lyle Schaller
United Methodist minister and parish consultant

2

[On the growing influence of Protestant "megachurches"]: It's revolutionary. We were trained since the Civil War to look to denominational headquarters for help. [Today,] the model of how you do church is coming out of the megachurches.

The New York Times,
4-29:1.

Louis P. Sheldon
Presbyterian minister; Chairman, Traditional Values Coalition

3

[On President Clinton's statement that religion should not be barred from having a place in public schools]: [The President's comments are] too little, too late. He came on at the level of the caboose, and we're here at the engine driving this thing. We've already revealed the level of hostility [against prayer in schools], and we need an amendment [to the Constitution affirming the right to have prayer in schools]. His is only an initiative, and it will be inadequate.

July 12/
The New York Times,
7-13:(A)10.

Loren Siegel
Public education director, American Civil Liberties Union

4

[On criticism that the ACLU is anti-religion because of its efforts to separate religion from government-associated endeavors, such as its stand on prayer in public schools]: We would and will take the case of any child in a public school who is told he cannot say grace before lunch. But we would absolutely oppose a graduation ceremony that would have a clergy person or anyone [delivering a prayer for the assembly].

The New York Times,
7-8:8.

Leonard I. Sweet
Chancellor,
United Theological Seminary,
Dayton, Ohio

1

[On the growing influence of Protestant "megachurches"]: These megachurches are becoming teaching churches, just as you have teaching hospitals.

The New York Times,
4-29:7.

Tad Szulc
Author, Journalist

2

[On Pope John Paul II's penchant for making saints]: Making saints is part of John Paul's strategic genius, a way of making the church as an institution more personalized and keeping it before the public. From the outset, he has sought to make it popular, active and as public as possible.

Los Angeles Times,
1-5:(A)6.

Paul E. Tsongas
Co-chairman,
The Concord Coalition;
Former
United States Senator,
D-Massachusetts

3

[Organized] school prayer is the way for a Jewish student to feel inappropriate when they do the Lord's Prayer. But I think the idea of a moment of silence, that you acknowledge a Higher Being, in whatever way that you wish—then you give legitimacy to the instinct to be spiritual. As opposed to make it seem nerdy or inappropriate or uncool, or something you do when you're off by yourself. Certainly the unabashed spirituality of the Founding Fathers never seemed inappropriate.

Interview, Boston, Mass./
The Christian Science Monitor,
1-9:19.

Dallas Willard
Adjunct professor
of spirituality,
Fuller Theological Seminary,
Pasadena, Calif.

4

Much modern thinking views spirituality as simply a kind of "interiority"—the basic idea that there is an inside to the human being, and that this is the place where contact is made with the transcendental. In this view, spirituality is essentially a human dimension. [But] Christian spirituality is centered in the idea of a transcendent life—"being born from above," as the New testament puts it. This idea of spiritual life carries with it notions like accountability, judgment, the need for justice, and so on. These concepts are less popular, and they certainly are more difficult, than a conception of spirituality that simply focuses on one's inner life.

Interview/
Christianity Today,
3-6:16.

James Williams
Executive director,
Church of God World Service

5

Our people 45 years old and younger have grown up mesmerized by materialism. There's tremendous pressure on families to spend, spend and spend . . . I've heard that the generation that believed in the tradition of tith-

(JAMES WILLIAMS)

ing is in three places: retirement homes, nursing homes, or cemeteries. Whether the newer generations are going to pick up on [tithing] is yet to be seen

Christianity Today, 4-24:49.

David Wulff
Psychologist, Wheaton College

1

Various religions encourage healthy practices like abstaining from smoking. But the [healthy] effect from religion remains after you control for such health habits. It seems to be the sheer optimism or hopefulness that's part of the religious outlook that makes a difference . . . [Generally,] higher levels of religious practice are usually associated with better health.

The New York Times,
2-4:9.

Science and Technology

Bruce Alberts
President,
National Academy of Sciences

1

There's always going to be an over-supply of scientists. My own view is that the system *has* to be competitive. Getting government funding is a privilege. The stiffer the competition, the better the chance that only the best are getting grants.

The Washington Post National Weekly,
1-9:6.

Neal Barnard
Member,
Physicians Committee
for Responsible Medicine

2

Scientific curiosity is such a powerful drive it causes scientists to step over ethical boundaries. I wish it weren't so, but I believe it is.

U.S. News & World Report,
9-18:80.

Garrett W. Brass
Executive Director,
United States Arctic
Research Commission

3

[On the decision to make available U.S. nuclear attack submarines for civilian scientific research under the Arctic]: The submarine is a fantastic greyhound that can race around and find things you can't possibly keep track of any other way. This agreement is going to produce a fantastic increase in our ability to monitor the changes that are going on in the Arctic . . . I'm still surprised that it happened. This started out as a blind date with this girl [the Navy] to see if we got along. The good news is that we did.

The New York Times,
2-21:(B)5.

Robert L. Dorit
Biologist,
Yale University

4

[On a study that concludes that modern man originated 200,000 to 300,000 years ago, not more than 1,000,000 years ago as previously theorized]: It suggests that we really are an extremely recent species on this planet. We are definitely rookies . . . noisy, but new.

Los Angeles Times,
5-26:(A)1.

Ervin S. Duggan
President,
Public Broadcasting Service

5

There is happening in the world a set of technological and marketplace changes in communications that seem to me as sweeping and profound as the Industrial Revolution of the 19th century was for the textile industry. Now, in 19th-century England, the weavers in their cottages were local and autonomous. But every one of them who imagined that he could sit at his loom, oblivious to the ships pulling up at Liverpool with bales of cotton from the American South, and to the

(ERVIN S. DUGGAN)

humming of the factories, paid a price. And sometimes the price meant extinction.

Interview, Alexandria, Va./
The New York Times,
6-26:(B)1.

Peter Gabriel
Rock musician

1

[On the technology revolution in interactive and personal computers and other hardware for which he is currently involved in producing software]: I believe one of the key issues in terms of economic growth for the world and political stability and peace will be determined by whether the technology stays in the hands of the West and whether it is really shared. What's exciting about technology is that with a few PCs and a small satellite up- and down-link—which should be very cheap—it's possible for any village in any part of the planet to, in a very short space of time, be part of this information revolution. So my dream is that the First World will be foresighted enough to realize that it is in their own basic economic interest to develop technology in emerging countries.

Interview,
Los Angeles, Calif./
Los Angeles Times,
3-8:(D)9.

Newt Gingrich
United States Representative,
R-Georgia;
Speaker of the House

2

[Criticizing proposed legislation that would impose strong penalties on those using computer online services to distribute pornographic material]: [This proposal is] clearly a violation of free speech and . . . a violation of the right of adults to communicate with each other. I don't agree with it and I don't think it is a serious way to discuss a serious issue.

TV broadcast,
June 20/
Daily Variety,
6-22:1.

Daniel S. Goldin
Administrator,
National Aeronautics
and Space Administration
of the United States

3

[On proposed new deeper cuts in NASA's funding]: I'm going to fight it. [When I read about it,] I couldn't get out of bed, I was so frustrated . . . Americans have to decide whether they want to have a space program. [If the proposed cuts go through,] the next step is to shut it down. I shouldn't have said that. [But] this [NASA] workforce has been whipsawed for too long . . . We've got to stop this continual cutting by the yard.

Interview,
Washington, D.C., May 12/
The Washington Post,
5-15:(A)17.

4

[On U.S. and Russia cooperating in building a space station]: People say they're worried about the Russians. I'm a lot more worried about the [U.S.] Congress canceling the space station [for budget reasons] and having to tell our allies. This is a litmus test for America's willingness to be a real interna-

(DANIEL S. GOLDIN)

tional partner. [If it's canceled,] it will have a chilling effect not just on space science, but on science across the board.

Los Angeles Times,
6-19:(A)15.

1

[On the current cooperative space mission of the U.S. and Russia, during which an American space shuttle will link with a Russian space station]: You can't make this unbelievable transition from pointing weapons at one another to working together without bumps in the road. But the relationship is rock solid. This proves that if you put your mind to something and search for common interests, you can build bridges.

Interview, June 27/
The New York Times,
6-28:(A)11.

Doyal A. Harper
Chief administrator,
Center for Astrophysical
Research in Antarctica

2

[On the arrival of the Internet computer system at the U.S. scientific station in Antarctica]: It's absolutely essential to tie together the men and women who work here, and the scientists outside Antarctica who use our telescopes, into effective working teams. The people in the States must remain engaged in the problems and realities of life down here, and the winter-over people who work here must not feel cut off from the outer world. For the first time, E-mail will let them communicate not only with the professional people outside Antarctica, but with their families and friends. We have begun a new era. The Internet is changing the flavor of science in Antarctica.

Interview,
Amundsen-Scott
South Pole Station, Antarctica/
The New York Times,
1-10:(B)9.

Reed E. Hundt
Chairman,
Federal Communications
Commission

3

It's one thing to say government should remove all of the concrete barriers [of regulation] between the lanes of the "information highway," and I completely agree with that. But when you take the barriers down, there's nothing convincing people to cross the lanes and compete . . . What you [as the government] can do is make sure fair rules of competition exist that will attract competition.

Interview/
The Christian Science Monitor,
5-3:4.

Daniel Kevles
Professor of humanities,
California Institute
of Technology

4

[Saying the Cold War forced the U.S. to invest trillions of dollars in scientific research]: In a sense, the [now-ended] Cold War was one of the greatest stimulants to Federal investment in lots of good things that we've ever had in the United States. It's ironic, but it's true.

Los Angeles Times,
5-24:(D)4.

Gennady Kozlov
Deputy Minister
of Science
of Russia

1

[On cutbacks in Russia's financing of scientific research]: When I worked as a scientist, salaries increased with seniority and academic qualifications. They weren't linked to the practical success of research . . . Ten years ago you would see lots of people everywhere in the scientific institutes. Today a lot of the rooms are empty, but in others some very good work is going on. The picture used to be homogeneous. Now there are islands of high activity.

The Christian Science Monitor,
8-2:7.

Sondra Lazarowitz
Associate professor
of microbiology,
University of Illinois,
Urbana-Champaign

2

[Criticizing cutbacks in funding for scientific projects that are risky in favor of those that are "sure things"]: Creative grants are nit-picked to death because everyone knows there are insufficient funds. Worse yet, they are trashed based on containing an element of risk. Frankly, the most creative science is that which takes risks. The situation is favoring the lemmings who copy what has been done and is safe.

The Washington Post
National Weekly,
1-9:7.

Leon Lederman
Nobel Prize-winning physicist;
Former president,
American Association
for the Advancement
of Science

3

[On the slowing of U.S. scientific funding]: If we persist on this course, we can expect to see America's position in the world gradually weaken. We will watch as our technology-based products become less and less competitive in world markets.

The Washington Post
National Weekly,
1-9:6.

John M. Logsdon
Director,
Space Policy Institute,
George Washington University

4

[On the increasing cooperation in space missions between the U.S. and Russia]: These early missions are a test of our willingness to do things that make sense despite problems in other parts of the relationship. We're no longer strategic rivals. Russia is no longer a threat to our security or world leadership, so we ought to be able to deal with it more pragmatically. The general idea and even the specifics of exploring together have been in the works for decades. There's an underlying logic to this collaboration that's been obvious to [U.S.] Presidents for over 30 years. Now the conditions finally seem right for our being able to do it.

Interview/
The New York Times,
2-7:(B)10.

Jean-Marie Luton
Director General,
European Space Agency

1

[On the planned international space station "Alpha," in which a number of nations, mainly the U.S. and Russia, will be involved]: We are acutely aware that the space station is a test case [for future international cooperation]. The problem is [the need for] a long-term commitment of vast magnitude . . . We need some patience.

The Washington Post,
6-24:(A)8.

John B. MacChesney
Researcher,
AT&T Bell Laboratories

2

Two hundred years ago, James Watt by himself invented the steam engine and launched the Industrial Revolution. Today, the work [inventors] do rests on the work of hundreds of others, and it takes deep [financial] pockets, and a long time span, to produce the kinds of inventions we're hearing about [nowadays].

At New Jersey Inventors
Hall of Fame induction,
Newark, N.J., Feb. 17/
The New York Times,
2-21:(A)12.

Kumar N. Patel
Vice Chancellor for research,
University of California,
Los Angeles

3

Near-term profitability pressures have led to a significant downsizing of [industry's scientific] research staff. Even those high-technology giants who built their industries on the results of basic research have substantially reduced fundamental research activities.

The Washington Post National Weekly,
1-9:7.

Marc A. Pearl
Spokesman,
Information Technology
Association of America

4

[On a new Connecticut law making it a crime to harass someone through computer communication]: Connecticut's approach is probably going to be followed by other states. The proliferation of on-line systems and usage will mean there will be as many crazies—perverted individuals—using that means as now use the mail and the phone lines.

June 12/
The New York Times,
6-13:(A)10.

Shimon Peres
Foreign Minister
of Israel

5

In historic terms, we are nearing an end to the season of hunting in human experience and entering the season of creation. What makes a person or a nation strong today is science and technology, rather than land and natural resources. Now, science, technology and information do not have sovereignties and do not have borders and do not have flags. They're available to everybody. So I think the struggle in the future will be very much of a spiritual and intellectual nature.

Interview/
"Interview" magazine,
July:88.

Henry Petroski
Chairman,
department of civil
and environmental
engineering,
Duke University

1

New things arise from old things, and inventors, engineers, designers see faults in those existing things and try to remove them. Like the zipper—it took 30 years for it to get to the point of just working reliably, and then another 10 or so to be generally accepted . . . I don't think anybody'll come up with the perfect anything. In engineering and design, generally, there are so many competing objectives. You want something to look nice, you want it to function well, you want it to be inexpensive, you want it to be long-lasting, durable, non-toxic—it's a never-ending list, and the more complicated the object or the structure, the more complicated the list.

Interview,
Durham, N.C./
Publishers Weekly,
9-4:44.

Robert B. Reich
Secretary of Labor
of the United States

2

There is nothing about technology that leads us inevitably down one path or the other. These are choices we can make as a society. Technology can upgrade the value of people and make them worth more in the marketplace just as it can downgrade their value and even replace them.

USA Today,
7-28:(B)2.

Howard Rheingold
Authority on
computer communications

3

[On why the Internet has become so popular]: Because it allows many people to reach many other people. It's kind of a publishing forum. It also allows you to communicate very easily with those who share your personal or professional interests, no matter where they are in the world or what time it is. It crosses a lot of barriers. If you have an interest in photography or raising roses, there might be a grandmother in Prague or a 14-year-old kid in St. Louis or someone in Tokyo with similar interests. Now you can all communicate. And "communicate" is the important word here. Information is useful and educational. You can make money or entertain yourself with it. But I think that it is 99 parts interest in people and one part interest in information that has kept the Internet going.

Interview,
Marin County, Calif./
American Way,
10-1:94.

Brewster Shaw
Director of Space-Shuttle Operations,
National Aeronautics and
Space Administration
of the United States

4

[On the new U.S.-Russian cooperation in space]: We've learned that the Russians are not as schedule-oriented as we are. Our people stand around and feel they're being slowed down a bit. [The Russians] have a different way of viewing the world than we do. It's kind of like getting married.

Time, 7-10:56.

Christopher Llewellyn Smith
Director,
European Nuclear
Research Center (Switzerland)

1

[On cutbacks in Russia's financing of scientific research]: Russia has a unique scientific, mathematical and technical culture. If Russian scientific culture were to die, it would be like losing a language.

The Christian Science Monitor,
8-2:7.

Koa Tasaka
Assistant professor
of chemistry,
International Christian University
(Japan)

2

Science education, especially in graduate school in Japan, tends to be just research-oriented. It produces people who are interested in chemical reactions only. That is wrong. We should teach these people more common sense and ethical values—at present they lack that aspect. They don't have the power to differentiate what's illegal and what's proper.

Los Angeles Times,
3-30:(A)6.

Albert H. Teich
Director, division of science
and policy programs,
American Association
for the Advancement of Science

3

[Expressing concern about future Federal funding of scientific projects and research]: For many years we had a protective umbrella of members of Congress who understood science, were sympathetic toward it and were associated with it. But now we have an awful lot of new people in Congress who don't have any connection with science. It's up to the scientific community to try to reach them.

Interview/
The New York Times,
8-29:(B)5.

Sherry Turkle
Professor of sociology,
Massachusetts Institute
of Technology

4

[On the possibility of legislation banning "indecency" on the Internet]: There are so few places in our society where people can have a little play space. Part of the appeal of online life is its sense of openness, and now it seems in danger of being closed down.

Los Angeles Times,
12-11:(A)15.

Edward O. Wilson
Biologist,
Museum of Comparative Zoology,
Harvard University

5

[On the idea of "naturalism"]: [It] is the philosophy of realism informed by scientific knowledge of the world as it actually is. Naturalism does not require atheism. It can be fitted easily to existing religious beliefs. But it is devoted to taking a much more hardheaded view about where humanity came from in evolutionary terms, how we fit into the environment, the natural environment especially, and what measures we have to take as a species to continue to survive and to promote individual fulfillment. Naturalism places a strong new emphasis not only on rational be-

(EDWARD O. WILSON)

havior, but also on deep understanding of the sources of our emotional behavior, and how the two are connected. It also calls for a realistic assessment of the dire need to control human population growth and preserve the natural environment, on the grounds that this was the environment in which our genes were assembled, the theater of human evolution.

Interview,
Cambridge, Mass./
American Way,
1-15:50.

1

I believe we are currently in the midst of one of the great [species-] extinction spasms of geological history. There have been five up until now, and we are, I think, in the sixth. The most recent, about 65 million years ago, was caused when a meteorite struck Earth. This led, among many other things, to the extinction of the dinosaurs. Each of those extinctions has been catastrophic for Earth because it's taken an average of 10 million years to recover from each of them. The difference between the previous great extinctions and this one is that the latter is caused by the actions of man—who may ultimately be among its victims . . . We are presently losing species, losing the diversity of our ecosystems, at an alarming rate. There have always been extinctions of what you might call a "natural" kind. Species that cannot compete or find a niche disappear. But as these species become extinct, others come along; so the trend is, increasingly, toward diversity. Since the appearance of human beings, however, the rate of extinctions has increased somewhere from 1,000 to 10,000 times. I often say that, as a biologist, I sometimes feel like an art curator watching the Louvre burn down.

Interview/
Modern Maturity,
May-June:63.

Sports

Sparky Anderson
Baseball manager,
Detroit "Tigers"

1

[Criticizing the possible use of replacement players in the coming season if the current long players' strike continues]: There's no place in our game for replacement players . . . Please let's don't think of such a horror story that we're going to have baseball with replacement players. If our game does that, there's going to be a lot of us who have been in this game a long time that are going to be truly, truly hurt.

News conference,
Lakeland, Fla.,
Feb. 17/
The New York Times,
2-18:33.

Charles Barkley
Basketball player,
Phoenix "Suns"

2

All you ever hear [about black college athletes] is we run for 1,000 yards and we dunk . . . But you make straight A's in the same school, they [the media] don't even know you're there. And that's sad.

U.S. News & World Report,
1-23:23.

Joseph R. Biden, Jr.
United States Senator,
D-Delaware

3

[On baseball, in light of last season's player strike and the resultant acrimony between players and owners]: I have not gone, will not go and would not consider going to a baseball game. I'm just so sick of them all.

USA Today,
8-4:(A)1.

Bobby Clarke
President,
Philadelphia "Flyers"
hockey team

4

[On team owners who demand that cities give them special perks or the team will relocate]: It's become blackmail. They say, "Build me a building. Pay for my losses or I'm leaving." I think the business is still screwed up.

Los Angeles Times,
6-1:(C)2.

Bill Clinton
President
of the United States

5

[On the current long strike by baseball players and the upcoming new season]: I just keep telling them to play ball. It's time to go. It's just a few hundred folks trying to figure out how to divide nearly $2-billion. They ought to be able to figure that out in time for the rest of America to enjoy this baseball season.

Washington, D.C.,
Feb. 6/
The New York Times,
2-7:(B)13.

Len Coleman
President, National (baseball) League

1

We have to create a greater focus on the game for the fans so they can enjoy the game and not have to hear as much rhetoric about the business aspects of baseball. We have to understand that the business of our game *is* the fans.

Ebony, June:128.

John Conyers, Jr.
United States Representative, D-Michigan

2

[Saying Congress should become involved in settling the baseball players' strike]: Congress always has been very cautious to intervene in collective bargaining. With the new Republican majority [in Congress] and their almost Pollyanna belief to allow the marketplace its own will, passing [a bill affecting baseball's work rules and antitrust aspect] will be difficult. [But] an increasing number of members of Congress are beginning to understand [that] the future of baseball as we know the game in our lifetime is in peril. That fact encourages Congress to act and perhaps act dramatically.

The New York Times, 1-5:(B)6.

Lenny Dykstra
Baseball player, Philadelphia "Phillies"

3

[On the effect on fans of the recent players' strike]: All they want to do is pay to watch a baseball game. We stripped them of that chance. We have to pay the fans the respect they are due.

USA Today, 4-7:(C)2.

John Ellis
Chief executive officer, Seattle "Mariners" baseball team

4

[On the new "wild card" system in baseball in which the team with the second-best record in each league is also eligible for the playoffs]: There was an outcry by the traditionalists about the new format, but when you think about all the problems baseball has had this year, the wild card has been the savior of the last half of the season. It's fascinating to me we [Seattle] can be in a race with New York [for a wild-card slot] that both cities are watching with bated breath.

USA Today, 9-15:(A)2.

Eliot L. Engel
United States Representative, D-New York

5

[On meeting a number of baseball players at a recent meeting between players and Congressmen arranged by the players' union]: It makes you feel like you're 10 years old again. I meet heads of state and have been doing this for seven years, but I'm not as impressed as when I meet ballplayers.

The New York Times, 2-4:32.

Chris Evert
Tennis player

1

The money [in tennis] is even bigger now [than when she was in her prime] and there are more demands on the players. Many of the players don't want to deal with the pressures and are always looking for ways to avoid it. They'll take week-long vacations in the South of France or St. Barts to get away from it all. I don't think I ever took a vacation when I first played. But then playing on the circuit was fun . . . There were no entourages or coaches, so we'd warm each other up, play our matches and have dinner together afterward. But the players are younger now. And there is so much more focus on them . . . They may take more indulgences now, but they also have more to deal with.

USA Today,
4-10:(C)3.

Donald Fehr
Executive director,
Major League (baseball)
Players Association

2

[On the current player strike]: The [team] owners' position has as its premise . . . that the owners are not capable of adequately managing the business and . . . we [players] should accept a salary structure well below what the owners admit players would otherwise be paid.

The Washington Post,
2-6:(A)10.

3

[On the current player strike, which began last season and may extend into the new season]: The [team] owners are determined to open the season with [player] replacements and see how many players cross the line. That's the reason they haven't been negotiating . . . Utilizing replacement players . . . denigrates the game and makes reaching an agreement much harder. It ought not to be something which is employed.

USA Today,
3-24:(C)2.

Stuart Fishelman
Physician;
Specialist in sports psychology

4

Retirement affects athletes in different ways. The highs an athlete gets from the highly selective field makes it hard for them to settle into another pursuit. These are young people who have achieved a lot of emotional and economic success at an early age, but they never think about their careers ending. The psychological "high" and its addiction is parallel to people who become addicted to cocaine or a smoker who has a dependency on cigarettes. Players rarely give much thought to life after football. It becomes quite a shock.

Los Angeles Times,
1-8:(C)4.

Rodney Fort
Professor of economics,
Washington State University

5

[On the recent labor strife in major-league sports, such as the current players' strike in baseball]: Now that it's really a matter for the courts and labor law, the [baseball] owners are going to get slapped around one more time. It will all come out in the wash that sports [players'] unions in America simply are not going to be turned back. The ability of the

(RODNEY FORT)

NFL Players Association to disband, bring individual players' lawsuits against owners, then get right back again, that's another indication that unions are not going away.

USA Today,
1-9:(C)2.

Otto Graham
Former football player;
Member of football's
Hall of Fame

1

[On the modernization of today's football games and the spectacle made of the Super Bowl]: I'm glad it's them and not me getting all that attention. I've reached the age in life where I look at the game and think you've got to be crazy to play it and stupid to coach it. I'm just happy I'm no longer involved . . . When I played, there was none of this stuff. It was just a football game. Now it's all big business, and the football game is almost incidental.

Interview,
Miami, Fla.,
Jan. 29/
The Washington Post,
1-30:(A)7.

Russell Granik
Deputy Commissioner,
National Hockey League

2

[On recent labor strife in major-league sports]: We are in a period where the dollars have become so large. All the leagues are trying to re-examine the underpinnings of the business. I certainly hope that once we get through that period, we can get back to a state of some normalcy for a long time.

USA Today,
1-9:(C)1.

Jim Harrick
Basketball coach,
University of California,
Los Angeles

3

[On being a coach]: Teaching is what you do from 3 to 5:30. Coaching is what you do during the game.

The New York Times,
4-4:(B)12.

Bob Huggins
Basketball coach,
University of Cincinnati

4

The main point I try to get across [to the players] is that effort can beat talent. The problem is that everybody tells himself he's trying hard, but not many actually do. If you really put out—run faster, get to where you're going quicker—there are darned few things you can't accomplish. If you do it every day in practice, you'll do it in a game as a matter of course.

Interview/
The Wall Street Journal,
1-13:(B)10.

Rob Huizenga
Former physician,
Oakland "Raiders"
football team

5

I would say most of the [team] doctors are first-rate professionals, but they can fall into a trap from the huge pressures of [team]

(ROB HUIZENGA)

owners and the millions of dollars involved, especially in big games. Doctors can pressure players who don't think they will ever get hurt or the ones who think they have only a few years left to make money.

Los Angeles Times, 1-8:(C)4.

Davey Johnson
Baseball manager, Cincinnati "Reds"

1

[On his team's recent trade with Cleveland, which took place during the current player strike, in which Cincinnati got five "replacement players" in exchange for "future considerations"]: Cleveland got the better of the deals. They didn't get anybody.

Newsweek, 3-13:19.

Bert Jones
Former football player, Baltimore "Colts"

2

Everybody goes into [football] realizing that two things are going to happen: Either one day you're going to be cut because you're no longer good enough, or an injury is going to cut short your career. If anybody tells you anything different, then they are dumber than I think they are.

Los Angeles Times, 1-8:(C)4.

Stan Kasten
President, Atlanta "Braves" baseball team

3

[On the current long players' strike]: This isn't a negotiation with these players. It's not even business. It's a religious war. They've never had to compromise in the past, and they don't want to start now. And so we're all very close to damaging another season . . . I swear to God, we're [owners] not looking for a win here. We're just looking for a tie.

Interview/ Los Angeles Times, 3-12:(C)9.

David Klatell
Chairman, broadcast journalism department, Columbia University

4

[On the late controversial sportscaster Howard Cosell]: Yes, he was a revolutionary and yes, he transformed the role of the on-air personality and yes, he took controversial stands and yes, he was grandly egocentric. But I believe he operated from two bedrock beliefs. The first was in himself. The second was that television and radio sports needed to be shaken out of their complacency, and it was his self-appointed role to do just that. He had a fascinating combination of beliefs and brains and he came from a background that did not include working for a team. And he was never an athlete. I don't think a broadcaster like him will ever come along again because I don't think they'd let it happen again. That's a condemnation of the industry. There are not any risk-takers anymore . . . People also have fewer illusions about sports, so the need for an illusion-shatterer is greatly diminished.

April 23/ The Washington Post, 4-24:(C)10.

John Lopez
Former trainer,
Baltimore "Colts"
football team

1

The impact and velocity of some collisions [between players in a football game], normal Americans can't appreciate because they are not on the field. It's like someone putting your body on I-695 at 6 p.m. and letting it get bounced around by traffic.

Los Angeles Times,
1-8:(C)4.

Peter Magowan
Owner,
San Francisco "Giants"
baseball team

2

We [team owners] cannot afford to have large [financial] losses with no light at the end of the tunnel. And unless the system is to be changed, that's our future.

The Washington Post,
2-6:(A)10.

Don Mattingly
Baseball player,
New York "Yankees"

3

[On team owners' proposal to use replacement players in the coming baseball season if the major-league players' strike is not settled by them]: I'm not going to be intimidated by replacement players. I haven't taken them seriously in any respect. I haven't watched them. I don't think there are any concerns about replacement players. I thought [the striking players] might be intimidated by this, but I haven't heard a scant thing about replacement players. Nobody's taking it seriously. The caliber of baseball that's being played [in spring training by replacements] is bad: I've talked to people . . . on [the] management side; they're talking low "A" ball at best.

News conference,
Orlando, Fla., March 15/
The New York Times,
3-16:(B)6.

Oliver Maxwell
Heavyweight boxing champion
of the world

4

In my mind, everyone should serve an apprenticeship in this business as a sparring partner. [As a sparring partner,] I never went [through] the sparring-partner syndrome—get busted up, get knocked down, get punched like a bag. I didn't soak up punishment, so I soaked up knowledge. It's a good route to the top if you're talented.

Los Angeles Times,
3-30:(C)9.

Mark McGwire
Baseball player,
Oakland "Athletics"

5

[On winning back the loyalty of fans following the recent player strike]: We are going to have to take time for that extra handshake, that extra autograph. We are going to have to recognize the fans more than ever.

USA Today,
4-7:(C)2.

Shane McMahon
Owner,
World Wrestling Federation

6

Wrestling [today] is two guys in their

(SHANE McMAHON)

underwear in a room beating themselves over the head. We're not wrestling anymore. We're sports entertainment.

USA Today,
6-26:(B)7.

Brian McRae
Baseball player,
Kansas City "Royals"

1

[On the possibility of team owners using replacement players in the forthcoming baseball season if the player strike is not ended]: If they play with replacement players, they might as well put a tent over the stadiums. It's going to be a circus.

Los Angeles Times,
3-4:(C)2.

Daniel Patrick Moynihan
United States Senator,
D-New York

2

[On the proposed repeal of baseball's antitrust exemption]: It may not solve all of baseball's troubles, but it is a necessary step and one that is decades overdue.

Jan. 4/
USA Today,
1-5:(C)1.

Martina Navratilova
Tennis player

3

The players today don't seem to have as much fun as we [veterans] did. They take the game too seriously. My matches against Billie Jean [King] and Chris [Evert] were just as competitive, but we seemed to enjoy ourselves more. Players now have blinders on. They feel there is so much at stake that they don't let their personalities come out . . . I told both Monica [Seles] and Jennifer [Capriati] that if they come back, they should do it because they love to play the game.

USA Today,
4-10:(C)3.

4

I think you start out dreaming that you're going to be this great tennis player, that people are going to recognize you for the tennis player that you are; but what happens is fame takes over and they don't recognize you as a tennis player. They just recognize you as somebody that's famous. Sometimes you feel like you're a little animal on display . . . People want to touch you and say, "Oh, I touched somebody famous." They forget that you're a human being. But when you're on the court, all of that stuff goes out the window, because you just want to perform, and that's where the life of the game takes over. That's why you feel like the court's your sanctuary. Even though you're completely on display, you are doing what you know and what you love. It's like your safety zone. And I think that's why Monica [Seles] is having such a hard time dealing with what happened to her [she was stabbed by a fan at a tournament two years ago]. It's not the injury itself; it's the fact that she got stabbed at her sanctuary.

Interview, Aspen, Colo./
"Interview" magazine,
July:98.

Byron Nelson
Former golfer

5

[On his winning a record 11 tournaments

(BYRON NELSON)

in a row in 1945]: I would never [think] that something I had done somebody else couldn't do. Except this. I don't know if it's the greatest feat in golf, because there have been a lot of great ones. I'll tell you, though, I don't think anybody will ever win 11 tournaments in a row again. They could play much better than I played and still not win 11 in a row.

Interview, Roanoke, Texas/
Los Angeles Times,
3-11:(C)12.

Roger Noll
Professor of economics,
Stanford University

1

The only way to get and keep major-league sports franchises in this day and age is [for cities] to subsidize them. It's as simple as that. There are so many cities willing to court them, and many fewer franchises than cities who want them . . . I doubt that any city is aching to throw money at sports franchises, but they really have no choice. The reason the subsidy is politically viable is that people in this country *really care* about sports.

Los Angeles Times,
5-1:(A)3,19.

Jim Otto
Former football player,
Oakland "Raiders"

2

[On the serious injuries he sustained while he was a player]: There have been times when I've said, "Why'd I do this?" [play football]. But I wasn't going to lay there and whine. Football is a contact sport, and injuries are a part of the game. And if you can't take the injuries, get the hell out. Yes, I'd do it all again. It's not for whiners.

Interview/
Los Angeles Times,
1-8:(C)4.

Steve Palermo
Former baseball umpire,
American League

3

[On recently announced plans to speed up baseball games, including instituting some rules changes]: The action that takes place in a baseball game happens right now in 3 hours and 4 minutes. The action is going to be compacted into a smaller time-frame now. It's still going to be the same action, but it's going to be a nice tidy package now.

June 8/
The New York Times,
6-9:(B)14.

Drew Pearson
Former football player,
Dallas "Cowboys"

4

Once you leave the game, people forget about you quite quickly. No matter how many passes you've caught or touchdowns you've thrown, that's nice, but it doesn't mean anything in the real world.

Los Angeles Times,
1-8:(C)4.

Cal Ripken, Jr.
Baseball player,
Baltimore "Orioles"

5

Sports for me has always been a combination of love and persistence. That's who I

(CAL RIPKEN, JR.)

am, how I approach things. I was brought up a certain way. If I wanted to play, and I *could* play, then I would. With no questions asked. It's hard finding someone who feels the same way about training as I do. That even goes for something as simple as playing catch.It's hard to find someone whose commitment matches your own . . . I just think of myself as playing as much as I can for as long as I can. It's as simple as that. I want to sit back when it's all over and look at my whole career and say I did all I could. We all have only so much time we're allotted when our skills allow us to play. I've talked to a lot of retired guys and guys getting toward the end of their careers, and the question I most often ask is: Do you have any regrets? You know what answer I get? "I wish I'd played more."

Interview,
Reisterstown, Md./
Esquire,
April:50,51.

1

[On his breaking Lou Gehrig's all-time record by playing in 2,131 straight games]: Some may think our strongest connection is because we both played many consecutive games. Yet I believe in my heart that our true link is a common motivation: a love of the game of baseball, a passion for your team and a desire to compete on the very highest level . . . Whether your name is Gehrig or Ripken, [Joe] DiMaggio or [Jackie] Robinson, or that of some youngster who picks up his bat or puts on his glove, you are challenged by the game of baseball to do your very best day in and day out. And that's all I've ever tried to do.

At celebration
of his breaking the record,
Baltimore, Md./
U.S. News & World Report,
9-18:17.

Bud Selig
Owner,
Milwaukee "Brewers"
baseball team;
Acting Commissioner
of Baseball

2

[Criticizing proposals to end baseball's antitrust exemption as a way of solving the current player strike and preventing future ones]: When you look back at the antitrust exemption, this [proposal] doesn't create any potential solution; that's total mythology. But more important than that, you're dealing with arguably the most successful union in labor history [the players' union]. They've achieved unbelievable gains with baseball having this antitrust exemption. The fact is we need a collective-bargaining agreement. This [antitrust controversy] is mere diversion and doesn't contribute to that end at all.

Milwaukee, Wis., Jan. 4/
The New York Times,
1-5:(B)6.

3

[On the current player strike, which began last season]: If there is no agreement, the [new] season will open with [player] replacements. I'm not fond of replacement baseball, but it's the best alternative we have . . . I did not realize the mistrust, the long-term animosity between the [team owners and the players] . . . There are so many things that have come together to make it so difficult. And yet, you would think there are enough assets there to work this out quickly, because it's in both parties' interest to do [it].

USA Today,
3-24:(C)2.

George Steinbrenner
Owner,
New York "Yankees"
baseball team

1

[On the current player strike and whether the owners will lock out the players at the start of the new season]: I'm not sure that I would vote for a lockout. I think the way to settle this whole dispute is through negotiation. For whatever reason and for whoever's fault it is, the negotiations have not been productive and, to me, it's an embarrassment. I'm embarrassed for the players and the owners.

Fort Lauderdale, Fla.,
March 27/
The New York Times,
3-28:(B)15.

Andre Thornton
Former baseball player,
Cleveland "Indians"

2

There are so many more unhappy players now, guys with a chip on their shoulder. I see too many young stars who had a poor relationship with the game and the people in baseball. You have to stand up to the scrutiny. Young players need to understand that people will write and say bad things about them when they play poorly—and they can't take it personally. If they accept the praise for playing well, then they have to take some of the criticism when they don't. They can't just say, "I'm not talking to anybody." They make it such a business. It is disturbing when I hear a young player say, "I'm going to play five years and then retire." To me, that is like the guy saying he can't stand the game—that he is playing because he has to. You wonder what is eating at some of these guys.

Los Angeles Times,
10-26:(C)5.

Tara VanDerveer
Women's basketball coach,
Stanford University

3

[On the growth of women's college basketball]: The perception of the game has changed. It has been shaped by the media and the development of high-school programs. Fifteen years ago, people said women's basketball was as exciting as watching paint dry. Now there is more opportunity for young people to play sport. We still have a long way to go. As women's coaches, we have to ask where we want the game to be. We want to keep the good things in the game but still grow.

The New York Times,
4-4:(B)14.

Fay Vincent
Former Commissioner
of Baseball

4

[Baseball-team] owners have never been able to control costs. The pressures are not just economic. They don't like to be pilloried for not spending. It's hard to be a popular owner and run the team as a business. It's a

(FAY VINCENT)

political, social and cultural position to be an owner.

Interview/
The Washington Post,
2-6:(A)10.

Corliss Williamson
Basketball player,
University of Arkansas

1

When I step on the court, I block off the whole world. As I have gotten older, that's the attitude I have taken. I want to make it my world.

The New York Times,
4-4:(B)12.

Miki Yaras-Davis
Director of benefits,
National Football League
Players Association

2

[On injuries sustained during their careers by football players]: [Many former players] can't walk through an airport without the metal detectors going off [because of various artificial parts in their bodies inserted during injury surgeries.] Almost no one leaves this game unscarred either physically or mentally . . . You ever go to a retired-players association convention? It's an orthopedics surgeon's dream. They all have the crab-like walk, and it's hard to believe they were once these feared gladiators. Forty-year-old players are having the same problems as 80-year-old men.

Los Angeles Times,
1-8:(C)4.

The Indexes

Index to Speakers

A

B

C

D

E

F

G

H

I

J

K

L

M

N

O

P

Q

R

S

T

U

V

W

Y

Z

Index to Subjects

A

C

**Many references to Bill Clinton are not listed in this index due to the numerous routine mentions of his name throughout the book. Only references that are specifically about him, personally or professionally, are listed here.*

D

G

H

I

J

K

L

N

O

P

S

T

Y

Z